Praise for

THE MEASURE OF OUR AGE

"This is a brilliant, urgent, and much-needed book that will occupy a special place on my bookshelves. In a rapidly aging country, the clear-eyed wisdom alone of *The Measure of Our Age* would make it exceptional, but M. T. Connolly also happens to be the rare expert who can write movingly and beautifully. I learned from this book, I loved it, and I'm sure I'll be reaching for it again and again."

—David Finkel, Pulitzer Prize winner and
author of *Thank You for Your Service*

"Our current systems are failing older people and their caregivers. This book reveals the new realities and challenges of aging today with invaluable insights to help us live both long *and* well. *The Measure of Our Age* is a humane and hopeful guide for anyone navigating the complexities of aging and care—who, in time, will include all of us."

—Ai-jen Poo, president, National Domestic Workers Alliance;
executive director, Caring Across Generations;
and author of *The Age of Dignity*

"With a lawyer's understanding of complex systems, a caregiver's heart, and an advocate's passion, Connolly has written a book that individuals, organizations, and government leaders can use to make aging easier, better, and safer for all of us. An essential addition to this universal topic."

—Louise Aronson, MD; professor of geriatrics, UCSF;
Pulitzer Prize finalist; and *New York Times*–
bestselling author of *Elderhood*

"This book is a revelation. It invites us to change how we think about caring, about aging, and about how we spend our time. With deep knowledge, humor, and heart, *The Measure of Our Age* shows us how to grapple with the hard parts of aging as well as its unrealized potential. This profound, life-enhancing invitation is one Connolly extends to us all."

—Adrian Nicole LeBlanc, author of *Random Family: Love, Drugs, Trouble, and Coming of Age in the Bronx*

"Connolly is without doubt our nation's preeminent guide to aging well. *The Measure of Our Age* is a singular testament to the power of purpose, meaning, connection, interdependence, and, above all, love. All that plus a roadmap to fixing the systemic problems that make aging so much harder than it should be. A compelling read from start to finish."

—Marc Freedman, founder and co-CEO, CoGenerate, and author of *How to Live Forever*

"How can we assure safety, dignity, and good care for people as they age? Building on her extraordinary career as a leading advocate for the rights and protection of older people, Connolly provides real answers to this question. *The Measure of Our Age* seamlessly blends compelling stories of unforgettable individuals with careful research and inspired policy analysis. If you are looking to unravel the complexities of aging today, Connolly is the person you want by your side. *The Measure of Our Age* is a unique combination of profound insight, fresh ideas, and lived experience that should be read by everyone negotiating life in an aging society—that is, all of us."

—Karl Pillemer, professor of human development, Cornell University, and bestselling author of *30 Lessons for Living: Tried and True Advice from the Wisest Americans*

the

MEASURE

of

OUR AGE

*Navigating Care, Safety,
Money, and Meaning Later in Life*

M. T. CONNOLLY

PUBLICAFFAIRS
New York

PublicAffairs
Hachette Book Group
1290 Avenue of the Americas, New York, NY 10104
www.publicaffairsbooks.com
@Public_Affairs

Printed in the United States of America

First Edition: July 2023

Published by PublicAffairs, an imprint of Hachette Book Group, Inc. The PublicAffairs name and logo is a trademark of the Hachette Book Group.

The Hachette Speakers Bureau provides a wide range of authors for speaking events. To find out more, go to hachettespeakersbureau.com or email HachetteSpeakers@hbgusa.com.

PublicAffairs books may be purchased in bulk for business, educational, or promotional use. For information, please contact your local bookseller or Hachette Book Group Special Markets Department at special.markets@hbgusa.com.

Print book interior design by Jeff Williams.

Library of Congress Cataloging-in-Publication Data
Names: Connolly, M. T. (Marie-Therese), author.
Title: The measure of our age : navigating care, safety, money, and meaning later in life / M. T. Connolly.
Description: First edition. | New York, NY : PublicAffairs, 2023. |
    Includes bibliographical references and index. |
Identifiers: LCCN 2022044622 | ISBN 9781541702721 (hardcover) | ISBN 9781541702745 (ebook)
Subjects: LCSH: Aging—Social aspects—United States. | Older people—United States—Social conditions. | Older people—Government policy—United States. | Older people—Services for—United States.
Classification: LCC HQ1064.U5 C611355 2023 | DDC 305.26—dc23/eng/20220915
LC record available at https://lccn.loc.gov/2022044622

ISBNs: 9781541702721 (hardcover), 9781541702745 (ebook)

LSC-C

Printing 1, 2023

To Heidi for the loving care

To Danny for the loving tech support

To Fiona, Nathan, and Gabriel
for lighting the fleeting days with love

Oh Lord, make me know my end and what is the measure of my days; let me know how fleeting I am.

—Psalm 39

The manner in which a society behaves with its old people unequivocally reveals the truth . . . of its principles and its ends.

—Simone de Beauvoir, *The Coming of Age*

CONTENTS

PART III: CHANGE 247

PROLOGUE

The Oxbow and the Ice Floe

Time is the substance from which I am made.
Time is a river which sweeps me along, but I am
the river.

—Jorge Luis Borges, *Labyrinths*

On her eighty-eighth birthday, my mother-in-law, Janet, sat in the bow of a green canoe paddling down the Brule River. That day, our family flotilla of canoes and kayaks also carried my own parents and the three grandchildren they shared. From the stern of Janet's canoe, my brother, the family naturalist, pointed out common mergansers and the bald eagles that have returned to that part of northern Wisconsin, where I, too, have returned to our cabin every summer since childhood.

I didn't know it then, but we were paddling very near the continental divide: While the Brule flows north to Lake Superior, the St. Croix, just a few miles away, runs south into the Mississippi and on to the Gulf of Mexico. A small move can make a big difference in where you end up.

As the river curled into an oxbow, we paddled to a little island inside its U-shaped curve. The kids leaned toward shore to pick wildflowers for a bouquet, fashioning a crown that their grandmother

I

rested on her white hair. Then we held fast to one another's boats and sang, voices full over the water, "Happy Birthday to You."

"You're all very kind," Janet said with a stricken laugh. "But as you sang so beautifully, I suddenly thought, 'This is it. They're going to leave me here on this muddy little island.' I know it sounds crazy, but for a moment I was sure it was true."

Longevity has taken varying forms in my family. Janet kept on living in her Chicago apartment, enjoying friends and seeing clients in her therapy practice until age ninety-five, when she began to need help. My mother lived fully until she died of cancer at eighty not long after that day on the river. And my father survived a host of health crises into his nineties, when many evenings still found him, night-cap in hand, reciting long stanzas he'd memorized in his youth—Shakespeare, Byron, Shelley, Keats, and Yeats. Tennyson moved something new in him in old age, and he bookmarked "Ulysses" in his worn anthology: "Tho' much is taken, much abides; and tho' / We are not now that strength which in old days / Moved earth and heaven, that which we are, we are."[1] Given that which he was, he was adamant about living alone, a fragile freedom made possible by good medicine, house calls, and the loving care of my sister, Heidi.

Even with the cushion of resources for aging in my family, Janet's fear on the river shook me—evoking legends of elders in the far north consigned to ice floes when their tribes deemed that their burden outweighed their benefit. Janet had known loss. Her father had abandoned the family when she was a teenager, and two husbands had died young. She'd also lived long and well and saw life clearly—both the inner and aerial views—in all its contradictions. But her reaction to that muddy island was something different.

Between 1900 and 1999, Americans gained, on average, thirty extra years of life. "Eighty is the new fifty," we're told, and octogenarians and nonagenarians at the peak of their powers and relishing life prove the point. We've enriched old age with new knees and hips, e-readers with large type, and video chats connecting distant family and friends. For millions of people, there has never been a better time to be old.

Studies also show that we grow happier as we age, at least through our seventies, as our priorities sharpen and we more appreciate what we have. Still, the years take their toll. We strive for longevity but feel conflicted about old age. On the one hand, there's the beloved, even revered, elder, living with purpose, good care, and love. On the other, there's the older person as a millstone, resented for taking up space and resources, for staying alive.

Our longevity means that millions more people will need care than ever before. Here, too, at first, our era seems a good one to grow old. We have abundant options, we're told: tens of thousands of facilities, with expert staff to meet residents' every need, and for the majority of older people who prefer to "age in place," skilled nurses and aides to come to the home. But when the time of need arrives, many families find the options woefully wanting and often unafford-able. By the time many of us learn this, it's too late to make a change.

For some the realization comes after a loved one moves into a facility only to learn that the care is substandard. So, they advocate. Or they supplement the care. Many try to avoid facilities at any cost, meaning that the vast majority of eldercare is, as it ever was, provided at home by family and friends, an "informal" and unpaid workforce, more than forty million people strong. Those caregivers, with little support, allow older people to stay at home longer and spend less time in hospitals, rehab, and long-term care facilities, saving money for Medicare, Medicaid, and private insurers. But all those "free" services, valued at about $500 *billion* a year, come with high unacknowledged costs to the caregivers themselves. Those costs are measured in time, money, jobs, health, and stress.

Whatever care people cobble together, most find the systems fragmented, with baffling options of uncertain quality. Trying to synchronize the various systems that come into play in old age—like health, housing, services, finances, and law—is harder still.

Like many people, I was surprised by just how complicated, onerous, and sometimes cruel navigating those systems can be. Their brokenness often eclipses what matters most in late life, leaving many people feeling like they've "failed" at aging or at caring when in fact they've been failed by society's unprepared and sometimes corrupt aging machinery.

Aging can be hard, to be sure, but it's been made infinitely and unnecessarily harder by our failure to build the infrastructure we need to age well. A central question running through this book is: *What makes aging so much harder than it should be?* My goal is to map the terrain to give us a better sense of where we are now and where we might be headed, in hopes that doing so will help readers to forge a more just, gentle, and joyful old age for themselves and for those they love. Understanding the systems—how they work and how they don't—can help us spot potential pitfalls sooner, and steer around them. It can also help us see and navigate toward aging's many positive aspects and, in the process, push the culture to do so as well.

Both my work and my personal life have exposed me to scores of examples of how things go wrong, how they go right, and the approaches that can lead us toward better long lives. In working as a civil prosecutor at the Department of Justice (DOJ), I had an inside view of cases against nursing home chains that mistreated residents, revealing forces that subvert good care. In heading up DOJ's Elder Justice Initiative, I saw policy being shaped—from sterile conference rooms to the halls of Congress—and tried to shape it myself. In launching a research program, and later working on research teams and building new solutions, I saw the importance of asking "what works?" and of collecting data to answer that question. In working with experts from medicine to services, from finance to forensics, I saw the challenges and rewards of aging through their eyes, giving me a multifaceted view of what progress could look like. And in working on the Elder Justice Act, I saw how just introducing a new bill could coalesce its proponents into what became known as the *elder justice field*.

Still, even after the bill was enacted in 2010, funding to implement it was negligible. The law itself foundered for years, along with many other of my aspirations, leaving me frustrated, again and again, by the creeping pace of change. I wanted to understand what was going on. Tracking the arc of a law, the arc of long lives, and the arc of change itself took me on a journey of awakening consciousness to many unexpected places. This book also chronicles the hard-won lessons of that search.

When I'm asked why I do this work, my usual answer is that the challenges are vast and growing, millions of people are suffering from preventable causes, and there's much we could improve if we set our minds to it. But I think there's also another more primal force: my mother.

My mother was a doctor, as were her mother, both of her sisters, and several of their daughters. Medicine was the respectable line of work for the women in my family. My parents fully expected me to fall in line and follow my mother into psychiatry. But after my first year of college, I was having doubts. I took a break to learn more, and signed up for an immersion program, moving into the state hospital in Rochester, Minnesota, my hometown, to be a resident volunteer. For volunteering twenty hours a week (which more often turned into forty or sixty), I got room and board on PS1-A, a general admission psychiatric ward where the bedrooms, including mine, had stone walls, shatterproof windows, and beige metal doors. The cafeteria food and social scene there were not unlike many high schools— including the one I'd graduated from, just a few miles away.

I'd spent lots of time at that state hospital while growing up. My mother worked there, in a different building. I saw it through her eyes, and to her neither the place nor the people who lived there seemed frightening. She recognized humanity in inhumane places and embraced people others preferred to look away from. Some of her patients, when they were discharged, became our car mechanics and babysitters. It was a different time and boundaries were never her strong suit.

As a volunteer, I did odd jobs for the nurses, many of them devoted and smart, and went on outings with the patients. But mostly I hung out—with the nurses in the staff room late into the night when the ward got quiet, and with "the ladies," as the patients were then called, in the "day room," gossiping, smoking, drinking thin coffee, and doing puzzles, the TV always blaring. When gaggles of nursing students came through, the ladies and I laughed about the anxious way they asked me questions, assuming I was a patient. In fairness, it could be hard to tell. One of the ladies looked like an administrator with a taste for high fashion. Another sent herself a dozen roses weekly, from a secret admirer. A third reminded me of a college classmate.

A warren of tunnels linked the buildings on the sprawling campus. One underground room was used for weekly dances—patients, staff, and volunteers reeling around to waltzes and polkas. Another was used for electroshock, gurneys ringing the perimeter. A bevy of white coats moved from patient to patient. They knew the steps—thread the IV, attach wires, sedate, slip a rubber tube between the teeth, step back, jolt, seizure, stillness. Patients woke up woozy, memories blitzed. Like the hospital itself, it was another era's remedy: for some an antidote, for others a travesty. For me, then nineteen, just witnessing those shocks that passed for good intentions was deeply unsettling. But my eyes were way out ahead of my brain's ability to fathom what I'd seen.

When I returned to college, I talked my way into a class in mental health law. We visited California's state hospitals and debated how to balance the liberty and safety rights of vulnerable people. I learned that lawyers (like my professor) were using the law to shift norms in medicine and mental health care. Ephemeral words strung together into laws could take on real force. They could improve or undermine the health and well-being not just of one person but of millions.

I decided to go to law school.

I didn't connect the dots until much later, but living at the state hospital, in all its humanity and horror, kindled in me an abiding interest in how society treats vulnerable people, the institutions and systems we create "for" them, and how we can find more humane and effective ways of doing things. Those issues, I learned, are as critical to aging as they are to mental health. And yet, also like mental health, although we've known for decades that robust community-based services and supports make all the difference, we put our resources elsewhere. Even when we know what works, we often fail to do it.

Why haven't we done more to prepare for society's aging when we've long seen it coming? In large part because of our pervasive animus toward aging itself. Pioneering physician Robert Butler coined the term *ageism* in 1968 and defined it in his 1975 book, *Why Survive?*, as a "process of systematic stereotyping of and discrimination against people because they are old, just as racism and sexism accomplish this with skin color and gender." The tragedy,

Butler explained, is not getting old but that aging "has been made unnecessarily and at times excruciatingly painful, humiliating, debilitating, and isolating."[2]

Almost a half century later, in *Caste*, author Isabel Wilkerson described the problem using another word: "Even the most privileged of humans in the Western world will join a tragically disfavored caste if they live long enough. They will belong to the last caste of the human cycle, that of old age, people who are among the most demeaned of all citizens in the Western world, where youth is worshipped to forestall thoughts of death. A caste system spares no one."[3]

By whatever name, the fear, shame, and disgust that cling to aging like a toxic mold diminish its humanity. The bias then compounds itself, producing and perpetuating the very conditions the prejudiced find so repellant. Deprive the enslaved of education, then castigate their lack of learning. Idolize women's looks, then diminish their fixation with appearance. Neglect the old in body, mind, and spirit, then feel disgust for their decline and decrepitude.

In measuring ageism's impact, researchers have found that it shortens lives and costs billions. It also seeps into the culture where it's magnified by our institutions. Our personal choices about aging aren't made in a vacuum. They're made in the context of the culture and the options available to us. So, improving how we age in our own lives means pushing our systems to improve, too.

Too often we think of old age as an island when in actuality we age not only as individuals but also as parts of families and communities, its repercussions rippling through both. And although we tend to freeze "old" in time, how we age is entwined with what happens earlier in life. Unaddressed problems build over the years. By late life, the snowball has become an avalanche. For well-being in aging, we need to better support people—caregivers and care recipients—through the whole life cycle.

This story of American aging is also shaped by another American story: our preoccupation with independence. By elevating adamant self-sufficiency to a singular virtue, we set traps that ensnare us in isolation and loneliness despite ample evidence that it's in fact *inter*dependence that leads to better health and well-being.

Another cultural inclination that serves us poorly is that we tend to wait until trouble happens and then react, instead of trying to get out ahead of it. Identifying the kinds of early and midcourse adjustments that might prevent trouble could do much to enhance our long lives.

Unlikely as it sounds, I found an illuminating model in automobile safety. When car companies started installing seatbelts, auto fatalities dropped. But medical examiners who investigated car crash injuries found patterns revealing that not all seatbelts were equal. Forensic analysis made the invisible more visible. Lap belts were better than no belt, but they didn't protect upper bodies from catapulting into windshields and steering wheels. Such observations, and research confirming them, changed emergency medicine, car manufacturing, consumer safety practices, laws, and eventually social norms, preventing millions of traffic fatalities.

Reducing harm required looking closely at the grim aftermath and analyzing what went wrong, not just once, but many, many times to reveal the patterns. I wanted to trace the problems with aging I encountered back to their sources, try to discern the patterns, and better understand what progress might look like.

Aging plunges all of us into new worlds, each one with its own language and ways. Families often split up its diverse demands—care, finances, errands, insurance—depending on who's closest or best suited for what. No one can know or do it all. A similar dividing up of responsibility happened in my professional life. The translators and guides who helped me understand the many worlds of aging and how these worlds intersect—among them a doctor, a criminal prosecutor, a social worker, an elder lawyer, and a banker—are characters in this book.

The book also has nonhuman characters—the fragmented systems that for now primarily appear in the role of villain. Systems are abstract and often obscured as we struggle to navigate them. But the harm they inflict is real. And their life-saving power when they do work is real, too.

In writing about people and systems, I inhabited a liminal role—simultaneously participant and observer, colleague, and chronicler. I tried to write what I knew, but as I looked more closely, instead of finding clear answers, often I found deep questions about the meanings of autonomy and safety, of compassion and justice. I learned how the trade-offs between them can evolve over a life, and how those trade-offs differ by person, family, and culture. What I learned changed me, too. For one thing, I started out as a prosecutor and emerged a "preventionist." This book tells that story, as well.

What my colleagues and I came to understand was that trouble often grows from the kernels of very common aspects of aging—caregiving, health, housing, money, and the struggle to balance competing interests. Part I describes those challenges with an eye on ways to better navigate them.

Part II looks at how society responds when things go wrong in old age, the hard, sometimes shocking questions such cases raise, and some new ways to tackle them.

The subject of Part III is change, with examples from the community level to the level where federal laws are made, as well as a look at the mechanics of social change-making itself. The final chapter looks inward, at the intimate tools of change we possess in ourselves and in our relationships with others: the capacity to make meaning of time and aging through curiosity, purpose, stories, awe, and love.

As I wound my way from subject to subject, I found myself unexpectedly hopeful by the end. Powerful tools of change are already in the hands and hearts and minds of everyone who loves someone old, or who is aging. That is to say, all of us. By focusing more on what matters most and facing the future with less fear and greater generosity, we not only enrich our own lives but nudge the culture to do so as well.

In looking backward, successful change, like those shoulder belts, may seem obvious. But midstream, static and signal are harder to tell apart, especially when it comes to matters of longevity. Aging may seem imperceptibly slow, but it's an illusion. We can't feel ourselves hurtling through space as the earth spins or hurtling through time as we age. But we're hurtling nonetheless. Paying attention to where we want to end up, and helping others do the same, is central to the business of living. Even small moves can make a big difference.

But for now, there's little social support for that kind of refocusing, despite the profound benefits it can yield.

In the pages that follow, I have tried to lay out both challenges and gifts of aging, in hopes that a more nuanced understanding can light a path for us—us as a society, us as families, and us as individuals—to improve our odds of a better old age.

Part I
CHALLENGES

The privilege of living long lives comes with challenges. There's the practical stuff: how to get the right care, where and with whom to live, and how to pay for it all. There are autonomy-safety balances to strike. Driving gets the most attention, but risky decisions about money, sex, care, and where to live are just as fraught. The institutions that are supposed to protect us as we age—like guardianship, powers of attorney, and nursing homes—too often harm us instead. And the biggest culprits are often hard to see—like our social norms that do more to undermine than enhance our well-being as we age. Understanding these varied challenges is the first step to charting a better course through later life.

Chapter 1

CARE

There are only four kinds of people in the world:
those who have been caregivers, those who are
currently caregivers, those who will be caregivers,
and those who will need caregivers.

—Rosalynn Carter

What did I know, what did I know
of love's austere and lonely offices?

—Robert Hayden, "Those Winter Sundays"

Love and Duty

Like a shift in the seasons, it's hard to pinpoint the moment
when things begin to change, as time and need recast our
relationships, and then recast them again. But whoever we
become as adults, some part of who we were with our parents shadows us if they live long enough to need our care. The role exists in a
time warp, one that millions of us will at some point inhabit.

The more I learned about aging, the more caregivers assumed
center stage. They often determined whether older people in ebbing
health flourished or came to harm. Their contributions, most unpaid
or underpaid, are measured in hours and days, in years and decades.
Their work is composed of countless tasks, rendered from near and
from afar.

There's little discussion, let alone consensus, about profound questions that attend the work. What should be expected of caregivers? Can they meet the high demands? At what cost to them or the people they care for? For how much, if any, compensation? And what guidance and support should they be entitled to receive?

Similar questions rumbled through my own family. After my mother died in 2008, my father stayed in Rochester, Minnesota, where he'd lived since emigrating from Ireland in 1951, to practice cardiology at the Mayo Clinic. That's where my seven siblings and I grew up. In the mid-1990s, he and my mother had moved from our family home to an apartment, thrilled to have less housework, no more snow shoveling, and a warm garage. When he rounded ninety, my father said he'd lived longer than anyone else in his family ever had. That's true in many families these days.

At one time, only the exceptional few reached what's called old-old age. In the twentieth century, Americans' life expectancy jumped from forty-eight to seventy-eight (with a dip to seventy-six in 2021 due primarily to COVID-19).[1] This increase, as the historian Steven Johnson has pointed out, is "a result of progress at both ends of the age spectrum: Children are dying far less frequently, and the elderly are living much longer."[2] In 1800, almost half of the children born in the United States died before they turned five. Today, the rate is less than one in a hundred. There are also fewer deaths among people in the in-between years.

Johnson argues that the resulting longevity is humanity's single greatest achievement of the last century but doesn't get the attention it deserves because it's slow moving and made up not of one feat but a multitude: People learned how to pasteurize milk and to boil and chlorinate water. Our nutrition and education improved, and we reduced industrial toxins and sewage. We started using refrigeration and seatbelts. Then, of course, there were vaccines, drugs, and surgeries. Also, critical to extending our lives were less-tangible efforts by the people who pushed good new ideas into practice, changing norms. The cumulative impact on aging has been nothing short of astounding.

Societal changes further transformed aging in America. Government programs like social security reduced poverty in old age. Medicare and Medicaid improved access to health care. Employer-based pensions and tax-deferred savings accounts like 401(k)s supplemented retirement income. The housing industry developed vibrant elder-friendly communities. And a massive long-term care industry promised older people convenience, community, and care under one roof, with the vigilance of a hospital and the comfort of home.

As the twentieth century gave way to the twenty-first, my father's cohort—people eighty-five and older—became the fastest growing segment of the US population. Their number—just 1.5 million in 1970, and 6.6 million in 2019—will balloon to 18 million by 2050.[3] We are living among a whole new old-old population unprecedented in human history.

Still, the victory is a qualified one. Our life spans exceed our "health spans." Improvements in trauma care and infection control mean that fewer people die suddenly or young, but progress in reducing chronic illness—like diabetes, arthritis, and heart failure—has been more modest. Whereas the life expectancy in the United States in 2019 was seventy-eight years, the *healthy* life expectancy was just sixty-six years.[4] And both life expectancy and healthy life expectancy are lower for the poor, poorly educated, and people of color.

The result? Almost three-quarters of people eighty-five and older have some "functional disability." More than half will require some paid assistance.[5] It's not just our physical health we're outliving, it's our brain health, too. Physical and cognitive disabilities mean that tens of millions of people already need more care than ever before, and their numbers are rising.

At some point in their lives, about a quarter of older adults will receive two or more years of paid long-term care at home or in residential care facilities that go by names like nursing homes, assisted living, and group homes.[6] Residential care is a double-edged sword. Sometimes it's great; sometimes it's awful. Whatever their reasons, most older Americans—including my father—want nothing to do with it. Three-quarters want to "age in place" and get care at home if they need it.[7] Another one in ten prefer to get care at the home of a loved one.[8] How to provide all that home-based care in a way that preserves the well-being of care recipients and caregivers alike are questions we haven't yet answered.

When I visited my father, he worked and read at his desk in his office for several hours a day while I did the same at my mother's old desk. She used to get up before dawn, so had angled her desk to welcome the sunrise, facing the stone windowsill where Daddy's brown, dry cactus now sat. He claimed it was still alive, which became a running joke among my siblings and me although we half suspected he might be right.

His frailty snuck up on me. It was discombobulating. He had always been so dominant, so unyielding. He had disapproved of my choices and was shocked when I didn't bend to his wishes—about religion or profession. For him, those demands were existential; good children acceded to their parents' wishes. He hadn't counted on the provocations of raising a family in a world so different than the one he'd known. But those grueling years of conflict had long since healed over. Old age and frailty brought forth a new pacifism and sweetness in him, and in me a new tenderness for him, mingled with anticipatory grief. A little like the sensation when you first notice that the leaves have begun to fall.

Writing about caregiving from my mother's desk was surreal, the term's vast range made manifest. I was sitting at the cushy end of the spectrum. I ran errands and cooked. We ate meals and watched baseball. And he recited poetry, the compendium in his head a hundredfold that in mine, his mind sharp, his body patched up a dozen times courtesy of his Mayo Clinic colleagues.

I was just a reinforcement. My sister Heidi, a cardiologist who lived a few blocks away, was the front line. She visited him almost every day when she was in town and called when on the road. "That'll be Heidi now," Daddy would say when the phone rang—and it always was. Despite her own busy work and life, Heidi somehow found ways to help Daddy get where he needed to go and procured his medications, special candies, and brandy. Heidi bought him fancy Hennessy. He bought himself the off-brand stuff in plastic half-gallon jugs. On many a Saturday night, Heidi had him over for dinner, often along with Dean, his priest and friend.

Heidi was caregiver, care manager, and field general. She scheduled medical appointments and directed the troop movements, not only of doctors, nurses, and aides, but also of us siblings and other family and friends who made the pilgrimage to see him. This required not only lots of time and thoughtful planning but also the weight of being in charge, always on call. She was the one to whom Daddy and the rest of us looked.

My brother Danny, who lives in Minneapolis, was Heidi's deputy. He was Daddy's Sunday short-order cook, rustling up eggs and bacon or Irish rashers for dinner. They often ate—cheering or commiserating—while watching the Twins or Vikings play. Danny was also director of tech support, the one Daddy called when his computer slowed to a crawl. Danny diagnosed the problem—2,000 open solitaire games—and closed each one. The other six of us who live on the coasts rotated in and out, as needed or not. We knew we were lucky to have the home team there, close and with expertise.

CAREGIVERS

Visits when my father's health was bad could feel weighty. But even by one of the less demanding definitions of *caregiver*, I didn't log nearly enough hours to qualify as one. The National Alliance for Caregiving and AARP estimate that 41.8 million Americans, most of them family, provide an average of twenty-four hours of "informal" or unpaid care every week for a person fifty and older, over an average of four years.[9] That's more caregivers than the entire population of California. The estimated annual value of all their care is about $500 billion.[10] And they lose an estimated $522 billion in income a year due to caregiving.[11] That massive unpaid labor force provides care that health facilities once supplied. It facilitates older people's longevity and shores up our national health and social service systems. Many people don't sign up for the job and get little notice before it's thrust upon them. Forty-four percent felt they had no choice.

I wondered: Who are caregivers in general? In a 2022 study of people using caregiver resource centers in California, they were adult children (51 percent), spouses (35 percent), partners (1.1 percent), other relatives (10 percent), and nonrelatives (2.6 percent).[12] The "typical" caregiver profile is a middle-aged woman who provides unpaid care on top of working her own job. For the 39 percent of caregivers who are men, the job usually entails cooking and laundry, handling finances, and care management. Women handle those tasks and, in addition, are more likely than men to handle the heavy lifting, literally—bathing, "toileting," and dressing. Many juggle eldercare with childcare. Women also perceive caregiving as more burdensome, feeling more hostility and stress than their male counterparts. Caregiving spouses tended to be older than other caregivers and in poor health themselves.

Women have been overrepresented among caregivers for millennia, of course. Research shows that having a daughter or daughter-in-law as we age is good for our health. But today that gender disparity comes with unprecedented pressure as more women are in the workforce with families dependent on their income. With birthrates falling and families dispersed, households are smaller, so there are fewer people around to share domestic work, just as millions more older people need care.

Women also provide care for more hours than men and it affects their careers more. They reduce work hours and pass up promotions. They take leaves of absence, cut back, or leave the workforce entirely. Those changes reduce caregivers' current economic wherewithal *and* reverberate into their own old age by reducing their social security income and retirement savings. Women's pensions are about half those of men's, in part because they spend an average of twelve years out of the workforce raising children or caring for older adults. Women fifty and older who leave the workforce entirely for eldercare lose an estimated $324,000 compared to $284,000 for men. "Free" care isn't free after all.

People of color also are disproportionately caregivers, "often lead[ing] to an inability to create generational wealth."[13] In general, they're also younger, provide more care, have fewer means, care for people who are sicker, and report worse health than their white counterparts. They also tend to get more help from family and friends and have a stronger sense of filial obligation. Though African American caregivers report lower levels of caregiver burden and depression, Hispanic and Asian American caregivers report higher rates compared to their white counterparts.

People in the LGBTQ community disproportionately serve as caregivers too, and male caregivers report providing more hours of care than female caregivers. "Families of choice" also often figure into caregiving arrangements.

Help Me!

Caregiving's demands have escalated with longevity. It's not all running errands and flipping TV channels. A 2016 National Academies of Sciences, Engineering, and Medicine (NASEM) report on caregiving found that older people's homes have become "*de facto* clinical care settings."[14] More than three-quarters of the caregivers serve as "care coordinators," trying to glue together a coherent whole from the fractured multitude of systems. They schedule appointments, arrange transportation, and negotiate with insurance companies.

Fifty-eight percent of caregivers say they performed medical tasks, with 40 percent reporting high-intensity caregiving.[15] This isn't so surprising as people today are discharged from hospitals and rehab *sicker and quicker* than before, leaving caregivers to perform nursing and medical tasks. They handle IVs and give injections. They manage feeding and drainage tubes. They change dressings on gaping wounds and thread catheters into bladders. They suction tracheostomies and adjust dials on breathing machines. With little training for these intensive jobs, they worry about doing too little or too much, about making lethal mistakes.

Despite its massive toll, caregiving-the-issue remains hidden in plain sight, gaining little traction as an issue of public health, economic security, jobs, or gender equity. Politicians and policy-makers rarely consider or are held to account for how their actions affect caregivers or the quality of care they provide. Families get scant support or guidance for how to plan for this often long, many-staged, arduous—and sometimes unexpected—phase of family life.

The job is often so complex that even people with lots of education and resources feel overwhelmed. And they're the lucky ones.

I learned a lot about eldercare from geriatrician Laura Mosqueda, a doctor at USC's Keck School of Medicine specializing in the health of older people, like pediatricians specialize in kids. On clinic days, her exam room fills not only with her older patients but also their partners, children, and caregivers. Because they too are central to her patients' health, she's attentive to their roles and concerns as well.

Laura, with whom I began working more than two decades ago, thinks that our cultural obsession with "independence" is misguided. Our lives are entwined with those of others (whether we admit it or not). Laura believes that aiming for "appropriate interdependence" leads to a better old age. That philosophy is infused through her practice, where caring for one person often means caring for many.

That's why Laura was taken aback by "Colette," the daughter of one of her patients. Colette's mother hadn't been easy to care for, Laura said, even before dementia had set in. Colette was smart and thoughtful. She'd stayed on top of her mother's care for years. Then, at one appointment, Colette slipped Laura a hot-pink three-by-five card on which she'd written: "HELP ME! I am overwhelmed."

"She was so together I totally missed her level of distress," Laura said. "It also made me wonder how often I was missing signs of distress in other caregivers."

Colette told me that she gave Laura the "HELP ME" card after her mother fell nine times in four weeks, once sliding down a full flight of stairs. Colette has painful arthritis, so she had to call neighbors to help her lift her mother each time. Nights got harder, too, as her mother needed care every two hours. "I had no medical background," Colette said. "It was a rude awakening."

Many caregivers set boundaries only to watch them shift. Initially, Colette decided that she wasn't going to help her mother shower. Then she thought, "I'll hold the shower handle, but she can clean herself." That shifted to: "I'll help her clean her back, but not everywhere." Colette crossed that line, too.

Eighteen months into caregiving, Colette's mother's dementia had progressed, so she was unsafe alone at home. Colette quit her job in her family business, losing salary and benefits. By the time Colette slipped Laura the hot-pink card, incremental steps had turned into ten years. At that time, more than a decade ago, resources for caregivers were even scarcer. After filing reams of paperwork, Colette was paid $72 a week for almost around-the-clock labor. Laura increased the frequency of their appointments, connected Colette with a geriatric social worker to help arrange for more support, and gave Colette her own cell number, saying "call anytime."

When Colette's mother died, she emerged from her caregiving decade "like Rip Van Winkle." Though she chose to be her mother's primary caregiver and was deeply dedicated to the enterprise, our conversation exposed the magnitude of caregiving's toll: financial loss, sleep deprivation, health problems, anxiety, guilt, boredom, loneliness, physical labor, exhaustion, fear, and isolation. "Caregiving knocked the starch out of me," she said.

Caregiving, like aging, unspools in stages. "These are often not six-month, but six-year experiences," said Kathy Kelly, head of the Family Caregiving Alliance. "Families have different needs at different times throughout the journey." The 16,000 families who used California's Caregiver Resource Centers wanted counseling, legal and financial consultations, support groups, and respite services that gave them a break.[16] Millions more caregivers who don't have access to resource centers use websites and videos for advice about dementia care, fall prevention, and lifting without injury or seek out caregiver support groups. But we still have much to learn about how best to help caregivers.

One overarching principle—in caregiving as on airplanes—is to put on your own mask before assisting someone else. You can't help if you can't breathe. Yet services, to the extent they exist, focus on *individuals* instead of caregiver–care recipient pairs. Our systems don't recognize that their health and well-being are inextricably linked.

Illuminating those links is why Rajiv Mehta developed the Atlas CareMap, a process that helps you map "who you care for—and who cares for you."[17] Mehta believes that drawing such maps has two benefits. First, you can better *see* the needs, your own and others, and what additional people and services you need to stay ahead of the challenges. Equally important, says Mehta, and more surprising to many people, is that mapping helps you identify, appreciate, and celebrate who and what's good in the current situation.

There are many reasons to take stock of the gaps and the full scope of the job. Caregiving's toll is written on the body. The labor and stress lead to more heart disease, worse immune systems, and a 63 percent increase in premature mortality. It's also written on our minds and hearts. Between 40 and 70 percent of caregivers experience depression.[18] Many more suffer anxiety, loneliness, anger, and sometimes PTSD.

One friend who had an agonizing caregiving journey told me about talking with other caregivers who separately confided that they were contemplating suicide if it would spare their own children the burden of caregiving they'd experienced. Of course, suicide replaces one agonizing familial legacy with another.

At a broader level, we're not doing honest math about caregiving. We measure the savings but not the costs, costs that we could do much to lessen by providing better support.

Like any group of forty million people, each caregiver has a range of skills and proclivities. Countless—like Heidi—are skilled, valiant, and compassionate. They know how to ask for help when they need it. For many, caregiving is hard but manageable. Some are flattened by it, even while providing great care. Some who appear poorly suited for the job rise to the occasion. Some who appear well suited can't, sometimes because of past trauma. Some find the work deeply meaningful. For some, it heals old conflict. For others, it drives new ones. And a few take advantage of the imbalance in power or ability to steal, bully, or worse.

Lauren Fuller, Chief Investigative Counsel for the Senate Special Committee on Aging and my primary colleague and partner in drafting the Elder Justice Act (discussed later), was in the first group. Her mom, a former actress and teacher, had been thrown out of two Texas assisted living facilities for shouting at other residents and lighting cigarettes under the fire alarm. In her third facility, she was placed in an Alzheimer's wing. "I thought, '*She* doesn't have Alzheimer's,'" Lauren said. "I had this vision of padded walls. But when I visited the first time, I met all these lovely, interesting, well-dressed older people. You didn't really know they had Alzheimer's until you talked to them for a while."

Things went well until Lauren's mother got a roommate at whom she yelled incessantly. Bathing was a fight, too. "She felt like she was being disrobed by a different stranger every day," Lauren said. Which wasn't entirely wrong. After much thought, Lauren and her brother moved their mom into a modest group home that included three older women and a caregiver. It was a good fit. "She knew everyone she lived with, had her own room in a comfortable house, and got great care," said Lauren. "She was happy there."

But after being hospitalized for pneumonia, Lauren's mother was too ill to move back to that home. The hospital discharge planner, under pressure to swiftly dismiss patients who were costly to the hospital, like Lauren's mother, wanted to send her to a nursing home. "I'd investigated one too many bad nursing homes for *that*," Lauren said. So, her mother moved from Texas to Virginia to live with Lauren and her family.

Lauren built a suite in the basement of her Virginia home where all the corners were rounded and the carpeting was thick enough to cushion any fall. She installed a stair-lift, grab bars, anti-slip surfaces, extra-wide doorways, an alarm that trilled when any exterior door opened, and oxygen tanks for her mother's emphysema. The woman who'd previously babysat Lauren's daughter returned to care for her mother while she was at the Senate. She paid the woman from her mother's funds.

"When mom was still of sound mind," Lauren explained, "thankfully she'd assigned my brother and me power of attorney," giving them the legal authority to make decisions on her behalf. "That POA made things much easier. Thank God, we didn't have to go to court and go through a big, expensive guardianship proceeding." Lauren also became her mother's representative payee (Rep Payee)—the person authorized to receive social security checks on behalf of an incapacitated beneficiary.

I asked Lauren what compelled her to care for her mother: love, duty, something else? "Both, I think," Lauren said, "though they're hard to tell apart." What compels us to care is a question that animates novelists, philosophers, and, today, millions of American families.

Familial and cultural customs and mores differ about how money and possessions are shared or not shared, and when assets should transfer from one generation to the next. Some caregivers dip into parental assets now and then. They buy a few extra groceries or gallons of gas figuring they've earned it. Or pocket a keepsake figuring it won't be missed. But for Lauren there was no gray area. She tracked her mother's accounts meticulously. "I never paid myself for her food, lodging, or care, or bought anything for myself with her money," Lauren said. "But there was absolutely no oversight over what I did as POA."

The Social Security Administration furnished little more scrutiny. "They sent me a survey once a year to ask how it was going as Rep Payee," Lauren said. "That was basically it. It was a great lesson for me in how easy it is to exploit someone in my mom's situation. I had control over all her money, what she ate, where she slept, what medical care she got, who she saw, everything. I could have done anything."

That lesson informed Lauren's thinking as we worked on the Elder Justice Act.

As It Ever Was

Much has changed, but most old-age care is, as it ever was, still provided beyond channels of official commerce. Despite its centrality to our lives, there's little public recognition of this $500 billion shadow economy. We rarely consider its impact on workplaces and health systems, or ask what is owed caregivers by their families, employers, or society. Do we exploit caregivers by not compensating them? Do we pervert bonds borne of love and loyalty by injecting money into the equation?

These aren't new questions. Legal historian Hendrik Hartog analyzed a century of disputes about caregiver compensation in New Jersey courts from the mid-1800s to the mid-1900s. Family, housekeepers, and neighbors provided care—sometimes for decades—in exchange for a pledge that they'd be written into the will. The cases Hartog studied arose when caregivers who didn't get what they believed they were due went to court. Over time judges distinguished between *labors-for-hire* and *labors of love or duty*. "Normal" labors like cooking, cleaning, and companionship were less likely to be compensated than "exceptional" ones, "something peculiarly repellent," as

Hartog vividly describes.[19] By admitting they loved the person they cared for, women often torpedoed their claims for compensation.

Lauren confronted one type of "exceptional" labor Hartog wrote about when her mother refused to wear diapers as Alzheimer's robbed her of bladder and bowel control. The resulting mess prompted Lauren to cover everything in plastic. Her mother also clawed and screamed at anyone trying to bathe her, so the caregiver left the task to Lauren.

Caregiving touches not only its providers and recipients. It also ripples through the lives of other family members. As caregivers struggle, their children and partners absorb the stress, and often feel like they've "lost" the caregiver to caregiving. Sometimes, it upends family life. Dinner was once the only time Lauren's family gathered after hectic days. Then it was overtaken by her mom's "sundowning," the increased agitation and confusion that can be triggered by the fading light. So they took to eating in their separate rooms.

Almost six million Americans have some form of dementia. From the Latin for "out of one's mind," *dementia* refers to a cluster of diseases that impair memory, language, and judgment. It changes personalities and makes it hard to pay attention or solve problems. It also leads to physical decline. Alzheimer's disease is the most prevalent form, but there are others, too, like Lewy body and vascular dementia. The symptoms span a broad range, but all dementias are progressive.

The same "modifiable risk factors" that decrease heart disease and cancer, like diet, sleep, and exercise, keep the brain healthier, too. Evidence suggests that reducing stress and depression and staying socially connected can reduce risk. Even improving vision and hearing by wearing the right glasses and hearing aids seems to help. But with the population aging, more people have dementia now than ever before, especially women and people of color.

The hundreds of billions of dollars spent on studying dementia cures have yielded disappointing returns. So far, there's nothing to stop its grim march. Drugs may treat some symptoms, but they're not very effective, and those showing promise come with high risks. As many as half of people who reach eighty-five will face some cognitive impairment. The gods hardly could have invented a crueler way to mock our relentless quest to defy aging and death.

As Lauren's mother's disease progressed and death approached, she stayed in bed more and pleaded with Lauren to stay by her side 24/7. Some nights she moaned for hours. If Lauren snuck upstairs to her own bedroom, the moans often escalated to shrieks that ricocheted through the house. Exhausted, Lauren knew it was the disease screaming, but she couldn't help feeling manipulated. The guilt about not doing enough to help her mother competed with the guilt about not having enough time for anything else: her teenage daughter, her husband, her work, her friends, or herself.

Yet, hard as it was, Lauren was grateful for the time with her mother. And occasionally, usually late at night, she was rewarded with a few lucid words. Like standing on the platform when the train passes through carrying someone you love who's headed somewhere far away. Was the wave one of recognition? And what words do you say in that moment, through the open window, before the engine hurtles back into the night?

ILL-SUITED

"Do you have a minute for me to tell you about a case?" Laura Mosqueda, the geriatrician, was calling me from her car at dawn, driving from Pasadena to Orange County, where she then headed the program in geriatrics at the University of California, Irvine. Laura was upset about a case she'd learned about during a meeting of a forensic team she had formed. The team included law enforcement, prosecutors, and Adult Protective Services, which is responsible for responding to reports about vulnerable adults at risk. The case involved an eighty-eight-year-old woman with severe dementia who had lived with her granddaughter with schizophrenia. It was one of those tragic cautionary tales about the peril of two people with escalating needs isolated together without support.

Laura explained: "The grandmother took in the granddaughter decades ago and was utterly devoted to her." Both women had lived off the grandmother's social security and pension income for years.

As the grandmother's cognition declined and dementia got worse, she needed more help than her granddaughter could provide. The grandmother had been in a nursing home once but had tried to leave every day and begged to be taken home. The granddaughter relented and promised not to send her back. Both women told anyone who asked that they had no intention of being separated, that they'd manage. But their bills were stacking up unpaid.

This is the moment we see the difference a more caring, coherent system could have made. The women could have managed with simple support—occasional bill-paying assistance and some in-home personal care.

Instead, they were evicted and began living out of the grandmother's car. The granddaughter worried that her grandmother might wander off, so while doing errands sometimes locked her in the car, knowing that she could no longer figure out how to open the door.

One hot day, a passerby peering through the smudged car windows saw the grandmother crumpled on the back seat and called 911. Someone broke a window, releasing a blast of heat and stench: the car was a furnace, and the grandmother was filthy and unconscious. Paramedics rushed her to the hospital where she soon died. The granddaughter told the detectives that she'd done the best she could. Prosecutors charged her with neglect. She pled guilty and was given a suspended sentence. What should justice look like in such a case?

Although such dreadful scenarios are not commonplace, the issues that set them in motion are. No one really wants to talk about it, but people who end up, by default, in a caregiver role are sometimes the family member least suited for the job. Whether due to mental illness, intellectual disability, substance use, or something else, many adult children long depend on older relatives for housing, money, and emotional support. Often the older relative feels responsible that things didn't work out better, that the child or grandchild depending on them didn't get the help they needed. Siblings or other family members may worry but want to respect their parent's choices or don't know what to do. Such scenarios are okay until they're not. As the older relative's function declines and their needs mount, first slowly, then in leaps, suddenly everyone's in over their heads. Whatever the prelude, overload can happen fast; be shrouded in good intentions, loyalty, or indecision; and have terrible consequences. Many "overload" calamities are preventable. The grandmother and granddaughter just needed a little help.

Poorly equipped caregivers, like the granddaughter with mental illness, present one kind of peril. Another arises where there's unresolved past trauma. Sue Hall Dreher, the former executive director of Sexual Assault Support Services of Mid-Coast Maine, told me about a support group she led for survivors of sexual assault where every group member was caring for a parent who'd abused them in the past. The issue came up, by chance, during intake interviews. "Several of the caregivers-to-be said, 'I don't know how I'm going to take care of this parent,'" Sue told me.

The enormity of early life trauma is hard to absorb: About one in seven children is abused or neglected, 90 percent of them by someone they know.[20] More than half of women and almost one in three men experience sexual violence during their lifetimes.[21] And millions of children are exposed to domestic violence that occurs in one in five intimate partnerships. Research indicates that these cycles of abuse extend to "adult relationships and finally to care of the elderly."[22] Childhood trauma often unleashes lifelong physical and behavioral health issues that, if untreated, mushroom over time. Some victims wind up dependent on their abusers. Some end up caring for them. Sometimes it's both. Professionals and even family members may not know what lurks in the past. All this affects relationships down the line and makes it a bad idea to pressure anyone into caregiving. *Everyone gets on the bus with all their baggage.*[23]

Old enmity and trauma don't just vanish. "Past abuse doesn't mean caregivers will neglect or abuse a parent," explained Sue Hall Dreher. "But it tells me it's a high-risk situation. I also ask, 'What have you done in your own healing process? How will it work for you to care for them? Will you ask for help if you need it? What will you do if you find yourself getting ready to explode?'"

The moral math is complicated. Many abusers were abused themselves. What goes around in families often comes around. We must consider how to weigh past wrongs on present scales. The shadows of the past inform, but don't excuse, future harm.

Navigating Expectations

Rifts in families occur for countless reasons other than trauma, such as mismatched expectations relating to caregiving and assets. In his book *Fault Lines*, Karl Pillemer, a Cornell University sociologist, describes his research on family estrangement. One woman whom Karl interviewed, a single mother, "Grace," was the primary caregiver for her parents, but resentful and "incredibly disappointed" that her only sibling "wouldn't live up to her obligations." After their mother died, their father, who had Alzheimer's, couldn't live alone. Grace wanted to sell the family home to pay for his care, but her sister wanted to rent it out because she might want to live there someday. "I felt that she should give me more say," said Grace, "since I had been the one who did all the caregiving work." In the ensuing confrontation, "I said some things, and she said some things." They sold the house but lost the relationship. Even sitting vigil at their father's deathbed, Grace's sister wouldn't acknowledge her.[24]

This case neatly maps many of the landmines families encounter: the hard work of care, disposition of the family home, its freighted contents and memories, and divergent feelings and expectations amid the existential upheavals of illness, care, and death. Caregivers may feel that they have both the knowledge and the moral authority for their decisions to be given greater weight, but their siblings may feel that they too deserve a say, care notwithstanding. Families careen through infinite variations on this theme, many painful, often leaving resentment and division in their wake. Karl told me he advises families to consult an objective third party.

I've come to think that we need "family caregiving navigators," professionals who combine the skills of a mediator, care coordinator, therapist, and coach. Among other things, they need expertise in aging issues, local options, negotiations, and communications to help families navigate complex sensitive matters productively. Families need more guidance as they traverse this increasingly common and onerous phase of adult life.

Karl's research showed estrangement in 27 percent of families. Caregiving was just one cause, joining a host of others. Although such estrangement research is relatively scarce, it suggests that people these days more readily sideline or sever painful or troublesome family relationships, a kind of emotional decluttering to enhance personal growth and health. Our very idea of *the family* is in flux, becoming less a bond of "mutual obligation" and more one of "mutual understanding." Said another way, family bonds increasingly are seen as less obligatory than optional. Whether one embraces family depends on what it has to offer. Many people also build or join "chosen families." But how all this plays out in elder caregiving, and what's expected of whom, remains in flux.

Whatever the situation, it's worth asking a few questions before embarking on caregiving and to keep asking them throughout: What was your relationship with the person you're caring for? Will it work for you to care for them? What kinds of support do you need? Other family members should aid those on the front lines. And remember, care needs usually escalate with time. It's helpful to think a few steps in advance.

Cognitive impairment also deals wild cards when it comes to caregiving. Adult children who finally reach equilibrium with a difficult parent may suddenly be called on to help. The parent may no longer remember the conflict, scrambling hard-won boundaries. Sometimes it goes in the opposite direction, an unexpected silver lining. One friend told me, "Alzheimer's transformed my solidly C– mother into an A+. I started calling her 'the Dali Momma.'" With dementia, some hard memories disappear while others fuse with fantasy. Others still, suppressed or long kept secret, roar back with new, raw force.

Even amazing caregivers who adore the person they're caring for may find it hard not to become annoyed by dementia's challenging behaviors. They may understandably feel hurt and angry if the person for whom they provide loving care wrongfully accuses them of theft or abuse. Or cuts them out of the will. Or is more generous to others, especially if those others have harmed more than helped. They may become resentful if other family members don't assist or show appreciation. They may feel overwhelmed and trapped in a role they'd underestimated. This is where a process like CareMapping can reveal that the care all goes one way: that the caregiver might need to be offered and accept some care, too.

Caregiving for someone with dementia is like being in a little boat on the open sea when the compass you once relied on doesn't work as it did before. It takes time to recalibrate and to find your sea legs. No matter how well you pack and who you can call, navigating is hard. Some days are sunny and you sing and remember. Supply boats bring fortifications. You eat well. But other days, waves drench you and squalls blow through. You try to keep everyone safe and hang on for dear life yourself. Even full of love and grateful for the time, it's hard.

If we want to live long lives, we also need to plan—as individuals, families, and a nation. There's a gargantuan unpaid eldercare workforce who needs our support. And we're going to need them, too.

A BIG JOB

After my mother died, my father refused help from anyone other than family, fervently guarding his privacy. But once he reached ninety-one, cancer, surgeries, a colostomy, near blindness, and a large open wound left him with two choices: go to a facility or accept help at home. When he returned to his apartment from the hospital after surgery, my sister Heidi arranged for nurses to come in twice a day. In addition, he needed help with meals, cleaning, and errands: the domain of aides, another aspect of caregiving. The nurses were covered by Medicare for less than three weeks. Then he paid out of pocket. The aides weren't covered by Medicare at all.

Just figuring out the various players—who does what and according to what rules—requires a tutorial. There's *home health care*, which is provided by nurses, physical therapists, and other health professionals, usually in coordination with physicians. Then there are home health and personal care *aides*, also called home care workers, who do housekeeping, go grocery shopping, and help people bathe and stay socially connected. Some also, with supervision, take blood pressure, help with range of motion exercises, or remind people to take their medication.

The Bureau of Labor Statistics reported that there were 3.6 million personal care and home health aides in 2021.[25] They're among the fastest-growing occupations, even as there are dire shortages of such workers in some parts of the country. And while agencies that hire nurses must follow federal standards to get Medicare reimbursement, that's not the case with aides. For aides, the rules are up to individual states and are inconsistent and sometimes nonexistent.

Only about half of the states require aides to be trained. A third or so require in-home reviews of aides' work, and fewer than ten states ensure that aides have the basic knowledge required for the job. That leaves a lot of room for poor care even by diligent aides. And though many agencies charge high hourly rates, they often pay staff poorly and don't provide benefits or invest in their education or supervision.

Getting paid help at home is expensive. People with long-term care insurance may have coverage, but such insurance is costly too—about $3,000 per person per year—and it often doesn't cover what people need when they need it. In 2021, the average annual cost to hire a home health aide was $61,700 and a homemaking aide, $59,500. A full-time aide is beyond the means of most people sixty-five and over whose median annual income is only $30,000.[26] The savings and income of people of color are lower still. Perversely, people less able to pay for long-term services and supports, or LTSS, are the very ones most likely to need them.

My family was fortunate in being able to afford to hire aides. Still, finding the ideal candidate wasn't easy. Before my father was discharged, the hospital staff had given Heidi the name of a personal care agency. Given my work, you'd think that when I called, I would have asked about qualifications and background checks. But no. Like many families, we were searching during a crisis. I explained to the agency representative that we needed just the right person, and fast. My father was not thrilled about the prospect of strangers in his apartment, I explained. We hoped to find someone reserved with good judgment, and a sense of humor.

That agency wasn't my only call. When our children were young, we found our best childcare providers by word of mouth. With that in mind, I started dialing. I interviewed several independent aides who offered more flexibility than the agencies. They got rave recommendations and included—given the Mayo Clinic's proximity—several retired nurses. Called *private duty home care*, or the *gray market*, such aides are employed not by agencies but directly by consumers, and rarely background checked or formally trained and supervised. Many work off the grid and some are undocumented immigrants.

There's talk about robots easing caregiving shortfalls by dispensing pills and leading exercises or reducing loneliness with AI-driven chats and visits from a cuddly robot-seal named Paro. And virtual reality goggles could lessen boredom by offering any adventure from the couch. But so far, this is all more theory than practice. Venture capital and start-ups also are bidding to enter the eldercare market, raising millions for new companies that boast they're the "Uber of" home care. But at this writing, no health or tech entity has found a silver bullet in a business that, unlike rides to the airport or ordering takeout, is high-touch and deeply personal.

There's little data about this informal army of workers, making it hard to study or even count. PHI, a leading caregiver nonprofit, estimates that there are about 2.6 million home care workers, not including those employed directly by individuals or households through the gray market (because those employment relationships are generally unreported).[27] The RAND Corporation estimates that nearly a third of Americans rely on gray market aides for eldercare.[28]

There's also little data about the quality of care aides provide or rates of abuse, neglect, or exploitation. We also don't know how quality correlates with training or working conditions. But there are countless stories. My work confronted me with far too many of the horrid ones. I wanted to learn how a caregiver with a great reputation approached the job.

When I first saw a posting on my neighborhood Listserv about a fantastic caregiver named "Ayana" looking for work, I forwarded it on to a friend looking for an aide to help his mother who had late-stage dementia. He hired Ayana. The job wasn't easy. "She always felt emptiness and could get very upset," Ayana said. "It's part of the sickness. It was a hard time for her, not for me." Ayana had driven for Uber and run a food truck before finding a vocation in eldercare. "My goal," she said, "is to put myself in the person's position and to imagine their feelings. That gives me insight."

"We love love love Ayana," my friend said. "She's incredibly kind and very religious. She answers to a higher authority. Care is her calling." Originally from Ethiopia, Ayana raised three children in the United States, one of whom is now in law school. Although she's an unwavering optimist, her life has been precarious. In my friend's words, "one car wreck away from calamity." When she first told him her salary, he said, "We'll pay you more than that." Caregivers' expectations often reflect the low value society places on their work. After my friend's mother died, Ayana went to work for his mother's best friend for whom she still works full-time. Word of mouth is the gray market engine.

Ayana never got any training, but she takes an analytic approach to her work. "I study the behavior of the people I take care of. And I have a technique. Give them time. Give them patience. Give them love. It's about love." I was curious about her approach to delusions. "For them it's real," she said. "I don't oppose it. I listen and accept it." Sometimes she finds it helps to change the subject. She might talk about nature or an animal. But most important in caregiving, she said, was trying to make a human connection.

"If you show them love, they see it." Then Ayana apologized and said she had to go. It was her day off; she'd been talking to me while taking her granddaughter to a doctor's appointment and they'd just arrived.

To learn more about patterns in the issues facing aides, I attended a conference of the National Domestic Workers Alliance and its sister organization, Caring Across Generations, both directed by Ai-jen Poo. The event resembled a United Nations convention of hundreds of women. Many wore headphones for simultaneous translation of both speeches and audience comments into English, Spanish, Tagalog, or Filipino. People of color were in the majority on the dais and in the audience. Workers told of egregious hours, chronic fear of deportation, no overtime, not being paid for their work, and wages so low they struggled to care for their own families and health. Some told of indentured servitude, false accusations, and abuse. Many caregivers encountered racism and sexism from the people they worked and cared for. Biases, even ones long left behind, can reemerge or be exacerbated by the disinhibition and paranoia that sometimes accompany cognitive decline.

Then there's the pay. The median wage for home care workers (primarily home health and personal care aides) was $14.09 per hour in 2021, according to PHI's analysis of data from the Bureau of Labor Statistics.[29] Their median annual income was $19,100 in 2020 and almost half live in low-income households. Nearly nine in ten home care workers are women and more than six in ten are non-white. Many workers suffer from unpredictable feast-or-famine hours. During the pandemic, they lacked personal protective equipment (PPE) and juggled impossible decisions involving income and the health of their employers, their families, and themselves.

Ai-jen Poo is the most public face of the movement to protect direct care workers in the largely unregulated industry. She has pushed, in some places successfully, for a minimum wage of $15 an hour. In the wake of the pandemic, grave worker shortages have resulted in modest increases in pay, but it's not clear how much the industry, or the quality of jobs, will change.

Poo's organizations, the Service Employees International Union (SEIU) (which represents home health workers, among others) and PHI, headed by Robert Espinoza, all point out that caregiving is hard work that deserves respect and equitable compensation. And data suggests that better jobs mean better care. "The vulnerabilities of older adults and care workers are commingled," notes anthropologist Elana Buch in her book, *Inequalities of Aging*. "Low wages and poor working conditions render workers' lives precarious. In turn, high turnover and endemic worker shortages translate into waiting lists and lower quality care for older adults. In home care, the fate of older adults and the working poor are connected, entangled by the broader indifference of a society that devalues both aging and care."[30]

To care well for others, workers must be treated well themselves. Here, too, theory and practice often clash. We believe, in principle, that aides should be fairly paid, but not that *we* should have to pay them well or assure reasonable hours, benefits, or training. One type of guidance few gray market aides receive relates to the legal and ethical considerations in accepting or seeking gifts from those for whom they care.

That issue arose for a caregiver who'd witnessed human rights abuses in Congo so terrible that she was given asylum in the United

States. Once approved to work, she got a job caring for an older woman. There was much mutual affection. About that much every-one agreed. Everyone also agreed that the caregiver got money from the older woman in addition to her wages. When the older woman's son who handled his mother's finances but was otherwise uninvolved in her care, noticed, he became enraged. His mother, whose cognitive abilities were waning, wanted him to let it go, but he reported the caregiver to the police and fired her. The caregiver claimed that the older woman had given her the money voluntarily.

Such scenarios are common and variably characterized as theft, undue influence, an investment, or a token of gratitude in a caring relationship, often between people of lopsided means.

Prosecutors filed charges but offered the caregiver a chance to plead to a "non-deportable misdemeanor" that would allow her to stay in the United States. Her public defender pushed her hard to accept the offer, but she was adamant in her refusal. She believed she hadn't stolen anything and would not say she had. At trial, the jury convicted her of theft with an enhanced sentence because of the victim's age. She served a year in prison but was not deported due to a technicality in the law.

While working for DOJ, I urged that more financial exploitation cases be prosecuted, but I came to wonder how effective cases like this one were in preventing future harm or advancing justice. What lessons should we take? Certainly, that aides need more training in the often-complex aspects of caring for people with dementia and in the ethical and legal rules accompanying the role. And that fam-ilies need more guidance about what skills aides need for the job. Many families struggle to clearly communicate expectations and limits, which is to say they struggle to be good employers. There's little guidance for them either.

When we searched for an aide to help our father, I initially leaned toward hiring a private duty or gray market aide, given their greater flexibility and lower cost. I interviewed several candidates who got great reviews. Then Heidi, who travels a lot, pushed back. She asked what we would do if the aide got sick, went on vacation, or got snowed in. Who would do the training, orientation, and oversight with every new person? Heidi was right. An agency aide made more sense.

I called back the scheduler for Home Instead, a national company with a Rochester franchise. She said, "I think I found just the right aide for your dad," a retired nurse who liked working with older people. When the scheduler and aide arrived together at his apartment for an intake interview, my father said a quick hello, then, ever shy, retreated to his office while I talked with them. That was how my father's caregiver started coming to his apartment four days a week for two hours a visit. We got lucky. Her quiet competence and gentle ribbing soon overcame Daddy's reticence. His apartment was cleaner than it had been in years. He had more fresh groceries, healthier meals, and fewer questionable items lurking in his fridge. We got prepaid credit cards for her to shop, and she left receipts for every purchase on the kitchen counter with sweet notes and smiley faces. He declared her to be "fantastic." "I never thought of myself as his caregiver," she said. "He always treated me as a friend." When we visited him and asked her how things were going, she'd roll her eyes, grin, and say in her thick Minnesota accent, "Oh you know, it's really tough. But I do the best I can." And they'd both laugh.

But also, when it comes to aging, no decision ever stays made.

Chapter 2

HEALTH

Medicine has been slow to confront the very
changes that it has been responsible for—or to
apply the knowledge we already have about how
to make old age better.

—ATUL GAWANDE,
"The Way We Age Now," *New Yorker*

Although I dashed my parents' hopes by going to law school,
in a sense they had the last laugh: I ended up working for
health anyway, just using different tools than they had. I'd
like to say that some noble impulse set things in motion. But DOJ's
Nursing Home Initiative, which became the Elder Justice Initiative,
began as an effort in damage control—one political party deflecting
efforts by another to score points off dire reports of decades-long
nursing home calamities for which both bore blame.

Self-interest motivated me, too. I hadn't quite gotten around
to practicing mental health law as I'd intended. After going to law
school and clerking for a judge, I'd gone to DOJ's Civil Frauds section to learn how to be a lawyer. Then I had three children, one
with serious illnesses after her premature birth. While embroiled
in a big research fraud case against the University of Minnesota, I
realized that although DOJ was a great place to be a lawyer, litigation's incessant conflict was too corrosive for me. And prosecution
was a blunt instrument that only came into play after other systems
had failed to stop trouble. Prosecution was a last resort; I wanted

work that focused further upstream, that looked forward, not back. I wanted to see more of my children. I wanted more control over my time. To shore up my intention to change my life, I told my boss, Stuart Schiffer, that I planned to leave DOJ when the University of Minnesota case was done. I had no clue what I'd do next.

Schiffer was a big, jowly, curmudgeonly man with a shambling gait, who smoked in his office long after it was outlawed. His irreverence could mask his abiding faith in public service. Just before we signed the final settlement agreement in the Minnesota case, I picked up my phone to a typical Schiffer rapid-fire patter *in medias res*, no preliminaries. His sales pitch that day went like this: "It sounds like a fucking depressing nightmare but then again you like that sort of thing and at my advanced age, I figure I'll need all the help I can get. Since you've decided you don't want to do real work anymore, the Deputy's office has a nursing home project, another brainchild of some genius upstairs who thinks he reinvented public service in his long year of sacrifice."

It wasn't that Schiffer recognized in me some latent skill for taking on nursing homes. Initiatives were viewed by career lawyers like him as whims of the political classes, inessential to the department's core mission of investigating and prosecuting cases. By enlisting me before I got out the door, Schiffer could mollify the higher-ups and produce a body without squandering a productive lawyer. For my part, I was a litigator, accustomed to learning on the fly. I figured, "I'll read up on it. How hard can it be?" The fact that I had no expertise or experience for the job was never raised by either of us.

GERIATRICS

When Laura Mosqueda first took over the program in geriatrics at the University of California, Irvine (UCI), in 1998, it was just her and a half-time geriatrician, along with a psychologist and a part-time social worker all crammed into a small, run-down space—hardly equipped to serve Orange County's more than 300,000 residents sixty-five and older. Laura's first priority was to revive the "sad little group" and build a robust Senior Health Center. But geriatrics had meager clout inside the medical center; it didn't bring in enough money. So she got a leadership grant and asked the dean to be her mentor, giving her entrée to high-level meetings where she got a glimpse of what factors drove decisions. One thing in her control was the quality of care she provided for her patients. She told me about a new patient, "Mr. Blue," in his late eighties, who'd come into the geriatrics clinic to sort out mobility, metabolic, heart failure, and dementia-related issues. He was accompanied that day by his much younger girlfriend and his son.

"You walk into the exam room cold," said Laura. "I'm not just thinking about medical and function issues. I'm also wondering— What are my patient's goals? How do the son and girlfriend's goals mesh with his? Do they get along or disagree on what's right?" Sometimes Laura offered to have a "family meeting" to troubleshoot and sort out goals and roles.

One major concern was that Mr. Blue's walking had worsened. Function is fundamental to geriatricians, like blood pressure is to cardiologists. It's measured in two kinds of increments: *activities of daily living* (ADLs) or the ability to carry out life's basic tasks to care for yourself—eat, bathe, walk (or move), dress, and toilet (used as a verb)—and *instrumental activities of daily living* (IADLs) or skills you need to navigate the world—the ability to use the telephone, manage finances, shop, prepare food, manage medication, do house-work, and navigate transportation. Once we master these skills early in life, most of us take them for granted. Until they ebb, that is. Then they're a big deal again. Losing function skills is cause for concern and helps inform what kinds of support we need.

Function is pivotal in other ways, too. "The more we can help people retain function," said Laura, "the less they need to depend on others to eat, bathe, use the toilet, pay bills, buy groceries, or use ATM machines." Reducing the number of people with access to such personal aspects of one's life reduces the risk that someone might exploit that access.

In the same way that, medically speaking, kids are not just small adults, older people are, in Laura's words, "not just wrinkled adults." Drugs get metabolized differently. Brains change. Seeing and hear-ing fade. Walking teeters. This is where geriatricians come in. They're trained to see how the parts interconnect. Often, it's not one big thing they do that makes a big difference, but a combination of many small things.

A good example is how they chip away at the risk of falls, which can be calamitous. There are things you can get—like walkers and glasses, hearing aids and handrails. And then there are the things you can do—like exercise, adjust medication, and remove trip hazards like throw rugs. Prevention is not glamorous or heroic. Providers get no awards for preventing falls. Insurance companies send them no thank-you letters for saving them the cost of broken hips. Grateful patients endow no buildings in honor of prevention's incremental steps. Still, prevention pays huge if invisible dividends.

Laura's patient, Mr. Blue, had recently fallen. He had bruises all over and, since the fall, spent a lot of time in bed. Laura had to consider diagnostic questions and how the broader context of his life influenced his health: His son lived out of state but was in close touch. Paid caregivers came in several days a week. His girlfriend lived with him, but her contributions weren't clear. Laura had long since learned that another set of questions was also relevant to her patients' health: Was Mr. Blue's son or girlfriend getting money from him? Were they pressuring him for it? Did he have the capacity to give it away? Were they getting him the right help?

"You don't want to be suspicious of everyone," said Laura. "But you don't want to miss stuff either." She wanted to examine and talk with Mr. Blue privately, so she asked his son and girlfriend to step out. During the physical exam, Laura also took a closer look at his bruises and kept an eye out for any other worrisome marks. This too was easier in theory than practice. There was little data about what was suspicious. Aging itself confounds the analysis. As we age, skin loses elasticity. Capillaries burst more easily. Bones break more readily. Bruises and fractures can look like abuse when they're not, and can look like accidents when they're not. "Aging can both mask and mimic signs of abuse" is how Laura puts it.

ASKING NEW QUESTIONS

Over the years, countless families have asked Laura whether they should worry about those bruises on mom. Or whether those pressure sores on dad were caused by facility neglect. The lack of evidence to answer such questions has launched untold agonizing investigations, countless lawsuits, and sometimes wrongful accusations.

Laura's interest in the subject had started with a patient. While she was doing her geriatrics fellowship in Los Angeles, a patient with mild dementia came in for an appointment. They had a warm, open rapport, but when Laura asked about the strange-looking bruises on the woman's arm, she got tearful and silent. Slowly, she explained that her caregiver had hit her with a phone and imitated the slamming motion for Laura with an invisible receiver.

Laura searched the scientific literature for any evidence to help her figure out if the dozens of bruises she saw weekly were accidental or inflicted. She found studies on suspicious bruising in children but none on bruising in older adults. In fact, she found no research to guide her in assessing *any* kind of suspicious condition in her older patients—fracture, brain bleed, or pressure sore. That piqued her curiosity. "What is it that makes me think some injuries are not okay?" Laura asked herself. The dearth of answers tipped her career in a new direction that would in time intersect with mine.

Because California law made Laura a mandatory reporter of elder abuse, she explained to her patient that she had to report the injury to Adult Protective Services. APS is the public agency that takes reports from families, neighbors, and professionals when they're concerned about a vulnerable adult who's at risk. When her patient returned a month later, Laura asked how things had gone with APS. "She didn't remember anyone visiting," Laura said. "So I contacted APS to follow up. She was right."

Laura complained to the APS manager but was surprised when the manager laid into *her*, too: APS never had enough workers, training, or resources. Everyone complained about APS, but no one helped—especially not doctors. "They were as frustrated with us as I was with them," said Laura. "*That* got me interested." She learned that APS workers faced complex medical and cognitive questions about their clients every day without adequate training and rarely with access to medical specialists to help them. Laura offered her services, but again no one followed up.

When she signed on as head of the program in geriatrics at University of California, Irvine, Laura planned to contact APS, but this time APS beat her to it. Rebecca Guider, director of Orange County's large APS program, was accustomed to doctors dismissing her. "I'd call to say, 'your patient is living in squalor, covered in bedsores, and starving,'" said Rebecca. "And the doctor would tell me, 'She's senile and going to die anyway,' and do nothing." For fifteen years, Rebecca couldn't get doctors to pay attention to her concerns.

Then she met Laura. "I thought I'd died and gone to heaven," Rebecca said. "Here was a doctor actually making herself available to my staff." Their work together began informally—Rebecca called Laura with medical questions, and Laura rode along with Rebecca's APS workers, wanting to see the world they saw. Then Laura, Rebecca, and their staffs formed the first of several teams: the Vulnerable Adult Specialist Team. They called it "the VAST."

Word of Laura's work also rippled down the coast. In San Diego, a child abuse pediatrician assembling a team to train medical professionals about family violence was looking for a doctor to teach the sessions on elder abuse. Most such trainings just ignored the subject. "They forgot old people are part of the family," Laura quipped. But that pediatrician persisted, calling a dozen California district attorney's offices to ask: "Who's your expert in elder abuse cases?" Eventually her calls produced a single name: Laura Mosqueda.

In 2000, I undertook a similar search while organizing the first ever forum on the "Medical Forensics of Elder Abuse." Janet Reno, then the attorney general, had agreed to participate, helping us entice some thirty leading experts to attend on short notice with no compensation or reimbursement. I wanted a lawyer and a doctor to co-facilitate to model a forensic collaboration. Finding a lawyer was easy; DOJ was crawling with them. Finding a doctor took longer, but a series of calls eventually led me to Laura.

Laura saw different aspects of elder abuse through her medical lens than I did through my legal one. Forensics—where law and science intersect—was our common ground. It took a while for me to see how the art and science of geriatrics were central, not just to my work but to anyone striving for a better old age. At first, I saw Laura's role mostly through that forensic lens. Maybe it was my myopia. Maybe that was all she revealed at first. She wasn't easy to know. She was by turns abrasive and funny, impatient and patient, guarded and warm. She refused to indulge perfectionism and was vigilant about time, making her extravagantly productive, as though working for two.

Laura's growing knowledge about forensics caused her to add a few new questions to the repertoire she routinely asked her patients. When a patient had dementia, she asked the questions in a way they could answer. Now, she asked Mr. Blue, while alone with him in the exam room: "Are you getting the help you need?" ("Yes.") "Is anyone hurting you?" ("No.") "Are you scared of anyone?" ("No.") "Is anyone using your money without your permission?" ("No.") Mr. Blue said he wished he saw more of his son and that he loved his girlfriend and was so glad she lived with him. He didn't seem fearful.

DIFFERENCE, DRUGS, AND DELUSIONS

Another unique aspect of geriatrics is *heterogeneity.* "If you look at a roomful of two-year-olds, developmentally almost all of them can do the same things," Laura explained. "But if you look at a roomful of ninety-two-year-olds, there's huge diversity in their functional status. We become more different as we age."

Another aspect of heterogeneity is that common illnesses present in uncommon ways. "I had to figure out why my patient had trouble getting out of bed," Laura said of Mr. Blue. "Was it a metabolic, orthopedic, balance, fear, depression, a medication issue, or some combination of them?"

Getting medications right is critical. "His depression wasn't well-controlled," Laura explained. "A different antidepressant might work better and also reduce his incontinence." (Some meds have positive side effects.) "And his orthopedic meds were interfering with the cardiac ones."

Polypharmacy is an epidemic among the old. Parades of doctors prescribe different drugs, often unaware of potential drug interactions or one another's prescriptions. There's a movement in geriatrics called *deprescribing,* but it's slow going. Laura asks her patients to bring in everything they take (prescribed and over-the-counter) *in the bottle*. Sometimes labels don't match what's inside. Or patients take wrong doses because they're confused or can't afford more. Laura considers what each drug is supposed to do and whether it's achieving the goal. "I stop more medications than I start," she says.

Such overuse may arise from ignorance, convenience, or neglect. Laura had a patient in a nursing home who was unable to move or communicate. The staff called her to say, "He's agitated; can you please prescribe something for his agitation?" Before doing so, Laura went to examine him first and found he had an infected ingrown toenail. "He couldn't say, 'Excuse me, my toe hurts,'" she said. "Agitation was the only way he could communicate. But he could easily have ended up on antipsychotics instead of getting treatment for his toe."

Another of Laura's patients was convinced that Secretary of State Colin Powell regularly consulted her for advice—a specific repeating delusion caused by dementia. The medication to manage it would have had serious side effects. The Powell conversations were the only "problem behavior" she manifested. "The delusions didn't bother my patient," Laura said, "but her caregiver-daughter was upset by them and wanted me to medicate her mom." Laura helped the daughter reframe what was going on. "I'll give you that it's weird and incorrect," Laura told the daughter. "But her delusions aren't hurting anyone." Laura's advice in such circumstances is *acknowledge-pivot-distract*. For example, say something like: "What an honor that Secretary Powell wants your advice. I love the sweater you're wearing. Is it new?"

Some people fear they'll perpetuate delusions if they go along with them. That's not the case, Laura explained. In fact, it can be upsetting to the person to dispute or correct what they firmly believe to be true. In such instances, entering another person's delusion can be an act of generosity. In my extended family, cousin Jay has a gift for this, earning him the (loving) moniker, *the dementia whisperer*. He might for example ask, "Is that Colin Powell bugging you again? What does he want this time?" In embracing the older relative's delusions, he became a kind, adventurous companion, like Don Quixote's Sancho Panza, along for any expedition of the mind.

Laura was relieved when her patient's daughter finally came to uneasy terms with her mother's delusions. "It just seemed wrong to medicate the mom to treat the daughter's anxiety."

"I want to help my patients figure out the optimum level of functioning they can achieve," said Laura, "and whether there's any excess disability we can reduce to help them be their best." This is central not only to geriatrics but also to all sorts of work with older people: to focus less on the losses and more on making the most of what remains. The geriatricians I know are a life-half-full lot. Researchers find that people drawn to geriatrics value enduring relationships, complexity, and teamwork, and get satisfaction from "seemingly small but nonetheless important changes in people's lives."[1] Geriatricians consistently report having among the highest levels of job satisfaction of any medical specialty. Their ethos is both profoundly practical and suffused with big questions about meaning.

When Laura saw Mr. Blue, who'd come in with his son, she couldn't eliminate his dementia but could reduce his depression and incontinence and maybe improve his walking. "I also adjusted his cane, which was too high," she said. "He really should use a walker, but he isn't willing to yet."

Laura also asked him about his goals, what kept him going. "He said he wanted to live as long as his identical twin. I told him, 'If you fall again, you might not.' That seemed to get through." It can be hard to stay focused on what matters most. In those moments, Laura tells her patients, "What you need now isn't physical therapy; it's metaphysical therapy."

We underestimate the power of specialized geriatric care to improve old age. In *Being Mortal*, Atul Gawande describes a 2001 University of Minnesota study revealing benefits so stunning we'd bottle them as an elixir if we could. "Patients who had seen a geriatrics team were a quarter less likely to become disabled and half as likely to develop depression. They were 40 percent less likely to require home health services," Gawande wrote. "The geriatrics teams weren't doing lung biopsies or back surgery. . . . What they did was to simplify medications. They saw that arthritis was controlled. They made sure toenails were trimmed and meals were square. They looked for worrisome signs of isolation and had a social worker check that the patient's home was safe."[2] Gawande asks, "How do we reward this kind of work?" Soon after releasing the blockbuster study, the University of Minnesota closed its geriatrics program for being financially unviable.

Fortunately, it has since launched a new Division of Geriatrics, Palliative, and Primary Care. Like many other medical centers' programs, Minnesota's combines geriatrics with palliative care, a newer specialty focused on relieving patients' pain, symptoms, and stress caused by serious illness, and on aiding their families to find the help they need. Palliative care and geriatrics specialists often work together, have overlapping goals and philosophies, and sometimes are trained in both subspecialties.

Public health experts have for decades warned that we're not ready to meet the growing demands of an aging population, but only a few entities heeded the clear demographic signs. One of them, the Department of Veterans Affairs (VA), saw that it needed to prepare for the aging of World War II veterans. In 1975, the VA persuaded Congress to create Geriatric Research, Education, and Clinical Centers (GRECCs). Those GRECCS have been knowledge hubs, spearheading geriatric research and interdisciplinary innovation. The VA also plays a role in the education of many of the country's geriatricians.

Still, despite geriatrics' manifest power to improve health and independence, and the burgeoning cohort of patients, it's a specialty in decline. It's on the bottom rungs of medicine's reimbursement ladder, which matters more as the average medical school graduate teeters under more than $250,000 in student debt. In 2022, 57 percent of the country's geriatrics fellowship slots were not filled.[3] "Medical students quickly learn," Diane Meier, a geriatrician and pioneer in palliative medicine, told me, "that procedures, devices, and drugs linked to income and venture capital are what's valued in medicine. Nobody wants to take you out to dinner if you're a geriatrician."

All that translates into serious shortages: In 2020, the United States had about 7,400 geriatricians, only half of them full-time. We already need more than triple that number. In 2034, the number of

Americans sixty-five and older will outnumber those eighteen and younger for the first time in history.[4] By then we'll need more than 30,000 geriatricians, but be nowhere close, whereas we'll have more than 50,000 pediatricians.[5]

Those shortages have consequences that are hard to quantify but can be measured in the burden of reduced function, independence, and health. The consequences also ripple on, as we've seen, to those who love and care for older people, and likely also on to the public programs they rely on for support.

In the face of the scarcity, geriatricians have had to decide where to allocate the existing expertise. For now, the triage plan is to focus on the frailest, most complex patients and work on training other medical professionals to handle the rest. Laura calls it the *Desk Test*. "When you look at your list of patients for the day and see a name that makes you want to hide under your desk because their needs are so difficult, those are the patients who most need geriatric care." But this triage approach means that geriatrics' power to prevent trouble goes largely untapped.

Given what I'd learned, I wanted to know what happened to that Senior Health Center Laura wanted to build. "I gradually learned the politics," she said, "and put together a business plan that showed cost savings and how geriatrics was important to *their* planning process. We also provided really good services and got good press for UCI. That made them happy about the work we were doing." UCI gave geriatrics shiny new offices and tripled the staff.

We have ways to make old age better. But most of the elixir remains in the bottle.

What Would a Geriatrician Do?

Anyone who has tried to help someone they love get good care knows how hard it can be. Even when things go well, it's tough. When faced with difficult decisions, patients often ask, "Doctor, what would you do?" I've asked the question many times myself—as a woman, a mother, and a daughter. Medical professionals have become better at giving patients information. But we patients often don't really know how to weigh what doctors tell us or to figure out what they're not saying. I wanted to take a closer look at how *the* experts navigate the fraught terrain of eldercare.

In her book *Elderhood*, geriatrician Louise Aronson describes having been gone for two weeks and returning to find one of her patients with dementia in a rehab and nursing home facility close to death. The patient was bedbound and drugged. She looked malnourished and had a huge, infected pressure sore. "I should have been more emphatic about the consequences of choosing the wrong nursing home," Aronson wrote.[6]

Aronson applied that lesson in her own family. "Even when I fought to get my own father into one of the better places in the city after his surgeries, we remained with him," she wrote, "taking turns to ensure one of us was there 24/7 initially, and then hiring someone to help overnight once the worst was over. I had spent enough time in hospitals and nursing homes to know that if we didn't, bad things were likely to happen."[7]

Laura told me something similar. In the mid-1990s, her mother, Gloria Frankl, a prominent radiologist and mammographer, noticed changes in her thinking too subtle for tests or her family to pick up. "She knew something was off," Laura said. "A few years later it became more apparent to the rest of us, too."

Even as Alzheimer's encroached, taking a visible toll on Gloria's memory and balance, her husband and children, like her, all doctors, were matter-of-fact. The elder Frankls' lives remained abundant. They went to the symphony and read books. Friends still came over for dinner.

The day I stopped by Gloria had laid an impeccable table with white linens and fine china bearing fruit and pastries. I didn't notice her dementia. It can be an intimate disease in its early stages. You only know if you know. Gloria and her husband, Hal, who'd passed along his gap tooth and yen for adventure to Laura, told me about their rugged family trips. Gloria wasn't a camper when they first met but grew to love their expeditions. She told me, "We took two very nice trips, one in the high country and one down the Rogue River, while Sally was still alive." Sally, Laura's identical twin, died of a brain tumor when the girls were eight. For Laura, Sally's death came as a total shock. She knew Sally was sick, but she had no concept of death or clue it might come. Even after Sally died, there was little talk about what had happened.

Almost fifty years later, among the Frankls' photographs was one, faded black and white, in which Laura and Sally are three. With their curly hair and gap teeth, both look surreally like Laura's adult self. They're holding harmonicas. I once asked Laura who was who. She shrugged. "I don't know."

Travel helped to heal the family and was formative for Laura. On a trip to the Galápagos Islands, they stayed on a boat, docked beside the home of a naturalist and his wife who lived with a colony of half-tame marine iguanas. The islands imprinted themselves on Laura, then ten years old. She swam with penguins and seals and stroked the shells of giant tortoises. "The great feeling inspired by these creatures was that of age: dateless, indefinite endurance," wrote Herman Melville after his own encounter with them. "What other bodily being possesses such a citadel wherein to resist the assaults of Time?"[8]

There, among the descendants of Darwin's finches, Laura, like scores of visitors before and since, came under the thrall of the ways that living creatures adapt, thrive, and age. Back home, dreaming of becoming a vet, she volunteered for the Los Angeles Zoo. In college, she nursed an injured fledgling sparrow back to health in her Occidental College dorm room, carrying it around in her pocket. She initially thought about becoming a large animal vet, but, she said, "I started thinking I could be happy in medicine and maybe do something useful there."

HOSPITAL

A few months after I'd had breakfast with Laura's parents, her mother fell at the Los Angeles Philharmonic. The fall marked a new chapter in life for Gloria and her family and set in motion a common circuit of old-age care—home, hospital, nursing home or rehab, and back home again. Laura met her parents at the hospital. Her mother had fractured her hip and was hallucinating that someone was after her. "She was grabbing at me frantically, pulling my clothes. She was calling for help," said Laura. "It was a wild night." On top of the dementia, the broken hip also triggered psychosis—probably brought on by pain and morphine. The cacophony of high-pitched sounds and patient laments amplified her confusion and panic, all common in older adults in the wake of serious injuries.

Laura finally convinced her father to go home, promising to stay the night. Had she not been there, her mother almost certainly would have been restrained physically or chemically, magnifying her distress and delirium, which is usually, but not always, transient.

Gloria Frankl was one of about thirty-six million older people to fall each year, one of more than two million whose falls land them in emergency rooms, and one of more than 270,000 whose falls cause hip fractures.[9]

What such fractures leave in their wake is often more destructive than the injury itself. There's disability and depression. And patients becoming dependent on others to meet their escalating care needs. Hospitalization alone exacts a toll. Researchers have found that rates of cognitive decline more than double after hospital stays, as though, the study's authors said, "people became ten years older from a cognitive standpoint, than they were before a hospitalization."[10]

What causes the decline? Probably some mix of injury, illness, immobility, *and* just being in the hospital. In one study, even older people hospitalized for noncritical illnesses were more likely to be discharged with a dementia diagnosis. It's not always clear whether hospitalization *causes* or *uncovers* the cognitive decline, but research shows that delirium prevention measures can be successful both face-to-face and remotely.

Neuroplasticity makes us hopeful. We can learn to speak Italian or play the cello deep into old age. But it has downsides, too. Similar to how childhood trauma can scramble human circuitry, late-life trauma also can blaze new, harmful trails through fragile, shrinking gray matter. Delirium, generally considered to be transient, may be less temporary than once believed.

ADVOCATING

Laura tried to reduce the cascading risk of harm after her mother's fall. "After hip repair surgery, my mom didn't need the ICU medically," Laura explained, echoing Louise Aronson, "but we gave her what I call 'the human ICU,' not technology but people—someone with her all the time." Laura and her father took turns sitting with her mother at the hospital, supplemented by a hired aide.

Rigid institutional routines are hard on confused older patients. Little things add up. "First, I tried to balance not being 'that annoying family' with advocating," Laura said. Then she just advocated. "When my mom hadn't slept for two days, I said, 'No, I don't want you to wake her to check her blood sugar now. It's not urgent. The test can wait.'"

Laura also refused to allow the staff to insert a catheter to check for urine retention. "I told them, 'Use ultrasound.' So, they used one of those little portable handheld ultrasounds. It took five minutes. They didn't need to hold her down and get her even more agitated or do an invasive procedure for no reason. And guess what, her bladder was empty."

Being a patient advocate requires a tricky balancing act, even for doctors—sometimes especially for doctors. Aronson wrote about being unable to get the hospital staff's attention when she suspected her father was bleeding internally so she did a rectal exam on him herself and then marched out to the nurses' station holding up her hand with the bloodied glove. "What is most interesting," she wrote, "is how much more comfortable I felt performing an intimate procedure on my father than demanding the attention of the professionals assigned to care for him. Abiding by the unspoken rules of medical etiquette, I had quieted my internal alarms. . . . I had prioritized wanting us to be seen as a 'good family' over being a good doctor-daughter."[11]

Aronson explains that the culture of medicine rewards patients who acquiesce to medical professionals' decisions. "This definition," she wrote, "runs counter to what we know about truly good care as a collaborative process." Questioning doctors can seem disrespectful, especially in a culture like ours that reveres them and presumes that medicine holds the answers. We fear their disapproval or even avoidance. But, Aronson explains, "active participation of patients and families is essential to optimal outcomes. [People] who are considered high-maintenance, challenging, or both are simply trying their best to manage their own or their loved ones' illness."[12]

Like Laura Mosqueda and Louise Aronson, I have been both a patient and a patient advocate. Unlike them, I wouldn't have known to suspect internal bleeding or to ask for an ultrasound to check for urine retention. Nor do I think the hospital staff would have been receptive to my diagnostic assessments. (They likely weren't enthused about the geriatricians' suggestions either, but at least they're medical experts.)

Most of us who act as patient advocates aren't doctors, but we can still strive to advocate for the best care possible. And all of us are experts in what's going on with ourselves and those we care for. My daughter is alive today because when I was pregnant, I called Julian Safran, my ob-gyn, with a gut check. Something felt off. I apologized for bothering him. He told me to come in, saying, "If it's important enough for you to call, it's important enough for us to check you out." He and I were operating on hunches but also on trust. I trusted him enough to call, and he trusted me enough to take it seriously. And Fiona, who was gravely ill in utero, lived.

Fiona's rocky start catapulted me into being an advocate—first for her three-plus months in the NICU, followed by years at home with oxygen, monitors, medications, nebulizers, and doctors on speed dial, as well as surgeries and many hospital trips. The terror-relief-question-doubt caregiving cycle changed how I moved through the world. For one thing, I learned that you don't need a medical degree to gain the insight that close, long-term observation of someone you know well provides, and that such knowledge can supply invaluable information that a medical professional's fleeting contact cannot. We had great doctors who knew that such information and partnerships were critical to good care, especially with long-term illness. They respected the art and science—the telling, asking, and careful listening—of shared decision-making.

Still, being advocates doesn't make us medical experts. We should ask questions without taking too much of our providers' time and make reasonable requests. We can try to educate ourselves about what's "reasonable," but take with a grain of salt what's floating around the Internet. Learning how to have an effective voice in medical decisions takes time and attention.

It takes preparation, too. If even doctors like Louise Aronson feel intimidated into silence, the rest of us may have a hard time speaking up. I have found, when seeing doctors myself or with someone else, that showing up with a short list of prepared questions helps me to use the limited time more productively. If I'm lucky enough to have someone with me taking notes, especially about any follow-up, all the better. Far from being rude, this can make things clearer and avoid the need for repetition later. No one is more invested in our health or that of someone we love than we are.

Most geriatricians wear two hats—they're both primary care providers for their own patients and consultants on aging issues for colleagues from other specialties. Primary care is medicine's most powerful tool to lower mortality, morbidity, and medical costs. The more complex a patient's needs, the greater the benefit. "For lung disease you may see a pulmonologist," explains Laura. "But my job is to remember that your lungs are attached to the rest of your body." Studies show that people with primary care providers have better prognoses and live healthier for longer. And the benefits multiply as we age. Primary care providers also serve as connectors and ambassadors when it comes to finding and communicating our needs to specialists. Not having access to the multiple benefits of primary care also exacerbates health inequities.

Another core component of advancing health—the collaborative process—is already part of primary care and certain subspecialties, like geriatrics. But that collaboration won't happen broadly, Aronson writes, "unless the healthcare system begins valuing and rewarding the time that clinicians spend talking to patients and families."[13] Time and trust are the secret sauces that build solid relationships and make care more effective. They require little overhead, but we disincentivize them by valuing and reimbursing more for procedures, devices, and drugs. Medical practice follows the money. What we reimburse reflects what we value. And it isn't primary care or geriatrics. *By their budgets and their reimbursement rules ye shall know them.*

Nursing Home and Rehab

After hip-repair surgery and a few days in the hospital, Laura's mother was discharged to a rehab and nursing facility for short-term physical and occupational therapy to help her regain mobility. Reimbursement rules put a lot of pressure on hospitals to discharge patients quickly, often while they still have significant care needs. From a medical perspective, such transitions come with risk. Just as one group of professionals gets to know the patient—medically and as a human being—a new team starts over. When handoffs from hospitals to nursing homes are sloppy, patients miss their medication and physical therapy. Their humanity can get lost in the shuffle.

Then there's the question of where to go. Many nursing homes have moved into the rehab market. It's more lucrative than regular long-term nursing home care. But nursing homes' results are worse overall than places specializing just in rehab. When the moment of need arrives, there's rarely time to do much research and little user-friendly-in-a-crisis consumer data. Most people just do whatever the hospital discharge planner suggests.

Even for someone as informed as Laura, sleuthing out a good place wasn't easy. The federal five-point nursing home rating scale has useful information, but some of the underlying data is self-reported by nursing homes and has been found untrustworthy. The nursing home rehab facility where Laura's mother went got five stars and looked good in terms of staffing levels and "incident reports." But as her mom was being admitted, Laura was struck by something harder to measure: "Nobody was mean or harsh as they examined her body," said Laura. "Fine. But my mom's lying there and they're just lifting up her clothes. No one's talking to her. Nobody's explaining anything. It was striking how little warmth or human interaction was there. It was like they were inspecting a car."

Laura stayed overnight. "That way, if Mom woke up, I could tell her where she was, help her to the bathroom, that kind of thing." As Laura went foraging for something to sleep on, she was seized by déjà vu. Twenty years earlier, as a young doctor, she'd stayed overnight in the hospital with her grandmother and gone on a similar hunt. Now, with her mother as the patient, she again found herself dragging a Naugahyde recliner down a hall.

But rest was scarce as the night filled with sounds of need. Once her mom fell asleep, Laura took leave of the recliner. "If something bad was going on, I couldn't just ignore it, right? One woman wheeled out of her room, and said, 'Can you help me? I'm in so much pain. I pressed my call bell, but nobody came.'" Laura went to the nurses' station to ask someone to help her.

Like for most people, going from home to sharing a room with strangers was hard for Gloria. The TV blared. People came and went at all hours. And like in double rooms everywhere, deeply personal information spilled through flimsy curtains unchecked by the vast armament of health privacy rules. And not just secrets about health.

"I overheard someone sweet-talking a raft of manipulative B.S. to get money from my mom's roommate," said Laura. "Later, just as I was dozing off, I heard her sobbing, so I went to talk to her. She told me, 'I can't believe he's pressuring me for money. He knows the problems I'm having.' She was fine cognitively but lacked the strength to resist her son."

Laura gave the roommate information about who to contact for help and urged her to tell someone she trusted. When the woman's daughter visited a few days later, they talked with Laura about ways she could protect herself.

"I don't know if it was legal," said Laura, "but I was just trying to help people get their needs met. I came away thinking that we need a trained comfort squad. It wouldn't cost that much for people to go up and down the halls responding to residents as human beings."

"That experience was a real eye-opener for me," Laura said. "You could see how people were fed, bathed, and dressed; what happened when they called for help. It was a perfectly good place and got the maximum number of stars. But none of those stars told you if you'd be treated like a human being or a chair."

As Gloria's delirium subsided and she grasped that physical therapy was her ticket home, she wasn't to be stopped. The staff "premedicated" her so therapy would be less painful. One day, the therapist said her blood pressure was too high to do her exercises. Gloria said, "I plan to do them with you or without you, so let's go." Gloria and her family understood the risks. They had expressed clear goals to the staff. The exercises went on. Gloria progressed so quickly that she was ready to leave in five days instead of the expected fourteen.

HOME

Patients are generally thrilled to return home, but when they have complex care needs and caregivers are unprepared, such transitions can be both difficult and risky. Things can go south fast when warning signs go unrecognized, appointments are missed, and treatments get out of whack. Caregivers who need help the most are often unaware they need it or are most reluctant to ask for it. Eric Coleman, a Colorado geriatrician, has made a science and practice of improving transitions. With input from family caregivers, he created an evidence-based, ten-question checklist to "foster more productive interactions between health care professionals and family caregivers."[14] As discharge time nears, the checklist helps staff and family have conversations about what care will entail and whether the caregivers are prepared.

Laura and her dad, both physicians, were uniquely qualified. But they too found themselves scrambling to get ready. What kinds of services? How often? For how many hours? Did they need a hospital bed? Would the pharmacy deliver? What would Medicare or insurance pay for? The list went on and on.

They lined up home health, physical therapy, and personal care. But finding reputable agencies is just the first step. "We had to orient every new person to my mom, my dad, the house, and supplies," said Laura. "And everyone had to get used to one another, which isn't easy with dementia." Finding the right aides was also a challenge: One was a lovely warm person but unreliable. Another, "in a well-meaning way, infantilized my mother, talking to her like a baby." A third mostly chatted on her cell phone and watched the Home Shopping Network. "She just sort of did things *to* my mother." Laura modeled how to help her mom undress. "Instead of just yanking her shirt off, you explain what you're going to do.

'Mom, we're going to take your shirt off now.' That aide wasn't mean or rough. She just didn't seem to think of my mom as a person." Then they found the superstar caregiver. "When she helped my mom get ready for bed, she'd say, 'Oh, don't worry, Dr. Gloria, just take your time.' She was just a very kind, capable presence."

The job wasn't easy. Gloria's mobility improved, but her Alzheimer's and mental health worsened. "There were weeks when my mom was agitated and hallucinating," said Laura. "She was very angry at times; there was no way to calm her down or reason with her. Antipsychotics helped somewhat, but it was tough."

Still there were also occasional moments of connection. "After thirty hours of complete nonsense, suddenly she'd pop out with something coherent. She'd say, 'What's happening to me?' or 'I've had enough. I want to die.' Or after I helped her get ready for bed, 'Thank you so much, Laura.' Was it true recognition? That's of course how I wanted to interpret it," said Laura. "But it could be coincidence that she happened to say a phrase that made sense in that moment. Dementia destroys your brain. If one of my patients' families told me stuff I saw with my mom, I wouldn't have believed them. It was great when she smiled, but I don't think there was any sort of sustained happiness for her. But you don't know." There are few reports back from the front lines of advanced dementia.

Payment was another stressor. Laura's parents were fortunate to be among the few people fifty and older to have private long-term care insurance.[15] "They paid a lot into that policy for a gazillion years," said Laura. "But it was just one hoop after another. They made it ridiculously hard when my parents were most vulnerable. How can my dad fight with the insurance company when he's physically and emotionally exhausted?"

Some people, after decades of paying for insurance, then pay a benefits expert to help them get what they're owed or learn that what they need isn't covered. Many just give up and pay twice, or forgo care.

Laura worried as much about her dad as about her mom, given the toil and stress of caregiving. "I'll support you 100 percent if you want to move mom to a nursing home," she told him. She wasn't dogmatic about facilities. She'd seen lots of them, good and bad, as a nursing home medical director, a physician whose patients went there, an expert witness testifying against them, a volunteer long-term care ombudsman advocating for residents (after a two-week training stint in 2016), and, now, as a daughter. "It's a hell of a lot easier to be a geriatrician than to have an aging parent," she once told me.

Laura knew that putting her mom in a nursing home was a gamble, but she feared her dad had reached the point when caregiving had become too much, and a nursing home was the painful best option.

Chapter 3

FACILITIES

Most of the nursing home scandals involved
financial chicanery and political influence. But the
indifference, neglect, and physical abuse of patients
continues.

—BRUCE VLADECK, *Unloving Care:
The Nursing Home Tragedy*

Nursing homes get close to $100 billion from taxpayers
a year to care for some of society's most vulnerable people. But we don't really know how they spend those public
funds, or how much goes to resident care, even though the quality of
care is largely dependent on how much is spent on it. We often don't
even know who owns the facilities. In the wake of the pandemic's
200,000 long-term care deaths, there's been much agonizing about
why nursing homes aren't better. To answer that question, we need to
follow the money, which, for now, we're not able to do.

For decades, the nursing home population hovered around
1.5 million. In COVID-19's wake, it dropped below 1.3 million,
due to deaths, departures, and greater hesitance to use them. But
they're not going away. To live our long lives well, we need a long-
term care system we can trust. This includes reliably decent places
for people with intensive care or supervision needs. Families cannot shoulder the entire responsibility, nor can they be omniscient
about the merits of any given place.

When I was at DOJ, we investigated large nursing home chains for abuse and neglect of residents and for defrauding Medicare and Medicaid, which supplied two-thirds to three-quarters of their revenue in exchange for providing the care and services residents need. Working on those cases gave me an insider's view of the patterns that emerge when things go wrong. Those patterns, which often sabotage care, only came to light using powerful DOJ and FBI investigative tools. It's virtually impossible for families to see what's happening behind the scenes when choosing a facility, even if that backstage action has everything to do with the quality of care.

Staffing—the ratio of caregivers to residents—is the single most important factor in nursing home quality. Today, direct care workers are in short supply in many regions. But even before such shortages, many facilities cut costs and maximized short-term profits by putting staff on the chopping block.

To be a resident in an understaffed facility, or to love someone who is, is to experience its cruelty. Without enough help to eat and drink, residents become malnourished and dehydrated. Without enough help turning and repositioning, residents get pressure sores and frozen joints. Without enough help getting to the bathroom, more residents fall and soil their beds and clothing. Without enough help to change sheets, or help people bathe, hygiene declines and infections rise. Without enough meaningful connection and activities, residents become isolated, lonely, and helpless. Neglect is not a random event. In facilities, its root cause is understaffing.

Lawsuits can reveal what otherwise would stay hidden and be powerful instruments of change. This chapter tells the story of two cases that taught me about the corrosive machinery in our nursing home system. We will not be able to fix nursing homes until we weed out the bad ones, replicate what the good ones do right, and hold owners accountable for how the public's money is being spent.

GeriMed

Geriatric & Medical Services, Inc., or GeriMed, once owned twenty-seven facilities across Pennsylvania and New Jersey and was Philadelphia's biggest nursing home operator. Its business philosophy was "heads in beds" by whatever means necessary. It was no surprise that Alison Hirschel, then a young attorney at Philadelphia's Community Legal Services, started hearing from desperate family members of GeriMed residents in the early 1990s. One was a daughter who'd reluctantly moved her mother—ninety-three years old, diabetic, and immobile—to a nursing home. She chose a GeriMed facility nearby so she could visit often. Once there, her mother (whom Alison called "Mrs. G") deteriorated quickly: a broken arm, infections under her neck brace, skin breakdown, a bruised face. She began missing doctor's appointments and her medical records disappeared.

Mrs. G's daughter implored the facility to provide better care, but for naught. She couldn't bring her mother back home. The care would be kinder but she couldn't manage it physically. So, she consulted Alison.

Alison was fourteen when she began volunteering at a nursing home. Residents who wanted to go outside could steer their wheelchairs to face in one of two directions: overlooking a highway or a graveyard. There, Alison befriended Mr. Bluth, a gentlemanly, sharp resident who was lonely after losing his wife and many friends. He and Alison went to the movies, and he joined her family for Thanksgiving dinner. Then Mr. Bluth had three strokes in a week and could no longer feed himself. Aides kept putting his meals on the table in front of him and picking them up an hour later untouched because there weren't enough staff to help him eat. "No one seemed to notice any change in him," said Alison, "that he'd gone from this lovely alert man to entirely incapacitated and vacant." But teenage Alison noticed and has kept on noticing. "That nursing home still exists," she said, "and it's still crummy."

Understaffing and neglect are the predictable consequence of greed and mismanagement abetted by low wages, profiteering, political maneuvering, and failed policies. GeriMed and other bad facilities didn't change largely because the government kept funding them as they were. And while the industry had power, the residents had virtually none, making it not so surprising that nursing home scandals kept erupting into public view, only to subside and then erupt again.

State and federal surveyors are responsible for overseeing nursing homes. They collect lots of revealing information, some of it now synthesized on a federal website.[1] But Alison's calls to the Pennsylvania Department of Health surveyors about GeriMed "did little." When the surveyors eventually visited Mrs. G's nursing home a few weeks later, they were alarmed. But it was too late for Mrs. G. Her pressure sores and gangrene led to sepsis, an often-lethal systemic infection. She went from stable to dead in twelve weeks.

GeriMed was unusual in how bad it was and in the detailed accounts of varied players' attempts to improve it. The case also laid a foundation for a new approach by DOJ and the Department of Health and Human Services (HHS) in such cases.

No solitary advocate can turn around a terrible home like GeriMed, so Alison teamed up with others, including long-term care ombudsmen. Ombudsmen, whose job is to advocate for residents and their families, have access to facilities and their records and know how the complex long-term care systems work.

Alison began working with Diane Menio, an ombudsman supervisor in Philadelphia, who was also fielding awful reports about GeriMed. But even with them working together, there wasn't much they could do. "The Health Department had the real power," Diane told me. "And it didn't force GeriMed to change." Regulators' failure to hold bad actors accountable is an old refrain persisting through this day.

Desperate for accountability, Alison and Diane referred GeriMed for criminal prosecution. Diane knew her boss would disapprove. "We didn't go to prosecutors then," she said, "but I felt it was my job to do *something*."

When the GeriMed case arrived in the Pennsylvania's attorney general's office, it landed on the desk of Ron Costen. A rare prosecutor with a social science PhD, Costen understood that breakdowns in oversight could worsen neglect, and that neglect could kill. He hired Garrett Speaks, an undercover agent, to take a nurse aide training course and then apply for a job at a GeriMed home in a low-income, majority Black neighborhood in West Philadelphia. Speaks earned $3.85 per hour, a meager wage even in 1991. What he saw was alarming. Food was on floors. Call bells were broken. Residents were tethered by restraints, unable to clean or hydrate themselves as they lay in their own waste in ninety-degree heat. And that was on the day shift.

Then Speaks moved to nights, on a different unit with sicker residents but even fewer staff. Immobilized residents weren't turned or repositioned, so their joints froze in place and they developed pressure sores. The one wound care nurse couldn't keep up.

It wasn't that GeriMed didn't know what was expected. One day, the facility administrator told staff she expected a Health Department inspection. GeriMed headquarters deployed a corporate SWAT team to erect a Potemkin façade, creating an illusion of adequate care. They conjured extra staff to clean rooms, bathe and shave patients. They trimmed fingernails, filled in charts, and piped in soothing music. White tablecloths appeared in the dining room. One aide told Speaks she wished the state would visit all the time. When the inspection was over, the process played in reverse: The parking lot emptied. The faux staff vanished. The music no longer played.

One law of understaffing is that neglect compounds itself. The more residents are neglected, the more medical problems they develop, the more care and staff time they need, the more staff have trouble keeping up, and the more residents' snowballing needs go unmet. A physician and nurse who reviewed GeriMed's practices put it this way: "Typical nursing home residents, although medically 'simple' on admission, became complex because of the lack of basic care."[2]

One method unscrupulous owners use to divert funds away from resident care and to themselves is by forming or buying subsidiaries, called "related parties," that are part of the same corporate family. This allows one arm of the corporation to buy (often overpriced) services from another. GeriMed bought all sorts of goods and services from its subsidiaries: ambulance transport to hospitals, medical equipment, temporary agency staff, pharmaceuticals, nutrition and rehab, and diagnostic testing services. Without external checks, related vendors could charge inflated prices and then funnel the profits back to the same corporate parent. GeriMed's real estate venture sold residents' homes when they went into its facilities, making it harder for them to leave. And its check cashing van came around on payday, allowing GeriMed to profit twice by shortchanging its staff—first by paying low wages and second by charging a fee when staff cashed their paychecks.

As his concerns grew, Speaks snuck a camera into the facility and photographed the human tragedy.[3] The prosecutor, Costen, faced an ethical quandary. Should he continue the investigation and strengthen his case, allowing the atrocities to continue, or shut down the undercover operation and file charges in hopes of stopping it. Costen filed.

Costen presented the case to a grand jury, which charged two administrators, two head nurses, and a GeriMed management entity with involuntary manslaughter. Alison thought she'd be thrilled that GeriMed was finally being held to account. "But I felt queasy see-ing those employees led across city hall courtyard in handcuffs," she said. "They weren't the ones profiting off the bad care. They'd done their best under impossible circumstances. GeriMed filled its coffers paying related parties' inflated prices but didn't give facilities enough money for staff."

That's how it often goes in such cases. Occasionally employees do neglect or abuse, but when the people working the controls choke off funds, it's impossible for even good staff to provide decent care. They're cogs in bigger machines. Higher-ups often point to "a few bad apples" to deflect blame from themselves. For prosecutors, too, low-level employees make easier targets than those who sit on the top rungs, insulated from accountability by layers of human and cor-porate shields. The way it often goes, the bad apples are tossed out, but the system stays rotten.

After the court dismissed Costen's cases against two of GeriMed's employees, he dropped his cases against the other two, and let the company plead "no contest" to two counts of involuntary manslaugh-ter and pay a $120,000 fine: $100,000 to cover the investigative costs and $20,000 for egregious neglect that resulted in the deaths of two residents.[4]

Costen declared victory. The case had led to more public aware-ness, more oversight, new standards to simplify prosecutions, and a new nursing home task force funded by the GeriMed fines. Alison was more circumspect. "The task force was great," she said, "but $10,000 per person killed seemed pathetic. How much did GeriMed earn off of everyone they hurt? Is dying in agony only worth $10,000 if you're a nursing home resident? It made me feel sick." The calls that kept coming from anguished GeriMed families made her feel even sicker. "The case didn't stop the abuse."

A year after Costen's criminal case ended, a GeriMed resident was admitted to a hospital malnourished, dehydrated, and in searing pain with twenty-six pressure sores. He barely clung to life. Appalled emergency room staff notified the ombudsman. This time Alison and Diane went to David Hoffman, formerly chief counsel for Pennsylvania's Department of Aging who'd recently moved to Philadelphia's hard-charging federal prosecutor's office. The move armed David with a prosecutor's swagger and a new weapon to take on nursing homes: federal law.

David sued GeriMed for defrauding Medicare and Medicaid under the False Claims Act—a law dating to the Civil War to protect the Treasury from fraud against federal programs and procurements. Just as the Department of Defense shouldn't pay for a fighter jet that won't fly, so too, the theory goes, Medicare and Medicaid shouldn't pay for "worthless" care or services. In this instance, it's not the bad plane or the bad care that triggers liability, it's filing claims seeking reimbursement for something worthless or nonexistent.

GeriMed, denying any wrongdoing, paid $575,000 to settle David's fraud case. It was a paltry sum by False Claims Act standards, even in 1996. What was new, and a big deal, was that the settlement required monitors with expertise in geriatrics to oversee the problem areas and to work with GeriMed to improve *future* care at not just one but nineteen facilities. Signing a consent judgment meant court supervision, so if GeriMed violated the agreement, David could ask that it be held in contempt of court. His aim, he told me, was to "create a separate enforcement mechanism so the failed regulatory system was no longer the only enforcer."[5]

By the time I took over DOJ's Nursing Home Initiative in early 1999, David was on his seventh case using the False Claims Act. He also used photographs and video, which many tort lawyers have deployed in suing nursing homes for damages on behalf of residents and families. David's cases made my bosses at DOJ's Washington, DC, headquarters, or Main Justice, nervous by seeking prospective remedies. The mistrust was mutual. David saw us as risk-averse, bureaucratic wimps to be held at arm's length lest we meddle in his good works.

Using the False Claims Act and analogous criminal statutes in those cases felt a little like prosecuting Al Capone for tax evasion—a valid use of the law, if not the best tools for the job. But as I studied our options, I was amazed to find that there really weren't any others. For all the thousands of pages of federal statutes and regulations, there was no federal abuse and neglect law to enforce. The powers that be could be wary of David, but he'd found a way to fill that gap. I drafted language for a new law in hopes of making such cases easier to bring, but it never went anywhere. So, we kept using old laws in new ways, often making it up as we went along. We hoped that our cases would do some good, even though we knew they did little to fix the root causes of the problem.

Financial Free Fall

I'd never worked on a nursing home case before taking on the Nursing Home Initiative, so a few weeks into the job I asked my DOJ colleagues in the Civil Frauds section to tell me about theirs. We met in our basement conference room one afternoon in February 1999 under harsh fluorescent lights that made the already stark discussion seem even starker. A crisis was brewing in the industry. GeriMed was small compared to the nursing home cases then flooding into DOJ, many of them against multimillion- and multibillion-dollar behemoths. Several operated 300 or more facilities, housing more than 30,000 of the country's most vulnerable citizens. I'd expected to hear about fraud and failures of care. What jolted me was that many of the chains under investigation also appeared to be in grave financial trouble. Their plummeting stocks made creditors antsy and set business pages buzzing with talk of insolvency.

In August 1998, a nursing home chain named Chartwell, with more than twenty facilities in Texas, Florida, and Missouri, had collapsed. It was, I'd learned, more complicated and hazardous than your standard bankruptcy. Chartwell's owners had stopped paying staff and vendors and run out of medication, food, soap, and supplies. "These are not patients who can just shop around for another place to live," said an HHS official. When Chartwell staff walked off the job, the Texas Department of Human Services took control of its Texas homes. Regulators later said that mismanagement and financial improprieties led to Chartwell's downfall. One of its executives later pled guilty to tax fraud.[6]

All moves are hard for frail residents, but the "transfer trauma" of sudden chaotic moves—possessions crammed in garbage bags—can kill them. One Texas official likened the impact of Chartwell's collapse to a major hurricane. In the end, they forestalled closure, but the case helped me understand how just the threat of shutting down, and the lack of alternatives, had given the industry powerful leverage over regulators for a long time, with an impact on residents that's hard to trace.

Like GeriMed, Chartwell also was small compared to any of the five huge chains teetering on the brink of insolvency about which my colleagues told me on that afternoon. No health care company as large as any one of them had ever filed for bankruptcy. Financial crisis is tough in any industry, but it doesn't usually put lives in immediate peril. This one did. One huge corporate chain in financial straits was a big deal. We had five on our hands. Cumulatively, their potential closure threatened to trigger a public health crisis. John Bentivoglio, then DOJ's lead health care fraud lawyer, had joined the meeting that day. Afterward, we made several calls: to HHS officials in charge of nursing homes, to DOJ's bankruptcy experts, and to the Senate Special Committee on Aging staff, then closely monitoring both nursing homes and federal oversight of them.

A BRIEF HISTORY

How did we wind up with a system where owners of for-profit corporations and powerless residents compete for the same dollars?

In the nineteenth and early twentieth centuries, older people in need of help had few options. They could hire caregivers if they had the money. If not, they could rely on the generosity of family and friends or submit to charity at "rest homes" like the Quaker Indigent

Widows' and Single Women's Society, *if* they had the right sort of social status—the "worthy poor." The rest landed in purgatorial poorhouses, wandered the countryside, or succumbed.[7]

The New Deal ushered in laws like Old Age Assistance and the Social Security Act that reduced the endemic poverty of late life. But Congress prohibited those funds from going to any "inmate of a public institution," like a poorhouse. Drafters of those laws wanted to help hardworking pensioners but not taint them with the stigma of lumping them in with poorhouse paupers on the public dole. That's why Congress mandated that only *private* entities could get funds, like those "rest homes," thus casting the die for today's chiefly private long-term care industry, although one predominantly funded by taxpayer dollars.

When I began working on the Nursing Home Initiative, I was confused. Why did so many nursing homes still exist? For decades there'd been about 15,000.[8] Their for-profit status helps explain it. Most state hospitals, like the one in Minnesota where I'd lived, were *public* entities. As part of the push to deinstitutionalize such places, most had been closed long since. (Mine shut down in 1982, reopening in 1984 as a federal prison, where my mother cared for yet another group of shunned and confined people.) The idea was to replace those hospitals with a community mental health system, but it never materialized. Patients who left often lost the only home they knew, the only society that would take them in. Many wound up on the streets, in prisons, or in nursing homes.

In the decades since, lawsuits and changes in law and public opinion decreased the census of those *public* state hospitals by 95 percent. What confused me was that many nursing homes were just as institutional and bad as those state hospitals. Why weren't they closed too? The answer lies in part in that public-private distinction. The nursing homes were mostly *private* entities and thus less susceptible to such pressures. They also had something those public institutions lacked: power and money to lobby for their own interests, including their existence, use, and funding.

By the 1950s, most poorhouses were gone. Congress changed the law, allowing funds to flow to public institutions, but too late. Today,

70 percent of nursing homes are for-profit, 23 percent nonprofit, and 7 percent public.[9]

Although a cut above poorhouses, early nursing homes were little more than human storage lockers. To improve them, Congress dangled financial incentives to make them more like hospitals and required states to set and enforce standards. That helped, but still few homes provided much by way of actual nursing.

Medicare and Medicaid's arrival in 1965 was no silver bullet, either. Medicare was never intended to fund long-term care, paying only up to 100 days for limited services in nursing homes, like rehab. Medicaid, a program for the poor, quickly became the largest funder of nursing homes. Medicaid's joint federal-state funding roughly doubled their number within six years—but not their quality. Bleak revelations kept rolling in through the 1960s and 1970s. Residents were drugged and tied to beds. Dozens were killed by fire and food poisoning. And again and again, greed and mismanagement begat neglect, always neglect.

Nor was improving them a high priority for Congress, although a few members tried. David Pryor, then a young Arkansas congressman, went undercover as a nurse's aide and then denounced what he'd witnessed from the House floor. House leadership refused to hold hearings on the abuses or create a House aging committee, so Pryor rented two trailers, parking one by a gas station three blocks from the Capitol, and in 1971 held mock-hearings in his "House Trailer Committee on Aging." Eventually, Congress created real aging committees in the House and Senate whose investigations revealed rampant misdeeds and misery. But implementation of their proposed solutions stalled, the House later disbanded its aging committee, and reformers' hopes sank again.

Advocates also entered the fray. Ralph Nader found summer projects for six teenage girls who'd just graduated from the posh Miss Porter's School. They worked as nursing home aides, conducted eighty-five interviews, and reviewed boxes of documents. Under Nader's tutelage, the "Maiden Muckrakers" used their fleeting celebrity to draw attention to their findings. They gave splashy press conferences and testified before the Senate. Their 1971 report, "Nursing Homes for the Aged: The Agony of One Million Americans," and book, *Old Age: The Last Segregation*, lambasted both the industry *and* government regulators for non-enforcement of laws.[10]

After more than a decade of hearings, the Senate Special Committee on Aging, led by Senator Frank Moss, released its 1974 report: *Nursing Home Care in the United States: Failure in Public Policy*. "It's impossible to be more succinct than that," wrote Bruce Vladeck, in *Unloving Care: The Nursing Home Tragedy*, a 1980 book that remains eerily contemporary.[11]

The heat of those scandals cooled, with no fix. "Exposé is not reform," cautioned sociologist Amitai Etzioni in 1977. Nursing home residents had a political problem. "They have had no such means of political expression, while the owners and administrators are well organized," Etzioni said. If they wanted change, reform advocates had to "organize and act."[12]

This was not easy. Nursing homes then as now wield money and political connections to influence officials who can determine their fate. GeriMed, for example, hosted lavish annual holiday parties for state officials and doled out generous contributions to them. They gave awards to Philadelphia's district attorney, the governor's wife, Pennsylvania's attorney general, and the state official responsible for licensing facilities. Neither residents themselves nor any group representing them had comparable clout or cash.

Nonetheless, "organize and act" was precisely what Elma Holder, a former "Nader's Raider," tried to do. In 1976, she formed the National Citizen's Coalition for Nursing Home Reform, now called the National Consumer Voice for Quality Long-Term Care, then as now the leading consumer group working to improve nursing homes and other long-term care. Elma's first goal, working in a coalition with dozens of other groups, was to pressure Congress to pass federal nursing home reform legislation. The eventual Nursing Home Reform Act was tucked into the Omnibus Budget Reconciliation Act of 1987 (OBRA '87).

The law created a "bill of rights" that entitled each resident to the care and activities they needed to "attain or maintain the highest practicable physical, mental, and psychosocial well-being."[13] Supporters hailed the law as an antidote to a long-stubborn problem. Opponents, mostly industry, argued that it intruded on doctor-patient relationships and that its oversight requirements were too onerous. After OBRA '87 became law, its opponents shifted their sights to stalling its implementation, and they were often successful. Although OBRA '87 made real improvements, it ducked the issue most critical to quality: staffing. Rather than requiring minimum staff-to-resident ratios, Congress punted, ordering HHS to do a staffing study. Eleven years later, there was still no study until Iowa senator Chuck Grassley, then chairman of the Senate Special Committee on Aging, demanded HHS to produce one. Finally released in 2002, that study found that 50 to 90 percent of nursing homes were understaffed at levels making residents unsafe.[14]

Another congressional investigation Grassley requested found that almost a third of California's 1,370 nursing homes provided care so bad it put residents at risk for potentially life-threatening harm.[15] President Bill Clinton announced the Nursing Home Initiative following prodding by Grassley, who planned two days of dramatic hearings in July 1998 spotlighting those failings.

Clinton promised that HHS would improve its oversight and that DOJ would review cases involving "severe violations of quality of care" and investigate and prosecute "where appropriate."[16] HHS had the larger role given its stewardship over Medicaid, Medicare, and nursing homes. But it was DOJ's Initiative that occupied me.

OVER A BARREL

When I met with my colleagues on that February afternoon under the fluorescent lights, one name that kept coming up was Vencor, a chain then operating about 360 facilities against which DOJ had twelve cases pending around the country. It's worth looking at what happened with Vencor because it reveals how the big chains had leverage over the government and how the government tried to use a new tool designed to improve quality.

At its peak, Vencor was a Fortune 500 company and home to some 50,000 residents in forty-six states. For its headquarters it commissioned architect I. M. Pei to design a $60 million Vencor Tower in downtown Louisville. But beneath this prosperity was a grisly foundation. Public oversight records recounted that Vencor routinely understaffed its nursing homes and long-term acute care hospitals so severely that they were unable to maintain even basic hygiene, much less high-level care.

Two nurse whistleblowers told a stark account of residents left soiled, unfed, unbathed, and unmoved for shift after shift. But their pleas to Vencor for more staff were in vain. So, they collected evidence, quit, and hired a lawyer. In June 1997 the whistleblower nurses filed a lawsuit using the False Claims Act's qui tam provisions that allow private citizens to sue on behalf of the government.

The evidence led investigators from Vencor's Los Angeles facility to its headquarters in Kentucky, where a corporate drama was unfolding. Vencor had recently spent $1.4 billion to buy another national chain with 360 facilities. Like many nursing homes, these facilities bought lucrative respiratory, physical, occupational, and speech therapies for their residents. The rub was that Vencor bought those therapies from another Vencor subsidiary. Vencor was paying itself for services and billing the government. When the Balanced Budget Act of 1997 phased in reimbursement changes, making those therapies less profitable, Vencor found itself in a bind.

With financial trouble on the horizon, Vencor's owners engineered a cunning corporate mitosis in 1998, moving the company's substantial real estate assets into a new Real Estate Investment Trust (REIT) named Ventas, which the owners kept for themselves. The remaining entity—first called New Vencor, and then again just Vencor—was responsible for operations and management, leaving it with what one attorney described as "all the liabilities and a bunch of bedpans." Ventas became Vencor's landlord. In the years that followed, REITs would become increasingly common industry-wide and a way for owners to stash valuable assets even further beyond the reach of anyone trying to hold them accountable. And new investors, like private equity, often were more interested in the chains' real estate holdings than their "operations," that is, providing care.

By the time my colleagues told me about their Vencor cases, the company was already skidding toward bankruptcy, buckling under the debt of its grandiose aspirations and its poor preparation for the reimbursement changes. It never built that I. M. Pei Vencor Tower. And the New York Stock Exchange delisted its stock as creditors wrangled to save their investments in the company.

A July 1999 meeting in New York City about Vencor's imminent bankruptcy left little doubt about what was really at stake. Some two dozen lawyers and bankers—mostly white men in fine suits—gathered around a conference room table with stunning views of Manhattan. Vencor needed an infusion of several billion dollars to survive, and its creditors wanted to find the money to keep it afloat so that they'd be repaid.

The creditors weren't the only ones after Vencor for money. HHS had overpaid Vencor by $100 million and wanted to be repaid, too. The feds were a creditor with a difference. Taxpayers, mostly through Medicare and Medicaid, supplied the lion's share of Vencor's revenue. If those spigots were shut off, Vencor would close, Ventas would lose its main tenant, the shareholders and creditors would lose their investments, and God knows what would happen to the residents.

Up in the rarefied air of that Manhattan skyscraper—the cumulative amount earned by the lawyers and bankers for their day of work exceeding what an average American earned in a year—there was scant mention of Vencor's reason for existing: to care for tens of thousands of vulnerable people. So, I was surprised when one banker said that a potential multibillion-dollar bridge loan rested in part on whether Vencor could provide adequate care for residents. This was no devotion to human rights. The banker calculated that good care attracted new customers, filled beds, and generated income. Bad care meant lawsuits and less profit.

In September 1999, Vencor became the largest health care corporation ever to file for bankruptcy. That filing marked opening day of a somber season, with other chains soon following: Sun Healthcare Group (with more than 320 facilities) filed the next month. Mariner Post-Acute Network (with more than 400 facilities) filed in January 2000. Integrated Health Services, Inc. (IHS) (with more than 400 facilities), filed in February 2000. And Genesis Health Ventures, Inc. (with more than 350 facilities, including the GeriMed homes it had bought a few years earlier), filed in June 2000.

Five of the country's seven biggest nursing home chains were insolvent, and many smaller ones were, too—about 1,600 facilities in all. Some 10 percent of the industry was bankrupt. Most of the companies blamed reimbursement changes, but entities that depended less on billing for lucrative therapies had done fine.

Bankruptcy wasn't the chains' only problem. Many also faced DOJ cases alleging that they'd defrauded Medicare and Medicaid. When they said they couldn't pay our fraud claims—cumulatively hundreds of millions of dollars—we responded that bankruptcy shouldn't provide blanket amnesty for all financial misdeeds involving taxpayer dollars. "Then we might have to close," a few responded.

I was never sure if those "we'll close" threats were serious. That Texas official had compared the sudden closure of Chartwell's eight Texas homes to a natural disaster. With that omen echoing in my head, those discussions sometimes felt like hostage negotiations. The industry had government *and* residents *and* their families *and* taxpayers over a barrel and had for a long time.

When I first got involved in the Nursing Home Initiative, the issues seemed new. But they were only new to me. In fact, fear of closing facilities had led to lax enforcement of nursing home standards since the 1950s. In 1965, only 12 percent of nursing facilities met the requirements to receive federal funds. Instead of demanding better care, HHS lowered the standards to keep the public faucet flowing.

MONITORS

When DOJ sued *public* institutions, like state hospitals and prisons, for violating the civil rights of institutionalized persons, the remedy usually involved monitors who oversaw the changes. The innovation in GeriMed was to require monitoring in a *private* institution. But Vencor was more than ten times GeriMed's size. Two monitors couldn't keep track of 360 facilities.

So, Lewis Morris, counsel for HHS's internal watchdog, the Office of Inspector General (OIG), adapted the monitoring process to those mega-chains, recruiting monitors with bedside, boardroom, and data expertise. David Zimmerman, director of the University of Wisconsin Center for Health Systems Research and Analysis, became Vencor's lead monitor. He knew the minutiae of staffing and care, understood the power structure of corporations, and could find red flags in massive nursing home data sets. Those agreements critically located accountability at the corporate level instead of just the facility level, like the usual regulatory process.

Vencor was the first big chain to file for bankruptcy and to sign a monitoring agreement. It emerged from bankruptcy in 2001, paying $104.5 million to settle multiple False Claims Act "failure of care" cases, while denying any wrongdoing. Then it arose with a new name: Kindred Health Care. Reformers were briefly hopeful about those monitoring agreements. But some of Vencor's industry colleagues saw its willingness to work with monitors and OIG as traitorous.

We hoped that monitoring's added oversight and accountability at the headquarters level would improve resident care. My admittedly biased hunch is that it did, but I failed to convince any independent researcher to evaluate the process. That meant we could never declare victory and call for replication or admit defeat and look for a better way. Since then, monitoring has waned. Between 2000 and 2006, some 1,600 facilities were under monitoring agreements. By 2023, it was a fraction of that number.

The legacy of those big chain cases still shifts and shimmies in my head, but one regret stays sharp: Not one of the 36,000 frail, sick, mostly old, defenseless people who called a Vencor facility home was at the negotiating table. Nor were their representatives. They were voiceless in their own remedy. Yet they had the most at stake in the outcome—not just their money, but their lives.

PRIVATE EQUITY AND PROFIT

Over the decades, nursing homes' dominance in the long-term care industry has given way to a range of other options that include assisted living, rehab, hospice, and home care. The boundaries among them are porous. Often, they're housed under the same corporate roof, are owned by the same corporate entity, and have overlapping functions. Private equity has acquired a growing stake in this sprawling industry, now owning an estimated 5 to 11 percent of nursing homes.[17]

Vencor's heir, Kindred, sold assets including its nursing homes to a private equity firm in 2018. Kindred's home care and hospice business, after initially being purchased by the health insurance giant Humana, was resold to a private equity firm in 2022. Corporate goliaths swapped ownership in health entities like so many trading cards.

Research suggests that those sales aren't great news for residents. On average, for-profit nursing homes provide worse care than nonprofits, data show, and for-profits owned by private equity firms provide worse care still. In fact, researchers found that private equity ownership led to an estimated 20,000 excess deaths.[18] What does this mean for the people who call those places home? The human toll after a beloved nursing home was acquired by a private equity firm is chronicled in sad and sordid detail in a 2022 *New Yorker* exposé. The investigation chronicled staff cutbacks and declines in residents' health and happiness. One resident, unable to get attention when her oxygen tube fell out, resorted to calling 911 for help.[19]

Hospice quality similarly has suffered. Its origins melded compassion and common sense to aid the dying and the grieving toward more serene, less high-tech costly ends. But we are learning ever more about how rapacious operators are corrupting hospices' reason for being, causing untold suffering and making a mockery of oaths to first do no harm.[20] The math isn't that complicated: the more money owners pull out of a care business, the less there's left for care. Private equity's model is to purchase entities with substantial profit potential, to squeeze them, to "increase efficiencies," and then to flip them.

A chilling insight is laid out in a 2019 Senior Living Innovation Forum session titled "How to Make 42% Profit Margin in Senior Housing," where the CEO of Eldermark, a tech firm that bills for residential care facilities, explained to the audience: "You have to dehumanize the fact of the person and call it a unit."[21]

That's a daunting business model if you're a taxpayer or a family member or, God forbid, a "unit."

Pushing Drugs

Big money dictates the fate of residents in other ways, too. In 2013, Johnson & Johnson and its subsidiaries (J&J) paid the US more than $2.2 billion to resolve criminal and civil liability arising from allegations that it falsely marketed its antipsychotic drug to nursing home residents, people with dementia and disabilities, and children; it denied all wrongdoing except conduct it admitted to in criminal guilty pleas. According to DOJ, J&J used an "ElderCare sales force" to push the drug, claiming "excellent safety and tolerability," despite internal data that it "posed serious health risks for the elderly."[22]

DOJ claimed that Johnson & Johnson not only made "false and misleading statements about the safety and efficacy" but also paid "kickbacks to physicians to prescribe Risperdal" and "speaker fees to doctors to influence them to write more prescriptions for Risperdal."[23] This is one reason it's a good idea to ask about the drugs being prescribed, especially powerful ones that can be used to reduce staffing needs by sedating residents. A 2021 *New York Times* investigation found that "21 percent of nursing home residents are on antipsychotic drugs," often justified by phony diagnoses.[24] Neither residents nor their families can know when inappropriate incentives have influenced what drugs or treatments they get. They have no choice but to rely on the facilities and the entities that oversee them.

It's an old scheme. When I lived at the state hospital all those years ago, there was a night nurse who overmedicated the patients at bedtime so he could sleep in the staff room undisturbed. I reported him—twice. The first time nothing happened. The second time he got a paltry suspension, but I got the sense that the administration was more irritated with me than with him.

Old Patterns

The types of failures described in this chapter, and variations on them, often are part of long-standing patterns. Some entities' names keep reappearing, like the 220-facility chain Life Care Centers of America that's owned entirely by one man. Selling long-term care has made Forest Preston a billionaire. DOJ sued Life Care in the early 2000s and again a decade later. The second case was settled for $145 million in 2017. The allegations in those cases included failures of care, fraud, high-pressure sales tactics so residents got unneeded costly therapies, and corporate coercion to provide medically unnecessary services. DOJ also claimed that Preston improperly "borrowed" tens of millions of dollars from the company. Defendants denied all wrong-doing. The nation's first COVID outbreak occurred at a Life Care facility in Kirkland, Washington. A 2021 Emmy-winning VICE News documentary, *Aging, Inc.*, traced trouble at Life Care to examine why the same problems have plagued nursing homes for so long.

Where's the Money Going?

Nursing homes and continuing care retirement communities earned $181 billion in 2021, about two-thirds of which—more than $100 billion—came from public funds. But there's no record of how they spend those public dollars or who's earning what. Owners' roles and even their identities often are covered up by layers of corporate Russian Matryoshka dolls. Those layers also buffer them from liability and responsibility for their stewardship of public funds.

"We need greater transparency and accountability," said Lori Smetanka, head of Consumer Voice, the leading long-term care advocacy group. "Nursing homes get billions in taxpayer dollars every year, with little to no scrutiny." We also don't know how much of those taxpayer dollars actually reach the bedside. In her twenty-five years of advocating for consumers, Lori has come to see her work in David and Goliath terms. "The industry has more money than God," she said to me, "giving them infinite resources to avoid being held accountable." So far, owners aren't required to report, much less certify, how they spend taxpayer dollars as a condition of getting more of them.

Staffing

What proportion of those funds they allocate to staffing is another open question. Research suggests not enough. Similar to prior findings, a 2020 study again found serious shortages. Half of nursing homes are understaffed, one-quarter of them at dangerously low levels.[25] Quality of care relates not just to the number of staff but also to how they're trained, supervised, paid, and treated. Nursing homes run on the labor of nurse aides, more than 90 percent of them women, more than 50 percent people of color, and 20 percent foreign-born. They're three times more likely to be injured on the job than other

US workers, often by lifting residents.[26] Dire shortages of direct care workers in many regions pose an ongoing challenge and were exacerbated by the pandemic. Lori Smetanka, the consumer advocate, points out that shortages are worsened by turnover rates between 52 and 94 percent.[27] This means that, on average, facilities must replace between half and all of their direct care staff every year. "If they could just keep the staff they have," said Lori, "they wouldn't have to find so many new people." Understaffing also perpetuates itself. Lori describes hearing from people who wanted to keep their nursing home jobs but couldn't bear working in a place where understaffing and neglect were pervasive.

Low wages and poor working conditions also exacerbate staffing shortages. For their arduous work, the average hourly wage for nursing home aides in 2021 was $14.41 and for assisted living and group home aides was $14.11. Many aides work part-time without consistent income or benefits; their median annual earnings of $23,000 to $25,000 mean they often must work several jobs to survive.[28]

That cruelty led to more in the pandemic. Staff became vectors of COVID-19, carrying the virus from job to job to home. Pressure on staff to work while ill, scant infection control, amassed health disparities, and the broken system killed staff, along with residents, in disproportionate numbers. And, like unprepared soldiers thrust into brutal battle, those who'd chosen the work of caring became parties to a calamity—mass death and solitary confinement, frantic families, and decisions about who got care, who got to say goodbye, and who died alone. Experts in suffering drowned in it, many now, like soldiers too, scarred by the "moral injury" of what they'd seen and done.

A Human Rights Issue

Nursing homes' flaws were never hidden, but COVID-19's death toll made it harder to look away, reminding us that this isn't just a regulatory or business conundrum. It's an ongoing civil and human rights imperative. Anyone who understood long-term care was petrified as the pandemic loomed. Residents weren't the only ones with preexisting conditions. Our long-term care system is riddled with preexisting conditions too, multiplying the peril. The results are now well known. More than 200,000 long-term care residents and staff died.[29] Millions of residents languished in isolation. Without visits from family, ombudsman, or surveyors, few people witnessed what went on inside. Some residents said they wish that they'd died rather than live as they did.[30] Nor did COVID-19 kill equitably. Death rates in homes where more African Americans lived were triple those of whiter homes.[31]

Seeing the carnage, the country briefly awoke to the problem. In 2022, there were two steps forward. The National Academies for the Sciences, Engineering, and Medicine issued a blistering report laying out a vision and specific recommendations for nursing home reform—thirty-six years after another of its reports led to OBRA '87's Nursing Home Reform Act—that an ambitious new "Moving Forward" coalition is working to implement.[32] And the Biden administration issued fact sheets and nursing home policy proposals.[33] We have a blueprint. But can we muster the political will to implement it? Will exposé become reform?

AGING DOES NOT WAIT

When titans like government and industry clash, the human impact is obscured. But even a titan's small steps have a huge impact on people's lives. What happens in facilities, and what does not, also shapes what happens at home—how people assess their options, how they make vital decisions about care, how they feel about those decisions. Bad nursing homes draw more attention than the good ones (of which there are also many), making people scared to use any of them. Letting poor care fester in so many homes does several types of harm. First, there's the actual harm of substandard care. Second, there's the harm of driving people who desperately need a nursing home to stay at home even when it's unsafe there. And third, there's the fear and guilt that engulf those who turn to a facility when they've run out of choices.

Laura Mosqueda knew the risks. Yet, despite all the problems in facilities, she believed there was no shame in using them. She knew from both professional and personal experience that when care needs exceeded what a family could manage—whether due to present challenges or past trauma—a facility might be the best option. The decision was intensely personal. Perfection wasn't attainable. It couldn't be the standard.

There's a subtle distinction here. It's not okay to run roughshod over an older person's desire to avoid a facility. But it's also not reasonable to expect family to forfeit their own lives to manage a loved one's care at home, a complex, time-consuming, costly, and health-depleting job. When people ask Laura for advice, and sometimes when they don't, she urges them to consider carefully what they can realistically manage and to not take on more than that.

So, when Laura told her father that she'd back him 100 percent if he thought it was time for her mother to go to a nursing home, she meant it, with love. Her dad saw it differently. "He looked at me in horror," she told me later, "and said, 'Absolutely not.' I told him, 'Fine. But I just want you to know it's okay with me. I'll support you whatever you decide.'"

Laura worried about her dad a lot. She tried to pry him away from her mom's side, but he was reluctant to leave. It was his old yen for adventure that finally provided a respite offer he couldn't decline. Over the years, Hal and Gloria had spent countless meals and holidays with Laura, her husband, Robert, and Robert's mother, Emilia Mosqueda, whom everyone called Millie. Toward the end of Millie's seventy-ninth year, she announced to Laura that for her eightieth birthday she wanted to go skydiving. Laura and Robert were all in. Laura encouraged her dad to join them, expecting him to decline. To her shock, he said yes.

On the appointed day, they put on blue jumpsuits and their small plane climbed to twelve thousand feet. First Millie, then Hal, vanished from a door in the plane's belly, each tethered to an instructor. Laura was next. She plummeted at a hundred miles an hour, arms outstretched, laughing in the roar. A few wispy clouds hung high above her, and below, the earth's crust had fractured into three deep fault lines running parallel to the coast—wonder and rupture, always there flanking us together.

Laura saw Hal and Millie's parachutes inflate as she hurtled toward them still in free fall. Then with a snap, an unfurling, a jerk, she sensed she'd stopped in midair. But the ground still drew closer as she swayed beneath her nylon canopy, surrounded by mountain, sea, sky, and the people she loved, all suspended for a moment, floating toward earth.

Caring for another person is a profound act, impossible to fully fathom in advance. That care, what animates it, and how we feel about it are inextricably bound up with the options available to help us. The failures of our long-term care system should be measured not just in the needless suffering of residents but also in the secondhand suffering it inflicts on others, and in the superhuman effort it demands of the people who actually provide the care—of facility staff, of caregivers like Hal Frankl who cared for Gloria at home until she died two years later, and of all the others who love them.

We can work to make the world better, but we can only live in the world as it is. Laura's admonition to think carefully about how much we can manage and set limits accordingly, even if that means that a loved one ends up in a facility, sounded hard-hearted to me at first. But I came to see it as a form of wisdom, even mercy. Of permission to live life without being buried by caregiving or by the shame of not doing more. Good enough is good enough.

Chapter 4

HOME

Where Thou art—that—is Home—

—Emily Dickinson

*"Home is the place where, when you have to go there,
They have to take you in."*
*"I should have called it
Something you somehow haven't to deserve."*

—Robert Frost, "The Death of the Hired Man"

F inding the right place to live as we age confronts us with a
bewildering range of choices. I learned this in my own family. My mother-in-law, Janet, who'd kept traveling and seeing
friends and clients into her early nineties, had started slowing down.
Her walking weaved and her friends were less numerous. Not getting
her driver's license renewed was wrenching. The cooking, cleaning,
and laundry were harder to keep up with. The woman who'd helped
her for decades had gotten older, too, and had her own health issues.

Occasionally we broached the subject of where she wanted to live
in her next chapter. She loved Chicago, her home of more than ninety
years, and being surrounded in her apartment by her books, art, and
her crisp blue and white bedding. She could see a small slice of Lake
Michigan from one window and Chicago's skyline from another, until
a building went up across the street. But she also considered moving
closer to one of her children, to a place that offered more support. It

would mean trading one kind of community for another. Janet couldn't decide. We wanted to be useful but also to defer to her.

When she visited one Thanksgiving, we went to see some places nearby. In one continuing care retirement community (CCRC), we toured the various "neighborhoods" starting with the independent living apartments. They might have been in any well-appointed, co-op building or retirement community. CCRCs are one-stop housing, with access to assisted living, "memory care," or skilled nursing, depending on one's needs. "It's like choosing the right college," the sales rep chirped: large or small, rural or urban, meals in the dining room or cook for yourself, close to or far from family and friends. Her pitch seemed targeted to us as much as to Janet.

Another place a few blocks from our house had a courtyard with rhododendrons that bloomed in the spring and live music before dinner. Janet talked with a lovely woman who, like her, had studied and taught at the University of Chicago School of Social Work. "I do hope you come here!" she told Janet. Like a charismatic college tour guide, she gave us all a warm feeling for the place. As we walked around, the sales rep described a wide range of activities: movies, concerts, plays, readings, and exercise classes. She showed us a large conference room with comfy chairs where the active resident and family councils met, a good sign, like a robust PTA or student council.

Later we talked with a friend whose father started out in a fancy Sunrise assisted living facility. When his funds dwindled, his family found a modest, three-resident, family-style home that suited everyone at one-third of the price. "Call our care manager," my friend said. Although pricey, she'd helped his family navigate the baffling options. He was sure she'd saved them money and heartache in the long run. A good care manager is gold.

We called. She came to the house. She was smart and perceptive. She also knew the bewildering systems and the local lay of the land. We all had coffee together around the kitchen table. As it turned out, the place with the chirpy sales rep that had impressed us, she confided, had had high staff turnover recently; a resident had gone missing, unnoticed, and died. So much for first impressions.

She also talked with Janet privately, to learn more about what mattered most to her. I'd learned over the years that we too often make decisions *for* instead of *with* older people. Changing one's home late in life is a huge deal. A private conversation might give Janet more room to explore her concerns and desires without worrying about our feelings.

Home doesn't just provide shelter. It's bound up with identity. Our homes root us in a community and are vessels for shared history. In *Independent for Life: Homes and Neighborhoods for an Aging America*, Henry Cisneros described the elder housing landscape. Cisneros, the former Secretary of Housing and Urban Development, with his coauthors, wrote that in the past the housing and community needs of older people "could be ignored. Families managed on their own." But as the aging population grows, their numbers give them leverage to get "housing and care that offers the right environmental, emotional, and economic fit." What's needed, Cisneros writes, is that we "change our culture to support both old and young people so that very long lives are lived well."[1]

We've moved way beyond just the traditional retirement community with a golf course as the centerpiece, like Florida's The Villages, where about 80,000 residents, most of them older and white, enjoy "free golf for life."

Today's dizzying array of "age-friendly housing" options include accessory dwelling units, or ADUs, also called "in-law suites," where parents can live both together with and apart from their families. More older people are offering lodging to others in exchange for assistance or companionship, an arrangement so common it's now facilitated by apps. As grandparents today raise more than 2.3 million of America's children, some older people seek out multigenerational communities that support such "grandfamilies." There's housing specifically for aging LGBTQ people who are less likely to have biological families to rely on for care. SAGE, which advocates for LGBTQ elders, estimates this community will grow to seven million by 2030. Some older people live in private homes; clustered groups of houses or apartments called "pocket neighborhoods"; or in communities intentionally planned around shared kitchen, dining, and laundry areas called "cohousing." Architects are also creating designs to keep older people woven into (not out of) the fabric of their communities.

Senior housing options span the income range, from affordable options, like Karin House, which provides housing and support for forty low-income older people in Washington, DC, to luxury options that promise to turn retirement into a five-star resort stay.

PRIVATE HOMES

Then, of course, there's aging at home. Cisneros describes the bungalow in Houston, where he grew up and where his mother, Elvira, still lived in her mid-eighties. Modifications made for his father after a stroke—a ramp to avoid steep steps, a handrail, and a roll-in shower—helped his mom, too, as she aged. As did living next door to a friend and in an engaged neighborhood, "full of encouragement, ambition, and pride in our Latino heritage." Cisneros wrote that it "could well have been lifted from a Norman Rockwell painting, except that all of the faces would have been brown."[2] That's where his mother wanted to stay. But the cultural transformation Cisneros and his coauthors envisioned has yet to cohere.

"Aging in place" well as our needs increase requires planning resources and determination. Some people contact the Eldercare Locator or their local Area Agency on Aging to find help nearby (see the Resources section). AI could be useful in identifying local resources, explaining what they do, their costs, ratings, and contact info. But people also need nuanced judgment to help them navigate very personal and human scenarios. It remains to be seen how helpful AI can be with this. We also already have an array of useful tech options. Voice assistants can turn on lights, make calls, read *Middlemarch*, or play Oscar Peterson. Smart watches can sense when someone has fallen and call for help. And innovators are explaining new ways that technology can help. But for now, most people weave together the help of family, friends, and often aides. People who can't afford aides might qualify for home and community-based services, or HCBS, a program for which people who are eligible for Medicaid can apply. HCBS can vary from a few hours of help a week to daily around-the-clock care that enables people to stay out of nursing homes. They might entail personal care, like bathing or dressing, or doing errands. They might help someone get a ride to the store, install a ramp or grab bars, or get to the senior center for exercise classes. HCBS may also provide respite care to give family caregivers an occasional break.

Programs of All-Inclusive Care for the Elderly, or PACE, a Medicare- and Medicaid-funded program, also can help older people stay in their homes and communities by coordinating soup-to-nuts services and care. Residents can see a doctor, dentist, or physical therapist. They can go to the hospital if necessary, and PACE will help coordinate services to bring them home again. PACE helps arrange for social workers, Meals on Wheels, paid caregivers, and transportation. And the services are coordinated from a center where people gather regularly, doing double duty to reduce isolation.

Many geriatricians, like Laura Mosqueda, also help people age in place with an old-fashioned kind of doctoring—the house call—seeing patients for whom it would be difficult to impossible to come see them. In Washington, DC, the Geriatric House Call Program, run by the MedStar Washington Hospital Center, has long served elders living in some of the city's lowest income areas.

House calls may seem inefficient, but researchers have found that many of them, like DC's program, save money. In one study tracking 11,000 patients, researchers examining the Department of Veterans Affairs' home-based primary care program found that it not only increased patient satisfaction, well-being, and longevity but also reduced health care costs by 24 percent by reducing the length of both hospital and nursing home stays.[3]

The VA runs the largest health system in the United States. Of the 22 million veterans it serves, almost half are sixty-five and older. Its home-based primary care program, launched in 1972, is also the country's biggest house-call program. Teams of medical and mental health experts, social workers, dieticians, pharmacists, and rehab therapists help veterans with chronic conditions stay at home. Why isn't this kind of care more common? "The traditional fee-for-service reimbursement system makes house call programs nearly impossible to support without grant or donation funding," says Lena Makaroun, a VA geriatrician. "Being liberated from that system allows the VA to innovate in doing what's right for high-need groups without being hamstrung by rigid reimbursement structures." Mountains of data show that older people's health and well-being benefit from more integrated attention to their medical *and* social needs. But our siloed systems obstruct just that—even though data suggest that cutting back on social services stokes our out-of-control health expenses.

Another reason home-based care is effective goes back to trust. Older people and their families are more likely to have talked with the team while sitting around the kitchen table about possible scenarios and hard issues like DNRs and ICUs. There's more time for questions, contemplation, and to work through conflict. Having a foundation of trust and an understanding of priorities is invaluable when it comes time to navigate the inevitable crises. It helps reduce emergency hospital visits and pressured decisions that can lead to futile long-term intubations. It can help families avoid recrimination and regret. It can help them emerge intact, with acceptance and peace.

Another underappreciated care model is the old-fashioned phone call. Long before the pandemic, both at UCI and at the University of Southern California Keck School of Medicine where she began working in 2014, Laura handed out her cell phone number like candy. She gives it not only to patients and their families but also to colleagues and friends, and to their friends. She knows she has knowledge that many people want and need, knowledge that's in short supply. I knew the value of having a number to call. When Fiona came home from the NICU, still on oxygen and monitors and very ill, her pediatrician and pulmonologist gave me their personal phone numbers, *just in case*.

Laura is convinced that by giving out her phone number, she helps people get the care they need at home, reducing hospital visits and their costs. More important, those conversations help people stay focused on what matters most to them as they navigate the daunting systems of life and death. When Laura's twin sister died, the news had come as a "complete shock" to her when she was pulled out of class that day. She knew her sister was sick, but no one had talked to her about the possibility of loss. That stayed with her.

As an adult, she's had hundreds of such conversations. One involved a ninety-three-year-old patient with serious, almost certainly end-stage cancer and his three daughters. A physician was suggesting that the man try one more round of chemo. The family was agonizing. Laura talked with the father and daughters about their goals. How did they want to spend what might be their last weeks together? Was there anything they wanted to do or say as life's end approached? A decision to stay home and decline chemo wasn't "giving up," Laura explained. It was a life-affirming decision intended to enhance their remaining time together. Often just a few brief conversations—a small "dose"—can help people navigate decisions based on what's most important to them, and not based on the frequent medical system default mode to forestall death, regardless of what that might mean for life.

Supportive Housing

In addition to aging in place, millions of older people, and their families, also rely on residential facilities for care. Such places go by names like "long-term care," "congregate care," and, more recently, "supportive housing." I thought I understood the options from my work, but to look at such places with Janet, was to see the landscape anew. The terminology, costs, and options vary by region, but in general long-term care falls roughly into four broad categories.

Nursing homes typically offer twenty-four-hour nursing staff, aides, and consultations by physicians, as well as meals and activities for on average $100,000 per year. Some also offer short-term rehab. Alternatively, for 20 to 120 residents, *assisted living* offers private apartments with common areas and à la carte options for meal plans, activities, and assistance with housekeeping, laundry, and medication. But definitions vary; for example, some states have fewer residents and shared rooms. Assisted living costs on average $50,000 to $100,000 per year. *Group homes* are a lower-cost option offering older adults a single or shared room, in a private home with two to twenty other residents. Meals and personal care usually are offered on-site, around the clock, but nursing and medical care are not. Group homes cost on average $20,000 to $90,000 per year, and not all are licensed. Then there are *continuing care retirement communities*, or CCRCs, like the ones we visited with Janet. CCRCs offer a range of services, covering any eventuality—from independent housing (houses or apartments) and assisted living to memory care and skilled nursing. Their value is that they offer varying levels of care, so there's usually another area you can move to if your needs increase. CCRCs' costs vary accordingly, but they aren't cheap.

Many Americans are surprised to learn two things about long-term care. The first is that Medicare does not cover it, making it the biggest uninsured risk most Americans face.[4] Its high price puts it beyond the financial reach of many people who don't have decent long-term care insurance, which is expensive in its own right. Those who can't afford long-term care must rely on family or friends or be poor enough to qualify for Medicaid.

The second surprise is that you can be asked to leave if the place determines your needs exceed what they're equipped to provide, if they won't accept Medicaid, or if they've deemed you a "problem" resident.

MEDICAL MODEL TO CULTURE CHANGE

As we've seen, twentieth-century reformers advocated to make nursing homes more like hospitals, believing that the *medical model* would improve care. Medicine had vanquished disease, the thinking went. Surely it could also cure old age. Though well-intentioned, this was no panacea.

Many residents had conditions that couldn't be cured. And places that felt like medical facilities tended to define older people by their physical ailments and deficits, not their capacities or wishes. When a facility is your home, you don't want to feel like you're at a repair shop. You want to be seen for the whole of who you are, have meaningful relationships, and do things you care about. You want, in short, a place that provides assistance and feels like home. Hence the term *resident*.

Enhancing the medical model with elements of home was the goal of assisted living pioneer Keren Wilson. When Keren's mother had a serious stroke, she was shocked by the lack of privacy and choice at the nursing home, so she decided to do something about it. Keren got a doctorate in gerontology in 1983 and created Park Place in Portland, Oregon, which melded elements of health care, hospitality, and home.

Park Place wasn't fancy. It had common areas and humble apartments, with call buttons and lockable doors. Residents made decisions about when they wanted to eat, sleep, and bathe. They could socialize or keep to themselves, get a cat or (at that time) smoke. Residents' function and well-being improved. Their care cost government programs 20 percent less than in nursing homes.[5] Keren called her model "assisted living."

Over the years, assisted living's innovations helped to usher in *culture change*, a movement focused on respecting residents' wishes, treating staff better, and creating environments where people felt connection and purpose. Geriatrician Bill Thomas was an early culture change warrior. Seeing epidemics of loneliness, helplessness, and boredom in the facility where he was the medical director, Thomas convinced the administrator to let him bring more life into the place, including dogs, cats, parakeets, rabbits, hens, and plants. Residents cultivated flower and vegetable gardens and volunteered at the childcare center and preschool on the premises, bringing the world in and the generations together in shared purpose.

Direct care workers had a voice in decisions and attended to both the physical and emotional aspects of resident care. Mortality fell; drug use was cut in half. Thomas called his philosophy the Eden Alternative and formed a nonprofit to push similar culture change in facilities beyond his. Atul Gawande chronicled Bill Thomas and Keren Wilson's innovations to create places where people feel like their lives still have meaning, in *Being Mortal*; and journalist Moira Welsh, in her 2021 book, *Happily Ever Older*, described a smorgasbord of hopeful care models, better for both residents and staff.

Some large nursing homes took culture change seriously, splitting themselves up into "neighborhoods" with eight to twelve residents, consistent staff, and a cozier feel. Residents had private rooms and bathrooms, as well as common areas to gather, cook, visit, and share meals. They lived in places where their emotional and spiritual lives mattered as much as their physical problems.

Culture change also addressed another issue. Despite being surrounded by others, many people who live in group settings feel profoundly lonely and isolated, with serious negative consequences for their health and happiness. Incapacity and immobility make it harder to interact with others without assistance. Infrequent (or no) visits from family and friends make the situation worse, as does understaffing or inattentive staff.

Reducing isolation and building homelike communities drove the creation of "small houses"—where residents got skilled nursing in actual homes. Here again, Thomas was in the vanguard, developing what he called Green Houses with the motto, "real homes with meaningful lives and empowered staff."[6] The Robert Wood Johnson Foundation staked $10 million to expand Green Houses nationwide and study their impact. Today, there are more than 350 Green Houses. Studies showed their residents were healthier and happier. Staff found more meaning in their work.

GOOD PLACES

Whatever name we give "person-centered" approaches, many facilities long have known, and shown, how to provide great care. Some years ago, Laura introduced me to a woman, saying, "when I need a nursing home, I want to go to Feri's." I'd seen plenty of what went wrong in such places. I wanted to know what Laura thought Feri Kidane, the administrator at a nursing home where Laura was the medical director, did right.

Some people with dementia walk a lot. Worried they'll wander into danger, facilities have lots of locked, alarmed doors that convey, again and again: *No entry. No exit.* Feri's facility had many open doors, inviting residents to places both appealing and safe. "There were beautiful, enclosed gardens," Laura said, "and paths through them that led back to the living area, so residents could walk freely."

When Laura showed up in her white coat, retired physician-residents would sometimes join her for "rounds," walking through the place, discussing diagnoses, engaging in issues important to them.

Another colleague told me about a nursing home where an older man with cognitive impairment kept scaring other residents, popping into their rooms at 4:00 a.m. The staff spoke with his family and learned that as a postman, his ritual had been to get up before dawn, have a beer, and start his rounds at 4:00 a.m. The staff affixed mailboxes in various locations outside residents' rooms and bought some nonalcoholic beer, which they gave him every morning along with mail to deliver. That's creative care planning.

Like any kind of home, facilities have different "vibes." Several of Laura's patients went to a place that initially seemed "chaotic and crazy" to her. "There was lots of loud music. I thought, 'this can't be good,'" she said. But Laura's patients and their families loved the place, so she took a closer look. In fact, the staff were extremely engaged and clearly knew the residents well. They didn't just park them in front of the television. Laura would arrive to find residents dancing to live music. Others painted or worked with clay. "Some people with dementia need calm and quiet," Laura said. "But for social people it was great. There was nothing special to look at, but there was a lot of joy in that place."

Good facilities look different, but they share common traits. Some have cozy gardens where residents stroll, read, and gossip, while others revolve around card games and common room couches. The important thing is easy access to welcoming places. Don't be deluded by chandeliers. A careworn place might have better care and activities than a fancy one. A place with special mattresses might rely heavily on temporary "agency" staff who don't know the residents. Consistent quality and emotional connection are preferable to dazzling amenities. See *all* the places where you might spend time, not just the ones the sales rep showcases. And talk with several residents and their visitors, not just people the facility suggests you talk to. Make sure they have activities beyond bingo that give people purpose. Book clubs and setting up a gift shop to sell resident-made items are good options. Also, says one advocate, residents should be invited to participate in operations. It's their home, after all. This could include forming a committee to welcome new residents, sitting in on new staff interviews, or reaching out to local schools to get involved in class projects.

The best places have clear policies, communicated up front, about what's included for what cost and how decisions are made as residents' care needs change. The staff treat residents with respect and know what and who matters to them. And the management treats staff like they're doing an important job and like the people they care for are valued customers. People joke and laugh. They answer call bells. They serve appealing food and know the residents' favorite desserts. In the words of one advocate, "Nothing matters more to people than the food."

Observe how staff interact with residents, Laura told me. Do they mostly just sit behind desks? Some aspects of care are particularly revealing, she said. "Feeding someone is a very intimate thing. It's primal. Do the staff just line up residents and stick a spoon in everyone's mouth—'here's your applesauce'—with no interaction or warmth? Or do they sit down, take their time and lovingly feed the person, recognizing the nursing home resident as a fellow human being?"

Persistent Challenges

Despite some improvements, culture change and related models have remained more the exception than the norm. As of 2020, fewer than 2 percent of the nation's nursing homes were Green Houses and they cared for fewer than 1 percent of all residents.[7] Many large chains shrugged off the evidence of culture change's benefits or took only superficial steps. "It's more than just pets, plants, and ice cream stations," one advocate told me. "It's about how people treat one another and making sure that residents have meaning in their lives in the way they define it. Then the pandemic, and the staff shortages left in its wake, made culture change feel almost like a luxury.

I asked Alice Bonner, a former top nursing home official at HHS, now leading reform efforts, why culture change and its more humane practices hadn't taken hold in nursing homes. Big change requires incentives, she said. Culture change had neither carrots nor sticks. Reimbursement formulas didn't require or reward it, and the 5,000 state surveyors who do oversight visits weren't trained to inspect for it. Because it wasn't mandated, they didn't impose sanctions for its absence. Some even imposed sanctions for its presence, like citing a health violation for a cat curled up on a bed.

We know a lot about what good places do to be good. Pandemic-fueled reform efforts described in the last chapter give us a chance to reenvision how to use carrots and sticks to align the incentives with good care. We need definitions of success that align with what matters most to people. We need to measure not only mortality and meds but also meaning, joy, and whether people feel like they retain a role in shaping their existence. If we're ever to have places that provide succor and feel more like home, we will need to measure what matters most and reimburse accordingly.

PRECEPTORS AND PATHWAYS

Reform will require not just carrots and sticks but also innovations to expand the caregiving workforce. That's the aim behind the Health Career Pathways program in Contra Costa County, California. It provides intensive training and support for people with "addressable barriers" to become certified nursing assistants (CNAs) and helps nursing homes become better preceptors and employers. A troika of entities created and runs the Pathways program: a job training program, an adult learning center, and a long-term care ombudsman program. "We're advancing person-centered care with person-centered education," said Nicole Howell, ombudsman director and former executive director of Empowered Aging.

Sheri Ignacio, a single mother of two, was a Pathways student. Worried about her math skills, she sought academic support to meet the math requirements. The program's wraparound services were also critical for her. "Getting things like food bags, gas cards, and having someone to talk to," she said, "was very helpful."[8] The program offers meals on-site, healthy groceries for students to take home on weekends, and childcare. Getting professional support to bolster their school, job, and life skills also is integral. "These students have had few opportunities to succeed," Nicole explained. Some have struggled with substance use or homelessness. They need—and get—wraparound services.

They also learn restorative justice approaches to mediate conflict. Nicole told me about one student who cared for a resident who hurled racial epithets at her. "The old me would have started yelling at her," the student said later. But using the skills she'd learned, she walked away and talked through the incident with her peers.

Students get 303 hours of classroom training, almost twice the state requirement and more than four times the federal requirement. "We work with them as long as they'll come," said Nicole. In turn, the students push and are there for one another. At about $8,000 per student, the program's not cheap, but it's less expensive than understaffing and lifts people out of poverty into financial self-sufficiency. Ignacio now works as a CNA, earning $17 an hour with full benefits, including health coverage for her family.

Nicole also worked closely with nursing homes to help them be good clinical preceptors and employers. "As an employer myself," Nicole said, "I ask, 'how much responsibility do I have to create a good workplace?' A lot. That's what the industry has failed to see."

We will not have reliably decent care anywhere—not in facilities or at home—until we provide reliably decent wages, training, and quality jobs for the people providing it.

Assisted Living and Group Homes

Assisted living began as an innovation to change nursing homes, but its culture changed, too. Although it started as an idealistic innovation, with affordable options like Keren Wilson's Park Place, assisted living's profit-making potential soon became plain. People who could pay would pay a lot to avoid a nursing home, propelling assisted living into a more than $90 billion market by 2022, estimated to swell to $140 billion by 2030.[9] Although assisted living residents look a lot like nursing home residents from twenty years ago, the industry plays by different rules with less stringent standards. Also, far from its affordable origins, nearly all assisted living is expensive today, beyond the reach of most people. For them, there are group homes, family care, or whatever Medicaid will fund.

Assisted living has a rosier reputation than nursing homes, but this may be unfair. We don't have data to compare them. We don't have much data about assisted living at all, and even less about group homes. The laws and standards that govern those industries—like how much care consumers can expect, staffing requirements, and who can be kicked out, when, and why—vary from state to state. Regulation is rigorous in some places, lax in others. It's impossible to generalize. In most states, consumers are on their own in trying to figure out the track record for a single place, much less in comparing places to one another. AARP has created a "score card" that provides some much-needed information. Still, the lack of consistent validated data and the profusion of definitions and models make assisted living and group homes even harder than nursing homes to assess and compare.

Some places get great reviews, but there are also dark harbingers, even in places with chandeliers. "Assisted living is the rock we don't want to look under," said Catherine Hawes, a long-term care expert and researcher, quoting the head of a state licensing agency. A *Frontline* and ProPublica investigative series, "Life and Death in Assisted Living," explained the problem this way: Workers "manage complex medication regimens . . . and handle people so incapacitated they can be a threat to themselves or others, [yet] in many states, regulations for assisted living lag far behind this reality."[10]

Group homes get, if anything, less scrutiny than assisted living. I once had an Uber driver who complained he wasn't making as much money as he'd hoped from his side hustle—running a group home for older people. Taking in older boarders has long been a way for people to augment their income, but such scenarios get chancier as the boarders' care needs escalate. Called "board and care" in California and "adult family homes" in Seattle, such group homes are highly variable in name, standards, and quality. Here, too, there are signs of trouble that often come to light only because a cop, prosecutor, or journalist investigated. That's what led to a *Seattle Times* series called "Seniors for Sale," exposing abuses in hundreds of Seattle's adult family homes. The article spurred brief outrage but not systemic reform.

It's not clear why we don't have better data about these multibillion-dollar industries responsible for the care of a million consumers, many of them with complex needs unable to advocate for themselves. When it comes to assisted living and group homes, we have even less clue than with nursing homes how they spend taxpayer dollars. Most are subject to consumer protection laws and the jurisdiction of Medicaid Fraud Control Units, yet few are held accountable for false promises. Maybe it's that assisted living has accrued so much power as it has gained market share and thrown in its lot with the powerful nursing home lobby. Or maybe it's that problems in assisted living and group homes are harder to see and quantify than those in nursing homes, which get most of the attention. Or maybe it's that no one wants to replicate the Byzantine nursing home regulatory apparatus. Or maybe it's that lawmakers don't have much appetite to use their power to help such a powerless constituency.

Whatever the reasons, as reform efforts proceed, it's critical to remember that today's long-term care landscape is very different than the one OBRA '87 was written for. Assisted living, group homes, CCRCs, and other settings house about the same number of older people as nursing homes these days. Home- and community-based services continue to replace facilities. There are new models and new names for old models. Who can keep track? Not to mention that what happens in one setting is bound up with what happens in others. Real reform will require an integrated approach across the entire web of providers. We also need to reenvision how we define "success," how we dole out money, and measure both based more on how *residents* define their own well-being.

Consumers and policy-makers alike need meaningful and reliable data to inform their decisions. Government is supposed to assure that the work behind the curtain is done well enough so we can trust the entities we must rely on when we must rely on them. It's also supposed to exercise stewardship over how public monies are spent. So far, government and the industries it funds have failed on both counts.

Consumer Advocates: Ombudsmen and Elder Lawyers

Given all the challenges, getting good long-term care for yourself or someone else requires dogged advocacy. Sometimes you can be your own advocate. But the systems are so fragmented, complex, and unyielding that many people need help from experts. An older celebrated author and former professor who struggled with severe mental illness and was facing eviction from his assisted living facility was one of them. The writer's guardian had failed to arrange for the medical care or medication he needed to function and hadn't pursued the writer's book royalties, leaving him impoverished. Frustrated, furious, and far from the artistic and academic communities where he'd once thrived, the writer taped his book jackets to the door of his room to convey "I am still somebody."

With eviction looming, an absent guardian, and nowhere to go, the writer contacted an ombudsman who got him medical attention, arranged for him to obtain medication, and connected him to a lawyer to help him replace the guardian with one who cared about who he was and what he needed.

It's worth stepping back here to look at the advocacy systems. Every state has a long-term care ombudsman program with paid staff and volunteers who advocate for residents and their families. The ombudsman program the writer contacted was housed in the Michigan Elder Justice Initiative, or MEJI, part of a larger legal services program. MEJI was founded and is directed by Alison Hirschel, who'd worked on the GeriMed case.

Older people and their families navigate legal issues—from housing to benefits, from wills to powers of attorney. For those who can afford a lawyer, there are private elder law attorneys. For people who can't, there are legal services attorneys, like Alison. The Older Americans Act envisions that ombudsmen and elder law attorneys work closely together. That doesn't happen as often as it should. But Alison was determined to provide integrated advocacy through MEJI. That meant that the ombudsman representing the writer could just call a coworker down the virtual hall, to find a lawyer to petition to replace the writer's guardian.

Coordinated advocacy got the writer his meds, a new assisted living facility with a community he loved, and a new guardian, a compassionate and attentive private attorney, who respected his wishes and got him access to his royalties again. The guardian even helped the writer's son, who had nowhere to live, get back on his feet. "His life, which looked so bleak when we first met him," said Alison, "is now infinitely better in so many ways."

AGING DOES NOT WAIT

As we await better options to help us navigate life's late chapters, aging does not wait. That included many people I loved. The place where we visited with Janet that Thanksgiving and met the woman from the University of Chicago School of Social Work seemed nice. Still, its main appeal for Janet was being closer to her grandkids—to be part of birthdays, dinners, walks, and movies; to be entwined in one another's lives in the way that living close allows. Yet, she'd lived in Chicago for more than ninety years. She couldn't decide. This was, of course, her prerogative, but we worried that the clock was ticking. We wanted the big decisions about her life to be made *by* Janet, not *for* her. Not deciding is deciding, too.

I've been increasingly impressed by the healing power, the joy even, of finding the right place. As I worked on this book, two friends worried about their fathers who were caring for their mothers with dementia at home. Everyone was getting exhausted and isolated. Then one couple moved to a cozy, small, assisted living facility, the other to a huge CCRC. Neither place was luxurious, but both provided great care, with lots of options for engagement. Both friends' parents traded the comforts of one home for the comforts of another. Both friends said it was as though their parents turned back the health clock by two years. After my friend and my children's godmother Ricki helped her dad move into his assisted living facility, he became the home's informal mayor. He led exercise classes and Torah study groups. He negotiated menus with kitchen staff and Internet upgrades with administrators. A social man, he relished his new roles. He had new friends and daily calls from his daughter. His place in a warm community where he was well cared for enhanced Ricki's quality of life, too.

That sense of community also appealed to my mother. Many of her and my father's friends lived at Charter House, Mayo Clinic's CCRC; they visited often for meals and events. It offered nice apartments, Mayo-level care, and abundant activities. She liked the idea of cooking and cleaning less, of lectures and meals with friends, and of running into people she knew. My father was a shyer sort. He made us peek out his apartment door before he went to the elevator to avoid running into anyone. Only my mother's powers of persuasion—no trifling force—got him to pay the deposit to hold a spot on Charter House's long waiting list.

But soon after my mother died, my father dropped off the waiting list and got his deposit back. We worried about falls, and he did fall several times, spending hours on the floor, bruised but miraculously okay. We took turns pleading with him to wear a life alert. "*That* won't stop me from falling," he said. His wishes were clear. He confirmed them during a brief stint at Charter House for rehab after knee surgery. One day, he paged Heidi several times. Worried, she called back right away. "Heidi," he said, alarm in his voice, "can you please bring me my wedding ring?"

"Now . . . ?" Heidi asked, her afternoon swamped with patients and meetings. "Yes," he implored, "please." Several widows had joined him at his table for lunch, he said. He didn't want them to get the wrong idea.

What had appealed to my mother seemed dreadful to my father. He wanted to stay in his apartment, alone, for as long as possible.

We need a range of reliable, supportive housing options that offer quality care, meaningful engagement, and a sense of home. We need places that don't tear up families with the distress of having chosen the "wrong place." We need affordable places to live our long lives well.

Chapter 5

MONEY

Because that's where the money is.

—Willie Sutton's alleged response
when asked why he robbed banks

As my father got older, the daily stack in his mailbox grew—a dozen appeals for money some days. "When I get telephone solicitations," he said, "I put down the phone because I know I'm vulnerable." Yet, the entreaties that kept flooding his mailbox piled high on his desk. He was impossibly frugal with himself—frayed canvas shoes, a tattered windbreaker for all seasons. He abhorred wastefulness. When Heidi stopped by at night, she often found the apartment dark, except for a triangle of desk light under which he sat hunched over, reading through a magnifying glass.

Still, on many days, generosity eclipsed suspicion, meaning that he sent out a lot of smallish checks, and his drawers filled with the cheap pens, key chains, and notepads the so-called charities sent him to keep the checks coming. He kept sending those checks, too, despite knowing the score. In his early nineties, he told me, "I suspect they sell your information and then everyone asks you for money."

We're amid a tempest when it comes to separating older people from their money. Wealth is disproportionately concentrated among the old, as are brain changes that erode "financial capacity" and the ability to discern when something's fishy. Then there's the Internet. Social media allows predators more direct access to their prey and to invent any convincing scheme they can dream up. Younger digital natives are deft navigators of the online world, dismissing messages from unknown contacts. But elders have a harder time spotting fakes and are more likely to think it bad manners to ignore a question or a plea.

So, if you're a person who tries to get other people to give you money—a con artist, a fundraiser, or a relative down on your luck—you can easily sift through the demographics to improve your odds, which was why my father got so much mail.

SCAMS

Scams are now ubiquitous. People of every age fall for them. Some are incredibly convincing, others bizarrely obvious, but all have the same goal: to leave the recipient poorer than before. The people losing money are disproportionately sixty and older, with those eighty and older losing most of all. Con artists may impersonate a cop, lawyer, or hospital staff to make the mark nervous. Being "Grandma-ed" has entered the lexicon to describe elders getting a call to help a grandchild who needs money right away for some emergency. They may start with "Grandma, I'm in trouble, I need help. Please don't tell Mom." Often this produces a name right away—"Jeremy, is that you?"—oiling the machine for future use.

It's hard to stay ahead of the ever-evolving arsenal, or even to pin down numbers on how numerous and costly scams are. Most older people who report scams are those who *don't* lose money. The people losing money rarely make reports. Even among those who do, older marks lose much more than younger ones.

Organizations like the Federal Trade Commission (FTC) and AARP regularly publish "look out for this one!" lists with new guidance about scams to watch for, but it's like holding back the tides: In 2015, 3.3 million people, many of them older, fell for calls supposedly from Microsoft Windows to fix a virus. The personal information victims divulged cost them about $1.5 billion a year. In 2019 and 2020, there was an increase in social security frauds with scammers impersonating government officials. The FTC reported that "people in their 70s lose 40% more (and those 80 and over lose 93% more) than people in their 30s."[1] Losses from cryptocurrency scams increased five-fold in just the fourth quarter of 2020, although they weren't a leading cause of losses.[2] And in 2022 the IRS reported that thousands of Americans lost millions of dollars to IRS impostors claiming they'll put a lien on your house if you don't pay "overdue taxes."[3]

Other trends include fake inquiries about charges for online purchases like (ironically) antivirus software and cancer charities with legitimate-sounding names. The FTC fined four of those fake charities $187 million for defrauding consumers. There are fake health care providers offering "free" checkups that aren't free and that keep billing for care patients never receive. There are con artists who troll obituaries to catch the bereaved in their early disorienting grief. And there are an infinite array of "romance" fraud or "sweetheart" scams, the type of scheme to which people sixty and older lose the most money.[4] Con artists can easily figure out marks' favorite musicians or celebrities and then impersonate them. Some scammers use religious online dating sites like BigChurch, Christian Mingle, and JDate to find people looking for love who can't imagine being swindled by someone who shares their faith. As my father suspected, con artists often do buy and sell their marks' information. Slip up with one and they'll be selling your social security or credit card numbers to scores of others.

We've long romanticized the roguish ingenuity of cons with comedy—*The Sting*, *The Grifters*, and *Hustlers*. *New Yorker* writer Jia Tolentino called scamming a "definitive millennial ethos," core to the identity of a generation raised on the Internet's anything-goes attention economy. Also, many millennials have mortgage-sized debt from educations, without a house or a salary to pay it off. "It would be better, of course, to do things morally," Tolentino wrote in "The Story of a Generation in Seven Scams," an essay in her book, *Trick Mirror*, "but who these days has the ability or the time."[5] That's one side of the equation.

The Harm

For older victims on the other side, financial loss can spell tragedy. In *Being Mortal*, Atul Gawande wrote about Alice Hobson, his wife's grandmother: "The body's decline creeps like a vine. Day to day, the changes can be imperceptible. You adapt. Then something happens that finally makes it clear that things are no longer the same. The falls didn't do it. The car accident didn't do it. Instead, it was a scam that did."[6]

Hobson was scammed by men she hired to do yard and tree work. They overcharged her, then came back, wresting more than $7,000 from her in all. Neighbors, hearing raised voices, called the police. "The men were convicted and sentenced to prison, which should have been satisfying for Alice," Gawande wrote, "but instead the whole process kept the events, and the reminders of her growing vulnerability, alive and lingering when she would have dearly loved to have set them behind her."[7]

This is the key to why elder scams are so harmful to health. They tip lives from independence to dependence. In a sense, *falling* for a scam really is like a fall, but a financial one. Both physical and financial falls can happen at any age, although they get more common later in life. But there's more stigma attached to a financial fall. It can usher in hopelessness, dread, and shame: "How could I have been so stupid? How could I have caused so much trouble?" It signals a broader defeat. The game is lost. That's why scams can hasten mortality and sometimes lead to depression and even suicide.

Exploitation's toll isn't just psychological. It can have serious physical fallout, too. For Sherrie Kaplan's mother a scam lit multiple fuses. Sherrie, codirector of the Health Policy Research Institute at the University of California, Irvine's medical school where Laura Mosqueda previously worked, told me that her mother had done well living on her own, despite heart disease, mild dementia, and losing her husband. She had a robust network of friends and family. Sherrie and her brother stayed in close touch with her.

Then the mother's bathtub backed up. Not wanting to burden her children, she picked a plumber from the phone book. The first estimate of $800 ballooned to more than $8,000. The job grew, too. Suddenly men were digging up her driveway to "replace clay pipes"— but she had no clay pipes. Then came dunning calls and men banging on her door demanding payment. The insurance company wanted explanations. Still, she didn't tell her kids for fear they'd think she couldn't live alone anymore. Instead, she stopped going out, scared of running into the men. She missed doctors' appointments. She didn't refill her prescriptions and stopped taking her heart medication. Then her heart failed, requiring emergency cardiac surgery. She never totally recovered, losing not just her money but also her health and likely years of her life. Prosecutors declined the case telling Sherrie her mother wouldn't make a "good" witness.

What shocked Sherrie most was how big and hidden the problem was. "When I reported the plumber to the Better Business Bureau and the licensing agency, they told me, 'This happens all the time. That plumber charged another elderly client $1,000 to replace a faucet.' And that was just *one* insurance company and *one* plumber. It's like a huge dirty secret."

Mark Lachs found the same thing in his research. Mark, the codirector of geriatrics at Weill Cornell Medical College, found that elder abuse, including financial exploitation, triples rates of premature mortality in victims.[8] "Elder abuse tips over lives at a point when people lack the time, health, or income to recover," he said. Old age is often like Jenga late in the game: There are wobbles, but the tower still stands. Then some event yanks out a critical block, toppling the structure.

FINANCIAL CAPACITY

Fraud usually comes with warning signs. Today, sophisticated algorithms flag out-of-the-ordinary transactions. Even before computers took over, local bankers knew when their customers' money habits changed. But for years, financial institutions did little about elder financial exploitation. They hid behind customer privacy laws, arguing that what clients did with their money was their business. With 10,000 Americans turning sixty-five every day, they were more interested in the growing market of older customers.

That was why in 2006 Ron Long originally hired a gerontologist, someone who studies aging and the aging process. Ron was head of regulatory affairs for what in 2008 became Wells Fargo Advisors (WFA), the investment arm of the banking behemoth. The majority of its almost $1 trillion in assets were owned by people sixty and older, and Ron was curious about how they could be better served. He was surprised by "eye-opening statistics" the gerontologist relayed. "Most sobering," Ron told me, "was that financial capacity is one of the first skills to go as we age. A person can seem fine even when their financial acumen has declined." Sometimes the assets are gone before anyone even knows to worry.

Financial capacity refers to the ability to manage funds, like bills and assets. Financial capacity skills are controlled by several parts of the brain, like memory and executive function, that often decline with age. Then there's the scenario of an unexpected caller asking for money. Such exchanges require our brains to parse thousands of social cues. "Gut feelings" in fact emanate from the brain's anterior insula, like messages that "something's not right here!" Researchers believe that pathological aspects of aging can dim those warnings, or mute them altogether. Some people become less suspicious in old age.

It's another one of those double-edged aspects of aging: as we feel our time waning, we intentionally focus on the positive, explains Duke Han, a neuropsychologist at University of Southern California and Laura's colleague. Duke, who studies elders' susceptibility to exploitation, started with a caveat. "Our ageism causes us to forget that the decision-making capacity of most older adults is perfectly intact," he said. "And lots of people without cognitive impairment fall for scams." Duke wants to identify factors, especially modifiable ones, that account for this. Feeling financially insecure, or being unfamiliar with cultural norms about what's expected when a stranger calls, are two possibilities. Duke's research is a part of a small but growing effort to learn what steps we can take so that declines in financial capacity and "gut feelings" don't become preludes to misfortune.

PROTECTING OLDER CLIENTS

In the 1990s, with increasing numbers of Americans aging and scams on the rise, advocates pressed for laws requiring bankers to report activity they suspected might be elder financial exploitation. Bankers fought back, leading to stalemates in some states, like California. In Massachusetts, the opponents tabled their differences, and in 1996 the banking industry joined a task force that trained bank employees to spot exploitation. An Oregon coalition also trained bank employees and noted the importance of cultivating relationships with the state bankers association: "Bankers trust other bankers and will check with each other," its report advised.[9]

Coalition members also found that most APS workers lacked the skills to investigate monetary cases, so they recruited retired financial experts to help APS.

A decade later, the Internet had expanded scammers' ability to reach their marks. And Ron Long had learned about financial capacity and what made older people vulnerable to exploitation. Seeing a critical role for bankers, he changed his approach to his older clients at Wells Fargo Advisors (WFA) and to his life's work. He searched for a program to use as a model but, finding none at any major financial entity, created one himself, forming an in-house team of experts to review suspicious situations spotted by WFA's 15,000 financial advisors.

Teaching the advisors about elder financial exploitation was the easy part. Figuring out what they should *do* when they suspected trouble was harder. When should Ron's staff freeze accounts or slow down transactions? When could or should they contact a client's family or doctor? When should they report suspicions to APS or law enforcement? The laws were different in every state. "At the time," said Ron, "our legal department wasn't perfectly set up to handle these issues." After years of planning, and jumping through hoops, WFA finally launched its Elder Client Initiatives in 2014, the first such program at a major financial institution. Instead of squabbling about the nuances of mandatory reporting laws, they just reported suspicious activity.

The cases weren't easy. One financial advisor had a client who believed he'd won Brazil's lottery and had already wired $92,000 in "taxes" to get his $5 million in "winnings." The scammers were pressuring him to send another $80,000. The man wanted to augment his nest egg and secure enough assets to care for his ailing wife. He was furious at WFA for stalling his transfer of funds.

The advisor asked Ron to talk to the client. As Ron recalled, two arguments seemed to resonate: "He and his wife might lose their house and the same $5 million in winnings had also been offered to other people." That crisis was averted, but a few months later the client again sought to withdraw money, this time to pay "taxes" on volunteering for the Elks Club. Ron contacted the client again, pointing out that it made no sense to *pay* taxes for volunteering. The man got mad, shouting at Ron, "Dammit, it's *my* money. They're waiting for me! You're causing me to lose these funds." Ron said he wasn't allowed to participate in fraud, but if the man's attorney verified that the scheme was legitimate, Wells Fargo would cut a check right away. When the attorney called, Ron explained his concerns. The attorney talked to the family. The children hadn't wanted to intervene but now realized that, if they didn't, there'd be no money left to care for either of their parents. They petitioned the court for guardianship.

Curious, Ron dialed the man who'd been calling his client—from a 202 area code, Washington, DC, Ron's hometown. The man told Ron, "You can't stop me," and hung up. "His voice was chilling," Ron said. "And the bad thing is, he's probably right. These cases aren't getting the law enforcement interest they deserve. You can track down a lot of perpetrators if you investigate." Without support from law enforcement, or the FBI, it's virtually impossible to do so. But the FBI has the capacity to crack such cases.

It seemed only a matter of time before the plotlines of our appetite for reality TV and elder scams would converge. They did in Jen Shah, one of the Real Housewives of Salt Lake City. Federal prosecutors in Manhattan indicted Shah and others in 2021 for conspiring to defraud hundreds of victims, many of them older. Based on the FBI investigation, DOJ alleged that for at least seven years Shah sold "lead lists" (names of potential victims) to others knowing they would defraud the victims. The scam mostly involved selling services, like website design, to make the victims' "businesses" more efficient. Only, according to DOJ, many of the victims were elderly and did not own a computer. Shah shared in the ill-gotten gains, banking millions.

She and her coconspirators tried to hide their actions by communicating with encrypted messaging apps, caching proceeds in offshore banks, and using other people's names to incorporate entities. After her arrest Shah initially trumpeted: "The only thing I'm guilty of is being SHAH-MAZING!" But as her coconspirators pled guilty and the strength of the FBI's evidence became clearer, she changed her tune and pled guilty in 2022. She told the judge that she'd committed telemarketing-related "wire fraud, offering services with little to no value," purchased by the victims because of "misrepresentations, regarding the value." She said, "I knew many of the purchasers were over the age of 55. I am so sorry."[10]

Shah has begun serving her six year, six month prison sentence and must forfeit $6.5 million, and pay restitution of $9.5 million to the victims. Her case already has spun off a 2021 documentary, *The Housewife and the Shah Shocker*. Bravo cameras captured both Shah and FBI agents on the day of her arrest, and the crime remained a major plotline in the *Real Housewives of Salt Lake City*'s second season. The sad stories told in the victim impact statements received much less attention.

In its first year, Ron and the Elder Client Initiatives team fielded about 150 calls a month. The advisors then referred suspicious cases on to APS, which was harder than it sounds. Reporting requirements differed by state, sometimes by county. Some states required reports by phone, others by fax or hard copy, others via a website. Police had their own reporting rules, as did regulators, public health officials, and professional licensing agencies. WFA's headquarters compiled a huge manual of each state's procedures, convincing Ron that APS should create a centralized national reporting portal. "A firm as big as ours can manage it," he said, "but how do smaller firms figure out this morass? The current system is insane—a tin foil and chewing gum operation."

There was plenty of fault to go around: Some banks didn't give APS the financial records it needed to investigate or to stop assets from draining. When banks did report cases to APS with concerns about a client's cognitive decline, APS might deem the person to have "sufficient capacity" and close the case. Even when APS did investigate, it often lacked adequate financial expertise in-house or help from outside forensic accountants to follow the money trail.

Regulators were slow to require the financial industry to address the problem. Banks stoked mistrust by lobbying for immunity for *any* decision they made when elder abuse was alleged. Revelations that banks, including Wells Fargo, exploited their own clients didn't help build trust, either. Law enforcement and prosecutors also rarely held scammers accountable. Who lost in all this? As usual, older victims and their families.

Legitimate Entities Crossing Lines

Swindlers aren't the only ones after old people's money. Vast armadas of development professionals from the most decorous of institutions are vying for it, too. As they seek to fatten endowments and fund favored causes, few stop to consider if the putative donor has financial capacity. Do their fundraising tactics cross the line into "undue influence"? Are donors relinquishing funds they need for care or to stay independent? The rules and ethics that should govern legitimate fundraising protocols have gotten scant attention. For now, there's little inclination or incentive to patrol ambitious development campaigns when there are annual goals to meet.

One daunting example involved an Ivy League university's development associate who pressured a friend's aged mother for a donation. She had warm feelings about the school—her son and late husband were both alumni—and planned to remember it generously in her will. But she had planned to hold off until after her death to make sure she had enough money to pay for her long-term care of choice. But as the school ramped up the pressure, she donated $400,000 right away, not having intended to do so, and was either unable or too embarrassed to undo her mistake. The event became a source of keen remorse for her and her family.

No one has yet systematically and independently analyzed the trove of data WFA is gathering through its elder initiatives, but I asked if Ron noticed any trends. "Anecdotally, hairdressers are on my hit list," he said. "We've seen several of those cases; one was named power of attorney and then sole beneficiary not just for our client but for several older customers." Clients went from trusting dressers with their hair to trusting them with their money. "And unfortunately, more religious personnel are ingratiating themselves," Ron said. "All it takes is for one person who knows their financial and cognitive situation to be dishonest. Some people who take money are basically honest, but the money's too great a temptation."

Exploitation rose during the pandemic. It isn't surprising: when we're alone, the simple balm of human kindness is more likely to unlock our guard. *Grooming*, a term used to describe how pedophiles cultivate trust in prospective victims, also applies to setups for elder scams. The groomer calls and asks about health. There might be meals out, gifts, and flowers all to soften up the mark for the pressure that will follow. In Seattle, a broker for the investment firm Bankers Life groomed five older clients with such overtures and then stole $1 million that she had pretended to invest for them.[11]

Page Ulrey, a prosecutor in King County, Washington, brought criminal charges against the broker. Financial exploitation victims almost never get their money back, but Bankers Life eventually reimbursed all the victims its broker had duped. Even so, repayment didn't undo the deeper harm. Page was struck by how much destructive pain those losses caused.

Page was an unlikely prosecutor. She grew up on a farm in Pennsylvania, where her childhood job was tending the sheep. Sherlock was the first lamb she raised by herself. When he came of age, Page, then twelve, took him to auction, sobbing as she led him around the ring. He sold for $1.16 a pound. After that, a kind neighbor bought her lambs to save them from slaughter.

Page learned early on how vulnerability could shape fate. At twenty-two, she was diagnosed with multiple sclerosis, or MS. "I thought I was dying or at least would end up immobilized," she said. "By some miracle, it subsided and has stayed well-controlled, but I got a glimpse of what it's like to know your body's going to fail you."

The MS meant Page needed jobs with health insurance. She worked first with juveniles in legal trouble and then as a paralegal advocating for people incapacitated by asbestos exposure. Seeing the law's potential to redress harm propelled her to law school, and then to Seattle's Public Defender Association. She loved the job but was unnerved when she found herself empathizing with both her clients *and* the victims. "I dreaded having to defend child abuse cases," she said. Page hadn't thought of prosecution as "doing justice" before.

But in cases involving devastating harms, the prosecutors she went up against seemed to have "more leeway to find just outcomes than I did."

Certain divides in American professional life are seldom crossed; public defenders and prosecutors rarely switch sides. It's not that the skills aren't transferable, but the professional culture is so entwined with identity that changing sides can be deemed defection. Still, in 1998, after no small amount of agonizing, Page became a prosecutor.

In 2001, her boss offered her the chance to launch the office's first unit to bring elder abuse cases—a unit of one. Page threw herself into shaping the new job. To bring exploitation cases, she learned that she needed help from financial experts who knew what documents to subpoena. They could translate the numbers and complex transactions into flow charts and graphs, which told the story of the fraud in a way that helped her and jurors follow the money trail.

Elder abuse cases weren't new in King County, but most weren't prosecuted because they fell below the office's usual $100,000 threshold. Once people knew that Page was open for business, the cases began coming in. Every fraud that landed on her desk had its own sordid story, but there was a grinding sameness in the impact on victims and the despair of their families.

Page saw some cases where professional relationships started out valid but became corrupted, like the investment advisor. In other cases, the older victims had welcomed the exploiter into their lives as a friend or even a stand-in for family. That was what happened with a professional home organizer who befriended an older woman named Mariana. After Mariana's daughter died of cancer, the organizer exploited her grief, using lies about childhood trauma and a drug-addicted son as crowbars to extract money. The organizer stole everything Mariana owned. Her house was foreclosed on, and she declared bankruptcy. When Page visited Mariana in assisted living, she took Ellie along. Ellie was the service dog who lived and worked with Page. Victims of the crimes that Page's office prosecuted often were devastated; some took solace from the yellow lab's warm, calm presence. On many days, Page got calls from colleagues asking if Ellie was available for a victim interview. If so, they would pick her up from Page's office. Now, as Page and Mariana spoke, Ellie lay at Mariana's feet, earning an occasional belly rub, which seemed to please them both.

"If you're alone in life, you depend on friends, neighbors, caregivers, professionals, whoever happens to gain your trust," explained Page. Research bears this out. Having someone around to ask "Hey does this make sense?" or "Do you think I can trust this person?" reduces susceptibility to fraud. It's a way our bonds protect us. But those very bonds, when warped, expose older people to the greatest risk. Among those who take older people's money, one group outnumbers all the rest.

Family Money

I asked Ron Long about the leading culprits they were seeing through the Elder Client Initiatives. "Family, often daughters," he said. What he said evoked the caregiving data. "The daughters often are the ones still there after everyone else has moved away. They're taking time off work to take mom shopping, to the doctor, to the hairdresser. They're buying the groceries and supplies. They're on call 24/7 and the ones called in a crisis. Then if mom says she's dividing up her estate even steven among the siblings, the daughter thinks, 'That's not fair. I've been doing all the work.' It doesn't justify exploitation, but she has a point."

Within families, money has subterranean meanings that are rarely discussed. But they take on extra force between parents and kids. In young adulthood, gaining financial freedom from parents is a big deal about which kids have big feelings. I learned this myself at nineteen when I took time off college, an interlude now called a gap year that my father called "dropping out." He was angry at me—convinced I was squandering my life—but gave me $50 because he knew I needed it. I tore up his check. I wanted his faith, not his money.

Now I can see that he gave it with love. My rejection of his gift—that then seemed like a declaration of independence—now looks callow and stubborn. I want to shout back through time at my righteous self: "Just say thank you!" But neither my father nor I could say what we meant, nor grasp what the other was trying to say. That check carried a lot of freight that had nothing to do with its value.

As we age, money's meanings and its practical implications accumulate. Adult kids may feel ashamed about relying on their parents. Parents may feel ashamed about relying on their kids. Giving can embody duty, or love, and take on new meanings with the growing consciousness that time is short. My mother found joy in generosity. In her late years, she often pressed some bauble on us when we visited. When we were reluctant to accept, not wanting gifts to be divisive among us siblings, she'd say, "It's so much nicer to give it with a warm hand."

Money is also a stage where aspirations and grudges play out. People who take money from their older relatives may worry about their own financial needs, figure they'll "get it anyway," or feel entitled to an advance on an inheritance. They may feel they deserve assets or the parental house in exchange for help they've given. Sometimes they're settling a score. Or they may think, "Grandpa will never miss this." Countless drug, gambling, and shopping habits have been funded with an exploited parent's or a grandparent's retirement savings.

Money also spawns honest differences among the well-meaning. Family and friends may move money to safeguard it. When allegations start flying, it can be hard for those close, much less outsiders like APS, cops, or judges, to sort out who's a rapacious threat, who's sincerely struggling, versus who's serving a protective role.

Page was struck not just by the harm exploitation wreaked on older victims but also by its collateral damage on "concerned persons." She also saw how it fractured families. She worried that her prosecution of cases often deepened enmities.

In the presence of cognitive decline, injustice can result from greed but also from the opposite: a dedicated caregiver's proximity and good works. As we've seen, there's little guidance for families about what caregivers are owed and how families should support them. "I lean towards some payment for family caregivers," Ron said. "Those assets were amassed for something. It's a way to acknowledge that there's a cost to the caregiver and a value to the care. Families should talk about it together."

There's also the idea of respite. Ron suggested that other family members should offer to take over caregiving for a few weeks a year and pay for the primary caregiver to take a nice long vacation.

Families should also recognize that cognitive problems can cause paranoia and unfair accusations. If mom mistakenly suspects that her dedicated caregiving daughter is stealing from her and lashes out or tries to cut her out of the will, that's one kind of hurt. If the other siblings go along with it, then hurt becomes injustice.

But paranoid parents aren't always wrong. Overall, family members are responsible for more than 60 percent of elder financial exploitation. They steal on average twice as much as strangers per case.[12] Struck by Ron's comment about daughters, I asked Page if she saw gender trends in the cases she prosecuted. Again, there's no data, but Page's best guess based on her cases was that sons committed more neglect and physical abuse and daughters more financial exploitation, usually fueled by gambling and shopping addictions. "In one of my typical cases," said Page, "two sisters wiped out their mom's savings in a few days, losing $60,000 at the casino and bingeing on crappy Home Shopping Network jewelry."

One family's crappy jewelry is another's multimillion-dollar painting. When Liz Loewy headed the Elder Abuse Unit in the Manhattan district attorney's office, she saw variations on the themes Ron mentioned at all income levels. In perhaps the country's most famous elder abuse trial, Liz prosecuted Anthony Marshall, the octogenarian only child of New York philanthropist Brooke Astor. Astor's grandson Philip set the case in motion when he petitioned the court to replace his father as Astor's power of attorney and health care proxy. He accused his father of turning "a blind eye" to the 104-year-old Astor and "intentionally and repeatedly ignoring her health, safety, personal and household needs, while enriching himself with millions of dollars."[13]

The guardianship petition leaked. Scandal ensued. A three-year investigation led to charges that Marshall had taken advantage of his mother's diminished capacity and "abused his position of trust to steal from her," taking valuable paintings, bestowing on himself an almost $1 million "raise" for serving as her power of attorney, and, with his attorney's help, changing his mother's will by means of codicils that redirected tens of millions of her $185 million fortune to himself and charities under his control.[14] Marshall was convicted on fourteen counts including grand larceny and received a one-to-three-year sentence. He spent just eight weeks in prison before being granted "medical parole" at age eighty-nine.

While the media were drawn to Astor's name and celebrity friends-turned-witnesses, the case bore many hallmarks of elder abuse in any family. There were strained relationships. There was an adult child's exaggerated sense of entitlement to his mother's money who allotted insufficient resources to her care. And there was an older person, isolated, unable to resist the influence of someone she held dear. Marshall had restricted visits by his mother's friends and fired staff she loved.

Brooke Astor's world may as well be in another solar system from Appalachia's coalfields, but there too older people are exploited. In McDowell County, West Virginia, the median household income is $26,000 and 33 percent of the population lives in poverty. Communities lack all manner of support. Families struggle with high rates of addiction and mental illness. Unable to get the help they need, many residents end up imprisoned or dead of overdoses. Many children live with, and are supported by, grandparents. Sometimes the grandparents are too young to get social security, so great-grandparents house multiple generations on their benefits, which are often meager given their low wages earlier in life. Some resort to selling the prescription drugs they need just to pay the bills.

Keren Wilson, a coal miner's daughter, assisted living pioneer, and foundation president, called me a few years ago, concerned about fearsome trends she was hearing about in McDowell County. Children or grandchildren were robbing older residents and sometimes assaulting them in search of money for drugs. Crime spiked every month just after social security checks arrived. Some elders facing serious pain and end of life were declining hospice services, fearing that if word got out that they had painkillers in the house, they'd be robbed.

When I caught up with Keren again in 2022, she reflected, "It's not just a West Virginia problem. It's everywhere now and it's gotten worse. Drugs like fentanyl are more accessible and make users more unpredictable. They cause lots of behavioral disturbances." The devastation wreaked by opioids touches families of all income levels, engulfing not just the young but also the old.

We don't know much about how financial exploitation varies by socioeconomic status, but certainly the tools and spoils differ: In the luxe Astor world, powers of attorney and codicils to wills were used to extract "income" and paintings worth millions. In West Virginia's hollows, fear and force were used to extract social security benefits and drugs. The amounts stolen from poor people might be smaller, but they're a larger percentage of what they have—and often the difference between a home and no home, care and no care, pain relief and pain.

Like many corners of aging and elder abuse, more research needs to be done on the disparate impact of financial exploitation. The data that do exist are troubling. For starters, people of color appear to lose more to financial exploitation than white people. One study found that 23 percent of older African Americans were financially exploited, about twice the rate of their white counterparts.[15] A study of more than 3,000 Chinese older adults in the greater Chicago area found mistreatment rates of 15 percent.[16] And a small pilot study of low-income Latinos in Los Angeles found that 40 percent were victimized by elder abuse, including financial exploitation.[17]

In the mid-1990s, Evelyn Laureano noticed a trend. Evelyn was the long-term executive director of the Neighborhood Self Help by Older Persons Project (Neighborhood SHOPP) in the Bronx. She found that when elders who used SHOPP's programs asked for help, there was typically more to the story. "They came in because they were about to be evicted or their utilities were being cut off," Evelyn said. "Only after we asked how this came to be would we uncover that the money was going out the door to someone else, usually a family member." In 1995, Evelyn started SHOPP's Elder Abuse and Crime Victims Violence Intervention and Prevention (VIP) program, covering all of the Bronx.

"About 60 percent of our clients are Hispanic—Puerto Rican, Mexican, and Dominican," said Evelyn. "Most are Spanish-speaking.

As people get established, they send for their parents to care for their children, so several generations often live in the same home. More than 30 percent of our clients are African American and Caribbean-West Indian. And we're serving growing numbers of people from Bangladeshi, Korean, and Chinese communities."

Evelyn hired staff who spoke the languages and understood the cultures of the people with whom they worked. They learned not to assume cultural or linguistic uniformity. "Many of our clients identify heavily with their nuclear and extended families," Evelyn told me. "We may think it looks like financial exploitation, but then the client says, 'This is what we do in our family. The money is pooled. Our son takes care of it.'" Words used for "abuse" in English have different connotations in other languages. The staff shifted from generic questions to more specific ones, Evelyn said, like: "Is it the custom in your family to give paid caregivers tips? If not, why are you doing that? Is she coercing or hinting to pressure you?" Also, written materials, even translated, were only so useful. Explained Evelyn, "You can't assume literacy, even in the native language."

The SHOPP staff didn't just work with clients one on one. They also did outreach and education, attuning their presentations to the audience. Every day, some 150 to 200 older people came to Casa Boricua, one of SHOPP's senior centers, known for its innovative performing arts group. Inspired by a workshop on elder abuse, the Casa Boricua theater group wrote and performed a series of plays in the style of *Caso Cerrado*, a Spanish-language TV program resembling *Judge Judy*. In one play, warring sisters who'd taken over their father's home appeared before the judge. In another, a concerned neighbor told the judge that he heard screaming from the apartment next door when the woman's grandson came for money every month. The woman said there was no problem. What should he do?

The performances had a far greater impact than brochures. "It was like going to the theater," said Evelyn. "The plays were really funny, and people were laughing. But, wow, the impact on the seniors was jaw-dropping. We had phone calls from lots of people in the audience saying, 'This is happening to my neighbor; to my sister.' It was a real door-opener for us."

(Un)Accountable

Working at Adult Protective Services is not many people's idea of a dream job. Handling reports about vulnerable adults and elder abuse, neglect, and exploitation confronts workers with impossible decisions, which often put them in the center of conflict, and sometimes in danger themselves. The pay is low, the demands high, and the job often invisible and thankless. But for Ricker Hamilton, APS was a coveted destination. "I always wanted to do something with older people," he said, "but getting into APS, well, I just happened to be in the right place at the right time when Maine's APS law passed in 1981." Working in the state with the country's oldest population meant Ricker often got a preview of challenges facing an aging nation.

Ricker was raised on the second floor of his grandparents' house, which his grandfather had converted into an apartment. His Westbrook, Maine, home was the family's center of gravity. "My cousins, aunts, and uncles constantly visited," Ricker said. "My great-grandparents, too." Ricker inherited a Mainer's deep ties to the land. As a boy, he trailed after his father and grandfather, heading out before dawn to hunt. They only killed what they would eat.

Ricker also got his name from the land. Chebeague Island—one of the hundreds in Casco Bay and the place where his father grew up—stretches from Ricker Head to Hamilton Beach. When Ricker's father was nearing the end of his life, they went back to the island together. Ricker didn't trust himself to remember his father's stories. He wanted to preserve them to pass along to his young son. So, with his father at the wheel, Ricker asked questions and filmed his father as they drove from one end of Chebeague to the other.

Ricker knew the island well. When he was a child, his family went often on weekends, spending afternoons at Chebeague's cemetery. "We'd pull weeds and plant something new," he said. "I can still see my grandmother Hamilton tending the plots and gravestones." While they gardened, they told stories. "Then it wasn't just stone. It was a person to whom you were somehow connected. You were reminded of who you are and where you come from. That you were going there yourself and wanted someone to take care of you."

As an adult, Ricker settled on Casco Bay's southern shore, in Falmouth, a town that was also home to a retired teacher named Elizabeth Cashman. As Cashman's health declined, she could no longer manage her money or walk her dogs—with unfortunate results on both fronts. She asked a friend and neighbor to be her power of attorney, or POA. The neighbor helped Cashman move to a boarding home, negotiating the price down so that Cashman's modest pension would cover it. But the neighbor was older, too. When helping Cashman became too much, she withdrew as POA, and Cashman's nieces petitioned to become their aunt's guardians. Friends opposed the nieces' petition, predicting trouble. Cashman hadn't trusted them—they'd been too eager for her money—but the court appointed them because they were family. The nieces promptly went from the courtroom to Cashman's bank to purchase traveler's checks, converting their aunt's modest assets to cash.

By the time APS was called in, they'd sold her home, car, and possessions, drained her accounts, stopped paying her boarding home bills, applied for MaineCare (Maine's Medicaid), and were still dipping into her pension funds with an ATM card. Ricker petitioned the court to rescind their guardianship and install APS instead. Under Maine law, APS is the guardian of last resort when there's no other "private person willing or suitable to serve." As guardian, Ricker's first act was to block the nieces' access to their aunt's pension. That stemmed the bleeding, but Cashman's money was gone.

Given APS's confidentiality rules, most of Ricker's cases were hidden from public view. Few people had any clue about the desolate scenes Ricker saw. And he was increasingly frustrated by how little he could do to right those wrongs and how rarely anyone was held accountable.

Ricker referred the case of Cashman's nieces for prosecution, but the assistant district attorney, who wasn't accustomed to paper-heavy financial cases, declined to pursue it. Incensed, Ricker called Maine's attorney general (AG), whom he knew casually, who referred him to Brian MacMaster, the AG's head of investigations. But things moved too slowly for Ricker's liking, so he confronted Brian. When they met, neither man curbed his grievance. "Within minutes, we had to be held back," Brian told me. "We were shouting nose to nose, trying to get at each other over the table"—two not insubstantial middle-aged public servants braced for battle. Once they settled down—and it wasn't that day—Brian created a position in his office to handle cases like Cashman's with funds Ricker had applied for. Despite their rocky start, Brian admired Ricker's deep commitment. "He's one of my heroes," said Brian. "Although he still gets so excited, I sometimes get concerned for his health."

Leanne Robbin, a financial crimes prosecutor in the Maine AG's office, filed charges against Cashman's nieces, signaling that she'd go to trial if necessary. ("Being prepared to litigate is the best settlement strategy," one of my bosses used to say.) Cashman's nieces pled guilty.

Most of Ricker's financial exploitation cases involved small sums. The amount of money victims lost was traumatic for them but didn't involve the complex, multi-district scope that the AG's office usually handled. In theory, local prosecutors or civil attorneys were the ones who brought such low-dollar matters. In fact, many cases wound up in a legal no-man's-land—too small for one office, too big or "paper-heavy" for another. "I'd work with the detective and Ricker to get out subpoenas," Leanne told me. "By then, I knew so much about the case it didn't make sense to refer it to someone else, so I'd just handle it myself." Without a Ricker or Leanne there to shepherd them through, most cases fell between the cracks, all over Maine and all over the country.

"Ricker was that squeaky wheel," said Leanne. "He got a toe in the door by getting funding for a detective in our office to investigate these cases. He made everything possible, really."

But his determination also had professional fallout. "Activists in bureaucracies," Leanne's description for Ricker, tend to worry higher-ups. They're hard to control and rail about issues that, fairly or not, are awkward for their bosses. Squeaky-wheel Ricker wasn't promoted for almost three decades.

I understood the dynamic well. I worried my bosses for similar reasons. Mike Hertz, the longtime director of DOJ's Civil Frauds section who'd originally recruited me to work there and played strictly by the books, took to calling my Elder Justice Initiative work

"Your Rogue Operation." I tried not to embarrass him or others in DOJ's chain of command, and the powers that be mostly left me alone, but it was no secret that I thought the department should be doing more about elder abuse.

Mike was right in a sense: the Initiative was rogue in that it didn't exist in any one office. I operated in the interstitial spaces between the department's vertical chains of command. This gave me room to maneuver but left me bureaucratically homeless. I had a large portfolio but no country. Working in the interstices is the norm in elder justice. Few of us fit neatly into any single lane. Our doctors know forensics. Our lawyers know social services. Our bankers know cognitive tests. Our work requires elasticity and stretches our professional identities into zones where they overlap. Other people's rogue is our normal.

Mostly I tried to stay out of sight, and mostly my bosses forgot I existed until some event pushed me back into their sight lines, like when the Senate Special Committee on Aging chairman sent the attorney general a written request that I testify at a June 2001 hearing on elder abuse. Laura and Ricker also were slated to appear. The letter put DOJ in a bind. Generally political appointees, not career people like me, represented DOJ before Congress. But there was no political appointee familiar with elder abuse. Not knowing who'd deliver it, I drafted bland testimony about our cases and projects. I'd learned how to make words sound like a lot of action, but we were doing just a tiny fraction of what needed to happen given the magnitude of the problem. I'd seen an exposé produce a hearing and a hearing produce a report that changed little. I'd grown wary of the chasm between the theater of change and the painstaking unheralded work that actually made change happen.

A day before the hearing, my boss, Stuart Schiffer, called to say that the powers that be, whom he derisively called "the geniuses upstairs" regardless of administration, wanted him, as the acting Civil Division head, to testify. Later he called back to say that the geniuses upstairs forbade me from even attending the hearing. If I was in the room, the senators might try to question me directly, including about what more DOJ could or should do.

The next morning, Stuart testified first. Prosecuting elder abuse was mostly the domain of local and state prosecutors, he said. DOJ's role was limited to enforcing federal laws where they existed, like prosecuting telemarketing fraud and those False Claims Act cases against nursing homes. Other than that, DOJ's role was to fund research and training, and make grants to support state, local, and nonprofit efforts. Stuart didn't mention that Congress had passed no elder abuse law to fund such work or to expand DOJ's ability to prosecute.

Stuart left immediately after fielding the senators' questions before the other witnesses were even seated. Once back at his desk, he called me and left a voicemail: "Several people whose names I don't remember asked me where you were. By which they meant, 'Who the fuck are you and why didn't they send someone who knows something?' I don't think I did too much damage. Call me."

While Stuart was leaving that message, Laura told the senators about police and APS's need for more medical help in responding to people with dementia. Ricker described the Cashman case along with several other APS cases from around the country with particularly gruesome facts that prosecutors had declined to pursue.[18]

The hearing, like so many before it, resulted in no concrete change. By then, I'd become convinced that real change would require a new law and new funding. In my head, and with a few trusted colleagues, I referred to that aspirational law as "the Elder Justice Act."

The High Costs of Elder Abuse

In considering new laws, Congress wants to know about the cost of the problem and of the proposed solution. As I searched for credible data on the cost of elder abuse, I found studies calculating the financial toll of child abuse ($80–124 billion a year) and of domestic violence (between $6 and $63 billion a year, depending on what was counted and who was counting). A few studies measured limited slices of elder abuse. But no one had calculated the problem's overall economic toll.

Yet, the cases, and research, suggested that it caused steep losses—to older people and their families, to Medicaid and Medicare, and to housing and other public programs—while enriching profiteers, individual and corporate. When I talked with Ricker about financial exploitation's uncalculated costs, he told me about a client of his who'd done well in life. She and her husband had a lovely house in Maine, condos in Arizona and Barbados, and bundles of astute investments that had borne fruit like a well-tended orchard. When her husband died, he'd left more than enough to pay for anything she might need.

He'd always handled the finances, so when her sons—educated professionals with good jobs, experienced in managing budgets—suggested she give them power of attorney to manage her money, she said yes. Bit by bit, they moved her assets into their own names: "estate planning to reduce taxes," they said. Then the older son suggested that they sell her house and she move in with him and his new wife. Her house was where she'd lived the parts of her life that mattered most to her. She was reluctant to leave it and delighted in her independence, but he pushed. In the end, she agreed to his plan.

It was a terrible rending. At her son's house, she felt like an imposition simply by getting up each morning. As she became more depressed and confused, her son and his wife got less enthused about having her there and moved her to an assisted living facility. Neither son visited and then they stopped paying the bills. As her health declined, her needs surpassed what the assisted living staff could handle. She needed a nursing home, the staff said, but she was unable to consent to the move, and her sons had stopped responding. They'd allegedly moved out of state.

The staff couldn't just evict the woman or ship her off, so they called APS. Ricker also lacked the legal authority to move her, so he petitioned the court for guardianship. Once the court named APS guardian, he found a nursing home that accepted MaineCare and helped her move.

Telling me about the case years later, Ricker was still furious. "With all *her* money and a little support," he fumed, "she could have stayed home much longer, probably the rest of her life. And she wouldn't have declined so fast, either." The sons took her money and autonomy, stiffed the assisted living facility, and shifted the cost of her care to the public.

Financial exploitation also can unleash massive "tipping" costs when it leads to victims losing their independence and declines requiring acute and long-term care. That's what had happened with Sherrie Kaplan's mother who wound up in heart failure and lost her independence after her plumbers defrauded her. Researchers have found that elder abuse triples rates of hospital admissions and quadruples rates of nursing home admissions. At what cost? The average (non-rehab) nursing home stay lasts 2.4 years and costs about $100,000 a year. The average three-day hospital stay costs $30,000. Those numbers add up fast.

Other types of mistreatment are also harmful and costly. Neglect, for example, often lasts a long time and is hard to uncover. When it occurs in residential settings like nursing homes, it harms not just one person, but many. And it can cause appalling injuries that cascade into acute care needs. Corporate policies that set neglect in motion often seem innocuous, like offering bonuses for regional managers who "cut costs," creating incentives to lay off needed staff. But as we've seen, understaffing leads to worse care and more suffering.

Owners who siphon off funds intended for essential resident care set in motion two types of economic losses. The first is simple fraud—billing for services that are worthless or nonexistent. And second are the "tipping" costs caused when neglecting residents makes them sicker, so they need expensive acute and long-term care, like what happened to many GeriMed residents.

Uncounted older people and their families shell out large sums based on promises they'll get good care, only to be neglected. Each episode of such exploitation is itself a tragedy. *En masse* they amount to fraud and waste of taxpayer dollars, betrayals of consumer protection, and violations of human rights.

"Medicaid Planning" and Nursing Home Pipelines

Some people give away or spend most of their money to become poor enough to qualify for Medicaid so it picks up the tab for their care. When they do so intentionally, it may be called *Medicaid planning*. People's reasons for doing this differ. Some may be trying to protect spouses and pass on the nest eggs they've spent a lifetime accumulating. What illness a person has makes a big difference in how and whether it's covered. If it's cancer or diabetes, Medicare pays for medical interventions. But if it's dementia, Medicare won't pay for help with daily activities or long-term care, so many people impoverish themselves paying for it.

There are other motivators for Medicaid planning, too. Parents may be trying to please children eager to transfer their parents' resources to themselves. Or older people may be following the guidance of a lawyer or financial advisor they trust. Some advisors are great. But others lack expertise in the complexities of Medicaid and don't appropriately help their clients fully understand the risks, what it takes to make Medicaid planning work, or lay out the alternatives.

Medicaid planning can be valid or exploitive depending on how it's used. To become eligible for Medicaid is in fact to be poor. You limit your care options and eliminate the more appealing ones that only money can buy. And though Medicaid does pay for some home and community-based services, actually getting these services can be frustrating. Hundreds of thousands of people are on waiting lists for them nationwide. Medicaid also may not pay for enough care. Or aides may not work for the amount Medicaid covers. Any of those factors could mean a person winds up in a nursing home, which may be substandard, the last place they want to be. Alison Hirschel, the elder law attorney and long-term care expert, laments that poor Medicaid planning can be "a pipeline to nursing homes."

Older people and their families should go into Medicaid planning with their eyes open—understanding the potential consequences of doing so, said Alison. Attorneys should explain the risks and trade-offs clearly, she said, and help clients not just *become* Medicaid eligible but also navigate getting decent care once they are.

Guardianship—a legal process that gives one person the authority to make decisions for another, who is incapacitated—is another mixed bag. Research shows that good guardians save money both for those in their care and for public programs. Bad guardians do the opposite. They charge exploitive, often fraudulent rates. They profit from selling possessions those in their care treasure and the houses they want to live in or return to. And they ignore the person's wishes about how *they* want to live, sometimes by putting them in facilities unnecessarily. In extreme cases, they imprison their wards and take everything they have. And, said Alison, "abusive guardianships are another costly—and tragic—pipeline to nursing homes."

Too often, the very systems intended to help people are perverted by profiteers who use older people as commodities to extract personal and public dollars. Their treacly promises of "care" and "protection" make such practices all the more galling.

Responding

"Jane," a retired nurse and widow in Los Angeles, was horrified by the news from Ukraine as Russia invaded. In Facebook discussions, "Ted," a human rights lawyer, explained that donations to smaller, nimbler charities went further because big charities spent too much on overhead. Ted was from the United States, he said, but on the road a lot between Ukraine and the Hague to help refugees. Jane was impressed by his work. They connected first on Facebook but then moved to WhatsApp and calls. They talked almost daily, and not just about Ukraine. He wanted to know about her, too. His interest awakened something long dormant. When he told her he might be falling for her, her feelings tumbled out. She mentioned nothing to her adult children, worried how they'd react. But the growing intimacy between them changed how she felt about herself. He was exciting. She felt alive. The hook was set.

Then Ted said he'd be out of touch for a while. He was headed to Ukraine to meet with refugee groups. Would she be willing to contribute to his cause? She did some online research, and what she found looked valid enough to her. She wired $10,000, a huge amount for her. He sent an effusive note of thanks. While on the road, he said he'd call when he could, and that his sister, lawyer, or colleagues might also call to update her, too. Over time, a pattern unspooled. Jane got calls or emails describing great dangers, heroic feats, him missing her, and an urgent need for more money. Sometimes it was for medical supplies; other times it was for food, or a bus to move refugees. When Jane murmured concerns, he allayed them and she tamped them down, not wanting to lose him.

By the time Jane's children learned what was going on, she was in crisis and on the way to losing her house. They reported the situation to APS and law enforcement. APS in turn referred Jane to social worker Miles McNeeley, who provides individual therapy and case management to victims of elder fraud. Miles works for the Los Angeles nonprofit WISE & Healthy Aging, which started the country's first and longest-running support group for victims of romance fraud, which account for the biggest losses by older people in stranger scams. He has since expanded the group to also include victims of other "imposter frauds," also called catfishing.

Given such scams' prevalence, you'd think we'd have found effective ways to stop them. There's lots of descriptive and prevalence data, but there's little evidence about what interventions or prevention methods work—a damaging deficit in the elder justice field. Once, at a meeting with colleagues from across the country, Miles asked if anyone was aware of interventions being used for romance scams. Someone said she knew of only one and directed him to his own program in Los Angeles. So, Miles draws on what he's learned from his own cases. Victims generally fall into three categories, he believes, corresponding with their levels of insight. Those levels determine how he responds.

The first group, people who are *aware* they've been scammed, face two crises: financial and emotional. The financial crisis requires steps to prevent future loss: canceling credit cards, stopping payments, blocking access, freezing accounts, trying to recover money, and reporting the crime. "The emotional crisis means addressing the victim's suicidality and hopelessness," said Miles. "They feel so alone. It's like grief." It's a quadruple loss: money, love, self-esteem, and the fear of what falling for a scam portends.

The second group is people *in denial*. "There's no grief, no concern about finances," said Miles. "They can't see it and can't let go of the relationship or the hope that their investment will lead to big gains." With this group, he tries to build rapport and looks for other ways to meet the need that opened them up to exploitation. Professionals who've had careers in law, medicine, or finance seem to be at higher risk, according to Miles. He thinks this might be because they're accustomed to operating with high degrees of confidence in their decisions. "I've done the research," they tell him. "And it's real." For people in denial, the support group doesn't help much. Instead, Miles works with their families or other entities to try to put financial guardrails in place behind the scenes to limit the losses, like an account with limited funds or a prepaid credit card. Sometimes they also use power of attorney or guardianship.

With the third group, those *vacillating* between insight and denial, he said, it's harder to know what to do. Even "aware" victims can vacillate. When Jane talked about Ted, "she'd stop using 'scam language,'" Miles said. He could see her become animated as she recounted the air raids he'd survived, the refugees he'd saved. "It was like a novel," said Miles, "a page-turner, and she was in it." This is another key to romance scams. "Love" is often entwined with excitement and drama that are enticing too and hard to let go of. With this group, Miles tries to provide supportive and engaged relationships that meet people's needs in less destructive ways.

Although he organizes the meetings, Miles has learned that it's most effective when a group member who's been scammed leads discussions. They can tell victims like Jane that they know the shame and paralysis. They've gone through the cycles of rumination, too. They've also lost huge sums or their homes. Some group members' most useful advice to newcomers is practical: eat, sleep, take that walk, see people. "It's a roller coaster," they say, "but you'll eventually get your relationships back and find joy again." The group makes victims feel like they're not alone. In fact, they're among millions. "There's validation from the group that's hard to get anywhere else," Miles explained. "It's a place to talk about how good it felt to have someone care about them, someone else who says, 'I know, I thought he loved me, too.'"

Since Miles started his group, others have emerged. AARP has launched online support groups and a helpline, and offers materials on its website. Marichel Vaught, a victim advocate at Community of Vermont Elders, organizes a regular peer support group for facilitators of such groups. Most of the victims with whom she works, one

on one and in groups, live in extreme isolation. The person defrauding them often is the person they talk with most often, or the only
person. Marichel, Miles, and others who lead groups also ask experts,
like Debbie Deem, a former FBI Victim Specialist, to talk to victims
about the scammers' techniques. Hearing from authorities seems to
help, at least for a while.

I asked Laura how she responded to financial exploitation. Her
patients in the "aware" group also express mortification when they
realize they've been duped. "Don't be embarrassed," she tells them.
"Scammers use tactics calculated to cause high emotion that somehow causes the brain to bypass its usual thoughtful reasoning circuit." They manufacture urgency to evoke fear, financial insecurity,
and guilt. It's hard to stop and think when you hear your grandchild
is in jail or a hacker has stolen your passwords. A get rich quick
scheme might appeal to a retiree with money concerns. And a human rights advocate's need for medical supplies tugs on a generous
elder's inclination to share their good fortune. "Medicalizing the vulnerability helps to reduce people's shame," Laura said.

   She uses a similar approach in talking with worried family members, emphasizing that falling for scams is not a choice, or a lack of
discipline. It's usually a combination of organic brain changes and
tactics precisely intended to exploit them. "I recommend they *not* say
things like: '*How* could you do something like this?' Or '*What* were
you thinking?'" Blame may cause the person to hide future questions
or problems. Instead, Laura suggests conveying that you're on the
same side, facing a common enemy: "That jerk ripped you off. It's not
your fault. She targeted you because of your age."

   Laura finds the "falls" analogy useful in talking with families about
how to respond. When an older person falls, she says, "We don't say,
'How could you fall!?' We ask, 'Should we have that knee looked at?
Get you a cane? Move the throw rugs? Install an alert system?'" We
understand that falls are caused by changes in our bodies. Declines
in financial capacity are caused by changes in our bodies, too, especially the big organ encased by our skulls. But our ignorance and angst
about financial capacity mean that financial "falls" carry more stigma
than the other kind. Unfortunately, educational materials aren't a silver

bullet either in the face of cognitive decline. "Teaching people not to get exploited just isn't going to work for many of them," Laura said.

PREVENTION AND PLANNING

To slow the massive wave of elder financial exploitation, one important step is to interrupt the flow of money at the point of departure. Credit and gift cards or reloadable cards are used in more than half the scams extracting money from older people. "Just go to Walmart, buy a gift card, and send it here," scammers instruct their marks. Law- and policy-makers could tighten up rules to make such cards easier to track and come with warnings, but have not yet done so.

Wire and bank transfer frauds are rarer—used in fewer than 10 percent of fraud events—but they represent by far the largest transactions and losses, sometimes into six and seven figures.[19]

Without prevention data, families and policy-makers are flung into this battle like soldiers with outdated weapons. Finding more effective protections will require the commitment of many different groups. Government and private funders must focus on research to find effective preventions. Policy-makers must turn good ideas into good law and practice.

To shore up financial security in old age, one good place to start is to take stock of one's assets and to organize records to make them accessible. That makes it easier to figure out if something's gone missing. This also helps you consider your goals for the future. How much do you have for the Mississippi riverboat cruise on your bucket list? How much for golf or season tickets to the theater? Live solo in a condo or in a community with others? Knowing your assets and priorities helps you plan and budget accordingly. Here again, we see how aging respects no lanes. Geriatrician Mark Lachs wrote a book called *What Your Doctor Won't Tell You About Getting Older: A Doctor's Guide to Getting the Best Care.* Yet a doctor, writing about health, included not one but two chapters on meaning-driven financial planning because he has seen over and over again in his practice what the research also confirms: "in our later years, the impact of financial health on medical health becomes more profound."[20] Some of the steps and reflections Mark recommends one can do on one's own. And there are numerous guides now available to help people plan. But some matters require the assistance of a financial expert.

Unfortunately, financial planners are pricey and beyond the reach of the people who most need their help. That dilemma bothered Ricker; how, he wondered, could people of modest means also have access to financial assistance? Inspired by a volunteer-based model in Massachusetts, in 1996 Ricker worked with the Southern Maine Area Agency on Aging (SMAAA) to create Money Minders. Still in operation today, Money Minders is staffed with bonded and background-checked retired accountants and financial advisors. The volunteers help older adults create and maintain monthly budgets, pay their bills, and avoid overdrafts and financial exploitation. "It especially helped older people who were starting to make math errors, bouncing checks, and falling apart emotionally because their math skills evaporated," said Debbie DiDominicus, SMAAA's then-deputy director. "Lo and behold, what else did we find? A huge amount of financial exploitation. Retailers and shopping networks were taking advantage of them. Even more often, family members were swooping in and writing checks for new cars and whatever, to the tune of thousands of dollars. Often the older person didn't even know."

There are also other scenarios—people protecting older adults despite the rules, not because of them. One dutiful daughter labored for years so her father who had mental illness and dementia didn't lose all he owned. He was paranoid about everyone—his daughter, his caregivers, and his bankers, depending on the day—and called the bank often and irate, demanding action for imagined affronts including that someone was stealing his money. (No one was.) The patient banker and the daughter worked together to protect him, although not always according to official policy. "The rules often can't accommodate the humanity or allow bankers to act with the necessary agility and compassion," said the daughter. "But those bankers act at some risk to their jobs." She paused. "Of course, it makes for circumstances rife for scamming too."

BANKERS, BROKERS, AND PROTECTIVE BUFFERS

The more Ricker saw, the more he wanted to find better ways to stop financial exploitation before the money was gone. Money Minders was one kind of prevention. But Ricker thought if he could just educate people in the financial industry about the problem, *they* could stop it further upstream. In the early 2000s, Ricker twice barnstormed the state, along with a legal services attorney. They trained bank and brokerage employees about elder financial exploitation. One trust officer for a wealthy woman told Ricker that in a two-year stretch, five of his client's kids asked for $50,000 from their mother's account because "Mom needs a new roof." "The trust officer knew they were lying but gave each of them the money," Ricker said. "He was scared he'd lose the account if he reported them. There's a lot of that."

While barnstorming, Ricker found financial professionals receptive enough to his message. Still, he gained little traction in getting them to do something when they saw suspicious activity. What stopped them? Some feared losing accounts, like the trust officer who approved the five roofs. Others had privacy concerns like those that had thwarted Ron Long in the early days of launching his Elder Client Initiatives at Wells Fargo Advisors. Even after the lawyers blessed the program, many of WFA's 15,000 financial advisors worried that reporting suspected exploitation, and placing "temporary holds" on accounts to investigate, might violate client privacy.

Ron reframed the project as "an extension of good customer service to protect clients' hard-earned nest eggs." That helped, but he was up against an age-old ethos that to be a "good" banker or broker was to be a vault for client privacy, no matter the price. Regulators exacerbated the problem by being slow to clarify the rules. Their inconsistent messages also gave reluctant entities another excuse not to act.

Finally, Congress stepped in in 2018, passing a law that made utterly clear that financial institutions did not violate client privacy laws by reporting suspicious activity, provided they'd trained their employees to identify and report such abuse. "The Senior $afe Act," wrote Maine senator Susan Collins, who coauthored the law with then Missouri senator Claire McCaskill, was "based on Maine's innovative program."[21] Collins was referring to the Senior$afe® Training Program launched four years earlier by Maine's Council on Elder Abuse Prevention. Ricker had originally formed the council, but the Senior$afe® training was the brainchild of Judy Shaw, Maine's securities administrator, who joined the council in 2008. "Judy was a breath of fresh air," said Ricker. "She brought both financial expertise *and* regulatory power."

"I was like a child finding a secret garden," Judy recalled about joining the council. "I was welcomed in and found lots of good stuff in there. I also saw some weeds in a corner and thought, 'maybe I can pull those weeds and plant new flowers there.'"

Judy could do what Ricker couldn't: bring finance people to the table. She spoke their language and understood their concerns. She also regulated many of them. But Judy thinks it was telling her own family's story that won them over. Judy's mother, a retired law firm secretary in northern Maine, had always banked in person, chatting with Effie, the manager at her credit union. Then Effie noticed changes. Judy's meticulous mother started looking disheveled, and she set up automatic monthly withdrawals—something new for her. Effie was worried so contacted Judy's sister, whose name was also on their mother's account. It turned out that Judy's mother had early-stage dementia and, wanting to augment her income to avoid burdening her kids, had fallen for a "work from home" scam. She'd been promised lots of money in exchange for purchasing "needed supplies," for which she vastly overpaid the con artist. Effie's sharp eye and call stopped the scam early. The family made a plan to address their mom's dementia and put protections in place.

Early on in her tenure as securities administrator, Judy took a listening tour around Maine. After lots of this sort of field research, she and other members of Maine's elder abuse council partnered with banks and credit unions to launch Maine's Senior$afe® Training Program in 2014 to educate financial professionals about elder exploitation and introduce them to other players in the state who might help their clients. Suddenly, Effies at banks and credit unions all across Maine were learning who to call at APS, legal services, law enforcement, and their Area Agencies on Aging. They could refer clients to Money Minders or to the domestic violence and sexual assault agencies to get help. AARP rolled out its Bank*Safe* initiative in 2019, incorporating many similar elements. It's a good program, Judy told me, but it should be complemented by assuring that financial representatives know their local service providers. "The most important component is the holistic community approach," she said, "wrapping services around the person in need."

On her listening tour, one investment advisor told Judy that she routinely asked clients for the name of a trusted contact, like an emergency contact at the doctor's office. That way, if a client became incapacitated, the advisor had someone to call. Judy was intrigued to learn that the trusted contacts people named usually weren't family. "They named friends, pastors, fellow parishioners, lawyers, and accountants," she said. Their reasons varied. Some didn't have kids or wanted to avoid burdening family. Others couldn't choose among them or wanted to keep their financial situation private. But a sizable number also didn't trust their family members.

Judy promoted the "trusted contact" concept first in Maine and then nationwide as president of the North American Securities Administrators Association. Through NASAA, Judy and colleagues developed a model act clarifying that brokers should not only report suspicious activity but also, if appropriate, place temporary holds to protect clients' accounts and invite them to name a trusted contact. Judy insisted that *clients*, not brokers or bankers, should choose the trusted contact. "You have to ask," she said, repeating a familiar refrain. "You never know what's going on in someone's family." Approved by NASAA membership in 2016, the model act is now law in thirty-four states.

Still, financial institutions were slow to implement the protections voluntarily. So, in 2018, a government-authorized nonprofit named FINRA, which oversees broker dealers, made the protections mandatory for its members: 624,000 brokers nationwide who are responsible for billions of market events daily. The FINRA rule allows brokers to freeze transactions with temporary holds of fifteen to fifty-five days if they believe disbursement would result in exploitation.

It's rare for anyone to measure the impact of such a law or regulation, but researchers did in fact analyze FINRA's temporary hold rule. They compared results in locations that had, and had not, implemented the rule during its staggered rollout. The results were impressive. Just allowing brokers to place those holds decreased suspected fraud cases by 4 to 6 percent, with an accompanying 4.5 percent drop in personal bankruptcies. Women, minorities, and unmarried people benefited the most.[22]

Despite the proven positive impact, many big financial industry players remain slow to institute reporting, temporary hold, and trusted contact protocols. WFA and several other large *brokerage* firms—including Bank of America, Fidelity, JPMorgan Chase, and Raymond James—had been early adopters. But the *banks*, even ones under the same corporate umbrellas, like Wells Fargo's 7,800 branches, have been slow to follow suit. Theories for why vary. One is that bank accounts are more numerous and smaller than brokerage accounts, so implementation requires more effort for many smaller customers. Another is that banks fear that if they offer protections, but they aren't properly implemented or a client is still fleeced, they'll be sued. Then there's the role of the bank regulators. Unlike FINRA's requirement for brokers, bank regulators haven't required banks to implement the protections. So far, Bank of America remains the only major bank to have done so of its own accord.

In a hopeful sign, Wells Fargo in 2021 created a new position—Aging Client Services—not just for the brokerage firm but for the entire enterprise, and named Ron Long to the job.

But there's much more financial industry players could do to protect their best client cohort. Despite efforts to take on the problem, we're still losing ground. For starters we need to create better financial guardrails, not just *to* but *through* retirement, with at least three elements: automatic protections, fraud alerts, and effective user-friendly support.

The first element, *automatic protections*, is one that's familiar to us from other parts of our financial lives. All sorts of simple default options improve our financial decisions—like preset retirement savings, direct deposit of paychecks, and automatic bill pay. Behavioral economists and psychologists call this *choice architecture*. Making good decisions up front can keep protections running in the background, so we don't have to deal with them day to day, reducing our risk of loss. Figuring out what this might look like will require work, but one option is to allow older people to designate how much they want to spend in a month or year, creating financial systems to shore up that plan, and designating a trusted other to contact if necessary.

The second element, *fraud alerts*, is familiar to anyone with a credit card. Countless entities use algorithms that send notices when they detect unusual transactions, and sometimes freeze our accounts. These tools should be widely used to identify and prevent elder frauds and financial exploitation. We could also designate a trusted other to contact when such an alert pops up.

And third, the system needs a solid, functional *user-friendly support* and assistance line for people to contact.

Obviously, many of these elements already exist, but they're fragmented, expensive, hard to figure out, or not sufficiently elder-friendly. What I'm envisioning is an easy-to-use, free-or-nearly-free option that everyone is invited to sign up for at a designated time, say when they enroll in social security.

The innovations of public-private partnerships and the thoughtful deployment of AI will be integral to creating effective systems. Preventing elder financial exploitation is in all parties' best interest. Financial entities would retain more clients and their funds, advancing the common good in a way that advances their own interests, too. Government would save money if fewer people were forced into dependence on public programs due to financial exploitation. And millions of older people and their families would avoid preventable misery and loss.

Chapter 6

THE AUTONOMY- SAFETY CONUNDRUM

All liberty is laced with borderlines.

—Joni Mitchell, "Borderline"

You live and breathe paradox and contradiction, but you can no more see the beauty of them than the fish can see the beauty of the water.

—Michael Frayn, *Copenhagen*

As we age, routine aspects of life can become riskier, especially in the face of cognitive decline. Driving gets the most attention, but it's all complicated. Millions of older people and those who love them try to balance autonomy and safety in decisions about money, sex, who provides care, and where to live. We Americans are fervent believers in the sovereignty of the self, or *autonomy*, roughly the freedom from external control and the right to govern one's own life. And yet, older people we love might exercise their autonomy in ways that seem scary, at least to us. The right to make risky choices is sometimes called *the dignity of risk*. Often there's not so much a right answer as a right approach to balancing autonomy and safety. And perspective matters. *We want safety for those we love, but autonomy for ourselves.*[1]

Autonomy and safety shouldn't be mutually exclusive. Seeking safety at all costs leaves us dominated by fear and leads us to infringe on others' rights. But a sole focus on autonomy can mean we abdicate responsibility for those who need protection. We need goals and systems that support a nuanced approach. To remain safe *and* free as we age, we should strive for both. Nor are autonomy and safety all we want. We also want lives that contain beauty, joy and awe, purpose and privacy, humor, loyalty, and love.

Autonomy-safety conundrums aren't limited to aging, of course. They're with us all life long, woven into how we govern ourselves and live as individuals, families, and societies. Consider rules about helmets, traffic lights, and drug use. The limits we set aren't absolute; they're human constructs. We look to culture, law, and religion to ordain benchmarks for young people as they ascend toward independence. At thirteen, many religions deem you an adult. At fifteen, most jurisdictions say you can consent to sex with someone close to your own age. At sixteen, you can handle the lethal weapon we call a car. By eighteen, you can vote, enlist in the army, leave school, buy a gun, and make your own health care decisions. And at twenty-one, you reach the apotheosis of American adulthood—the legal right to consume alcohol.

There are no comparable benchmarks or rules in old age. Young people are presumed legally incompetent until the age of eighteen, but there's no age of presumption at the other end of life. Everyone ages differently, and adults are presumed legally competent until a judge declares that they're not.

Our prefrontal cortex, the brain's rational decision-maker, governs self-control. It's the last part to mature and the first to decline as we age. But the process is different for everyone.

Autonomy's enigmas are hardly new. When Sophocles was eighty-nine, it is written that his sons sought a court verdict "removing him from the control of his property." But after "the old man read to the jury his play, *Oedipus at Colonus*, which he had just written and was revising," he asked the jurors: "Does that poem sound to you like 'the work of an imbecile?'" And the jury acquitted him.[2]

Proxy Decision-Makers

Although today millions of people are grappling with such dilemmas, there's surprisingly little guidance for how we should balance our duty to help those in need with our duty to respect their sometimes risky choices. And the balancing gets harder as the stakes rise. Many families muddle through until it comes time to sign documents or make big decisions about health or assets. Then, they need something more formal. Here, two proxy arrangements often come into play: powers of attorney (POAs) and guardianships. POAs are private written agreements by which you give someone else the right to make decisions for you about finances, health, or both. You also retain the right to make those decisions yourself, as long as you retain capacity. Guardianship or conservatorship, a process many first learned about in connection with the pop star Britney Spears, is more onerous to create, requiring a court order. It's also more restrictive, legally stripping persons of authority to make decisions about their own lives.

POAs and guardianships are both insufficient in their own ways. Both come with little oversight or accountability, and are too easily twisted into instruments of exploitation. They also raise tricky timing issues.

You have to sign a POA while your capacity is intact. *Durable* POAs are effective right away. You can still make your own decisions without input from the person holding the POA and you can still revoke the POA. (The terms are confusing. Both the document and the person with the authority to decide may be called a "POA.") But, if you no longer have cognitive capacity, then it stays in force (it's "durable"), decision-making shifts to the POA, and you can no longer revoke it. Other POAs are called *springing*, that is, they're activated only on a finding of incapacity. But there can be confusion about what trigger should cause it to "spring" into force, sometimes adding another layer of confusion and delay. A good POA can protect assets and well-being, and is useful as a health and estate planning tool. Yet, urging someone to sign one can seem intrusive and paternalistic or worse, like a grab for control. Unfortunately, by the time some families realize they need one, it's too late.

The case of a Seattle artist illustrates the catch-22. The artist's friends and family cobbled together visits to help him stay at home as his memory and assets dwindled. His paintings had become valuable, but they began to disappear. The artist didn't know where they'd gone. While his ex-sister-in-law did the dishes one day, she heard him say, "What are you doing with that?" The artist's on-again, off-again boyfriend, George, a busker with some minor convictions, said, "You gave it to me." "No," the artist replied, "I did not give it to you. Give it back to me." But George took off with the painting.

At George's house, police seized eleven of the artist's oil paintings, several drawings, a letter to the artist from the poet Allen Ginsberg, and a self-portrait from William S. Burroughs. George claimed they were gifts of a close relationship. But the artist always signed his paintings before selling them or giving them away, and the paintings George took weren't signed. Also, George had started taking them only after learning that the artist had dementia.

After the exchange the ex-sister-in-law overheard, the artist's family had taken him to a lawyer to change his will and to assign her to be his POA. In the meantime—with his paintings held as evidence—he'd lost his primary source of income, which he needed given that he lived in low-income senior public housing. He also occasionally left romantic voicemail messages for George.

Page Ulrey's colleague, prosecutor Kathy Van Olst, charged George with theft. George's lawyers argued that if the artist had enough cognitive capacity to sign a POA and change his will, he also could give his boyfriend presents. The voicemail messages were, George's lawyers said, evidence of the nature of their ongoing relationship.

Conflicts over POAs reveal unclear borders. As we age, when should we designate a POA for ourselves? Who are good ones? And how should families, aiming to respect a loved one's autonomy, not miss the window to protect them? Page's inbox is full of cases where POAs were used as a license to steal. Various entities offer tips, but policy-makers have done little to create structural protections against POA abuses, leaving individuals and families to grapple with these challenges mostly on their own.

(Un)Due Process

Guardianships, also called conservatorships, are more labor-intensive and drastic. You'd think, given that courts are involved, that there would be more oversight and protection, but that's often not the case. Like POAs, guardianship can be a sword or a shield depending on who's wielding it. First, someone files a petition, usually in probate court, where judges specialize in wills, estates, and guardianships. The judge may appoint a family member, friend, paid stranger (often employed by a private firm), or public agency to serve as guardian. Some people indicate in advance who they'd like their guardian to be, if necessary. But there's no guarantee they'll get who they want.

Many dedicated guardians work tirelessly, often without compensation if they're family or friends. They also rarely get training for a hard job that requires many types of expertise (How can we reduce his chance of falling? Is she at risk of starting a fire in the apartment? Are his allegations against the caregiver real or imagined?) and navigating ethical questions (At what point should I override her wishes if she's in danger?). Guardians need much more guidance and support than they get about both practical and ethical issues. (As for the terminology, reform advocates suggest that the archaic term *ward* is diminishing and recommend instead "person subject to guardianship" once a guardianship has been imposed and "respondent" while the petition is pending.)

Guardians can protect and expand options, but they can also do harm. Even good ones can be neglectful when they get overwhelmed. The bad ones are controlling or greedy and often deplete public funds. They subvert the very well-being they're legally bound to advance, violating the person's rights, and panicking their loved ones.

Systemic flaws and backward incentives do a lot of harm, too. Guardianship is supposed to be the *last* resort, but it's easier for petitioners to seek, and judges to order, full guardianships—which take away *all* the respondent's rights—than to figure out which decisions the person can still make, sometimes with support. Judges rarely limit the guardianship to only those matters that require it. It's more complicated. Nor do they routinely ask if guardianship is even necessary at all. And it's rare for anyone to carefully examine if improper financial incentives lead to overly restrictive or exploitive conditions.

Many people were introduced to the laxity of guardianship oversight through the pop star Britney Spears's case. Her conservatorship stretched on for a decade, despite conflicts of interest and persistent allegations of impropriety that got considerable public attention. If it could happen to Britney Spears, what about the uncounted frail and mostly old others who have no one looking out for them, much less a Free Britney movement?

Lack of oversight and backward incentives aren't the only defects. Judges also may impose guardianship based on evidence from "experts" who aren't experts in what matters—neuropsychological and functional status. It's like an ophthalmologist deciding you need a heart transplant. Still, lots of doctors without direct expertise readily opine in such cases, even though a person's freedom hangs in the balance. In the health system, a psychiatrist needs to provide compelling clinical evidence to hospitalize mentally ill patients against their will for even three days. Yet in the legal system, doctors without professional expertise in cognitive capacity routinely tell judges to limit aging patients' freedom for the rest of their lives. Some judges impose guardianships based solely on a skimpy physician letter without ever taking testimony.

Despite the high stakes, some respondents don't have lawyers to represent them. Some aren't asked for their views. Some aren't even present in the courtroom when the fate of their liberty is determined.

There are other big questions, too. Some facilities petition for guardianship of a resident as a way to get paid. Is that a valid reason to strip someone of their rights? Some family members, like in Britney Spears's case, use guardianship (called conservatorship in California) to control another's assets or life. And sometimes guardianship is used as a tactic to gain leverage in family fights, turning respondents into pawns. What minimum due process protections should the Constitution guarantee in such matters?

Once guardianship is granted, in theory, persons subject to it have the right to appeal. But in practice, this right is illusory. Ken Brummel-Smith, former president of the American Geriatrics Society, told me about a rare successful appeal. The judge had imposed guardianship based on "expert" medical testimony that the respondent had Alzheimer's disease. In fact, he had a *temporary* delirium, a confusion induced by infection or a drug reaction. With Brummel-Smith's expert testimony, the man regained his freedom, but few respondents have the wherewithal to appeal or access to such an advocate.

In fairness, it can be hard to ascertain an older person's wishes and determine the best course. When family members squabble about who should be named guardian, some exasperated judges just appoint a professional. This may not be the best resolution if there is in fact a suitable family member or friend. Procedures to navigate such disputes vary by state. Some use court investigators or guardians ad litem. Others use eldercare coordinators or mediators, similar to those in divorce proceedings.

Guardians usually are paid from respondents' assets if they have any. When they don't, most states use public programs. As we've seen, in Maine, APS serves as the guardian of last resort. And California has a public guardian program. But some states either have no public guardians or not enough of them. That, too, can have dire consequences, as was the case with a Pennsylvania nursing home resident who had a small infection in her toe but lacked capacity to authorize the necessary surgery and had no immediate family to do so. (The number of such "kinless" elders is today on the rise.) The hospital wouldn't operate without consent because it lacked legal authority to do surgery absent a life-threatening crisis. Once the infection became gangrenous, they had to amputate the woman's leg to save her life. Five years later, the same thing happened again, and the woman's other leg was amputated. Access to a public guardian would have allowed for earlier treatment, preventing her appalling and unnecessary losses.

When it comes to private guardians, there also are few structures to screen or vet those who will have virtually unfettered control over powerless people. In one 2010 study, congressional investigators created profiles for two nonexistent people: one with bad credit and the other with a dead person's social security number. Both were approved to become guardians in the four states where they applied.

Once a person is under guardianship, there's also rarely any process to assure that the guardian will actually spend their funds wisely and advance their best interests. In general, guardians aren't required to submit a plan for next year. They don't need to report if the person they're helping got the hearing aids she needs, still goes to her painting classes, or sees her grandchildren. Not all must submit an accounting of how they spend the money. And even when they do, often no one looks at those reports. Oversight of guardians varies by state but in general is perfunctory. Even well-meaning guardians can benefit from routine guidance.

And yet, despite guardianship's many failings, sometimes it's impossible to protect people without one. A guardianship might have helped the artist get his paintings back from his ex-boyfriend George, whom jurors ultimately acquitted. They weren't convinced beyond a reasonable doubt that he'd stolen the artist's paintings and were peeved at prosecutors for getting involved in what seemed like an ongoing relationship.

There's also a question about when caregivers must have a guardianship just to protect an older person they care for. That may sound extreme, but the question came up in another of Page's cases, which, I was learning, often shed light through the holes in our social safety net. It started when Gerd Foerster's close friends, also his POAs, hired Sujinda Yahatta to massage Foerster's hand, partly paralyzed by a stroke. Even after the treatments were done, Yahatta occasionally visited Foerster, a widower, at the group home where he lived because of his dementia. One day Yahatta and a friend took Foerster out to lunch. A few days later, they returned; "lunch" again, they said. It was 10:00 a.m. The staff person was concerned so asked them to wait until she could contact Foerster's POA for approval. Instead, they packed him into their car and left.

On the first lunch date, they'd applied for a marriage license. On the second they headed to the courthouse where Foerster and Yahatta were married by a judge, and then went to Foerster's bank (but not his usual branch) and asked to withdraw all his assets. The teller became suspicious. Soon, the police and Foerster's POA-friends arrived. Foerster told the cops that he was married but his wife wasn't there. He didn't recognize Yahatta or remember marrying her. He did recognize and was happy to see his old friends. By the time Foerster's friends got him back to the group home, he'd forgotten what happened.

After mulling over the options, Page charged Yahatta and her friend with attempted theft and kidnapping. They pled not guilty and claimed that their gambit was motivated by "concern, love, and a willingness to help" and to protect Foerster's assets from his POAs, although there was no evidence of any wrongdoing by the POAs.

At trial, the judge found the women not guilty on both counts: On the attempted theft charge, he found Page hadn't proven that they planned to keep the money. On the kidnapping charge, the judge held that even a valid POA wasn't enough to give the group home staff authority to stop the women from whisking him away.

The implication? Only a guardianship would have been sufficient to safeguard Foerster. But requiring courts to impose guardianships as a condition of protecting or caring for vulnerable persons isn't feasible and would unnecessarily strip countless people of their rights—like using a sledgehammer to drive nails. Every day, countless cognitively impaired people are cared for without guardians. Caregivers are expected to prevent them from wandering out into the subzero cold or leaving with someone who means them harm. Millions of those caregiving arrangements are not codified in legal documents.

The floodgates opened by a mandate to condition care on guardianship would overwhelm probate courts. It would waste colossal family and government resources, leaving some people the system was intended to protect worse off. We need alternatives short of full guardianship to protect vulnerable people like Foerster and the artist from those who might exploit them.

As she saw more elder cases, Page noticed a pattern—"consent" defenses kept coming up, usually in one of three contexts. In financial cases, defendants argued that older people with cognitive impairment had "consented" to give away money or paintings. In neglect cases, defendants argued that victims had "consented" to not getting care and they were just respecting victims' wishes. And in sexual assault cases, defendants argued that victims had "consented" to sex.

Such defenses are nothing new in rape cases, especially when alcohol or drugs are involved. But their recent use in cases involving older persons with cognitive impairment has received little attention despite raising complex philosophical questions in how we define autonomy and safety.

Regulating Sex

Sexual assault is the least common form of elder abuse. Even accounting for underreporting, most victimization in late life isn't sexual or even physical violence, but instead financial, emotional, and neglect. Still, elder sexual abuse happens and is devastating for victims, and viscerally unnerving for those who learn about it. It also can raise challenging questions, as in a case Page faced involving an eighty-seven-year-old, bedridden nursing home resident with serious dementia. An aide who'd walked into the woman's room found her in bed, underwear down, gown up, while her gentleman caller, a "family friend" in his mid-fifties, yanked up his pants, washed his hands, and left in a hurry.

The woman called the man her "boyfriend" and said that he kissed her and told her she was beautiful. She also said she wouldn't have sex with him. The rape kit revealed evidence of anal intercourse. She said she welcomed his attentions. The staff thought he'd assaulted her.

For many older people, the only physical contact remaining in their lives is that with caregivers and health professionals, for some, a deprivation accentuating their loneliness. It's also an embargo that's not so easy to address, in part because people balk at holding notions of "elder" and "touch," or God forbid "sex," in the same thought. But growing old should not mean forfeiting physical intimacy or other human touch like massage or hugs. For many, a touchless old age is a profound loss.

In pondering whether to file charges, Page wanted to know more about each person's state of mind: Was the sex consensual but the woman ashamed to admit it? Was she traumatized and too ashamed to say she'd been assaulted? Did she know what happened or consider it to be sex? Was she trying to protect the man? Did she want to make sure he kept visiting?

The man must have known she was impaired. But what duty did he have to figure out her ability to consent? Does *yes* mean *no* in the presence of dementia? The nursing home reported the man to the police and banned him from the premises. Was that what the resident wanted? And what was the facility's duty? To respect her privacy to have (unchaperoned) visitors? To set up a procedure to ascertain consent in advance? There were so many questions.

Page and her colleagues discussed what to do. "We asked ourselves whether our reaction would change if the alleged perpetrator had been ninety," Page said, "or the resident had been fifty." Where should laws, and the people enforcing them, draw lines in such situations?

Disability rights advocates in Minnesota blocked a law that would have outlawed paid caregivers from having sex with those for whom they provided care on the grounds that prohibiting such sex unreasonably reduced the choice of partners and autonomy of people with disabilities. Courts considering similar cases also have leaned toward autonomy. In a 2015 case, a retired Iowa farmer was charged with felony abuse for having sex with his wife who had Alzheimer's. They married after both were widowed in their seventies. Now her family said he was a criminal because she could no longer expressly consent to sex. His family said he'd done nothing wrong. The case also divided advocates and experts. "Any partner in a marriage has the right to say no," one legal scholar wrote, but "at what point in dementia do you lose the right to say yes?"[3] The man was acquitted.

We have long underestimated and underused the power of loving touch to improve well-being in old age—perhaps because our first impulse in considering older bodies is to recoil or repair. Techniques that go by names like therapeutic touch, healing touch, compassionate touch, and massage therapy have been shown to reduce agitation, pain, and some "behavioral symptoms" of dementia, without drugs. Geriatrician Ken Brummel-Smith believes that facilities should offer safe and respectful human touch options as part of care planning, and hire screened and trained people to give hugs and massages.

The desire for physical contact is primal but often shrouded in shame and denial, especially as we age. "Her hardest task now as she grew older," wrote the novelist Jane Gardam in *Old Filth*, "was to deal with her longing to be touched—hugged, stroked by anyone, any human being—a friend, a lover, a child or even (and here she scented danger) a servant. Of either sex. She prayed about it, asking that God's encircling arms would bring comfort. They did not."[4]

"We have an obligation to do everything we can to preserve whatever pleasures we can for older people who have lost so much," said Daniel Reingold, the president and CEO of RiverSpring Living, which operates the Hebrew Home at Riverdale, a New York nursing home. "If they want more salt when they are 95, give them salt. Same with sex."[5] Under a long-standing "sexual expression" policy, Hebrew

Home staff are expected to "enable intimacy for residents, including those with dementia, while also protecting people from unwanted touch."[6]

Both the enabling and the protecting parts of the policy are critical. A 2012 study found that 40 percent of nurse aides witnessed unwanted sexual advances among residents, including people exposing themselves. Given that most residents in the study were cognitively impaired, some argue this is a form of facility neglect caused by insufficient staffing and care planning to prevent it.[7] With this in mind, Reingold has trained his staff to distinguish between wanted and unwanted attention, focusing on nonverbal cues that might indicate desire, pleasure, fear, or discomfort.[8]

Related challenges also arise at home. Sometimes, dementia makes one spouse newly sexually aggressive, leaving the other feeling violated and confused. A wife happily married for decades may be too upset and ashamed to ask for help. Adult kids who get wind of such trouble are often at a loss for what to do. *Call APS on Dad?*

I asked Laura what she advised in such situations. "Work with someone who really knows the potential medical, behavioral, and medication issues," she said. The behavior could be associated with Alzheimer's, Parkinson's, Lewy body dementia, or something else. A new medication might be playing a role. Or an environmental trigger. "I try to set realistic expectations," she said. "These issues are tough. The woman might have to sleep in a different room; and maybe put a lock on the door. People need to be safe."

In emphasizing the importance of ruling out medical issues, she told me about an assisted living facility that called to say a patient of hers with dementia needed medication for "inappropriate behaviors." He was masturbating constantly. In doing a physical examination, Laura saw he had a fungal infection in his groin area. "In scratching the itch," said Laura, "while he was down there . . . well, you get the idea. So, I treated his 'inappropriate behavior' with an anti-fungal cream."

Sometimes accusations of sexual impropriety are deployed to control older people's behavior. Ricker Hamilton often found himself in the crossfire of families' autonomy-safety battles, like when adult children implored him to use his authority to enforce *their* moral standards. "They'd say, 'My mother, my God, she'd *never* get in bed with another woman. You have to do something! It's terrible.'" Adult children may not be fully aware of their parents' sexuality or see a chance to control sexual conduct they previously couldn't. "But when you talk to the staff," Ricker told me, "you often learn that they enjoy the other person's company. They sleep better and are most content with that other person. Often the only ones who are upset are the family members."

Some cases pit present and past selves against one another, raising philosophical questions about the meaning of autonomy. If the woman now happily in bed with another woman would have been strongly opposed to such an attachment before she got dementia, should family or staff help her do what she wants to do *now*? Or should they impose limits on current behavior based on what they surmise she would have done *in the past*? This can get knotty quickly.

A woman with dementia who begins a new nursing home relationship despite having a longtime spouse at home is the subject of Alice Munro's story "The Bear Came over the Mountain" and its film version, *Away from Her*. It was also the subject of real life and the news when former Supreme Court justice Sandra Day O'Connor's husband, who had dementia, began a nursing home romance. O'Connor and her sons responded with generosity and grace. When O'Connor visited him, sometimes she held one of his hands and his girlfriend the other. The new companion brought him joy, they said. His quality of life was paramount.

Such scenarios can be very painful for the spouse left behind and for other family members. It may help to reframe the loss as one caused by disease, not rejection. Families who might disapprove of such new liaisons should know that separating those new older couples, whatever the reason, often triggers declines in both parties' happiness *and* health.

Page didn't charge the man for sexually assaulting the nursing home resident with dementia because the woman didn't consider the encounter an assault. (She did refer the resident's family to a civil attorney who sued the nursing home.) Law professor Nina Kohn concurs with Page's reasoning and criticizes efforts to criminalize behavior that older people consent to or don't consider abusive. After all, blanket rules that people with dementia can't consent to physical intimacy—a variant on statutory rape laws—would infringe on among the most central of human rights: adults' sovereignty over their own bodies. But if blanket rules don't apply, we need to develop more humane and fine-tuned ones that do.

PROTECTION AS DEFAULT

For a long time, the systems intended to protect older people—such as guardianship, nursing homes, and APS—leaned more heavily toward safety than autonomy, even when doing so overrode the wishes of the person ostensibly being protected. The reasons for this varied. Some of it was legal and medical paternalism—an ethos of *we know what's best for the vulnerable*. More benign reasons include fear of harm and lawsuits. Less benign reasons include indifference to the wishes of the persons allegedly being "protected" and financial incentives skewing decisions. To understand how we ended up with the current systems, it's worth asking who profits from "protection."

Ricker told me that in the early days of APS, clients deemed unsafe at home usually landed in nursing homes or boarding homes. This was the case all over. Although many such placement decisions turned on assessments of cognitive capacity, few APS workers had medical or neurological expertise or access to experts to help them make such calls. That was one reason why, in the late 1990s, Orange County's APS director had eagerly accepted Laura's offer to help.

As Laura rode along with APS workers, she met many older people who'd become so isolated or incapacitated that they no longer saw their own doctors. "Chet" and "Hilde," an older couple living in a nice suburban neighborhood not far from her office, met this description.

Chet and Hilde's house stood out among the manicured lawns on a broad, tree-lined street. An old woman peered from the battered pickup truck parked out front, surrounded by a toilet, a rusted condom dispenser, a cigarette machine, and tires. A chain of extension cords disappearing into a neighbor's window kept their fridge running. And an old school bus sat in the side yard, propped on cinder blocks. When the APS worker had visited the first time, Chet had chased her away with his old rifle.

Now, Laura joined APS to help sort out Hilde's medical ailments and cognitive status. As they pulled into the driveway, Chet rushed toward the car. Hoping to quell his anger, Laura asked him to show her the bus. That worked. It was his pride and hideaway. Following him up the stairs, Laura heard the thrum and felt a trembling in the air before seeing its source—a huge wasp nest hung like a gray balloon from the roof. She asked Chet if he might show her around the yard.

Chet told Laura that he'd been a handyman but hadn't held a steady job for years. Hilde had been the breadwinner and family air traffic controller. Her memory wasn't so good anymore. She'd been able to walk until recently. She had no cane or walker. They'd always liked animals but had too many now. Chet used to take medicine for mental illness, but it ran out ages ago. Hilde used to make the appointments and pick up prescriptions, but neither of them went to their doctors anymore.

Their adult children lived out of state, were busy, and didn't visit much. When their phone went dead, their daughter had called APS. Worried neighbors had called, too. After Chet scared off the APS worker, he wrote his daughter a postcard saying they were fine, and she should never again send out government meddlers.

Chet took caregiving seriously, though the house was messier than when Hilde had kept it. Chet carried Hilde to the truck every morning. In the pickup, she could watch life pass by on the street and listen to the radio. A few times a day, Chet brought Hilde food and lifted her onto the porcelain commode behind the pickup connected to nothing. He kept his gun close by in case anyone came around again trying to take her to a nursing home. That wasn't what either of them wanted.

Laura asked Chet how he was doing. It was hard, he said, but Hilde had done a lot over the years. It was his turn now. They'd manage.

As Laura followed him into the house, the stench and chaos hit her. With the gun, the wasps, and now this, she understood why some APS workers say they deserve danger pay. Detritus was piled three feet deep in some places—boxes, bags, papers, Styrofoam, bubble wrap, cans, mail, magazines, clothes—evidence, at least, that life went on. The dogs and cats had added to the mess. Getting around required climbing through mounds of hip-deep, stinking trash. The couch in the front room where Hilde slept was stained. Chet slept upstairs in the bedroom they'd shared for more than fifty years until Hilde couldn't get up there anymore. Chet didn't want Laura to go up; it wasn't fit for company.

Then Laura and the APS worker traded places. Laura introduced herself to Hilde as she climbed into the driver's seat of the pickup. She asked Hilde, "Did anything hurt? Was she dizzy? Could she move her legs at all?" Hilde smiled and tried to answer. Laura craned around the steering wheel with her stethoscope to listen to Hilde's heart and lungs. Then she got out, went to the passenger side, and opened the door to examine Hilde's feet. "I start with no clue what's going on, just trying to get basic info: Is her breathing okay? Does she have a broken hip? Is she paralyzed? Are her feet infected or her toenails too long or ingrown?"

After asking Hilde a series of questions "to get a sense of what parts of her brain worked, where she struggled," Laura determined that Hilde had dementia, but she couldn't tell why she couldn't walk. Like Chet, Hilde was thin and dirty but didn't seem to be in pain, distress, or imminent danger. She was clear about one thing—she wanted to stay at home with Chet.

Now APS had to decide if Hilde needed protecting. There were many factors to consider. Was anyone taking her money? Was she in danger? Could she understand her risk? Could she and Chet keep living as they were? Should help be forced on one or both of them? If so, based on what authority? Was there anywhere they could go together? How should Chet's needs or wishes be factored into APS's decisions? Was it a patronizing intrusion to force help on them? Or was it an abdication not to? Whose call should it be?

As Laura got in the car to leave, Chet handed her a worn red business card from his wallet. It read, "Don't Fret! Call Chet." She thanked him, briefly grateful that she'd been able to do what she set out to do. She'd examined Hilde. There'd been no sign of the gun.

But as they drove off, her sense of relief faded. The big question still hovered—what next?

Society has designated APS to respond when an adult is at risk. In the APS vernacular, Hilde was the *client*, but one without the sovereignty most clients enjoy. She could not decline the APS investigation or stop APS from referring her case to the public guardian who petitioned for guardianship and moved her to a nursing home. When Laura told me about the case a few years later, she said. "Now, I would have fought harder to get them the help they needed to stay at home. But things were different then. Once APS brought in the public guardian, a nursing home was usually the only option."

A massive factor in the lack of options for people like Hilde and Chet—the system behind the curtain—was reimbursement policy. In Medicaid's early years, if beneficiaries needed long-term care, they had to go to a nursing home to get it. In 1983, Congress authorized states to create waiver programs so beneficiaries also could use funds on some "home and community-based services" (HCBS). But for decades, states were slow to grant HCBS waivers, forcing many people like Hilde into nursing homes.

HCBS are far more accessible now than twenty years ago, with expenditures on HCBS and nursing homes about even. Still, Medicaid steers people to nursing homes because it pays for them, whereas to get HCBS one must get a slot in a Medicaid waiver program, for which there are often long waiting lists. Studies indicate that HCBS are often less expensive than nursing homes, but it's a system still playing catch-up. The powerful nursing home industry spent decades lobbying for policies for maximum revenue from "heads in beds."

When I asked Laura what had happened to Chet, she said, "I don't know."

THE SWING TOWARD
SELF-DETERMINATION

HCBS became more broadly available, due in large part to the efforts of relentless disability rights advocates who pushed Congress to pass the 1990 Americans with Disabilities Act. They also filed the lawsuit leading to the Supreme Court's 1999 *Olmstead* decision, holding that people with disabilities had the right to receive care in the least restrictive environment available. Although that movement's focus was on younger people with disabilities, its work changed the legal landscape and resources for older people with disabilities, too.

The APS pendulum was also swinging toward autonomy after long leaning heavily toward "protection." APS workers began seeing themselves as "self-determination advocates." But autonomy alone, without adequate community resources for those avoiding APS intervention or institutions, hollows out the victory with a different sort of human toll. No one has collected evidence to figure out what approach results in the best outcomes *for clients*.

Page thinks the pendulum has swung too far. She worries that overburdened APS workers sometimes use "autonomy" or an assessment of cognitive capacity without expert input to justify closing tough cases that later land on her desk. She's concerned that serious harm to or the deaths of profoundly impaired persons might have been warded off had APS taken action further upstream. One prominent geriatrician—a strong autonomy advocate—believes that "autonomy" is used by all sorts of professionals to duck hard cases, saying, "We're respecting people's autonomy to death."

CAPACITY TO DECIDE WHAT?

Cognitive capacity isn't a lights on/lights out affair. It exists on several spectra because different decisions require different sorts of capacity. It can vary depending on the hour, day, or week. And people with the same disease may have very different symptoms. That's why it's so difficult and so important to ask and really listen to a family member, a client, or a patient as they make decisions. The bigger the decision, the more important the process.

When I asked Laura for an example of how she asks and listens, she told me about a recent house call. Despite the dismal circumstances, or maybe because of them, many parents want to stay with their flawed children.

Laura joined APS, law enforcement, and a public guardian to visit an eighty-eight-year-old woman in her home. Her son, his wife, and their children lived with her. The place was a mess. The sergeant and public guardian spoke with the son and his wife in the front room while Laura and the APS worker spoke with the mother alone. She was thin and frail. Her room was filthy and trash was strewn everywhere.

"It took her six minutes to sign a consent form for me to do an evaluation that determined that she didn't have the capacity to sign the consent," Laura told me.

"When I asked, 'How are they treating you?' she burst into tears and said, 'They yell at me when I call for help.'"

"It was absurd," Laura told me. "She was hard of hearing, so I'm screaming my questions: 'IS ANYONE HURTING YOU?'" The woman said no.

"I told her, 'You don't need to live like this. You could live somewhere else. Or they could.' She told me, 'They depend on me for my money so I don't feel like I can leave.'" Her social security payments supported the entire family.

The critical question, Laura said, wasn't whether she had cognitive or financial capacity. Given her vascular dementia, that was highly improbable. The question was whether she could decide where to live, and under what circumstances.

"She knew they depended on her money and comprehended what was happening to her," said Laura. "I pushed her a bit. I told her, 'You haven't done anything wrong. You don't deserve to live like this.' She burst into tears again and told me no one had cared about her for a long time. But she was clear in her decision. She said, 'This is where I want to be.'"

"So I said, 'Okay, I understand you want to stay here. What can we do to help you?' She said her feet were cold. She wanted socks."

After talking with the mother, Laura and the APS worker traded places with the officer and public guardian. Back in the living room, Laura asked the son and his wife about caring for his mom. "He's going, 'I love her so much . . .' and the tears start," said Laura. "I'm thinking, 'the Academy Awards aren't for a few months, buddy.'"

As he spoke, his wife rolled her sunken eyes. "What's this like for you?" Laura asked her. "I'm the one who cares for her. . . . It's hard," she said. Laura asked to see the log the wife used to track the mother's pain meds. It covered just three days and was incomprehensible. Laura suspected the wife had a drug problem of her own.

As they talked, the mother kept yelling for them. "If she does that all day and night," Laura told me later, "that's not easy, either."

. After the visit, Laura said she thought the mother could grasp her situation well enough to decide to stay. The team agreed. Their effort to discern and respect the woman's wishes, despite her impairment, was one kind of progress in the two decades since Hilde had been sent to a nursing home against her will.

Laura would follow up with the woman's doctor, and the team would make sure a caregiver came in for a few hours a week. They'd also look for an adult day care program to pick her up on weekdays. "In the interim," said Laura, "how about we get her some damn socks?"

What can those of us without training do? As we've seen, most tools are too binary. They assume either you do or don't have capacity, that a surrogate does or doesn't decide for you. A method called *supported decision-making* has been used to help people with intellectual and developmental disabilities make their own, informed choices, usually with help from a trusted friend, family member, or supporter. But the method has not been used much with people who have dementia, which in any event presents distinct challenges. A new method—*interdependent decision-making*—is designed to account for fluctuations in older decision-makers' abilities and wishes, and in finding the right roles for others. It's also designed to reflect, and bring structure and ethical scaffolding to, what most of us do when we face hard decisions—talk with others we trust. The starting point is *decision-making capacity*—a person's ability to make a particular decision at a particular time, taking into account their ability to get, process, and retain information, deliberate among options, and express a decision. *Interdependent decision-making* (also called *deciding with others*) offers a hopeful new model as millions of us seek to strike the right balances in navigating complex decisions in aging.

GUARDIANSHIP REFORM

Alison Hirschel has represented the legal rights of older people for thirty-five years and believes that two broken systems—nursing homes and guardianship—have inflicted the most harm and anguish on her clients and their families. Both systems claimed to protect older people but often violated their rights, leaving them and their families helpless and outraged. Alison felt that there'd been modest progress in nursing home reform. But on guardianship less so, despite decades of efforts by advocates around the country and in Congress, including hearings, investigations, reports, and new laws. One challenge is that every state has its own ideas about how to run and reform it.

In 2017, experts convened by the Uniform Law Commission drafted a nonpartisan model guardianship law that states could use as a guide to reform their laws. In fact, many states already had decent laws, like Michigan. They just weren't being enforced. That was the backdrop in November 2018 when Marcie Mitchell filed a petition to become the guardian and conservator for her father and stepmother, Robert Mitchell and Barbara Delbridge. (In Michigan, *guardians* handle personal decisions, and *conservators* handle financial decisions.) Bob and Barb lived in their own home, but with Bob's dementia and Barb's psychosis and depression, the challenges were mounting. Marcie worried about Bob driving up north with his buddies to go hunting but wasn't sure how to stop him. Worried, some weekends Marcie picked up Barb, and the two of them drove up north, too.

Marcie hired and paid an aide and physical therapist to come three times a week, and she paid whatever bills she could find. There was no lack of funds. Bob and Barb had $2.7 million between them but couldn't manage it anymore. Their broker suggested that Marcie visit an attorney with them to get POA. But the attorney said that Bob and Barb could no longer understand what they were signing— they'd unintentionally put off seeking a POA for too long. The attorney suggested that Marcie petition for guardianship.

Filing that petition triggered a visit to Bob and Barb by a guardian ad litem (GAL), who explained the process to them and how they could contest it. Bob told the GAL he'd like Marcie to be his guardian. Barb was nonresponsive. Based on his interview, and Bob's stated preference, the GAL recommended that Marcie be named guardian and conservator for both.

That prelude was pretty routine as guardianship goes. Then came the hearing. Probate judge Kathryn George castigated Marcie for her deficient care and for letting Bob go hunting. Marcie's lawyer explained that without guardianship, Marcie had no legal authority to stop him or, in fact, to use their money to pay their bills or caregivers.

In naming a guardian, the judge was supposed to follow priorities set out in Michigan law: adult children and family members were near the top of the law's list. Marcie was both. She also was the guardian her father requested and the GAL recommended.

But Judge George had another idea. She named Caring Hearts of Michigan to be both guardian and conservator for Bob and Barb, even though, under Michigan law, corporate guardians are the *last* option. Marcie's attorney protested. And she asked the judge at least to name Marcie as co-guardian. The judge denied both requests and doubled down, forbidding Marcie from returning to court for six months to ask to modify the court's order. The hearing took less than a half hour. The only evidence before the court was the GAL report.

Catherine Kirk, Caring Hearts' owner, hired Executive Care to supply around-the-clock care for Bob and Barb with three full-time aides. Kirk also owned Executive Care, so was in essence hiring herself. Michigan law prohibits financial self-dealing by the guardian with respect to the ward.

The relationship between the guardian and family began rocky and got worse. For the first few months, they argued about visiting and traded accusations about mistreatment. Kirk had a six-foot "privacy fence" installed around Bob and Barb's home and restricted visits by family and friends. In April 2019, she banned the family from visiting.

Prohibited from returning to court, the family petitioned the public, creating a "Justice for Bob & Barb" Facebook page and going to the press. "They can't get out, we can't get in," Marcie's cousin told a local television reporter, standing in front of the tall privacy fence. "They can't take phone calls because their landline's been disconnected. Their cell phones have been taken; their cars were towed away. They're literally prisoners in their own home, and they've done nothing wrong."[9] In May, Kirk and Caring Hearts went back to court, represented by Kirk's husband's law firm. They sought sanctions and a restraining order, alleging that Bob and Barb's family had harassed and defamed them.

In prior years, there would have been little recourse for families like Bob and Barb's, but the same month as Marcie had filed her guardianship petition, Michigan voters elected a slate of officials who were finally willing to take on the state's entrenched guardianship system. In January 2019, Alison and a colleague submitted a lengthy memo to the Michigan Supreme Court—which oversees state probate courts—titled "The Case for Guardianship Reform," laying out the problem and ideas for solutions. A few months later, Michigan's attorney general and two Supreme Court justices did a twelve-stop listening tour. "They heard people from all over the state tell harrowing stories about guardianship abuse," said Alison. The Supreme Court chief justice launched a "have gavel, will travel" initiative where she and two colleagues sat in with probate courts to learn more about the workings of guardianship proceedings. And a tenacious TV reporter kept airing stories about failures in guardianship and every new twist in Bob and Barb's odyssey.

In June 2019, Michigan's AG launched an investigation into Bob and Barb's case—the first domino to topple. Thereafter, in rapid succession, Caring Hearts withdrew its petition for sanctions and withdrew as guardian, Judge George was removed from the case, and Kirk's husband was relieved of his position as the county's public administrator, who helped courts manage wills and estate matters, none of them admitting wrongdoing.

A few weeks later, Marcie was named as her father's guardian and Barb's sister was named as hers. For her seven months on the job, Kirk billed Bob and Barb $376,000: $46,000 for Caring Hearts, $263,000 for Executive Care, and $67,000 in legal fees for her husband's firm. Bob and Barb's family objected.[10]

In September, less than a month after completing the listening tour, Dana Nessel, Michigan's attorney general, took the unprecedented step of intervening in Bob and Barb's case, citing "the web of connections," blocking payment to the Kirks, and noting that the law was "very clear" that courts shouldn't appoint guardians who would benefit financially from providing services to persons under guardianship. Nessel also commended the TV reporter as "an excellent example of the incredible importance of journalism in our society."[11]

Barb and Bob died a few months later, within weeks of one another. In the middle of the following year, their families reached a financial settlement with the guardian for undisclosed terms. The

AG's case led to an injunction that dissolved Caring Hearts and barred Kirk and her employees from any future involvement in guardianship, to which they stipulated without admitting liability or wrongdoing. After a lengthy absence from the bench, Judge George retired in 2021.

I asked Alison in 2022 if she thought Michigan's calcified guardianship machinery would finally change. "I think so," she said, "which is astonishing after it's been ignored for decades." She described the AG's intervention in more cases, a dynamic new task force convened by the AG, and a move toward stricter standards. Finally the wheels of accountability had creaked into motion. "Without Dana Nessel being AG," said Alison, "the issue never would have seen the light of day."

It was real progress. Yet, in Michigan, like everywhere else, families and reformers still faced another challenge: neither researchers nor policy-makers could provide them with the most basic kinds of information to inform their efforts. Who makes a good guardian? What caseload can they carry? And how can we keep them more accountable? People need better information to do the right thing.

As I thought about the tools we use most often in our struggle to balance autonomy and safety, I kept going back to Chet's gun. It never went off, but what Chet had hoped most to prevent by waving it around had happened. The APS-to-guardianship-to-nursing-home chain reaction had been set in motion, in some senses as brutal and resistant to the nuance of human desire as the weapon he'd hoped would protect them. Hilde wound up in a nursing home. Chet wound up alone.

Chapter 7

LAGGING NORMS

Our prejudices are impressing themselves in our
institutions and therefore on the lives of all of us.

—MARILYNNE ROBINSON, *What Are We Doing Here?*

Old people just grow lonesome
Waiting for someone to say, "Hello in there, hello."

—JOHN PRINE, "Hello in There"

R everence for elders is central to many cultures. In Con-
fucianism, for example, filial piety is not just about honoring and caring for one's parents, it is also the philosophical
underpinning of a good society. Elders not only pass down crucial
facts, they also possess spirituality and wisdom about the greater
meanings of things. Experience matters.

In the twentieth-century United States, we take a dimmer view
of aging. Our norms have not kept pace with our longevity. In one
sense this lag is understandable. Seen through the lens of history and
evolution, today's longevity struck with lightning speed. Since 1900,
humans on average gained more years than since the dawn of the
species. At one time, old-old age was exceptional. Now it's common.
When families and communities were more integrated by age, there
was a greater role for older adults, ways they could contribute. In
hunter-gatherer societies, older women provided something of value

in caring for children, allowing parents to hunt and forage. And older men's knowledge improved the productivity of hunting parties.

But when families live apart, older adults become their own social and economic units. Once out of the workforce, they're deemed to have "outlived" their productivity and value. Their support is on them, sometimes with help from social programs and their families. As we've seen, those added years often bring new, bracing challenges that we haven't figured out how to navigate or finance.

Our attitudes toward aging compound the challenges. We approach it with resistance, fear, and shame, and associate late life with a waning of our humanity. The way we've organized our societal institutions leaves most older people outside the flow of civic and domestic life, either isolated or segregated by age. The structural challenges of isolation and segregation are magnified by cultural ones, like ageism and loneliness, making it harder still to age well.

STRUCTURAL NORMS
Isolation

Earlier in life, education, family, and jobs require us to interact with others. If we don't show up for work or school, someone asks questions. But as we age, life's command performances are fewer. We stay home more. We become less mobile. We hesitate to impose on others. We're less integrated into the ordinary flow of community and family life, resulting in widespread isolation. In 2020, the National Academies of Sciences, Engineering, and Medicine (NASEM) called *isolation*—having few social relationships and infrequent social contact—an "underappreciated public health risk."[1] NASEM estimates that one-quarter of people sixty-five and older are isolated. The same year, a study by the AARP and United Health Foundations found an even higher rate—two-thirds of older Americans. These numbers suggest that our cultural preoccupation with independence may be coming back to bite us.

As isolation creeps up on us—empty nest, retirement, spouse lost, friends moved—its risks creep up, too. Researchers have found that isolation leads to more heart disease and strokes and worsens mobility and immune systems. It leads to higher rates of depression and anxiety and increases our dementia risk by 50 percent. It also sets the stage for more mistreatment and premature death. Many programs can help mitigate the isolation of older people. The largest of them, the Older Americans Act's Aging Network, includes home-delivered meals, in-home services (like personal care and homemaker assistance), telephone reassurance for isolated older persons, senior centers, the Eldercare Locator phone line, State Units on Aging, and hundreds of Area Agencies on Aging, the "other AAA." Those AAAs, which go by varying names, serve as local hubs to connect older people with information, services, and other people.

Atlanta, Georgia's AAA runs an Empowerline that describes itself as "the front desk for people who need help navigating life changes" and obstacles in their homes, health, and communities.[2] When I looked at the offerings, there were classes for caregivers, training for older people to become volunteers, and a four-week course on the sculptor Auguste Rodin. The AAA also brings together old and young, like when a high school freshman named Akiva rode along with Meals on Wheels.

In addition to public programs, some communities organize grassroots, peer-to-peer groups, like the Villages Movement, where people help one another to find less-expensive services and care, arrange rides, and enjoy social and educational activities.

Religious entities also play a role. Churches organize "friendly visitors" and meal delivery for isolated elders. And large organizations, like JASA, or the Jewish Association Serving the Aging in New York City, aide tens of thousands of older people a year. But even all these and other anti-isolation efforts taken together don't come close to meeting the need.

Segregation

We have created a raft of institutions designed *for* older people, where they're welcome, recruited even. Such entities may reduce isolation, but they've evolved in a way that perpetuates structural age segregation. The intentions behind them weren't nefarious. Educating kids of like age and developmental stages together made sense. So did organizing vibrant retirement communities and senior centers around fun activities and relaxation after a life of hard work. Creation of long-term care and supportive housing, filled mostly with older people, was driven by economies of scale. We move through life with our cohort and have lots in common. Some prefer to congregate primarily with people their own age. But being with people of other ages stretches us and makes us happier in old age. "Intergenerational relationships can transform our future" is how a Stanford Longevity Center report on the subject puts it.[3] But old and young more often inhabit separate orbits these days, to the detriment of both.

"Old people need old people, but they also need the young, and young people need contact with the old," wrote Christopher Alexander in his 1977 classic, *A Pattern Language*, a fusion of architecture, design, and philosophy. "Contemporary society shunts away old people; and the more shunted away they are, the deeper the rift between old and young."[4] The young not only miss out on learning from and having loving relationships with the old. They're also deprived of witnessing the process and humanity of aging. Death too becomes more terrifying when it's shrouded, instead of seen as the last event of every life. When old age becomes alien, it turns into a stage onto which we project our fears, and its players become caricatured husks. This in turn leads to more dread, bias, and mistreatment.

"Built for Each Other"

"The old and young are built for each other," said author and social entrepreneur Marc Freedman, co-CEO of CoGenerate (formerly Encore.org). Marc builds entities to make that philosophy a reality, including Experience Corps, now run by AARP, which arranges for older adults to tutor young children to help them read.[5] AARP calls the program "a triple win" that helps "students succeed, older adults thrive, and communities grow stronger."[6] For older people—who often are made to feel they have little left to offer—helping young people can be joyful and transformative. And for at-risk kids, having a caring older mentor can yield benefits that last a lifetime. Research shows that forming positive relationships with older adults who aren't family is a key indicator of future success for all kids.

Such relationships may be homegrown or facilitated by an array of initiatives like buddy programs, book clubs, and oral history assignments baked into school curricula. The AmeriCorps Seniors RSVP program pairs thousands of older volunteers with change-making organizations. Becoming foster grandparents, whether through RSVP or other nonprofits, means older people hear secrets, give out jelly-beans, and get drawings for their fridges. They dole out hugs, help with assignments, and sometimes offer a consoling shoulder. One DC woman credits foster grandparenting with saving her life. Still, despite all their benefits, such intergenerational "triple win" opportunities remain more exception than norm.

Another type of intergenerational pursuit involves shared activism. Nuns & Nones began as an alliance between aging Catholic nuns and millennials who check "none" for their religious affiliation. For decades many sisters used their lands for teaching, nursing, and social work. But with their aging and diminishing numbers, they want to ensure that their devotion to social justice lives on. "How can we start to see things that might feel like burdens—buildings, land, things that are too big for us—not as problems but opportunities?" asked Christin Tomy, a Dominican Sister of Sinsinawa, Wisconsin.[7] To that end, the sisters and the millennials are exploring uses for the sisters' large properties that will advance climate and racial justice. To hear the sisters and the millennials extoll the profundity of their connection and shared values is to mourn the paucity of such alliances.

Another way to lessen age segregation is to co-locate institutions created for young and old, like when senior centers team up with elementary schools and libraries or long-term care facilities share space with childcare centers. There are countless models and robust evidence showing that co-location is good for the health of young and old alike, reduces isolation, improves people's sense of purpose, and might even reduce costs. I saw one such partnership in action when Ricker Hamilton took me to visit Gorham House outside Portland, Maine, where a Continuing Care Retirement Community is built around a preschool. Children call the residents "grand-friends." Young and old enrich one another's lives.

Polls show that 85 percent of Americans like the idea of inter-generational shared sites.[8] And HHS in 1995 urged expanding co-location in both the private and public sectors. Yet it remains rare—about 150 in the United States versus tens of thousands in countries like Japan, the United Kingdom, Canada, and Spain. Why? Slews of bureaucratic obstacles—reimbursement rules, zoning laws, regulations—make it burdensome and expensive to get programs off the ground.

In the meantime, we're barely aware of what we're losing. When older people's "ties with their own past become unacknowledged, lost and therefore broken," wrote Christopher Alexander, "their youth is no longer alive in their old age."[9] Older people will not be integrated so-cially if they're not integrated physically and "share the same streets, shops, services, and common land with everyone else." We should reorganize ourselves, he argues, so that people of all ages can live well, apart *and* together. This idea also animates the age-friendly or livable communities movement, launched by the World Health Or-ganization in 2006 and supported in the United States by AARP. Their goal is to create "great places" for people of all ages "to grow up and grow old."[10] To that end, AARP has created a score card to measure communities on factors like transportation, housing, health, and inviting public places and opportunities.

Maine has some seventy age-friendly communities, more than any other state, in part because it has the oldest population. Still, overall, instead of being the norm, communities that foster connec-tion among people across age and ability remain the exception— something we must advocate for, community by community and person by person.

My niece Charlotte reminded me of the ripples one person can set in motion. In the summer after tenth grade, she registered with Volun-teer Match and was paired with a nursing home close to her house—one that she hadn't noticed before. After lots of email, "a bunch of vaccines," and months of waiting, she started going twice a week after school, from 3:00 to 6:00 p.m. "Welcome to the dementia floor, honey," the head nurse told her when she arrived.

"It was terrible, at first," said Charlotte. "The residents looked at me but didn't talk. Then the nurse says, 'I'm going to lunch. Make sure they don't fight,' and leaves. One woman said, 'I'm not talking to you.' Another one was really upset. I wasn't prepared at all." But visit by visit, everyone got used to one another. The residents started telling Charlotte their stories; she felt she was getting to know them.

The residents usually passed time doing puzzles and watching TV. Often they just sat there. When I learned about Charlotte's volunteering, I gave her an Imagination Kit that she took in a few weeks later. The Imagination Kit is the brainchild of Anne Basting, a University of Wisconsin English professor and founder of the nonprofit TimeSlips.[11] The kit is one of Anne's many projects to "bring joy and meaning to late life," using a technique called creative engagement.

Charlotte didn't know what to expect when she pulled out the kit's "Beautiful Questions"—large type on colorful five-by-seven-inch cards. The open-ended questions with no right, or wrong, answers are designed to spark creativity and foster connection. As they contemplated the first question—"If you could have a superpower, what would it be?"—"everyone was still a little stiff," Charlotte said, "but then people really got into it." The question "How does music make you feel?" led into a conversation about favorite artists. One woman who loved the tenor Andrea Bocelli told a story about listening to him with her brother. "It got people talking to each other."

In response to "What is a place that calms you?," one woman who had lived in Montana talked about visiting the Pacific Ocean in the Northwest. "She described the sound of the waves and smell of the air," Charlotte said, "and that the coastline had 'real trees, not palm trees.'" A woman who couldn't hear read the questions and wrote down her answers. "She described her mother's kitchen in writing and then drew a picture of it with a little window and sink."

"They were all part of it," said Charlotte, "asking each other questions, and interested in what I had to say. And they were really into fairness, so everyone got to talk. It was cool how it evolved."

"I had no idea about dementia," Charlotte told me. "At first, it seemed like these people were always looking for their kids who weren't there. Or just staring into space. But now when I come in, they're like 'hi, how are you?' or 'how's school?' Maybe they don't remember my name, and maybe they don't remember that I'm not a boy, but I've become a familiar face. Everyone knows who I am now. They remember things we've talked about because they mention it when I see them. It's not like complete memory loss. Dementia's different for everyone, which is something else I didn't realize before."

Charlotte also started volunteering for the Digital Grandparents program. People of all ages gathered for a couple of hours a week at the New York Public Library to help older people with tech issues. Some needed help to connect with loved ones. She helped a man pair his iPad with his PC and unsubscribe from spam. As she walked him through the steps, he took notes. Their conversations also stretched beyond tech. "When I ask him questions about his career, his face lights up. He wants to help me. He knows so much and wants to share it." Then it was Charlotte's turn to take notes.

The way Charlotte put words to what she was learning changed, even just from one conversation we had to the next. "I've become more comfortable around older adults," she said. "They treat me like somebody they want to share their knowledge and share their stories with." At first, she wasn't sure if they'd want her there, but "everyone is really accepting across the board; they're interested in who I am. I learn more in volunteering than I do in school."

In the pressure cooker of eleventh grade—rigorous STEM school, college applications looming, long travel soccer hours—time with older people was a revelatory interlude. Unlike in a family, her relationships with older people in the nursing home and library came with no expectations. "They don't have to love me. I don't have to get along with them. It's that I genuinely like this person. They engage in what I'm interested in, and we talk about their interests. It's just like with friends but different generations." She paused. "It's not hard to see the effect that I'm having on them and they're having on me."

CULTURAL NORMS
Ageism

Antiaging animus, what psychiatrist Robert Butler first called *ageism* in 1968, is one of the least acknowledged forms of prejudice. Isabel

Wilkerson called the old "a tragically disfavored caste . . . among the most demeaned of all citizens." Pervasive in American culture, ageism causes untold suffering and has a high price tag. Yale epidemiologist Becca Levy calculates that ageism increases excess health care expenses by $63 billion a year. She also found that ageism turned inward shortens lives. The process starts early. In following young people until they turned sixty, Levy found that those who'd "taken in negative stereotypes about aging" at young ages doubled their risk of heart failure, stroke, and heart attack later on. People who held the most positive beliefs about old age lived 7.5 years longer than those with the most negative.[12]

Ageism is also damaging when turned outward. It's associated with an increased prevalence of violence and entwined with disgust that acts like a social toxin. When we feel disgust for a class of people, that emotion is excreted into our politics and culture, diminishing the humanity of those we find disgusting, and elevating their risk of bias, exclusion, and harm.[13] Ageism and disgust pave the way for elder abuse, neglect, and exploitation.

Ageism also combines with and accentuates other forms of bias, like prejudice against people with disabilities, also called ableism. Seven in ten people age eighty and older have at least one disability.[14] The interplay of ageism and ableism isn't well understood, but they appear to magnify each other's impact with devastating ramifications.

Older women suffer the double whammy of ageism and sexism. Not only are they considered to become less beautiful and desirable as they age, they also become invisible.

And nursing homes reveal how ageism combines with racism and socioeconomic disparities that accumulate over a lifetime. Research has long shown that on average older African Americans live in worse nursing homes than their white counterparts. COVID-19 multiplied those inequities with much higher death counts in majority minority facilities.

Ageism also compounds economic inequities. For one thing, disparate opportunities for accumulating retirement savings means many older Americans are economically unprepared for old age.

People in lower income brackets "get poorer by the year."[15] The National Council on Aging reports that one in three, or fifteen million, older Americans live at or below the federal poverty level. Even more older people of color and women live in poverty given historic wage discrimination and other inequities. Many can't afford to stop working.

It's worth noting that ageism—age-based bias—also can be directed toward the young. In terms of economic security and health care, we've done much more for older Americans than for children, younger adults, and vulnerable families. Older people exercise more political power than younger people and long have benefited from programs like social security and Medicare, while many younger people have lacked adequate education and health care, and endured trauma with little or no help to address it. These societal failures follow people life-long, making them more vulnerable in their own old age. They also compound the challenges of caregiving, when those who don't get treatment for mental health or substance issues wind up depending on older relatives for support. Then, if their older relatives decline, and need help themselves, such "caregiving" arrangements can be recipes for disaster. Troubles unaddressed earlier in life often mushroom over time. We need norms and more holistic programs that support people better through all life's chapters.

Ageism and Work

Two-thirds of older workers report age discrimination on the job, subverting their fulfillment at work and pushing many out of positions they're still well able to do, even though employers report that multigenerational workforces are more productive and profitable.

Retirement is great for some, but not others. Men's mortality increases in the two years after retirement. And overall, some 40 percent of people "unretire."[16] However it's not the norm in the United States to offer meaningful "encore" opportunities for late-career and retired people who want to keep contributing but work fewer hours with less stress and more flexibility. Some employers offer part-time or retire-and-consult options, but our American *all-or-nothing* work norms squander much human potential.

The desire to find a meaningful encore act propelled cardiac surgeon Charles Edwards when he developed a tremor that prevented him from operating at sixty-four. Having seen both of his parents struggle with Alzheimer's, Edwards got additional training at Johns Hopkins University in dementia and geriatric psychiatry and then opened the nonprofit Memory & Movement center in Charlotte, NC, where he, along with his wife and colleagues, cares for people with dementia, Parkinson's, and related disorders.

Our focus in later life leans toward questions like "Will the money last?" or "Should I take those statins?" These questions, while important, can obscure bigger ones about how we derive meaning. As we live longer lives, we need new policies and norms that give older people a broader array of options for meaningful encore work, if they're so inclined. Society's needs are vast, as are the untapped capacities and potential contributions of older people who could help meet them.

Ageism in Health

In health care systems, ageism, greed, and perverse incentives routinely undermine our health and well-being as we age. "We know how to improve care," said Terry Fulmer, president of the John A. Hartford Foundation and a practicing nurse. Terry believes age-friendly care is grounded in "the four Ms": what *matters*, the patients' goals and priorities; *medication*, reviewing each one for interactions, doses, and the chance to "deprescribe"; *mentation*, patients' memory, mood, and mental health; and *mobility*, moving and staying active.

"I've never felt more urgency," said Terry, who, through the foundation, is working to change norms and educate patients and their advocates about how to demand more appropriate care. She's also working with HHS and the American Geriatric Society to create incentives for health systems to adopt more age-friendly practices and expand the number of health professionals with expertise in meeting the needs of older adults.

Mere Exposure

Ageism infiltrates our institutions and our psyches like an odorless toxic gas. Unlike other biases, we don't even think we *should* think it's wrong. Yet absorbing its toxins makes it that much harder to take on the gathering challenges. Doing so will require fighting back against massive industries that tell us that aging is bad so they can sell us more potions, pills, and surgeries to stave it off. Shifting those attitudes won't be simple. Their roots run deep and are tightly coiled around our identities.

One antidote might lie in something called the *mere exposure effect*. Words, faces, and random shapes "presented more frequently were rated much more favorably than [those] that had been shown only once or twice," wrote Nobel laureate Daniel Kahneman, in *Thinking, Fast and Slow.* The effect occurs "even when the repeated words or pictures are shown so quickly that the observers never become aware of having seen them."[17] The explanation lies in our biological adaptation to a dangerous world. If we see something often enough and it hasn't harmed us, then caution fades and affinity grows. Exposure to more positive images of aging could reduce the harm of the fusillade of old-is-bad messages. It might even shift attitudes about aging.

I stumbled on a similar realization in writing this book. When Laura Mosqueda was a child, her grandparents were her primary babysitters. Ricker lived upstairs from his grandparents; many other older relatives lived close by so he saw them often. Page Ulrey spent long summers at her grandparents' farm. And Alison Hirschel volunteered at a nursing home as a teenager. The work they chose later is more than a fluke. There's nothing mere about exposure.

This was another reason I was thrilled to learn about my niece Charlotte's volunteering at the nursing home and library. Research shows that the simple act of connecting across generations changes not just the individuals but also the norms of the communities they're part of, reducing ageism. A critical element in moving the dial, research suggests, is having some common purpose, like shared activism. Museum outings, gardening, and pen pal letter writing are relatively simple, low-cost anti-ageism measures for any community. The options are limitless.

LONELINESS

Loneliness is another harmful norm in aging. Loneliness and isolation are related, but there's a distinction: isolation is structural; loneliness is psychological. Loneliness is rampant these days among people of all ages. In the wake of the pandemic, more than three in five young adults and half of young mothers report being profoundly lonely.[18] When US surgeon general Vivek Murthy did a listening tour around the country, he found that "loneliness ran like a dark thread through many of the more obvious issues . . . like addiction, violence, anxiety, and depression." No issue he worked on resonated more with the public than loneliness. The antidote Murthy prescribes is the "healing power of human connection."[19]

We tend to blame the pandemic, but even before its massive confinements, lots of older people were lonely: 43 percent according to the 2016 NASEM report.[20] And loneliness was even more damaging to older people's health than isolation—quadrupling premature deaths and increasing emergency room visits by 57 percent and hospitalizations by 68 percent. We are wired to be social creatures. Disconnection ruptures a basic fiber of our humanity. This book is shot through with the pitiless suffering that isolation and loneliness inflict.

What happens in our psyches is inextricable from what happens in our bodies. In his book, *Together*, Murthy looks at the evolutionary origins of loneliness. In short, our ancestors who banded together were more likely to survive. They could hunt together, protect one another, and share resources. Loneliness, the theory goes, is an early warning system, like smoke or pain, nudging us to rejoin our people. Only that's harder to do once we feel lonely.

Murthy describes promising initiatives to reduce loneliness, like Phone Pals, run by the CareMore health system, that calls loneliness "a treatable health condition."[21] Murthy tells the story of Virta, a desperately lonely and isolated woman who'd lost her home, gained weight, and was growing unhealthier. Talking regularly with a phone volunteer named Armando helped Virta turn her life around. She didn't want to let Armando down so tried to take better care of herself. "Without Mr. Armando calling," Virta told Murthy, "I don't think I would have made it." Human connection, even by phone, made all the difference. "Virta found it easy to be open and vulnerable with Armando," wrote Murthy, "because he listened without judgement and seemed to genuinely care about her well-being."[22] Many older people who fall for phone scams do so in part because they're lonely. Having an Armando to talk with could well reduce not only loneliness but also other types of losses.

As loneliness spirals out of control, the United Kingdom and Japan have named Ministers of Loneliness. Murthy describes how a British nonprofit created the Silver Line, an elder helpline with the motto: "No question too big, no problem too small, no need to be alone."[23] The Silver Line has served more than two million callers since 2013, and the number keeps rising. Some people call to bookend their days: to have someone to greet when they get up in the morning and say good night to before bed. Daytime calls tend to involve practical matters, but often those who call in the dark of their nights are in the vicious grip of loneliness.

We've managed to extend our years but to what end? We want to get old but not *be* old. Our lagging norms are a warning sign. If we don't change our approach to aging, there will be much more unnecessary suffering. Like much else, norms change in two ways: first gradually, then all at once. Being aware that harmful norms exist and need changing is the first hurdle. Here again, we shouldn't underestimate small steps. I've seen their long dividends in my own home.

When our children were young, we had many regular visitors, including my former law professor, Zipporah Wiseman, a brilliant pioneering lawyer with huge opinions, curiosity, wit, and heart. When Zipporah was on the cusp of ninety, she and my son Gabriel visited the Portrait Gallery together. "It was wild," he said. "While I wheeled her around, she talked about the art, and the history, politics, and culture of what we were seeing. She knew a shit-ton and was so eloquent and cool." My son Nathan was one of the countless young people who lived at Zipporah's house in Cambridge, Massachusetts. It was part kibbutz, part salon, part student housing. And when my daughter, Fiona, was down to the wire in deciding what college to choose, she called Zipporah and only then made her decision.

I recently asked Fiona why she'd called Zipporah. "I had my high school friends and my parents' perspectives," she said, "but Zipporah had a different set of life experiences. She had wisdom. I really trusted and respected her. She was part of my cabinet. She was my friend."

Fiona then dropped back in time and talked about how she saw Zipporah when she was a little girl. "For older people and kids, there's this stigma that you won't be taken seriously," she said. "But Zipporah was one of those people who really saw you. She took you seriously. She didn't care how old you were. You were just a person. And you saw this ageless person back."

Part II

DOWNSTREAM, UPSTREAM

Aging is a little like paddling a boat down a river. Laura Mosqueda, in her geriatrics clinic, usually saw patients and families while they were still in the headwaters, where she and her team could help them better understand the exigencies of aging and find ways to turn away from danger, toward channels with smoother waters.

Ricker Hamilton saw a small subset of older people downstream from Laura, only after someone had called APS or 911. The water was rough, but people and services still might help them steer toward branches of the river ahead with less turbulence.

By the time people got to Page Ulrey, their boats had been sucked under by rapids or gone over the falls. Those passengers who were still alive were injured or had their hearts broken by someone they loved. Some got help. More did not. And some died or disappeared under circumstances that should have raised questions but rarely did.

To improve the odds of a better old age, it helps to start planning further upstream than we usually do. Looking downstream provides hints about how to do so, and lessons about how things can go wrong. Understanding the why of it can help ward off trouble and inform how we work for change.

I have an unusual perspective borne of my varied work in law, research, policy, and programs—in trying to push them to better serve the people they're intended for. My colleagues, my professional "family," helped give me a fuller picture by letting me see what they saw from their varying perches, through their different lenses. My work changed how I saw the problems, the solutions, the institutions, and the potential paths for change.

Then, at some point, the pyramid in my head flipped. At first, my focus was trained on the pyramid's apex, the worst, most extreme tip of aging: elder abuse. But in time I came to see the problem and the cases I worked on more as symptoms—the ventilator patients and the dead—of a deeper disease: our denial, fear, and loathing of an entire segment of the human life cycle. The very prevalence of elder abuse, neglect, and exploitation—that it victimizes one in ten people sixty and older and almost half of people with dementia, hastening their deaths by 300 percent—was a sign. As was research showing that it caused serious stress for more than thirty million concerned family, friends, and neighbors trying to help.

These numbers are ill omens. But the numbers are so big they're numbing. Aging seems far off. We look away and hope for the best. Me too. Yet, my work, and the stories of friends and strangers, kept reminding me that the problems of aging don't just afflict "other people." Aging comes for all of us.

Many of the grimmest troubles can be traced back to our failure to find better solutions to challenges like caregiving, understaffing, financial exploitation, and isolation. While we wait for better prevention evidence, two things are worth keeping in mind: Older people with good social support are mistreated less often and are better off in other ways, too; the stronger the support, the more protective a role it plays. And, it appears, better support for caregivers can also reduce mistreatment. These are important bread crumbs in our quest to learn what works. We need more. Demographically speaking, our challenges are just beginning. If not addressed, they'll keep undermining the health and well-being not only of the old but of anyone who loves and cares for them, too. We may not be able to see the rapids yet, but we can hear them and feel the river begin to descend.

Chapter 8

WHO TO CALL?

Some paradox of our natures leads us, when once
we have made our fellow men the objects of our
enlightened interest, to go on to make them the
objects of our pity, then of our wisdom, ultimately
of our coercion.

—LIONEL TRILLING, *The Liberal Imagination*

L ots of people have never heard of APS. When I started working on the DOJ Elder Justice Initiative, I went from never having heard of APS to hearing about it all the time. It's one of those "worlds" that exists all over, mostly out of sight, until we fear that an adult we know is in danger and we don't know who else to call. The 1.3 million reports to APS every year nationwide involve a broad spectrum of human misery. As we've seen, APS investigates reports of hoarding and heatless homes, medical crises and evictions, and abuse, neglect, and exploitation.

SHAKY FOUNDATIONS

In the mid-twentieth century, more and more people fretted about how to respond to the growing numbers of older people "unable to manage," who had no one available or suitable to help them, or who would accept no help. Protective services had existed for animals since 1874, and for children since 1879. Beginning in the 1950s, aging experts advocated for protective services for older people, too. In

185

the 1960s, Congress funded seven demonstration projects to study the outcomes of various elder protective service models.

The most rigorous of those studies was led by Margaret Blenkner, the respected research director of Cleveland's Benjamin Rose Institute on Aging (BRIA). Blenkner designed a randomized controlled trial to test the well-regarded elder protective services BRIA provided, compared to the city agencies' normal fare.

It took courage for BRIA and its all-woman board to put their own best efforts under a public microscope, especially as year by year the data rolling in told an increasingly unsettling story. In 1974, Blenkner published findings that made the outcome starkly clear: clients who got BRIA's gold-standard protective services landed in nursing homes more often and died sooner than those who did not.

"The results shocked everyone," said researcher Georgia Anetzberger, the elder justice field's informal historian. "But really, none of those demonstration projects had notably positive outcomes for protective services. Later studies quibbled with the methodology, but basically confirmed the findings. And nobody has systematically examined APS efficacy since then. It's amazing we ended up with adult protective services at all."

I asked Georgia why protective services resulted in worse outcomes. "My take is because they eroded people's rights," she said. "In our country, with the emphasis on independence and individualism, you can't take away people's freedom and ability to make choices and expect to have positive outcomes. In another culture where decisions are made more in the context of the extended family, not the individual, maybe the outcome would be different."

Undeterred by the poor results, advocates and lawmakers kept pushing for that era's version of protective services. In drafting APS laws, many states just cut and pasted their existing Child Protective Services (CPS) laws and models even though CPS had its own problems, and the needs of the young and the old are very different. APS also inherited CPS's backward paradigm—a primary focus on investigation and response *after* problems are reported rather than trying to prevent the underlying ills causing the trouble. This approach led to untold preventable suffering. It also laid a trap for workers: Intervene too soon or aggressively and risk violating clients' rights.

Or don't intervene soon or aggressively enough and risk failing to stop harm or death in time. There was no consensus, much less any evidence to guide workers in navigating the "right" path among the fraught options.

Child advocates had fought mightily to legislate in more proactive ways. Led by Minnesota senator Walter Mondale, Congress had passed a law to help vulnerable children and their families, taking a preventive approach. But President Richard Nixon vetoed it in 1971. In 1974, Congress returned with the Child Abuse Prevention and Treatment Act (CAPTA)—highlighting deadly cases and trained more narrowly on reporting and investigating child abuse. That law Nixon signed.

This reactive instead of proactive approach—responding *after* the harm starts instead of fixing underlying problems—was part of a broader societal pattern that afflicted the elder justice field, too.

A New Bill

Congress's funding of protective services in 1975 had focused on older people "unable to manage." The darker specter of elder abuse was barely mentioned until Claude Pepper, Congress's champion on aging, took up the issue. Pepper, a Miami Democrat, chaired the House Select Committee on Aging and held hearings. Some advocates accentuated violent "spilled blood" examples. Although literal "spilled blood" cases comprised only a small fraction of elder abuse, the image drew more attention from politicians and press. Pepper predicted that the 1980s would be "the decade of the Battered Parent."[1]

In 1980, Cleveland congresswoman Mary Rose Oakar, mentored by Pepper, introduced the Prevention, Identification, and Treatment of Elder Abuse Act (modeled on Mondale's 1974 CAPTA) to "control the unwarranted violence against the aged." The law would have created a federal office mandated to compile research and training programs, provide technical assistance, investigate the problem's causes, and provide federal matching funds to states for APS.

Oakar and Pepper reintroduced their bill eight times between 1980 and 1991. It bobbed in and out of view and then sank for good. Congress's attention to elder abuse in the twentieth century peaked with a few hearings and reports, and a pittance to fund a National Center on Elder Abuse. (Laura Mosqueda is director of the NCEA now housed at USC.) Pepper's other consolation prize? Pepper's name for the problem—"elder abuse"—stuck, outlasting granny battering, battered parent syndrome, and King Lear syndrome.

Despite its reactive framing, the Pepper–Oakar bill also would have done real good, providing much-needed federal funds, a home for APS within a federal agency, and the leadership, personnel, and expertise that come with federal support. Such structure also would have meant data collection, research, more consistent standards, and training. But none of that happened.

Instead, APS evolved headless and helter-skelter, each program different. Within six years of Congress's 1975 funding push, every state had created an APS program and needed staff. As the newest kid on the social services block, many APS workers were totally green, like Ricker Hamilton, or coming from child protection, mental health, or juvenile justice jobs that had burned them out. Ricker received no training before becoming an APS casework supervisor. "Absolutely none," he said.

"It was the Wild Wild West then," an APS director told me. What workers lacked in resources, many made up for in ingenuity, scrounging to find their clients everything from medical care to food to women's undergarments, to the chagrin of one older male case aide. There weren't many standards then, either. Early on some workers bargained with clients who hoarded, trading bags of McDonald's for bags of trash. For some clients, APS was the last stop. "Often," Ricker said, "APS workers were the only ones at the funeral home when a client died."

Six months after Ricker started working for APS in 1982, the University of Southern Maine planned and hosted a national summit on Improving Protective Services for Older Americans. They convened two hundred of the nation's leading protective services experts for a "law and social work seminar." In a controversial keynote speech, legal scholar John Regan chastised protective services for due process violations and urged a philosophy of "minimal intervention." Regan's vision for protective services, which he also laid out in a congressional working paper, was for APS to work shoulder-to-shoulder with health professionals and lawyers to meet their clients' vast and disparate needs. But that vision hadn't come to pass in the years leading up to the Maine summit. Instead, when doctors and lawyers paid attention to APS, it was usually to criticize it. What Ricker, then twenty-eight, remembers best about the summit was the bitter clash over whether APS should have petitioned a court to let doctors amputate the gangrenous feet of a client, a seventy-two-year-old Nashville artist, to save her life.

That debate exposed deep rifts, pitting social workers, attorneys, health professionals, and scholars against one another. Attorneys lambasted APS for overriding people's rights while APS workers resented being cast as "the enemy of civil liberties." Those lawyers made lofty pronouncements about liberty from the comfortable distance of their offices while APS workers spent time with the people whose lives hung in the balance. Lawmakers had assigned APS the legal duty to protect society's most vulnerable adults. Now they were being accused of doing too much and too little. APS workers left the summit "feeling that they should be doing something different, which was equally undefined."[2]

The Welter

In the meantime, law- and policy-makers just kept piling one duty after the next onto APS workers' shoulders, without the resources to handle them. Today, most APS programs are mandated to serve not only older people but *all* vulnerable adults eighteen and older. Almost half of the states require APS to handle cases not just in homes but also in facilities. And almost a third of APS cases involve complex questions of cognitive capacity often beyond the scope of workers' expertise. Unlike child protection, where kids and their families can't decline a CPS intervention, APS's adult clients can decline *if* APS deems they have the cognitive capacity to do so.

In talking to dozens of APS workers over the years, I've been astounded by the breadth of issues on which they're expected to have expertise. It's a staggering list: medicine, cognition, mental health, aging, developmental disabilities, ethics, law, transportation, finance, forensics, investigations, crisis intervention, applying for benefits, finding housing and long-term care facilities, coordinating care, and navigating guardianship and other proxy decision-making. No one can do all that, much less without adequate training or assistance from people who have expertise.

Some, like Ricker, formed coalitions to expand their resources. If his clients needed a lawyer, a doctor, or a nursing home, he knew who to call. Ricker bolstered his own skills, getting a master's degree in social work at Boston College in 1984 while still working full-time at APS. Later, he also convinced Maine's law enforcement academy to include two hours of elder abuse training, which he helped teach. "I went through the law enforcement academy training myself," he said. "Then I wasn't just a fat old social worker. I was Reserve Officer Hamilton. What I said carried more weight."

Ricker's evangelizing and connector zeal occasionally were shadowed by private moments of doubt. He knew he helped some people a lot and others not at all. Still, he wondered—what approaches to the work were the most effective? What did the clients think? Were there better ways to do this hard work? He didn't know. No one did. Those were questions that only researchers could answer. And they weren't doing so.

All the while, APS muddled along, its structural flaws not so visible. Years of routine, like layers of wallpaper, had covered the cracks. But look closely, and the fissures revealed themselves.

Lawmakers also imported another type of law from child welfare to elder justice—mandatory reporting. Every state mandated some type of reporting to either APS, or in New York to law enforcement, without measuring the impact. There was a compelling argument for it. Many older victims are impaired or too frightened to seek help in life-threatening or destitution-threatening situations. But reporting also can breach trust and autonomy, increase risk, and bring unwanted government intrusion where it's feared or unwelcome. Early on, I pushed for mandatory reporting, too, but my views have been tempered. Such mandates funnel cases *into* APS but don't ensure that they'll be handled well once they arrive, or that they'll be handled at all. Such mandatory reporting laws are a cheap and easy way for legislators to *say* they've addressed the problem and check it off the list without doing the harder work of actually legislating meaningful change to reduce the problem. Such laws are yet another "solution" focused downstream, after the trouble happens, instead of on trying to prevent it further upstream.

TEAMWORK

Over the last decades, more and more APS workers formed or joined teams with other professionals, giving them access to different skill sets and resources. Laura's friend geriatrician Carmel Dyer founded the first medical center–based team in Houston in 1995: the Texas Elder Abuse and Mistreatment (TEAM) Institute. Laura founded what she called the Elder Abuse Forensic Center in Orange County in 2003. And Risa Breckman and Mark Lachs founded the New York City Elder Abuse Center in 2008.

Today, five hundred or so such teams exist in more than thirty states, most called multidisciplinary teams, or MDTs. They're housed in universities, APS and prosecutors' offices, and nonprofits. They not only give APS access to medical, legal, and financial expertise, they also give team members access to one another. Addressing these complex issues is a team sport, and though most teams don't provide services, they coordinate the efforts of others who do. Some teams specialize. Financial exploitation teams bring on forensic accountants, and fatality review teams work with coroners and medical examiners. Over the years, many MDTs have proven themselves to be valuable enough that state and local governments have begun to fund them—itself a form of success and a sign they're useful.

But while most MDT members *believe* that their teams improve clients' well-being, as with APS, no one has measured their efficacy or their impact on clients, and few are governed by consistent definitions of "success." And yet, there's little doubt that MDTs represent progress. "No one professional can handle these complex cases sitting alone in their office," said Risa Breckman, the founding executive director of the large New York City Elder Abuse Center. That's the practical point, but there's also another principle at work. Scholars of complex systems find that diverse teams consistently outperform homogeneous ones. The more complex the problem, the more important a role diversity plays. People with different experiences bring a broader variety of tools and ideas to the table.

Teams also can be engines of innovation by uncovering questions that need answers and then, sometimes, figuring out how to answer them.

Chapter 9

FORENSICS

One discovers the light in the darkness, that is
what darkness is for.

—James Baldwin, *Nothing Personal*

The world is full of obvious things which
nobody . . . ever observes.

—Sir Arthur Conan Doyle,
The Hound of the Baskervilles

At a multidisciplinary team meeting in Brooklyn, the assistant district attorney whisked photos and X-rays across the table to the team doctors asking again and again: "Is this elder abuse? Is *this?*" The doctors didn't know.

Every Injury Has a Story

In a sense such teams stand in for families. When older relatives have injuries and can't explain what happened, countless family members have asked staff in doctors' offices, homecare agencies, and emergency rooms: "Do you really think Mom fractured her hip in a fall?" "Grandad looks malnourished; is the staff helping him eat?" "Could all those bruises on Dad really have happened accidentally?"

The origins of unexplained injuries are hard to trace for families and professionals alike. As multidisciplinary teams brought people with different kinds of expertise together, their discussions raised new questions that only research could answer.

The Brooklyn assistant district attorney also had other questions, like about the fractured wrist of a man in his mid-eighties. He said his much younger girlfriend had hit him with a cane. She said he broke his wrist in a fall but didn't remember because of his drinking and dementia. "Who should we believe?" the prosecutor asked the team doctors.

They didn't know the answer, so one of them, Tony Rosen, an emergency medicine doctor at New York-Presbyterian/Weill Cornell Medical Center, asked a radiologist. The forearm has two bones: the radius on the thumb side and the ulna on the pinkie side. Older people commonly fracture the radius when breaking a fall with their hands, the radiologist said, or sometimes, the ulna breaks at the wrist. But this man's ulna was broken *in the middle*. Such mid-ulnar breaks also go by the name "nightstick fractures" because they were seen in people who held up forearms defensively when struck by a police baton. Tony saw the radiologist have a "come to think of it" moment. You almost never see an ulna fractured like that in a fall, he told Tony. Come to think of it, that break is more consistent with someone holding up a forearm to defend himself.

Every injury has a story. The first rule of *forensic markers*—injuries raising both medical and legal issues—is, "Does the injury fit the story?" As Tony started asking questions, he learned that radiologists saw lots of suspicious injuries in older people—for example, several injuries in various stages of healing, unlikely combinations like a broken jaw and ankle, or a defensive injury, like that ulnar fracture—injuries that didn't fit their stories. Radiology and emergency medicine professionals get the first glimpse of all sorts of harm and make calls all the time about what's suspicious. Usually, they have data to guide them. But that wasn't the case with older patients.

So, Tony decided to study the physical injuries of elder abuse, starting with a literature review. That didn't take long. There were four hits: a review article led by a Canadian radiologist and three articles relating to Laura's research on bruising.

BRUISES

One way we come to *see* what was previously invisible to us is through the organized collection and analysis of data. When I first met Laura, she was already wondering about bruises, such as the ones she saw on her own patients, like the woman whose caregiver hit her with the phone. There were also the bruises her patients' worried families called her about.

She was frustrated by the lack of data to help her tell the difference between accidental and inflicted bruises. No one had studied the issue in older people, so she decided to do so herself. Laura got a DOJ grant and kept her first research question simple: What do accidental bruises in older people look like? Collecting data to define "normal" is unglamorous but foundational work. It forms a baseline. Every morning for six months, researchers went to Freedom Village, a senior housing complex, to visit the same one hundred people whose average age was eighty-five. Researchers examined every inch of skin, measuring and photographing each new bruise, asking how it got there. They used paint samples from a hardware store to color-code each one, so their research notes were sprinkled with quirky paint names, like Burnt Umber.

Advancing knowledge requires not just questions, researchers, and funders but also legions of willing subjects. "I was really moved how people let us bother them day after day in such an intimate way to help us learn," said Kerry Burnight, one of the researchers on the study. Usually, people sat or lay down while Kerry examined them. But on one visit the research subject opened his door to Kerry, naked, his wife beside him, both smiling. "I'm ready!" he said brightly. As he stood and Kerry inspected his feet, he peppered her with questions. She wanted to respond, and for him to hear her answers, but wasn't sure how to do so without looking up.

The data showed that in bruising, as in real estate, the mantra is *location, location, location.* Ninety percent of accidental bruises were on the arms and legs; 10 percent on the torso. Most people didn't remember how the bruises got there, although they were slightly more likely to remember the origin of a bruise on the torso than on an extremity. Fifteen percent of the bruises turned yellow-green-purple in the first twenty-four hours, so color wasn't a useful tool to date them. Normal-looking bruises on arms, legs, and even torsos are rarely suspicious. But bruises in other places, with no plausible explanation, warrant a closer look and possibly reporting.

The article Laura published in 2005 in the *Journal of the American Geriatric Society* garnered little notice.[1] Geriatrician Mark Lachs knew the feeling. His trailblazing research that found elder abuse triples premature mortality had landed with a thud seven years earlier.[2] But Mark knew what Laura's paper represented. "It was," he said, "the first study ever to describe a forensic marker of elder abuse."

Having collected baseline data, Laura and her team next studied how bruises "inflicted" on APS clients differed from accidental ones. Quite a bit, it turned out. They were bigger, there were more of them, and they were often in unusual locations. They differed in shape and were sometimes "patterned"—or mimicked the shape of what caused them: fingers, hand, belt buckle, rope. They appeared in places accidental bruises rarely did—the head and neck, abdomen and buttocks, palms and soles, inner thighs and genitalia. They more likely crossed "multiple planes," like the front and side of the neck or the inner and outer parts of the arm. They also showed up in unusual combinations, were more numerous, and often accompanied other injuries. People also more often remembered their origins.

Laura had aspirations for her bruising data. "Research that sits on the shelf won't do much," she said. "We tried to get the information into the hands of nurses, cops, and APS workers. Doing the research is just the first step. You also have to disseminate it in a way people can absorb." She created color-coded body maps, videos, and an app (since adapted by DOJ, called EAGLE). She knew she'd made progress when she took her medical boards and got a question on her own study.

As the findings seeped into the world, the world had questions. Laura's inbox filled with inquiries from all over: "Was this abuse? Should I be worried?" As both author and consumer of her work, she often asked herself the same questions. Like when a longtime patient arrived for a routine appointment with a small bruise on her inner thigh. Laura talked to the patient and her caregiver separately.

She contacted the family. The bruise's location was questionable. The woman had no memory of how it got there. Dementia made her paranoid and anxious. She thought everyone was out to get her. But she was indifferent to the bruise and gave no hint of a negative association with it, nor any other sign of abuse.

Laura worried about the high stakes of making a wrong call. If there'd been abuse and she said nothing, she might leave her patient in danger. Laura was *Ms. Bruise* and a mandated reporter. If she didn't report a suspicious bruise, how could anyone else be expected to? But reporting wasn't a neutral event either. The family had cared well for the mother for years. Her dementia wasn't easy. They'd struggled to find the right caregiver. This one was well-screened, competent, and kind. The mother had fired others, or they'd quit in exasperation. This one stayed. The mother liked her. An accusation would almost certainly mean she'd leave. She might lose her livelihood or be deported. Without a caregiver, the mother might wind up in a facility, something she'd desperately wanted to avoid.

"The longer I do this work," Laura said, "the more I consider the consequences of everything I do really carefully. The options often are less clear than they seem at first. Good intentions can backfire, leaving the person we're trying to help worse off." Based on all she'd learned, Laura believed the thigh bruise was innocuous. The family concurred with her approach. She recorded it and wrote herself a note to follow up. That's another thing about forensic markers: *location, location, location* must be mediated by *context, context, context.*

SEEING LEAFY SEA DRAGONS

People sixty and older make about twenty-nine million emergency department (or ER) visits every year—more visits than they make to geriatricians. Hospital visits are often the rare occasion when isolated older persons come into view. But hospital staff rarely recognize signs of trouble. When I asked Laura and Mark Lachs in 2014 whether they got referrals from or were consulted by their medical centers' ERs about suspicious injuries in older people, both said no. Laura and Mark ran two of the leading national medical center–based elder abuse programs, but their own colleagues weren't then referring them cases—not fractures, brain bleeds, or bruises. The problem was invisible.

Laura uses a photo of an Australian fish that looks like kelp to make the point in speeches to medical professionals. "When I show them a picture of a leafy sea dragon in seaweed, no one sees it," she said. "But when I show them one swimming in open water, they clearly see that it's a fish. Then, when they see the original photograph again, they can spot it. They need to know what it looks like to see it."

This is not a new concept in medicine, although most doctors talk not in terms of fish but of "differential diagnoses"—the list of possible conditions they contemplate when a patient arrives with a complaint. If it's not "on the differential," whoever's looking won't even consider it. Tony Rosen thinks that ERs are ideal venues to spot issues and ask questions. They've long had medical-forensic protocols to detect other kinds of suspicious injuries, just not in older people.

Every problem under the sun turns up in a hectic ER. Discerning abuse or neglect, especially in patients who can't speak for themselves, is tricky. Researchers use catchy phrases to help busy clinicians remember. "Those Who Don't Cruise Rarely Bruise" is the title of one 1999 article. The findings? Children too young to move around seldom bruise, so their bruises warrant concern.[3]

"We know some risk factors now," Tony said. "One fracture isn't necessarily suspicious. But if I see multiple fractures in different stages of healing, I'm more worried. And then, if I learn that the patient's drug-addicted niece lives with her, well that's . . ." Tony paused. "Do you know the Bond villain Goldfinger?" he asked. "Goldfinger says: 'Once is happenstance. Twice is coincidence. The third time, it's enemy action.'"

After college, Tony worked for a horror movie production house named Troma and then started a tech business with friends. But he wanted something more, so enrolled in University of California, Los Angeles's School of Public Health where the university's injury center exposed him to injuries and violence nothing like the film genre. When a childhood hero, a judge, died by suicide after an Alzheimer's diagnosis, Tony said, "I began to realize the growing impact of aging and dementia on public health." He went to medical school and then on to the 24/7 noise and drama of emergency medicine. I had a vision of Tony as a gallant young doctor, reforming how ERs handled suspicious injuries in older people. Not so much, he said. "While I was a resident, I saw a zillion falls but never 'saw' elder abuse. When you're training, you're supposed to move faster and faster and see people who are sicker and sicker. I was just learning how to be a doctor." ER residents face a deluge every day. "There are lots of disincentives to slowing things down," he said. "If someone says, 'it's a fall,' you just agree." In time, however, Tony gained confidence and credibility as it became clearer that he was onto something.

Tony also realized something else. "Emergency physicians usually spend just a few minutes with the patient," he said, "so it's critical to train and empower the whole team. Triage staff, nurses, and radiology techs are often alone with the patient in ways that don't arouse suspicion. They could be trained to ask delicate questions if there are concerns."

I'd learned this firsthand when I fell down the stairs a few years ago fleeing a swarm of bees. I landed in the ER, body and pride badly bruised. A nurse and radiology tech on separate occasions asked me probing questions when no one else was in earshot: "What happened? Are you scared of anyone?" I wondered if my bruises would have prompted such questions had I been eighty-five.

Tony was especially interested in the role of emergency medical technicians (EMTs) who did what he referred to as "basically house calls" when someone dialed 911. EMTs notice lots of red flags. They can immediately see if the home is perilously full of garbage. They can check if there's food in the fridge or chat up a skulking nephew or an overwhelmed caregiver. EMTs also get private moments with patients in an ambulance.

In focus groups with EMTs, Tony learned: "They saw lots of worrisome stuff, including elder abuse, but when they spoke up, their concerns were ignored again and again, so they stopped saying anything." Studies show that futility breeds inaction. Medical professionals won't speak up if they feel like it won't matter. "Now we take their concerns more seriously," Tony said. "And we created feedback

loops, so they know that what they say matters and is acted on."
Another lesson of change-making, Tony learned, was to ask questions of and listen to *all* staff who spent time with older patients.

"The question is how best to increase the suspicion level from zero
to some," Tony explained, but it's important that it's not too high or
too low. "You have to decide what mistakes you want to make," said
Richard Gelles, a pioneer in the family violence field. Do we want
to over- or under-identify the problem? My first instinct was for
aggressive screening, but, Gelles cautioned, that too had unintended
consequences. People use ERs for medical emergencies, like strokes
and heart attacks, as well as for the aftermath of gunshots and sexual
assaults. Millions of poor people also use them for primary care. Because ERs screen for child abuse more vigorously than primary care
providers do, poor and nonwhite people who rely more heavily on
ERs for primary care are disproportionately screened and funneled
into the child protection and criminal systems. Gelles's concern is
critical to factor in as we begin to screen more for elder abuse and
grapple with the issues that attend such screening.

Lurking behind the scenes is another ethical dilemma: Should we
screen if we don't have evidence-based interventions to handle the
cases that screening identifies? For now, screening mostly funnels
people toward APS, long-term care, guardianship, or the criminal
justice system without knowing if the people referred emerge better
off. It's what Gelles called "marching victims into a vacuum." The
US Preventive Services Task Force does not recommend that health
professionals routinely screen older patients because "the current evidence is insufficient to assess the balance of benefits and harms of
screening for abuse and neglect in all older or vulnerable adults."[4]
Said another way, we don't know if the interventions we use help
people more than harm them.

But there's a difference between such routine screening and sending
up a flare if you see something alarming. "When I suspect a cardiac
issue, I refer my patients to a cardiologist," Laura told me. "These
issues are complicated. We need specialists whom others can consult
to help answer, 'Did something bad happen here?'" It's unreasonable

to expect busy clinicians to have the expertise to figure it all out. They just need to be able to spot suspicious signs and know who to call."

But *whom* should they call?

When it comes to suspected child abuse, hundreds of pediatricians have supplemented their training with fellowships in the grim underbelly of "non-accidental trauma." The American Academy of Pediatrics formally recognized the subspecialty of child abuse pediatrics in 2006, and gave it its own qualifying examination in 2009, citing decades of research providing a strong scientific basis in the field.

Child abuse pediatricians have dual citizenship in the optimistic land of child health and the netherworld of crime and punishment. Most doctors avoid legal entanglements at any cost. Their status and credibility, usually unchallenged, are impugned in lawsuits as a matter of course. The work child abuse pediatricians do is heartbreaking and often contested. Like anyone else, they can't always be right, and the stakes are impossibly high.

Still, by 2020, there were 350 credentialed specialists. More than twenty institutions, among them the most respected pediatrics programs in the world, offered three-year fellowships in child abuse pediatrics. Major medical centers without fellowship programs hired experts, including the Mayo Clinic, I learned while preparing to give a talk there some years ago. Today, five child abuse experts work at Mayo.

By contrast, there's not a single trained forensic geriatrician in the country, or any fellowship program to train them. The people I've written about, and a handful of others, have cobbled together the skills to step into that breach, but it's all ad hoc. Most medical centers don't have any expert on staff, and even when they do, their colleagues often don't consult them. Sometimes their colleagues don't even know that they're there to consult.

Ignorance compounds ignorance. There are already too few geriatricians, even fewer researchers with geriatrics expertise, and far fewer still researchers with dual expertise in geriatrics and forensics. This gap reflects norms within medicine: geriatrics is a low-paid, low-status subspecialty of family medicine and internal medicine. Forensic geriatrics, to the extent it exists, is a dark, even lower-status corner of a low-status subspecialty. This deficit of researchers leads to less inquiry, less knowledge, and more incorrect assumptions about injuries in older people.

The main reason for this deficit in people, brainpower, and knowledge is that the country's major research funders have contributed so little. Congress has appropriated only meager sums, and the big federal funders—like the National Institutes of Health (NIH) and the Centers for Disease Control and Prevention (CDC)—despite some recent improvement, historically have had other priorities. Private funders have contributed little. And advocates haven't exerted effective pressure to expand funding or change the priorities for the money that exists.

When it comes to research, the way institutions show they care is with money. Without money, it's hard to draw talent to a new field, and grueling eat-what-you-kill university rules mean that researchers often have to raise grant money to pay their own salaries and keep their jobs. Hustle that could go to data collection or project design goes to just staying afloat. Universities also take big cuts of what researchers bring in—often 50 percent or more for so-called indirect costs made up of overhead and the like. Keeping enough grant dollars flowing to sustain a research career is hard even in a field flush with cash like heart disease. Where money's scarce, it's even harder. Given those structural disadvantages, the modest gains in aging and elder justice research we've seen in recent years should be celebrated. But given decades-long deficits, there's a long way to go.

The most damaging and shameful consequence of this knowledge deficit is that we have virtually no evidence-based prevention tools to give millions of Americans desperately trying to ward off trouble for themselves and their older loved ones. That knowledge chasm will persist and take its largely invisible toll until we muster the political will and public voice to demand better.

Still, there are glimmers of hope. Several medical centers are participating in a "collaboratory" to improve how ERs respond to suspicious elder cases. And two hospital-based elder forensic teams are doing evaluations, documentation, and supporting patients in such cases 24/7—one team formed in 2016 by ER doctor Tony Rosen in NYC and the other, five years later, by his mentee, geriatrician Elizabeth Bloeman, at the University of Colorado Medical School.

In Weill Cornell's busy Manhattan ER, more and more colleagues are calling to ask Tony if he has a minute to discuss a case. They've begun seeing leafy sea dragons.

DEATH, THE REVELATOR

Postmortem inquiry has been used for centuries to reveal secrets about injury and disease. The seatbelt parable had taught me that the dead have much to teach the living if only the living ask. Medical examiners' questions about why people who wore shoulder belts died less often in car crashes than those who wore just lap belts led to changes in manufacturing practices and laws, shifting norms in ways that prevented millions of injuries and deaths. Could related analyses push norms to improve aging?

The medical examiner's main tool is the autopsy, a word from the Greek for "to see for oneself." An instrument of scientific revelation since ancient times, today, autopsies and death investigations fall into two broad categories: medical and legal. Despite what TV shows suggest, we err a lot in declaring causes of death. Autopsies, when we do them, unveil major misdiagnoses in 40 percent of cases—a rate unchanged for eighty years, despite our more sophisticated diagnostic methods. In one-third of misdiagnosed cases, the underlying condition would have been treatable if caught sooner. Death certificates are even less accurate, even though we use their data for a broad range of health and policy decisions. Studies show that more than half contained errors.

In contrast to *medical* autopsies, *legal* autopsies are done as part of an inquest into the cause of an unexplained or suspicious death. In that context, "autopsy" refers to both external and internal examination of the body, often accompanied by analysis of tissue and fluids, toxicology screens, context, and visits to "the scene."

When it came to car safety and accidents, a few individuals asking questions led to organized teams asking questions more methodically: "Why did this happen? Did something go wrong? How can we do better?" Car makers, medical examiners, and researchers began meeting regularly, calling themselves "fatality review teams." The model spread. Similar teams began analyzing child abuse and neglect deaths in the 1970s, and domestic violence deaths in the 1980s. The teams asked if "systemic weaknesses" had contributed to a preventable death, and, if so, they proposed policy fixes to address them.

Most people die in old age, so it makes no sense to investigate all or even most deaths. But some *do* warrant scrutiny. Ricker Hamilton saw many cases involving troubling deaths and was deeply frustrated by how officialdom responded, or more often didn't respond. For instance, in one case a brother kept his sister who had developmental disabilities confined to a squalid room for decades. She was found, at age seventy-eight, weighing fifty-four pounds and could only say twelve words. The three she used most often were "I hate you."

The prosecutor declined the case, saying that the brother had done the best he could. That rationale vexed Ricker. "They wouldn't say that if the victim was a child," he fumed. When older people died under suspicious circumstances, especially when they were incapacitated, the attitude Ricker often encountered was "Old people die. The dead are dead." When a human being dies under atrocious or questionable circumstances, regardless of age, shouldn't society respond in some systemic way, or at least ask questions?

When Ricker heard in 2003 that DOJ would provide seed grants for elder fatality review teams, he applied and received $5,000 to launch the Maine Elder Death Analysis and Review Team (MEDART). It was housed in Maine's AG's office.

Few APS workers have access to a state's chief medical examiner, but MEDART put Ricker at the same table as Maine's, on a regular basis. Before MEDART, the medical examiner's office never called him. Then, Ricker said, "They'll call and say, 'Ricker, have you heard of Sally Jones? She's on my table. I have my suspicions and wanted to check if she's someone known to you.'"

The team helped people connect the dots in troubling cases. In many instances, it also recommended changes, like after a nursing home resident asphyxiated when he became wedged between a bed rail and a poorly fitting air mattress overlay. MEDART recommended using emergency sensors and having the AG release a consumer bulletin. As with car fatalities, close observation followed by dry bureaucratic policy changes are the incremental steps that, over many years, can save countless lives.

A WAY TO IMPROVE NURSING HOMES?

Mark Malcolm, chief coroner in Pulaski County, Arkansas, had a theory that nursing homes would provide better care if they knew someone was looking. He wanted to use fatality reviews to prove it. In the 1990s, Mark started getting calls from family members claiming nursing homes had neglected an older relative to death. After Mark did an investigation along with Arkansas's long-term care and attorney general's offices, they persuaded courts to let them exhume and autopsy seven bodies. Each one showed some anomaly the nursing homes hadn't reported. Seizing the moment, Mark and his allies sketched out a new law requiring nursing homes to report, and county coroners to investigate, *every* nursing home death regardless of its cause, including any resident who died within five days of discharge.

"If the nursing home industry knew what a coroner's investigation was when we asked for that law, it would have been a whole lot more difficult," Mark said. But "no lobbyist from the industry showed up, no owner showed up. . . . We slid in there, got it done, and got out."

By the time I met Mark, he had a few years of investigations and learning under his belt. When they did toxicology screens that showed "drugs in our person that aren't prescribed to them, then we see if it's prescribed to the person in the other bed," Mark's deputy said. "That happened five or six times right away. As soon as we started bringing it to people's attention, boy, we cleared that drug problem up pretty quick." Simple toxicology screens that shed light on drug errors appeared to reduce them.

But, as I would learn with the Elder Justice Act, a law that creates new programs without new money to implement them can only do so much. Mark gave 96 percent of homes clean bills of health. He knew he missed cases. Research consistently has shown serious problems in about a quarter of nursing homes. But he lacked adequate tools and resources for the job. He had no specialized toxicology screen for drugs more likely to kill elders and, as we've seen, no research on forensic markers to inform which fractures and pressure sores were suspicious. Arkansas then had just three medical examiners for the whole state, so Mark only dared refer the worst three to five cases a year for autopsies, out of about 500 his office investigated annually. "If I asked for too many autopsies," Mark joked, "I might suddenly find myself in line for one too."

In fact, no one was looking in most of Arkansas's sixty-nine other counties. Many of Mark's fellow coroners ignored the law—it added work without adding resources. And unlike Mark, who was appointed, the rest of the state's coroners had to stand for election. Some seemed reluctant to do vigorous investigations that exposed questionable conduct, potentially antagonizing powerful constituents—like funeral homes, nursing homes, and ambulance services. Other coroners owned or were employed by the institutions they were supposed to investigate. These conflicts have led reformers to urge that all coroners and medical examiners be appointed.

Given the absence of reliable methods to improve nursing homes, Mark's claim that his death investigation law made Pulaski County "the safest place in America to be in a nursing home" was intriguing. While at DOJ, I funded research to analyze his claims, but the numbers were too small to draw statistically valid conclusions. Congressional investigators who studied the Arkansas law found it resulted in Mark's office identifying avoidable deaths that would otherwise have remained hidden.

I also funded focus groups with coroners and medical examiners from around the country to learn more about their approach to unexplained elder deaths. The researcher, Catherine Hawes, who'd devoted her career to improving long-term care, called me in tears. One participant told her, "I don't have much interest in investigating the death of an 85-year-old woman. Most cases are quasi-neglect." Another said a "mandate to review all nursing home deaths would destroy the system."[5]

Yet, somehow, for a while, the Pulaski County coroners handled 500 additional cases a year, investigating all nursing home deaths quickly, without extra pay. We take "our older generation and just shove them away there and say, . . . 'Just get old quietly and pass on,'" said one of Mark Malcolm's colleagues. "We're going to treat you with the same respect that we treat anybody else. And you're going to get every investigation of your death that you deserve."[6]

Chapter 10
PARENTS' KEEPERS?

this is not somewhere else but here,
our country moving closer to its own truth and dread,
its own ways of making people disappear.

—ADRIENNE RICH, "What Kind of Times Are These"

Most of Page Ulrey's cases are set in motion by a call from a family member and raise hard questions about what adult children owe their parents. That hot-pink card reading "HELP ME! I am overwhelmed" that Laura Mosqueda's patient's daughter slipped her speaks for many people these days. Criminal laws draw lines to define the conduct societies deem intolerable. Page's job was to enforce those laws. In families, the rules are different. Most people aspire to familial conduct that's better than intolerable, but how they define it varies. Page's work spans this unsettled terrain, so it's not surprising that her cases raise unsettling questions. And although the scenarios she sees are extreme, they're also cautionary tales for the rest of us with, broadly speaking, three lessons: Older people, including people with cognitive impairment, need purposeful activity in their lives. Isolation can be perilous. And families and caregivers need more accessible guidance and help.

When Moe Gorelick was ninety-six, his caregiver's daughter, Elle, persuaded him to invest in her business. Between May 2018 and May 2019, he gave Elle $900,000. Moe's parents had fled Russia and he had overcome polio to run a successful plumbing supply company with his brother. Investing in Elle's business was an engaging project and gave him a lift. She was encouraging and got him a phone, an iPad, and a laptop.

Moe's daughter who lived close by knew that her father's memory was faltering and he had trouble paying the bills. She suspected that Elle was exploiting him, but also saw that Elle made him happy. She saw her role as supporting her father. She was scared to confront him and initially didn't confide her concerns to her brother, Kenny.

When Kenny found out, he took a different approach. He took control of Moe's finances and pleaded with him to stop giving Elle money. He explained that Elle wasn't investing his money in her business but instead spending it on herself, buying a Range Rover, clothes, cosmetic procedures, and more. Moe seemed to absorb what Kenny said, but only briefly.

Elle, for her part, told Moe that his children were the enemies of his independence. "Elle promised their dad everything. All they could offer him was safety," said Page. "If it was really a scam, then he was no longer the savvy businessman he was invested in being." Rekindling that sense of purpose, Page said, had drawn him into Elle's scheme in the first place.

After Kenny took control of his dad's money, Elle's mother, who'd been Moe's trusted caregiver for decades, took Moe, almost ninety-eight, to an attorney she knew and had him revoke Kenny as POA and sign a new one with a broad gifting clause that named Elle's mother to be his financial decision-maker. When Page's office brought charges and the case went to trial, the attorney testified that she believed that Moe had capacity because he was awake, alert, cheerful, smiled, could name his children, and nodded or said "uh-huh" to the provisions they discussed. The attorney did not contact Moe's children or his longtime attorney. For Kenny, the POA transfer was the last straw.

Kenny had stopped the financial bleeding. But after Moe lost Elle, he resented Kenny; there was no longer a close feeling between them. Moe died a few months later. After charges were filed against Elle, the case attracted brief attention, likely because Kenny is the saxophonist Kenny G. But such cases are now so commonplace, even that attention was fleeting.

At trial, Elle cast herself as Moe's main protector. The jurors convicted her of two counts of theft from a vulnerable adult and two counts of securities fraud. At sentencing, Kenny said that she "took away our relationship with our dad" and hastened Moe's death. Elle said, "I never thought of harming Moe. He made me smile and taught me a lot." She said she considered herself fortunate to have known him and pleaded with the court not to separate her from her five-year-old daughter. Page argued that Elle's actions involved not just money but had ruptured the relationships between Moe and his children, an even greater loss. She also noted that Elle had had other convictions on related charges. The judge sentenced Elle to twenty-six months with part of the term to be served in community custody, on the low end of the guidelines.[1]

Page believes that our culture is a coconspirator in these cases. "It's hard to age with dementia and still feel valued," she said. "Basically, the message is 'If you have this disease, you're worthless.' Scammers tap into that sense of loss, which is one reason it's so common, when we are alone late in life." Her concern had become personal. Page's father had died recently and her mother lived across the country—alone. Page called her mom twice a day. "*She's* doing great," said Page. "But *I* worry." Given the cases she sees daily, how could she not?

In considering what offspring owe their parents, Moe's children's approaches are both valid. Such scams are often hard and painful to interrupt. The lack of protective systems and the dearth of data about effective prevention methods make it all infinitely harder on families. Page's point about the lack of purpose deserves more attention as we consider how to defend against scams that have both a financial and a psychic component. People need activity that has meaning for them. Cultivating that is crucial, maybe even the best defense.

Page's neglect cases raise a related set of hard questions about what adult children owe their parents and when their omissions cross a legal line. "Moe at least had his kids calling and stopping by," Page said. "He had resources, food, and some enjoyment in life. People with severe dementia are more isolated and unprotected than anyone else. If they happen to be in a good place, with a good caregiver, they're probably okay. But if they're in a shitty facility or living with a son with a gambling problem, God help them."

Laura Mosqueda and Ricker Hamilton, like Page, saw many troubling neglect cases. But unlike Page, their cases usually stayed shrouded from public view by medical and APS confidentiality rules, leaving them frustrated by how rarely anyone was held accountable, and how few people knew about what could go wrong. Those confidentiality rules mean that policy-makers and the public rarely see the full nature and scope of human suffering that neglect inflicts. We want to think that somehow older people will manage, but some don't, and sometimes terrible wrongs occur, demanding a public reckoning. Relying on prosecutors for society's response means we're targeting our efforts way too late. But Page's cases at least show the extreme outcomes of neglect, individual and societal. Change must happen further upstream, but for now the cases that cross her desk reveal things that are hard to see and hard to ignore once you've seen them.

CRIMES OF OMISSION

Twelve days before the Senate hearing in 2001 where my boss Stuart Schiffer had testified along with Laura and Ricker, Page became Seattle's first elder abuse prosecutor. Her boss, Norm Maleng, a moderate Republican and King County's prosecuting attorney for twenty-eight years, was an innovator. He'd created special units to prosecute sexual assault and domestic violence, and one to help victims. Creating an elder abuse position put Maleng in the vanguard again.

He wanted Page not only to prosecute cases but also to start a community council and work with other agencies involved in elder abuse. Page didn't even know what those agencies were. Paul Greenwood in San Diego, then the country's leading elder abuse prosecutor, had testified at the same hearing as Laura, Ricker, and Stuart. He'd also been the one to urge Maleng to create the elder abuse position. So Page headed to San Diego.

Paul's job had started with a campaign promise. In a politically savvy move, San Diego's public guardian and APS workers had elicited promises from both leading candidates for district attorney that if elected they'd prosecute elder abuse. After the 1996 election, the new district attorney called Paul into his office and told him, "You're in charge of elder abuse." "What's elder abuse?" Paul had asked. "He told me, 'I don't know either, but I want you to find it and prosecute it.'" Paul feared the move was a career killer and vowed to return to "real" crimes as soon as possible.

Prosecutors get most of their cases from law enforcement. By the mid-1990s, many large cities had police officers who specialized in child abuse, domestic violence, and sexual assault investigations, but not for elder abuse. When Paul wasn't getting matters referred, he visited police departments during roll call to say, "I'm open for business. If you see a victim over sixty-five who's physically, financially, or mentally abused, send me the case."

He heard all sorts of reasons why not to bring cases, like "the victim is ninety-four and would make a terrible witness." One officer told him, "If the son's abusing his mother, she's probably as bad as he is; the apple doesn't fall far from the tree." Other victims were scared or ashamed and didn't want to get their children in trouble.

Skeptical, Paul hired a victim advocate to review police reports involving older people and asked her to bring him any report that said "victim declines prosecution." Then Paul called the officers to say, "You wouldn't write that for domestic violence victims. Bring me the case and let *me* decide if she's a terrible witness."

"Ninety-five times out of a hundred, she's very credible," Paul explained. Furthermore, "Just because the victim doesn't want me to prosecute, doesn't mean I won't." Prosecutors, not victims, decide whether to press charges. And prosecutors differ in how much weight they give victims' wishes.

As word of Paul's work spread, cases started pouring in. By the time Page visited him, he'd been at it for five years, and his idea of a "real" case had changed. "It's exciting to walk into an uncharted area," he told her. "Get copies of every police report with an older victim. Do 'roll call' pitches. Get a contact in every precinct." This was a daunting prospect.

San Diego County only had two police agencies. King County, with its many towns and municipalities, had thirty-nine.

As Page reviewed the stacks of police reports involving older victims, she had no clear notion of where to start. It was an inefficient way to spot cases, but patterns emerged. Most cases involved financial exploitation or neglect, often both. There was a financial crimes unit in her office, but none to handle neglect, so she started there. The cases shocked her. Neglect was unlike other crimes and not as rare as she'd supposed.

In March 2002 a matronly woman in her mid-fifties called 911 to report that her mother, Margaret Brown, was vomiting and couldn't get up. The EMTs found a gray-skinned woman in her mid-seventies curled up on the floor, surrounded by mounds of trash, rotting TV dinners, plates of food, and rat droppings. They couldn't clear a path wide enough to wheel in a gurney, so they carried Brown to the ambulance—confused and cadaverous, her hair clumped, her body frozen in a fetal curve from lying so long in one position.

Emergency room nurses are hard to shock, but one described Brown's condition—caked in feces from head to toe—as the worst she'd ever seen. In medical terms, Brown was severely malnourished, dehydrated, hypothermic, unable to swallow, and in acute renal failure. Hospital staff described the daughter as "nonchalant" about her mother's condition. She had only called 911 at the insistence of her niece who'd stopped by to help her pick up Brown. As required by law, the nurses reported the case to APS.

Page joined the detective in executing the search warrant at the now-condemned house. In their white hazmat suits, carrying oxygen tanks and wearing masks, they looked like terrestrial astronauts picking through human debris. In that odd way of memory, what struck Page in retrospect was just how fat and clean the daughter's dogs were, how shiny their coats.

When the APS worker visited Brown in the ICU, she told him she was eating "fine," even though swallowing a single sip of water took five tries and caused her heart rate to plummet. Brown said her daughter had not mistreated her. She insisted that she could care for herself and just had gotten "sloppy" about bathing. The doctor estimated she hadn't bathed for six months to a year.

Brown accepted IV fluids but refused the dialysis and feeding tube she needed to survive. Could she understand that this decision would kill her? To assess her cognitive capacity, the APS worker asked her the questions on the Mini-Mental State Examination.

Laura and many other experts believe that exam, one of several options, sometimes does more harm than good. Although it assesses memory, it fails to pick up loss of judgment or executive function and thus gives testers, untrained in subtle neuropsychological evaluations, false confidence that their patients understand the impact of their actions. Despite the test's problems—including inconsistencies in how it performs among people of color versus white people— many APS workers, physicians, and other professionals regularly still use the Mini-Mental.

In the hospital, Brown knew the day of the week but not where she was. With the slender reed of the Mini-Mental assessment, APS determined she had a "basic understanding of what's going on," was "self-neglecting," closed its case, and referred Brown to a specialized geriatric team to evaluate her mental health. But she was ineligible; the team only offered evaluations for people living at home. This lapse shows the perils of fragmented systems and untrained professionals using flawed instruments to make decisions about patients' capacity. As for Brown, she didn't want to go to a nursing home. She just wanted to go home. Instead, eight days after arriving at the hospital, she died there.

The detective assigned to the case reviewed thousands of pages and interviewed dozens of witnesses. He believed he'd uncovered a financial motive for the neglect—the daughter was about to lose her job and stood to inherit half of her mother's estate, which was valued at $500,000 to a million dollars. The daughter resented her mother's "intentional laziness," he concluded, and felt that her mother used her as a private "catering service." The daughter's lawyer agreed that the mother and daughter's relationship had been fraught, but said Brown had been stubborn, controlling, and unwilling to accept her daughter's help. Brown had put her daughter in an impossible position. He cited old rancor, too. When the daughter was young and became pregnant, her mother made her give up a baby she'd wanted to keep, a baby who would have been her only child.

At that time, scarcely any medical examiner in the country would have ruled Brown's demise a "homicide." A few might have ruled it "undetermined"; most would have ruled it "natural," undermining any prosecution. Richard Harruff, King County's chief medical examiner, held off on ruling anything. As a pathologist and the public official charged with ruling on the cause of unexplained deaths, he wanted to see what the investigation turned up. He sent the detective twenty questions about Brown's condition, home, circumstances of death, and access to care. As a scientist, Richard wanted to bring more objective criteria and structure to analyzing this "new" type of case. As a human being, he brought curiosity and calm to work that immersed him daily in life's impermanence and loss.

Page was grateful for his rigorous interest and thoughtful approach. She asked him to help her start the King County Elder Abuse Council, guessing that local agency heads might take the council more seriously if Richard was involved. She was right. He cosigned her letter inviting them, and two dozen people showed up to meet around the table in the morgue's conference room.

The grisly reports and photographs appearing in Page's inbox were desolate fare, even by prosecutor standards. As she sifted through the unhappy facts of unhappy families, the cases challenged her notions of crime, punishment, and justice. She was a prosecutor whose instrument to respond to all that misery was criminal law. But getting charges to stick proved elusive.

There were patterns in the reasons why Page's cases collapsed. Some faltered under failures by someone in officialdom: people in agencies saw neglect but took no action. "If experts excused the neglect, how could I expect a jury to convict?" Page concluded. Other cases tanked when the caregivers themselves were incapacitated. (Page opened several gruesome neglect cases, only to learn that the adult children responsible had developmental disabilities.)

Then there was the middle-aged woman who, after providing loving, competent care for her parents with dementia, snapped one day and stabbed them both to death with a kitchen knife. When police picked her up wandering the neighborhood spattered in blood, she confessed that she'd ignited a terrorist attack that leveled

Seattle and triggered a global war. Page got involved in that case because it involved older victims with dementia killed by their caregiver. The daughter pleaded not guilty by reason of insanity. Page was taken aback by the outpouring of strangers urging leniency given the vicissitudes of providing such care.

Then came what Page described as "a blip of success in a sea of failure." Mac McKinney was an Air Force veteran and thirty-year Boeing engineer. As his health declined, his son Jack moved in with him, allegedly to provide care. Two daughters lived close by but rarely visited. Jack locked Mac's bedroom door from the outside, to stop his father's wandering, he said.

After a grandfather clock fell on Mac and broke his back, doctors said he needed 24/7 care. Jack thought his father was feigning helplessness, telling him, "Get your fat ass off the floor. I'm not going to break *my* back getting you up." Neighbors heard Mac calling out but did not help. One later told a reporter, "As a neighbor you offer your help, but you keep your distance. You can't force your way in."[2] Mac's daughters kept their distance too, while controlling Mac's money—in excess of $500,000, more than enough to pay for decent care. Although at least two of the siblings bought annuities for themselves, and Jack bought a motorcycle with Mac's money, they canceled the visiting nurses who'd cared for their father.

When one daughter stopped by, not having seen her dad for a while, she called the police to do a "welfare check," because, she said, "we had no idea it had gotten this bad." She then tried to cancel the request, but the police came anyway. Jack, drunk, greeted the EMTs, saying: "He's lying on the floor in his bedroom. He knocked over his piss bucket again. Put your gas masks on and go down there." The EMTs found Mac emaciated, wearing only a T-shirt and a garbage bag for a diaper in the hot room, filth everywhere. A spiral notebook contained Mac's written pleas: "Help, I don't know how the coffee machine works. Help, I haven't seen anybody for days." And this: "Help, help, help. I am alone."

With the specter of homicide charges if his dad had died, Jack quickly pleaded guilty to criminal neglect and unlawful imprisonment. (His sisters weren't charged.) Soon after, his father did die in the place Jack had promised to help him avoid: a nursing home. "I tried and failed," Jack told the court. "Looking back, . . . I would have put him in a nursing home."[3] Terror of nursing homes, and promises to help older relatives avoid them, was a dark current running through Page's cases.

In sentencing Jack to a two-year term, the judge said: "What we have here is a very dysfunctional family. All three siblings in one way or another were saying, 'I am not my father's keeper.' I am not sure if there is a moral distinction between the three of you."[4] There was, however, a legal distinction. Under Washington law, as the "custodial caregiver," Jack had legal responsibility.

The "custodial caregiver" issue was also central when it came to Margaret Brown's daughter. Under Washington law at the time, only custodial caregivers were liable, a vestige of child neglect laws where the person with physical custody of the child was deemed responsible. First, the daughter told detectives that she was her mother's caregiver, that they'd lived together for thirteen years. Her lawyer later "clarified" that she wasn't actually a *custodial* caregiver.

The investigation turned up clogged toilets in Brown's house, dirty, apparently unused showers and sinks. Utility bills showed negligible recent use of heat or water. It seemed peculiar that the well-coiffed, nicely dressed daughter would live in such cold and chaos. The detective learned that she traveled often to events for the Emblem Club, a women's offshoot of the Elks Lodge, but found no other home for her. He believed that the daughter knew how to provide good care when she chose to, citing her pets' "meticulous" grooming and up-to-date shots and vet visits.

Sixteen months into the investigation, medical examiner Richard Harruff ruled Brown's death a homicide. Page charged the daughter with felony manslaughter in the first degree, a domestic violence offense. Both Richard's ruling and Page's charge were firsts in King County. In persuading her bosses to let her charge manslaughter, Page relied heavily on the detective's investigation and his theory that the daughter was an intelligent, functioning woman motivated by anger and financial gain.

Still, the legal twists of neglect caught Page off guard. When a daughter snaps and stabs her parents, the cause and time of death and the wielder of the knife are clear. Neglect is harder to locate in time and space. Instead of a single event, it's comprised of countless omissions over weeks, months, and years, making it hard to pinpoint the ones that caused the harm or death. Naming the culprit is harder, too. Usually there's more than one person with a legal, ethical, or professional duty to act. Neglect invariably results in finger-pointing among family, friends, neighbors, and professionals. It's also complex medically. Which injuries were caused by neglect versus some underlying disease? Whose omissions caused what harm?

With the sweep of human shortcoming and the passage of time that neglect encompasses, motive is hard to pin down. One can imagine ludicrous defense arguments: "Your honor, the defendant's neglect was motivated 20 percent of the time by greed, 20 percent by ignorance, 20 percent by trying to respect her mother's wishes, 20 percent by resentment for past wrongs, and 20 percent by fury at her mother for putting her in this impossible position."

Neither Page nor the detective had ever handled a case with so many inscrutable health records. Brown had had strokes, kidney disease, and a swallowing disorder. She was dehydrated and malnourished, and likely had dementia and delirium. To prove manslaughter, though, Page would have to show that the daughter had "recklessly" caused her mother's demise. Page needed a good medical expert.

In Page's crash course on elder abuse, she'd twice heard Laura speak at conferences. Afterward they had dinner to discuss their mutual interest in and concern about such cases. Now Page tracked Laura down and was thrilled when Laura agreed to review the medical records. But Page's relief was short-lived. Laura agreed with Richard Harruff and the hospital doctor that lack of care had killed Brown, but she had another concern. The records suggested that Brown had refused medical care for fourteen years, Laura said, even while she was still cognitively intact.

Brown's sister had told the judge that she was sorry that Margaret died but that no one could have helped her because she "simply did not allow help." The daughter echoed her aunt. "My true crime was to respect my mother's wishes," she said. "I never would have dreamed of going against those wishes."[5]

But Page saw it differently. "If your mom is lying on the floor, vomiting, and can't eat or drink, and you're there," she said, "you have a duty to get her help, even if she refused medical treatment before."

Brown's son, through his attorney, said that he didn't know his mother was living in squalor. "If there is a lesson to be learned from this case," his attorney said, "it is that the laws and reporting procedures need to ensure that there is sufficient protection for vulnerable adults such as Margaret."[6]

But who would have reported or gotten help? The son lived close by but hadn't seen his mother for a year. Uninterrupted isolation can lead to points of no return.

Then Page's case took another hit. On the eve of trial, the ardent detective on the case was arrested for writing fake prescriptions to get painkillers. He'd had multiple injuries and surgeries, his lawyer said, and became dependent on pills so he could keep working through the pain. The detective's damaged credibility tarnished the evidence he'd gathered. The case had dragged on from 2002 to 2005, an eternity in Page's office. As it crumbled, she did the prosecutor's version of cut and run—she offered the daughter a misdemeanor deal.

Most prosecutors win a lot. They have broad discretion to choose cases, and most pick winners and then trumpet their 90 percent conviction rates as "justice." Page's office was uncommon in that she got no pressure from above for her string of defeats. In fact, her bosses fully supported her bringing hard cases that challenged our norms about aging. But the losses left her dejected. "In the beginning, I didn't know how to parse a viable case," she said. "I'd look at these horrible pictures, hear there was a caregiver who had let that happen, and think 'of course I'll file.'"

The losses took their toll. Page felt she'd failed her superiors, who'd trusted her to build a new unit; failed the detectives who worked with her; failed the medical examiner who helped her launch the Elder Abuse Council and risked ruling Margaret Brown's death a homicide. Worst of all, she felt like she'd failed the victims, living and dead.

In the end, the detective lost his job after fourteen years on the police force and was sentenced to a four-year term. The daughter he'd investigated received a two-month deferred sentence after pleading guilty to a misdemeanor for third-degree abandonment. A decade later, she became president of Washington state's Emblem Club. In that role, she chose two signature songs: "The Sound of Silence" and "Stand by Me."

Earplugs

Seven years after Margaret Brown's demise when Page charged another family member for a neglect death, there were modest signs of change. In June 2009, Christopher Wise called 911 at 12:23 a.m. to report that his mother, Ruby, was dead. After visits from EMTs and patrol officers, Detective Thien Do from Major Crimes arrived at 4:40 a.m. He interviewed the son and took photographs, one of which showed two orange earplugs beside a remote control. But even after looking through his manual, he wasn't sure what law applied.

A little after noon, Detective Do was surprised to see Richard Harruff himself, and not a more junior death investigator, arrive at the Wise home. Richard later told me that he wanted to do the scene investigation himself. "If we pass these cases off as 'natural,'" he said, "the coroner or medical examiner doesn't have to assert jurisdiction. It's an easy cop out, but that's just being lazy." After having ruled Margaret Brown's death a "homicide," Richard had reconsidered his approach. "If you call it 'homicide,' you draw argument and spend your time defending yourself," he explained. "If you call it 'undetermined,' you engage the jury. Then the jury has to answer, 'Is this homicide? Is this an acceptable way to treat your mother?'" Ruby Wise's death was if anything more dreadful than Margaret Brown's. Though she weighed seventy pounds and had terrible pressure sores, Richard still ruled it "undetermined."

Ruby had rented a lakeside cabin outside Seattle that she shared with her son, Chris. She had moved to Washington from Florida, where she had a daughter from whom she was estranged. When Chris stopped working as a computer programmer in 2002, Ruby's $2,000 monthly income sustained them both. He said he and his mother had agreed that she'd support him and, in exchange, he'd care for her. As Ruby's dementia and physical condition worsened, she relied on Chris for everything. Emails showed that he found caring for her strenuous and considered getting more help. "I guess I could use a 'home nurse,'" he wrote to one friend; "any connections?" But he never followed up.

Ruby's journals from that time reflect that she was in pain. So did the cries neighbors heard coming from the house for weeks. When they raised concerns with Chris, he said his mother had dementia and was "noisy" sometimes and he was looking into getting a nurse. So the neighbors closed their windows and moved farther into the interior rooms of their homes to muffle her cries. Chris put in earplugs.

At trial, Chris testified that he'd promised his father to care for his mom and that she didn't want to go to a doctor or a nursing home. He said, "I follow[ed] my mom's instructions."

But while she could still write, Ruby's journal entries belied his claims:

> "I need a new prescription. Hopefully soon . . ."

> "Out of heart and thyroid meds. Doctors need to get busy to help me. I have a good amount of pain I don't understand."

> "My feet hurt so bad and no one is listening."[7]

While Ruby still controlled her own life, unlike Margaret Brown, she visited her doctors regularly. She'd given Chris a list of her physicians, but once he took over her care, he ignored reminders of overdue appointments, let her prescriptions lapse, didn't get her the new glasses she needed to see, and ignored her pleas for help.

Just simple things might have restored to Ruby some function and dignity. With glasses she could have read. A trip to the doctor and the right meds might have meant less agitation and pain. But in the hands of a gatekeeper like Chris, Ruby was imprisoned in her incapacity.

In court, Chris cast himself as a martyr who didn't deserve "legal damnation." "I offered everything, and she made her choices," he testified, arguing his mother died "swaddled in love." Society was to blame, he said, for not creating standards or norms for how he should provide care.[8]

There is no excuse for Ruby dying as she did, but I wondered whether things might have been different if we had clearer standards about what's expected of caregivers. If we had better systems of caregiver support. If we had norms that encouraged caregivers to ask for help and encouraged other people to look in on them to offer it. Many caregivers don't have the wherewithal to say, "HELP ME! I am overwhelmed."

At trial, Page and her co-counsel, Patrick Hinds, argued that every morning brought a new day when Chris could have helped or sought help for his mother but decided not to—that he had recklessly caused his mother's death.

When the bailiff summoned Page to the courtroom for the Wise verdict, the quarterly meeting of the Elder Abuse Council was just ending. Page didn't have time to drop Ellie, the victim support dog, back at the office, so headed to court with Ellie in tow, grateful for her calming presence. Wise was the first case of its type to go to trial in King County. The harrowing facts and her track record in neglect cases had Page on edge.

The jurors acquitted Chris Wise of the most serious second-degree murder and first-degree manslaughter charges, finding that the prosecutors hadn't proven "recklessness." But they convicted him of second-degree manslaughter, given its lower proof bar. Afterward, the jurors, defense counsel, detective, and Page talked for more than an hour. The jurors were outraged by Ruby's fate, but because Chris had fed her bits of banana and tried, if ineffectively, to tend her wounds, they weren't convinced that he'd recklessly caused her death.

The dark evidence left the jurors rattled, so much so they kept getting together for months after the trial. And on that day, as they talked, some standing, some sitting on the wood benches in the hall outside the courtroom, one or other of the jurors patted Ellie's belly or scratched behind her ears the whole time.

At sentencing, a few months later, Chris Wise told the court, "My love and devotion might be antiquated." But the judge, who'd described the photographs of Ruby's body as the worst she'd ever seen, told Chris, "I am not convinced your mother chose to die this way," and gave him a twenty-seven-month prison term, plus another year because of Ruby's vulnerability.[9] Page was disappointed that the jury hadn't convicted Chris on the higher counts. But Richard

Harruff thought that just getting the jury to grapple with the issue in a public forum was a victory.

"One case can have a ripple effect," Richard told me. "These elder cases are an emerging problem, and not just for us and prosecutors. It's a pervasive systemic problem. But right now, most cases aren't recognized. Courts might not be the right venue to work out these issues, but other systems aren't getting involved." Richard likened presenting cases to juries in open court to the kind of public debate that occurred in the Roman Forum. "For now," he continued, "there's a benefit to getting cases exposed in a venue where society gets to look at them and ask, 'Is that right or not?' We need to determine what's normal, what's acceptable, and what's expected by society."

Drawing New Lines

One of the Chris Wise jurors had told Page she didn't think the law fit the crime very well. Page agreed. She believed the burden of proof should be lowered from "recklessness" to "criminal negligence," to make it easier to hold caregivers accountable for egregious neglect. Other agencies supported the idea, but, as the only prosecutor then bringing elder neglect cases in King County, Page needed to instigate the effort. In 2014 she reached out to AARP, the state's most powerful legislative advocate on aging issues. Ingrid McDonald, AARP's advocacy director at the time, helped Page rally support from allies and get a proposal on the legislative calendar. Page described the Wise case in her testimony before Washington's state legislature, which wound up revising the intent requirement in neglect cases from "recklessness" to "criminal negligence" in 2017. (Page and Ingrid's advocacy partnership also evolved into another one: in 2018, they got married.)

As was its protocol, the Department of Corrections set about notifying Chris Wise's next of kin just before he was released from prison. In so doing, it tracked down what hadn't been previously: the address of his estranged sister in Florida. "She found out that her mom was dead and that Chris was getting out of prison for neglecting her to death when she got that notice," said Page. Ruby's daughter called Page distraught and sobbing. Such surviving family members often feel that prosecutors connect them to the person they've lost. In one of their many calls, Ruby's daughter asked Page if there was anything that had belonged to her mother that she could have. There was nothing left of Ruby's modest estate but Ruby's journals, which were introduced at trial and were still sitting in a courthouse evidence room. Page petitioned the court for permission to give the journals to Ruby's daughter. Chris opposed the petition, but the court allowed the request.

As I thought about Ruby's daughter, I thought about all the ways people lose track of one another, even when there's love. We get busy. We're far away. We let time pass and feel guilty or stuck. Maybe we're hurt or angry. Whatever the reasons, if we're not in touch with an older relative, we want to believe that whoever's with them will do right by them and, if not, that warning bells will sound and someone will respond. We want to believe that people won't die like Ruby Wise, Margaret Brown, and Mac McKinney did. But they do.

The individual neglect is enabled by our broader social failures. A long-term care system people fear. Not enough support for care-givers. So many people so alone. Neglect implicates bystanders, too. Ruby Wise, Margaret Brown, and Mac McKinney all had neighbors. One had said, "You keep your distance." Another closed windows. Was Page right when she said they'd have reacted differently had the wailing come from a child—or even a dog?

Millions of concerned family, friends, and neighbors don't know where to go for guidance, even when they're worried and do want to help. Giving them a helpline was the brainchild of Risa Breckman, founding executive director of the New York City Elder Abuse Center. "You're their lifeline. We're your helpline" is the motto of the Elder Abuse Helpline for Concerned Persons.[10] "Often family, friends, and neighbors intervene on behalf of the older person or want to do so," said Risa. "These millions of 'concerned persons' need emotional and practical support." A specialized helpline like Risa's is very useful, but the exception. Conversely, anyone can call the Eldercare

Locator. And most communities have an Area Agency on Aging, APS, caregiver, or local aging groups to contact for guidance or help. Most useful of all is to start planning further upstream.

A DISAPPEARANCE

In early 2022, no one had seen the woman since 2019. Her husband had died a few years back, but her adult son lived with her. There were supposedly a lot of guns in the house.

When fellow parishioners missed her at church where she'd been active, they tried to call her. So did friends and neighbors. The son always allegedly had some excuse—she was on a trip, sick, asleep, shopping, visiting relatives, busy. Or he just didn't answer the phone or the door. They called APS, which went out many times but got no better answers and had no authority to do more. APS referred the matter to law enforcement, as the friends and neighbors had done, too. The police did numerous "welfare checks" but never saw the woman, either. And everyone was nervous to push too hard, given the guns.

When COVID hit in 2020, the mother was one of countless people who disappeared into their homes. Attention to police violence and a new state law making police liable if they lacked cause for forcibly entering a home during a welfare check made them unwilling to do more than knock.

In late 2021, APS, at wit's end, brought the case to the King County elder abuse multidisciplinary team (MDT). Page talked with Todd Salter, an enterprising agent for the US Postal Service with whom she'd worked on many cases. Salter, less reticent than the local police, assembled a team that included, in addition to Page and another prosecutor, federal postal and Social Security Administration agents, a police drone operator, local detectives, and reputedly the "best cadaver dog on the west coast." The mother and son lived on a compound with multiple buildings. Salter and his team didn't know what to expect.

After several planning meetings, the team of more than twenty met early on the appointed morning at a parking lot close to the house. Those slated to enter the home put on Tyvek suits, hoods, gloves, and masks. An advance guard, wearing bulletproof vests, went to the front, then the back door, knocked loudly, and told the son through a bullhorn to come out with his hands up. Getting no response, they broke down the back door. They found extreme hoarding, boxes and trash piled high everywhere, and the son lying in a bedroom in the back of the house with a sheet over him, alive but unresponsive. A dose of Narcan revived him and he was taken to the hospital.

They didn't need the cadaver dog or the drones. The mother's body was lying faceup on the bathroom floor, a blanket draped over her mummified remains. Her organs were dust, the autopsy showed, and there was no sign of trauma or pressure sores, although it was hard to know. She'd been dead at least a year. Where she lay on the floor, her hair had been neatly combed and fanned out around her head.[11]

When Page got home, she showered and then headed to the garden before dark fell. She layered straw onto the vegetable beds on the sunny side of the yard and then moved to the shade garden to prune the dogwoods and cut back the ferns. Page still hadn't eaten long after nightfall. Despite the hazmat gear, the showers, and the clean clothes, "the smell still seeped through."

Soon after the search warrant and the overdose, the son was back in the house. He will possibly face theft charges for allegedly claiming his mother's social security and pension payments long after she was dead.

This time, neighbors, friends, and APS tried to get help, but for naught. People are disappearing into homes and facilities with hardly a trace. We are losing track of one another.

These extreme outcomes could be avoided. We need places older people, caregivers, and those worried about them can go for help. Staying connected doesn't just improve well-being. It saves lives. Prevention is the cure.

Chapter 11

HARM AND HEALING

Victims are the members of society whose
problems represent the memory of suffering, rage,
and pain in a world that longs to forget.

—Bessel van der Kolk, *Traumatic Stress*

Two six-letter words—*trauma* and *victim*—pervade our culture these days along with debates about what they mean, who gets to define and claim them, and how to address them. Some people who've had terrible experiences don't feel that the words apply to them. And not every harm is trauma or every person harmed a victim. Yet, we use *trauma* and *victim* as a broader language to describe sufferers, suffering, and the odyssey to relieve it.

The ways that trauma and victimhood intersect with late life is called an *emerging topic*, the polite term for an issue that's been ignored. What we're learning about addressing that emerging topic holds hints not just for professionals but also for families trying to address the practical and emotional aspects of suffering in old age, of victimization, and of trauma, whether caused by recent events or by the returning ghosts of long-ago harm.

"Victim services" are a relatively new invention. "For centuries, criminal trials were, like civil ones, contests between individual parties: Victim v. Defendant," wrote historian Jill Lepore. Then things changed. "By the early modern era, the state had become the prosecuting party in criminal trials . . . State v. Defendant."[1] The criminal legal system was focused on uncovering the guilt or innocence of the defendant. That was justice.

For a long time, no parallel system existed for victims. The harm they endured was collateral damage. That began to change as medicine recognized trauma and its impact. Sigmund Freud and his successors believed that great fear could induce "psychic trauma." The plight of Vietnam veterans gave the condition a name and a psychiatric diagnosis: post-traumatic stress disorder, or PTSD. Evidence mounted of its sprawling harms, including that childhood trauma leads to a lifetime of worse physical and mental health. "After trauma the world is experienced with a different nervous system," wrote Bessel van der Kolk in *The Body Keeps the Score*. It "can result in a whole range of physical symptoms. . . . This explains why it is critical for trauma treatment to engage the entire organism, body, mind, and brain."[2] Trauma can even influence our genes and be passed from one generation to the next.

Along with the growing recognition of trauma's harms, two movements changed how we see and treat victims of crime, "a marriage of feminism and conservatism," in Jill Lepore's words. The criminal system, for all its claims of impartiality, for centuries rarely pursued some types of cases, like violence against women. As the women's movement gained traction, advocates argued that domestic violence and sexual assault weren't just private misfortunes but also crimes, and that a civil society should both prosecute perpetrators *and* help victims. To that end, in the 1960s and 1970s, women's advocates started rape crisis centers, women's shelters, support groups, and hotlines.

Around the same time, the attorney-activists at the Heritage Foundation launched a crime victim rights movement as part of 1960s and 1970s "law and order" campaigns, with support from Presidents Richard Nixon and Ronald Reagan. They framed the problem as one of defendants getting "too much due process" while victims got none. Like women's advocates, they too sought more help for victims and survivors whose lives had been upended.

They also had a more controversial demand: to give victims a greater role in adjudicating crime. That may sound straightforward, but stirring victim-impact statements could sway jurors toward convicting innocent people and imposing unjust sentences. Finding ways to honor victims' needs and rights without subverting justice for the accused raises profound questions that society has yet to resolve, including in the elder justice field.

LAWS
Victims of Crime Act

As advocates and researchers made trauma's damage harder to ignore, and victims gained social status and political clout, politicians took note. Nowhere was this more evident than in the passage of the 1984 Victims of Crime Act (VOCA), which created the Crime Victims Fund, paid for and continuously replenished by fines paid by defendants in federal cases. Between 2010 and 2020 alone, the Crime Victim Fund took in about $24 billion to fund assistance for victims, paying their medical bills and defraying their economic losses. The fund also pays people to help victims navigate the legal system and provides them with counseling, support groups, and emergency housing.

Most of VOCA's billions have been apportioned to states in large block grants, distributed by state administrators. Who got money often depended on who doled it out and who was asking. For a long time, one thing stayed consistent: VOCA funds rarely went to help older victims.

Violence Against Women Act

Enactment of the Violence Against Women Act (VAWA) ten years later, the result of decades of work by women's advocates, funded new responses to domestic violence, sexual assault, stalking, and dating violence. Reflecting its origins in the Crime Bill, VAWA also placed heavy reliance on arrest and prosecution of offenders and on enacting more mandatory arrest and prosecution laws. Much of VAWA's more than $500 million a year went to hire and train police and prosecutors.

When VAWA first passed in 1994, it included no funds for elder abuse. Its 2002 reauthorization included modest funds, but solely to train law enforcement and prosecutors about the problem. Four years later, the law allotted $4.2 million (and in 2017, increased to $5 million) a year that could be spent on multidisciplinary "coordinated community response" teams. In that way, one of VAWA's smallest programs, managed by DOJ's Janice Green since its inception, became the biggest elder abuse training program in the country. This also meant that VAWA's underlying principles, including its early heavy reliance on criminal responses, imprinted themselves on the elder justice field.

People in the nonprofit and university worlds go through contortions to find funds, often shaping their work to fit the funding source and to appeal to the predilections of the funders. This happens all the time, but it's especially pronounced in a cash-starved field like elder justice. This magnified the impact of VOCA and VAWA on the field.

Although victim services and adult protective services sound similar, they have distinct philosophies, owe their existence to different laws, and have roots burrowing back centuries to very different legal canons. APS's roots derive from the *parens patriae doctrine*—the state's power and duty to protect citizens who are unable to protect themselves. Victim services' roots, by contrast, originate in the state's *police power* to enforce laws and punish wrongdoers for the sake of social order. And victim services often are provided by law enforcement and prosecution entities. Understanding these divergent origins helped me understand the differing approaches and tenets of APS and victim services.

This chapter focuses on the latter, older victim services that went from nonexistent to cut-and-pastes from other fields, to slowly being modified for their intended beneficiaries, as people came to recognize that aging often changes what people want and need. We know that just importing other fields' philosophies and approaches doesn't work, but we're still in the early stages of figuring out what does. With no guidebook and with mostly anecdotal evidence about what works, people have innovated based on what they've learned and the resources they have. What follows is a mosaic of vignettes with examples of efforts to address the unmet needs, including *first*, adapting existing services; *second,* issues of trauma in aging; *third,* the role of identity; and *fourth,* the impact of words and stories.

ADAPTING SERVICES

Outreach

Ricker Hamilton spearheaded an early effort starting in the 1990s to ask older victims what they believed would help them. "I was constantly frustrated because there was no place for our domestic violence victims to get services," he said. "I couldn't even get the local domestic violence agency to help older women who'd endured forty years of spousal abuse. Often even their kids had tried but given up on them and moved away. So I started asking around." On the receiving end, this might have seemed more like "complaining around."

The local domestic violence agency's executive director got wind of Ricker's grievance and sent a board member to have lunch with him. "Next thing I know, I'm on the board," Ricker said, "and Family Crisis Services is the only domestic violence agency in Maine with a staff person dedicated to older victims."

Family Crisis Services also joined the elder abuse coalition Ricker then led. Older people weren't contacting those victim programs, so the coalition got a VAWA grant to find out why not. They surveyed 100 older women who talked about lives in flux—jobs, retirements, illnesses, caregiving, death, and financial hardship. But they avoided darker subjects about family violence. "What happens at home stays at home," said one. So, the interviewers changed tactics, circling their subject, asking, "What does safety mean to you?" For one older woman it meant keeping a mattress and food in the attic where she fled for days at a time to escape her husband's violent rages. For another it meant that the police would do more than just tell her husband to "walk around the block to cool off" after he beat her. One woman's mother had told her, "You made your bed, now sleep in it." And she had, for decades.

Some victim service providers started with groups that offered practical tips—about fall prevention and housing options, for example, or what to do when adult kids wanted to move back home. Once they built familiarity and trust, some older people raised darker concerns, too.

Parents' Groups

The Milwaukee Women's Center was one of the first entities to provide services designed for older victims, starting in 1991. The staff soon learned that people mistreated by their adult offspring didn't want to be lumped together in support groups with those abused by spouses. They wanted their own group. Such cases invariably involved all sorts of conflict. "Good siblings" got mad at their parents for not cutting off abusive kin, but many parents didn't want to abandon offspring in trouble and often felt that they'd caused their children's problems. Engulfed by heartbreak and regret, they resisted calls to press charges or evict, not wanting to add legal or housing trouble to their children's litany of problems.

Those parents often found in one another the most helpful support. They didn't sugarcoat things with one another, but their common cause left them feeling less alone. "Edna" and "Eula" were mothers who forged a friendship over drug-addicted sons who beat them up and took their money. Both struggled to create boundaries. Both kicked their sons out of the house only to let them back in, starting the cycle anew. "Parental guilt is the biggest barrier to getting safe," they agreed. As another woman put it, "I can divorce my husband but not my child."[3]

Shelter

Emergency housing, a place to go when home isn't safe, is another staple of victim services that needed adapting. The occasional elders who landed in shelters had mixed reactions to the hubbub of younger women and children in crisis and transition. Some liked the activity, but for others the racket and requests to babysit, cook, or sew could be daunting amid their own crises. "You take them out of a hell they know and put them in a new one" was how Ricker put it. "We tried to make things fit that didn't." Another issue was that few shelters, or transitional housing programs (for longer stays while people got back on their feet), could accommodate victims with disabilities. They didn't have ramps for wheelchairs or grab bars in showers, much less staff who knew how to help clients with dementia and a purse full of meds. Shelters that served older men—an estimated third of elder abuse victims—were almost nonexistent.

When Ricker had clients who were incapacitated and had nowhere to go, he'd plead with a local hospital or nursing home to do short-term "social admit." The Hebrew Home's Weinberg Center in Riverdale, New York, built a program around providing victim services inside its nursing home for about a dozen elder abuse victims a year too sick for other options. There's no designated wing; victims are placed in the facility depending on their needs. Other facilities around the country have adapted the model in what's called the Spring Alliance. Whatever the model, one issue remains consistent. Many older people are reluctant to use emergency housing because they don't want to leave their homes or communities, even when they're unsafe there.

Aging Services

Victim advocates understand trauma. The aging network and APS understand aging. Older people who've been harmed need both kinds of expertise. Too often expertise is siloed. Coordination multiplies the benefit. In Seattle, for example, Page and colleagues got one of those VAWA grants in 2009 to fund, among other things, elder victim services. They built the program inside the Area Agency for Aging (AAA), the local hub for aging services. Page, APS, and other team members were grateful to have somewhere to refer victims who couldn't get help elsewhere, like one older woman targeted on Facebook by a fake Garth Brooks. A huge fan, she sent him so much money "to plan their wedding" she lost her house. The victim advocate worked with her anguished daughter and detectives to stem the bleeding and help clean up her credit score so she could find new housing.

Even AAAs that don't have formal victim services programs can provide valuable help. Some are part of local multidisciplinary teams and get cases that way. Becky Kurtz, the director of the AAA in Atlanta, Georgia, told me about such a situation involving an older couple. The police had repeatedly been called to the house because the husband abused his wife for whom he was the primary caregiver. She elected to stay with him, but the AAA got her enrolled in in-home services so that she at least had ongoing professional care and someone to regularly check in on her well-being inside her home. The AAA also offered the husband free caregiver counseling, which he declined.

Legal Services

We've long had programs offering legal services to domestic violence victims who often need help to get a restraining order or a divorce, for example, or maybe to avoid eviction or get help in a custody dispute. Older victims too, when asked, consistently have said that they believe having access to legal services can make them safer, like help getting benefits to hire a caregiver so they're less dependent on, say, an addicted daughter. But no formal program provided such help until 2016, when the first two emerged. One, now housed at Equal Justice Works, offers two-year "elder justice" fellowships around the country. And the other, part of the legal services program where Alison Hirschel works, is called the Crime Victims Legal Assistance Project–Elder Justice and is funded by VOCA.

The first year was rocky, Alison said. The ten, mostly newly minted attorneys worked on complex cases housed in legal services offices all over the state. While the domestic violence attorneys had a deep bench of mentors and sample pleadings, the elder justice attorneys were new to the issues and had few precedents or mentors to guide them. But they soon learned the issues and built networks to help them help their clients.

One client had put her children on her bank account to pay her bills during a hospitalization. Instead, they stole most of her savings. The elder justice attorney filed a civil action, winning the return of all $41,000 she'd lost. Without the lawyer, the chances of her getting anything back had been close to zero.

The attorneys helped some clients stay out of nursing homes and helped others stay in, like a man for whom a nursing home had been home for five years. He needed the care and wanted to stay there. When the nursing home tried to involuntarily discharge him to his condemned, uninhabitable former home, the lawyer argued that the discharge notice was invalid, that the destination was inadequate, and that he had a right to stay in the facility. The judge agreed.

As word spread that the elder justice attorneys were open for business, more clients and legal questions came their way. Responding to the demand, Alison's program hired more lawyers. "Scaling up wasn't easy," she said, "but now we have a passionate, knowledgeable crew. Other legal services programs should apply for VOCA funds, too."

Navigating Court

Navigating legal proceedings is hard for all victims. Old age can make it even more challenging. Some victim advocates work for nonprofits, others for law enforcement and prosecutor's offices. Advocates who work for public entities help not just the victims but also the detectives and prosecutors working on their cases. For some victims, it's hard to get to or around the courthouse, especially if they have cognitive issues. Advocates help with that. They also make sure victims have any necessary medication or oxygen on hand, sit with them during interviews and long waits, ease pre-testimony jitters, and sometimes even keep their favorite chocolate on hand. They can also vouch for the prosecutors who, in the tumult of trial preparation, may have little time to spend with them. During one trial, an advocate monitored the victim's oxygen tank while she testified. And when defense counsel argued that seeing the victim in her wheelchair might unfairly arouse jurors' sympathies, there was a group effort to lift her into the witness chair before the jury entered, and stow the wheelchair out of sight.

Some advocates provide vital support long after trial, too. Page Ulrey prosecuted a corporate executive for brutal domestic and sexual violence that allegedly started only after the couple had grown older, with age-related changes and medications perhaps playing a role. "A year later, while I was waiting for a train," his by then ex-wife told me, "I saw a man in a pale blue button-down shirt like the ones I used to get him. Suddenly I couldn't breathe. I panicked and ran out of the station." She didn't want to bring her kids into it, so when the flashbacks overpowered her, it was the victim advocate she called, one of several domestic violence victim advocates who worked in Page's office. But for financial exploitation and neglect cases, Page had no advocate to call on. In 2021 her office employed twenty-six advocates to help victims in cases involving domestic violence, child abuse, sexual assault, and protective orders. But none for elder abuse, despite being a national leader in such prosecutions. Finally, in 2022, the office hired one half-time elder advocate.

Trauma and Aging

Past Trauma

Given the untold millions of older people who have experienced trauma at some point in life, there's surprisingly little guidance for families or caregivers who encounter its boomeranging pain. Some survivors haven't revealed their past trauma, even to their children for whom those late revelations can be accompanied by grief and guilt. One ninety-year-old woman had hidden the sexual abuse she suffered as a child until she entered hospice. Then she spoke about it constantly with her son. He wanted to be there for her. But in that case, it wasn't just the mother who experienced pain. Her son was devastated that the old incubus cast a pall over his mother's last days, and his last days with her.

Trauma expresses itself in many ways. Hoarding disorders and obsessive-compulsive disorder, for example, are more common among people who have experienced trauma, although we have much still to learn about its origins and effective treatments. Our understanding about how best to treat trauma in older adults lags far behind other age groups. But the research suggests that targeting treatment based on the type of symptom, like depression or anxiety, rather than the type of trauma that caused it is more effective, says University of

Texas researcher Ron Acierno. Ron's research also found that social support helps to reduce PTSD and the negative outcomes of elder abuse, improving mental health in older adults.

There's also a complex interplay between dementia and PTSD that's not well understood. It appears that PTSD increases the risk of dementia and that some dementias increase the risk that PTSD will reemerge or worsen in late life. In one study involving nursing home aides who cared for Holocaust survivors, one aide said: "Everyone has their memories, but when you have dementia, you cannot sort out what is what (a memory, recall, or an episode in the present time)."[4] Decades after these patients had escaped the Holocaust, it had caught up with them again.

There's limited data on how best to relieve such suffering. Some recommend walking, creating art, or meditation as calming activities. Reassuring persons that they have control over aspects of their lives like meals and grooming seems to help, too. The aides who worked with Holocaust survivors found that food could both trigger and soothe, likely linked with their starvation in concentration camps. Aides found food hidden in the bed sheets of some residents when they went to do laundry. Assuring that food was always visible and accessible, like a sandwich or a piece of fruit on the bedside table, seemed to ease the distress of some older survivors. Music and humor also could bring joy and help tamp down reemerging terror. In the words of Viktor Frankl, a psychiatrist and Holocaust survivor himself, "Humor was another of the soul's weapons in the fight for self-preservation."[5]

Dementia

Victim advocates realized in different ways that they weren't reaching older people. For the cofounder of the domestic violence agency called Human Options, the moment came while she was hospitalized. Her roommate's husband berated his wife every time he visited, undeterred by her advanced age, her serious illness, or the stranger in the next bed. The agency director wondered where older women like her roommate went for help. Finding no program in Southern California, she started one—Safe Options for Seniors—in 2000. When Laura Mosqueda formed the multidisciplinary Forensic Center a few years later, Safe Options for Seniors joined the team, including social worker Cristi Ritschel.

One of Cristi's clients, "Pearl," had dementia and lived in a facility with her husband who'd been controlling and abusive for decades. "He has a temper," Pearl told Cristi. Or "he just gets like this when he's worried." Then one night while Pearl slept, he beat her bloody with a frying pan and was shipped off to jail.

At Forensic Center meetings, everyone was both a student and a teacher. Cristi gained access to experts in aging and elder abuse, and a new set of community resources she needed to help her older clients. Sometimes APS workers or geropsychologists joined her on home visits. Cristi estimated that 85 to 90 percent of her older clients were referred to her by APS. Teammates also taught her about working with people with dementia.

Each time Cristi met with Pearl, she reintroduced herself, but wondered if her visits did Pearl any good. Pearl told Cristi that sleeping in the bed where she'd been assaulted gave her nightmares, so she slept in a chair, but not well. Cristi usually suggested that clients move away from the place of trauma, but with Pearl she held off because moves can be confusing and traumatic for older people with dementia. Finally, however, the toll of insomnia outweighed that of relocating. As Pearl changed rooms, Cristi worked with her on breathing and visualization exercises to soothe herself.

When Cristi reintroduced herself the next week, Pearl told her that imagining she was on a mountaintop helped her relax in her new room. "She didn't remember how she'd learned it," said Cristi, "but she remembered the technique and that it helped, so kept doing it." When Pearl said she missed having someone to sleep next to, Cristi suggested putting pillows beside her. The next week Pearl told her, "I put pillows next to me so it felt like someone was there. It was *better* than having him here! I didn't cry."

Then Pearl's husband died. She often forgot he was dead, but when she remembered, she grieved losing him (again and again) and losing the chance to ask, "How could you hurt me?" "She couldn't write down her feelings anymore," said Cristi, "so we did some talking to an empty chair as if he was in it." The next week Pearl told Cristi that she'd imagined taking a walk with him and telling him she was really angry at him and missed him. "She didn't remember me," said Cristi, "but she remembered the trauma and what helped. Somehow the deeper emotional aspects of the work were preserved."

The pooling of knowledge and skills helped Forensic Center team members ask better questions and build a broader repertoire of responses. Cristi and her predecessor and mentor, Carol Tryon, brought their experience with domestic violence, sexual assault, the tactics used by abusers, and trauma-informed services to the team. "Learning more about domestic violence tactics expanded how I looked at cases," said Laura. And Laura could explain to teammates how emotional memories take different paths through our brains than neutral ones, are stored differently, and may improve how well we remember something. In fact, emotional events may persist more clearly in the memories of people with dementia.

Techniques similar to those Cristi used also may be useful in scenarios less extreme than Pearl's. For example, they might help a person with dementia who had a contentious marriage without physical abuse move past perseverating about unresolved issues and realize that they're no longer current.

Emotional Harm

One of the most common ways older people are harmed is through emotional or verbal abuse. But services addressing it have been slow to evolve, in part because we underestimate its damage. Although less concrete than a punch, words have power to cause psychological pain. When aimed at older people, they're often infused with an acidic ageism: "You're disgusting. You've lost your mind. You're worthless. You can't do anything. If you don't do XYZ, I'll put you in a nursing home. Why are we wasting money on care for you? You've lived long enough. Just die already." Research repeatedly shows "that chronic emotional abuse and neglect can be just as devastating as physical abuse and sexual molestation," wrote Bessel van der Kolk.[6] This isn't so surprising given that harmful words break human bonds and undermine self-worth.

Researcher Charles Mouton found that for women aged fifty to seventy-nine, examined separately, verbal abuse was more detrimental to health than physical abuse.[7] Researchers also have found variations in what verbal exchanges people perceive to be harmful in old age depending on their cultural traditions and norms, yet another issue about which we need to learn more.

Faith

Faith communities are an often-overlooked potential source of support. Nine out of ten older Americans describe themselves as religious, and about half attend a religious service weekly. People who would never turn to APS or a doctor for help might trust their rabbi, pastor, or imam. With this in mind, the nonprofit Safe Havens works with religious organizations to reduce the toll of domestic violence among older victims, too.

Rev. Jesus Laguerra has done similar work as a Baptist minister and former intake worker for Self Help by Older Persons Project (SHOPP) in the Bronx. His role at SHOPP was not as pastor, but his pastoral role informs his work with older clients, many of them in distress. Jesus told me he listens for whether religion is among his clients' coping mechanisms. "Most Latinos have a spiritual tradition," he said. "People have mixed baggage with their faith journey. Sometimes their spiritual tools are helpful, sometimes toxic."

Jesus pointed to *marianismo*, the female gender role counterpart to machismo, as an example. Rooted in Christianity, marianismo encourages women to be spiritual and submissive, the family nurturers. Researchers have found that marianismo correlates with higher rates of depression and anxiety.

"Rent is expensive, so often the generations live crowded together," Jesus said. "It's hard to be seventy and living in the projects raising grandchildren." He talked about often seeing grandparents being abused by their grandkids. "It's an issue that hurts the most intense fiber of the human heart. But the mother or grandmother isn't focused on her own needs. *Sacraficio.*"

Jesus did outreach to churches while at SHOPP, but not as successfully as he'd hoped. "The church needs to be more courageous," he said. "Faith leaders see people over time and have access to households. They've taken on other problems but not yet the suffering of older people. The field is still in pampers. Rabbis, priests, ministers, imams, all need to use a more amplified repertoire to help their communities heal."

SERVICES PEOPLE WANT

Help for Someone Else

Some traditional services can be adapted. Other gaps are structural. Many older victims wanted help not just for themselves but also for someone else, sometimes even for the person harming them. One older woman had had a long, harmonious marriage, but dementia made her husband volatile and violent. She loved and worried about him. She also feared him. So she fixed him meals, left notes explaining how to heat them up, and fled to a domestic violence shelter. She told the shelter staff that he wasn't safe alone, and pleaded with them to get *him* help. They declined, explaining that the abuser wasn't their client. Victim services were designed for victims, and victims only, even if the victim herself wanted something else. Anxious about her husband's well-being, the woman returned home a few days later and that night her husband killed her in a delusional rage. It was a preventable tragedy illustrating a simple point. People need the kinds of services they want and will use.

Culturally Informed Healing Services

Though its importance is often overlooked, many traditions emphasize the family over the individual. Services uninformed by culture may leave victims with no help. "We offer clients to work within the family," said Evelyn Laureano, whose program served a 60 percent Hispanic population in the Bronx. Evelyn rooted her services and approach in the victims' cultural and familial preferences. "We ask, 'Would you like us to help that family member? If so, how? Is the family member open to a drug treatment program?' We use a family systems approach as opposed to the domestic violence world, where you often cut off connection with the abuser," she told me.

The failure of services to respond to the wishes of many older Black people is addressed in a 2020 "toolkit" entitled *Increasing Access to Healing Services and Just Outcomes for Older African American Crime Survivors*. Ms. Annette, who tells her story in a video that's part of the toolkit, was a grandmother with ten children. Her husband had abused her and their children, and she said she could have benefited from classes in parenting and anger management herself. In her old age, some of her adult children mistreated her. She said, "I'm struggling, barely managing." She could move away, she explained, but "I stay because of the grandkids. It's about them."[8] Our societal failures early in life fold back on themselves in old age. The damage done by our failure to protect children lasts a lifetime, again illustrating that elder abuse is a problem with intergenerational causes that requires intergenerational solutions.

Other blind spots are also harmful. "There's lots of community capacity that's overlooked," said Juanita Davis, the toolkit's lead author. Juanita explained that funding for victim services and research is often doled out based on the funders' values and culture. "In Black culture, people might seek help at their hair salon, barbershop, or church. What you might call the cops for, I might call my pastor for. But that's not who's getting funding. It's a misconception of what's needed in the community," she told me. There's research to support Juanita's point, including a study showing that Black men who worked with pharmacists they met at their LA barbershops significantly reduced their blood pressure in six months because they got care in a place they knew and trusted.

Juanita pointed out another issue, too. "Lots of services are for victims, not perpetrators. But perpetrators can be victims, too. By limiting those services, we lose opportunities to enhance well-being and quality of life." Juanita's point is echoed by many contributors to the toolkit. "Older African Americans don't see themselves as victims when it comes to their children," said LaTrice Buck, former director of the pioneering Milwaukee Women's Center. "They see their children as a reflection of themselves, and ask 'What did I do to make this happen?' A central factor in whether many people accept help is, 'Who will care for the grandchildren?'" Getting help for others may be a condition of accepting help themselves. "If you've done something for my son or daughter, *then* you can help me."[9]

Family issues are also central for Asian and Pacific Islander (API) elders, a diverse group representing dozens of ethnicities, cultural customs, and languages. Four million Chinese Americans form the largest subgroup. Tight-knit families help protect older Chinese immigrants from being mistreated, research suggests. In close families, adult children perceived caregiving as less burdensome. Filial piety was a shield.

In less cohesive families, by contrast, the older people were at greater risk. Old and young were often raised in different cultures with different expectations of what it means to be part of a family. This could lead to misunderstandings about what was expected and greater ambivalence about caregiving. Some older people feel marginalized in their own families. "The erosion of filial piety values," researchers found, increased the risk of mistreatment.[10] The cultural primacy of family also meant that older Asian Americans were less likely to seek outside support, fearing that doing so could bring shame or negative consequences for a family member or themselves. This further isolated them and magnified their risk.

There's much to learn about what effective prevention and services for Asian and Pacific Islander populations look like. What is clear is that providers should partner with people who understand the cultures and speak the languages of the people being served.

The existing research about older LGBTQ people suggests they face high rates of mistreatment. In one study, two-thirds of participants reported verbal harassment and more than a third said they were threatened with violence or physically attacked. Transgender elders and older gay people of color reported the highest levels of discrimination and mistreatment.[11] Some older LGBTQ Americans report that moving into a facility pushes them back into the closet. Others report bias such as denial of visitors or not allowing their partners to participate in medical decision-making. In addition, LGBTQ elders are disproportionately isolated and often reluctant to seek help. Here, too, there's still much to learn.

Words on Words

Some of what we've learned about providing culturally competent services is specific to race, ethnicity, and culture. Other aspects point to a broader need to reconceptualize the services we provide so that they better fit what older people want and need. Although it seems obvious to ask the intended beneficiaries for their views, that often hasn't happened. When they were asked, older victims said they hated flyers featuring broken glasses and bruises. They preferred positive messages, like a flyer saying, "You can do it!" The word *victim* didn't describe how many saw themselves, nor did *perpetrator* describe their troubled children—"That's no perpetrator; that's my son."

Concerns about language run deep. The term *victim* is a compelling shorthand. But cultivating an *identity* of "victimhood"— whether victims do so themselves, or whether it's foisted on them by politicians, advocates, prosecutors, or culture—can do insidious damage, reducing whole humans to one attribute of their complex personhood, an attribute that usually arose on another person's terms.

By fusing a person's identity with what's often the worst thing that ever happened to them, we risk inflicting more harm in the very process of trying to ameliorate it. The critic Jacqueline Rose has said: "Victimhood is something that happens, but when you turn it into an identity you're psychically and politically finished."[12] When people say they don't see themselves as "victims," we should listen.

Language and stories shape how we perceive the world. On this point, I wondered what it meant that thousands of people were introduced to elder abuse through the story of Miss Mary, a woman physically and sexually assaulted by her grandson for hours one night when she was ninety-six. He threatened to kill her, but she outsmarted him and got away. DOJ funded the making of powerful videos in which Miss Mary describes—in her own words—the crime, her life after it, and the help she got. The videos also feature interviews with the detective, prosecutors, and victim advocates involved with her and her case. Bonnie Brandl, a leading expert at the intersection of domestic violence and elder abuse, talked about Miss Mary in Senate testimony. Miss Mary's story was a vivid centerpiece in dozens of VAWA-funded trainings organized by Bonnie at which Page and Ricker often taught.

Some aspects of Miss Mary's case were common. She wound up in a nursing home for the last three years of her life. She said that her granddaughter-in-law (who wasn't charged) stole her burial down payments. There was conflict in her large family, and they initially disbelieved her. In trials as in weddings, observers often show their allegiance by where they sit. While Miss Mary testified, her entire family sat on "his" side of the courtroom. Victim advocates, worried the jurors might infer she wasn't sympathetic or believable, rounded up people to sit on "her" side. But other aspects of the case were less common. Sexual violence is the least prevalent type of elder abuse. And older people are much less likely to endure domestic violence than their younger counterparts.

In contemplating what lessons translate from one field to another, I struggled to figure out how elder abuse and domestic violence overlapped and how they were distinct. Should abuse by people with cognitive impairment or by nonfamily caregivers be considered domestic violence? And are there scenarios in which neglect, verbal abuse, or financial abuse *alone* could be considered domestic violence?

What lessons should we draw? For me, the many vignettes of innovation and adaptation in this chapter revealed an emerging picture—a mosaic of sorts—reflecting the breadth of challenges faced by older victims and by those trying to meet their needs. There's no silver bullet. We will need to collect data and study outcomes to draw the right conclusions. The vignettes are lots of beginnings. Their very diversity shows just how complex the issues are.

Maybe that helps explain why Miss Mary's story was so often a centerpiece. We have a hankering for clarity. Messy stories are hard. We want victims who are "all victim" and deserve our outrage without moral ambiguity. A "good" victim can make our work feel urgent, heroic even. A vicious crime is more likely to draw the fleeting attention of everyone from senators to prosecutors to the public. We're repelled by what Miss Mary suffered and buoyed by her resilience. She wanted her grandson to go to jail, and he did. For advocacy and training purposes, the case sends clear messages, free of the tangled desires and bewildering autonomy-safety issues that muddle our notions of justice in these hard cases and sometimes in aging itself.

So many cases aren't clean battles of wickedness versus justice. They involve conflicting frailties and unresolved pasts. They require us to hold several opposing ideas in mind at once, something our systems weren't built to handle. Jesus Laguerra, the Baptist minister who worked with older people in the Bronx, told me, "You need to use imagination to help families heal holistically." That's what my colleagues and I were trying to do.

Part III
CHANGE

Advancing elder justice will require change in our culture, in our legal codes, in our communities, and in our consciousness. As we've seen in Parts I and II, our norms and systems have not kept up with our longevity, sometimes with terrible, and usually preventable, consequences. When things go wrong in aging, many people feel like it's a personal failure. Yet it's often caused by inadequate systems related to caregiving, long-term care, and financial security, and made worse by norms that allow isolation and ageism to run rampant.

But change *is* possible—and some is even underway. Part III presents four approaches to change. The first two chapters tell the stories of efforts I've been involved with: one at the community level, the other at the level where federal laws are made. Chapter 14 then looks at ways we can advocate more effectively for social change to advance elder justice. The subject of the last chapter caught me by surprise, but I've come to think it's the most profound strategy of all: increasing our capacity to make meaning of aging, and of our fleeting time on earth, by paying more attention to the power of purpose, curiosity, stories, awe, and love.

Chapter 12

NEW MODELS

Rather than asking, "What law was broken,
who broke it, and how should they be punished?"
restorative justice asks, "Who was harmed? What
do they need? Whose obligation is it to meet
those needs?"

—SUJATHA BALIGA, "The Transformative Power
of Restorative Justice," *The Gray Area*

I had worked for "justice" for years, but the longer I did, the more
elusive it became, both as an idea and as a fact. Most of my
work had happened at the 30,000-foot level, and up there it
felt like *Groundhog Day*. Again and again the field said it wanted
the same two things: intervention research to learn if what we were
doing worked, and prevention research to figure out how to prevent
the problems we were seeing. We knew the questions, but we weren't
answering them.

Given the disappointing results of my 30,000-foot work, I
inverted my approach. I wanted to start building from the bottom up
more than from the top down. I hoped to translate what I'd learned
from my law and policy work, from my research and writing, into
action at the community level. In other words, while writing about
change, I also was trying to change things in real time.

GOALS

In 2015, I called Ricker Hamilton to pitch a project. After thirty years at APS, he was considered a national leader in elder justice, but in his own agency he'd held the same position for decades. Then he was promoted three times: in 2011 to be director of Aging and Disability Services, a year later to be Maine's Deputy Commissioner for Health and Human Services, and in 2017 to be Maine's Commissioner for Health and Human Services. Finding himself in charge of APS, Ricker fretted. "We *say* all sorts of nice things about being client-centered," he told me. "But are we really? Do our *clients* think they're better off?"

David Burnes, a University of Toronto researcher, told me he hoped to do a study asking APS clients just that question. APS often is reluctant to participate in research. It's time-consuming and who knows what it might find. So I called Ricker, who jumped at the chance to have Maine's APS program be part of the study. In asking Maine APS clients about their goals, it turned out, unsurprisingly, that the top priority for some was to get help for someone else—like a caregiver who needed treatment for addiction. But that was beyond APS's authority, so it had to respond, "Sorry, I can only help you."

That's what happened with a retired nurse in her mid-eighties whose son in his forties had an autism spectrum disorder. He cycled in and out of jobs, relationships, and housing, often landing back in his mom's house. The nurse's daughter encouraged her mom to set better boundaries and not to let him move back in. Tough love time. Mom felt guilty that she hadn't gotten him more help when he was younger, but services had been scarce in the rural community where they lived. Their relationship was fraught; he could be resentful and controlling. But she loved him, and she adored his four-year-old daughter who lived with them half the time.

The son's periodic violent outbursts scared them all. Someone called APS, but all the mother wanted was help for her son. His well-being was *the* dominant factor in her own. So, APS closed its case. Then one night, he had another violent outburst. The police showed up and took him away. She was bereft.

This case shows how siloed and binary the options are. For older people like the retired nurse, we have APS, long-term care, guardianship, and victim services. For her son, the alleged abuser, we have law enforcement and prosecution. Few organizations are equipped to help both individually, much less help them repair their relationships, even though elder abuse is defined to arise *in relationships of trust*. The way our systems have evolved, they often don't or can't respect people's complex wishes or meet their complex needs. We treat individuals, not families.

So, I went back to Ricker. At breakfast overlooking Portland's harbor, he said, "If my kid was taking my money, I wouldn't want APS or law enforcement involved. I'd want to get *him* help." Over the years, Ricker had agitated loudly for more reporting, arrest, and prosecution. Now in his sixties, over weak coffee, he spoke as a father.

I asked if he'd be willing to let us design and pilot-test a new program to offer support not just for the older person but also for others, including caregivers and even alleged perpetrators. "In a heartbeat," said Ricker in his thick Maine accent. Then, lowering his voice, he said, "Do it fast while I can help." The commissioner was about to resign. He was slated to replace her. "But," he said, "I don't know how long I'll last in the job."

Over the next months, David, the Toronto researcher, and I worked with Stuart Lewis, a geriatrician and researcher at Dartmouth, to design a new program of our own that was more flexible and could help families if that's what older people wanted. We had countless calls; we pored over existing programs and research; we studied interventions that showed promise in other fields. One of the models we looked at was created by Laura Mosqueda.

AIM

In the late 2010s, Laura and her colleagues created a model to simplify the complex situations they encountered and to aid others to see the big picture, too. She wanted to help people know where best to focus their attention. Over the years, certain types of scenarios have come to set off alarm bells in my head, like when a friend tells me about a declining parent who lives alone with a troubled sibling. It's not just me. For all of us in the field, certain combinations of factors set our brains clanging.

When Laura saw what seemed like a high-risk situation, she asked herself, "What exactly set off the warning bells? How could I help reduce the risk?" As we saw in Parts I and II, these fraught scenarios involve so many moving parts, it's often hard to know where to start. "It's usually a whole series of little things that can add up to a big important change for the person," said Laura. "Often there's so much going on, it's hard to know where to start."

Laura compares using her model to bringing order to a messy desk. "It helps you to organize your papers into stacks so they're less overwhelming and you can figure out where to start. You can't do anything about X, but you can about Y. So, focus on Y."

Over several years, she sketched dozens of different approaches on the butcher paper beside her desk. She wanted to create a visual representation to organize what she knew from intuition and experience. What emerged was the Abuse Intervention Model, or AIM.[1] It was deceptively simple—a large circle divided into thirds, each third representing a set of risk factors. I've listed them here, with examples, because they're of use in families:

1. **Risk factors relating to the older person:** These include cognitive impairment, isolation, loneliness, physical frailty, physical dependence on others, financial dependence on others, needing assistance that gives other people access to what was previously private, and difficulty in providing adequate self-care.

2. **Risk factors relating to another person, like a caregiver or trusted other:** These include inadequately treated mental illness, substance use, or trauma; financial or emotional dependence on the older person; history of violence or financial exploitation; lack of understanding about aging or dementia; inability to manage caregiving; or resentment, greed, and volatility.

3. **Risk factors relating to the environment or context:**
These include isolation, cultural norms (like marianismo),
limited access to transportation, a history of conflict, financial insecurity, and poverty.

Laura also color-coded the risk factors into ones that could be modified versus ones that couldn't. This helped her, and her families, focus
their attention and resources on where they could do the most good.
When I called AIM a "risk assessment" tool, Laura corrected me.
"It's also an intervention and prevention tool," she said. "If you can *see*
a risk, it's easier to prevent it and to know how to intervene." Although
Laura hopes to numerically quantify the amount of risk each element
contributes in the future, even as is, AIM allows us to plug in factors
present in our own lives and families to see the risks more clearly, and
to do something about them. Think of the risks as leafy sea dragons.

Designing RISE

Creating a new program is a little like creating a blueprint for a high-
rise apartment building. You want the concept to be solid before you
start construction, so you wind up with something that's both struc-
turally sound and that people want to use. As David, Stuart, and I set
about designing the new program, we organized a community meeting to get input from Maine experts and practitioners. We were all
squished around a table in APS offices with Ricker and Erin Salvo,
the APS director. National experts chimed in by speakerphone. After
the meeting, Patty Kimball, the executive director of the nonprofit
Elder Abuse Institute of Maine, stuck around to brainstorm. She
was excited about the idea of creating a more holistic approach, and
we were excited about her expertise in a practice called restorative
justice. A few months later, we asked Patty to join the team and run
the program. We called our new model *RISE*, named for the goals
and methods that it incorporated:[2]

Repair harm using *restorative justice* approaches to hold people
accountable while reducing harm in meaningful ways, a method used in criminal justice reform.

Inspire change using *motivational interviewing* to help people feel that change is possible, a method used in the mental health field.

Support connection using *teaming*, a process to strengthen informal and formal social support around both the older person and others in their lives, a method used in child welfare.

Empower choice using *supported or interdependent decision-making* by helping older people with cognitive impairment achieve *their* goals, a method building on approaches used in the disability rights field.

One thing soon became clear. Building trust was the threshold. The human connection during early encounters was what unlocked the possibility of change. Everything else flowed from it, so we recruited a leading expert in such engagement, Geoff Rogers from Hunter College's Silberman School of Social Work, to join our RISE team.

In implementing RISE, Patty proved to be a gifted leader, savvy about the big picture and.attuned to minute details. She guided the advocates to build networks with a multitude of people and entities to help them help their clients. This was critical to a key feature of the model: to build ongoing social support around clients—informal supports like a neighbor or niece stopping by periodically, and formal supports like arranging for Meals on Wheels or enrolling in MaineCare. This is one of the only methods shown to protect older people against mistreatment. As the advocates learned the ropes, other players came to value their unique approach.

We started by pilot-testing RISE in two randomly selected counties—Maine's most urban and most rural. Collecting elder justice data is notoriously challenging, and RISE was no exception. But there was a surprise. The advocates *wanted* to know the impact of their work on clients and were enthusiastic about collecting data to figure it out. Patty had created an environment of curiosity, where the culture valued research and the process of asking, measuring, modifying, and asking again. I've never seen anything like it.

The results showed that APS workers referred their most intractable cases to RISE advocates and that, even so, RISE clients' chances of a repeat APS investigation fell by more than 50 percent. APS workers valued the program because it was good for their clients and for their own well-being. More importantly, the older clients had an extremely positive view of the program. APS was so enthusiastic about RISE, it expanded the program from two counties to the entire state. Then, in 2023, RISE was written into the governor's budget to make it a permanent part of Maine's healthy aging system. "Without the thoughtful, research approach to the pilot," said Jeanne Lambrew, Maine's Health and Human Services Commissioner and a leading health policy expert, "we could not have proposed this next step." It was a lesson Lambrew had taught me before. When she worked for the White House Domestic Policy Council, I had proposed a "solution." She and her colleagues asked what evidence I had to support it. I admitted, I had none. I didn't want to make the same mistake again. That was one reason we made research a core component of RISE.

As word of the program spread, we expanded to other states and to specialized issues, like the role of substance use. We also adapted RISE to other systems, like cases in or diverted from the criminal justice system.

CRIME, PUNISHMENT, AND JUSTICE

The elder justice field has relied heavily on arrest and prosecution as a "solution," mirroring a broader approach both in society and in the domestic violence field that has influenced elder justice. But research has shown that such reliance leaves many poor and non-white domestic violence victims worse off. Some don't seek help because they fear involvement of the criminal system. When breadwinners are imprisoned, families may lose their only source of income. Victims often act based on what they believe is best for their children, not for themselves.

In 2020, forty-six state domestic violence coalitions signed onto a public document, titled "Moment of Truth," reflecting these concerns. In using "increased policing, prosecution, and imprisonment as the primary solution to gender-based violence," the coalitions stated, "rather than real community-based solutions that support healing and liberation," the violence against women movement failed to listen to Black feminists and other activists who cautioned against doing so. "We have invested significantly in the criminal legal system, despite knowing that the vast majority of survivors choose not to engage with it and that those who do are often re-traumatized by it."[3]

Many older people and their families fear involving the criminal legal system too, concerned they'll get a family member in trouble or worsen family strife. They worry what it might mean for them. Will they lose a caregiver and land in a facility? Will it unleash unintended consequences so they lose control over their lives?

When there's trouble, most older people just want the harm to stop and to regain their dignity and peace. Many want to repair relationships. But meeting those goals are not the role of prosecution. A prosecutor's role is to punish wrongdoing, seek financial restitution (almost always illusory in elder abuse cases), and preserve the public order.

As a nation, our overreliance on prosecution has had cruel results: Almost 50 percent of the incarcerated have mental illness, and 85 percent have an active substance use disorder or were incarcerated for a crime involving drugs or drug use.[4] African American and Hispanic people make up 32 percent of the US population, but account for 56 percent of the incarcerated population.[5]

Yet, when prosecutors don't prosecute certain types of crimes, that also sends a message. For much of history, family violence was considered a private misfortune, mostly shrouded inside families and occasionally social service agencies. Prosecution pushed it out from under the shroud, into public view. In the criminal laws we enact, and the cases we bring to enforce them, we make manifest, as a society, what conduct we deem intolerable. Jill Leovy argues in her book *Ghettoside* that not prosecuting murder and other violent crimes against men of color leads people to take the law into their own hands, causing even more violence. The failure to prosecute telegraphs that those crimes matter less, that those victims matter less, that society doesn't care. When crimes are taken less seriously because they injure people of lower social status, the practice is called "victim discounting." As a group, men of color, she argues, are discounted as victims.[6] Older people, especially those with dementia, are another sort of discounted victim. Their suffering too is taken less seriously and punished less vigorously.

Most prosecutors talk in terms of "justice" but measure success like sports teams—in wins and losses. Page Ulrey and her colleagues were different. They brought hard cases and wanted to know if their work led to more just outcomes, to safer families and communities. They collected data from four years and hundreds of elder abuse prosecutions, which were analyzed by Tony Rosen, the New York emergency medicine doctor, and his team. But those data didn't answer the big important questions about whether those cases advanced justice, improved people's lives, or made Seattle a better place to age.

When Page first started teaching other prosecutors in 2005 as part of a national training program, few were bringing elder abuse cases. She urged them to be more aggressive. Then in some jurisdictions, the pendulum swung too far. Page worried about the lack of a consistent definition of an "ethical elder abuse prosecution." She also worried that she was seeing more prosecution of "grossly inappropriate" cases. For example, when a nursing home resident fell as an aide helped her to the bathroom, the woman showed no bleeding, bumps on her head, or other outward signs of injury. When the resident died soon thereafter due to a brain bleed, however, prosecutors charged the aide with manslaughter.

Another case involved a couple who cared for an older gentleman living in a remote rural area. He considered the caregivers his de facto family and gave them a substantial gift. Prosecutors charged them with financial exploitation and arrested them, leaving the older man with no one to help him cook or shovel snow. He pleaded with the prosecutor to drop the charges, arguing that he had the capacity to make the gift. It was his choice. But the prosecutor didn't back off, so the man sought help from a legal services attorney. When the prosecutor proceeded to trial against the caregivers, the legal services attorney testified on their behalf, according to the older man's wishes, infuriating the prosecutor.

In a third case, an older undocumented immigrant without health insurance had incurred substantial expenses during an earlier hospital stay and feared saddling her family with more debt. So when she again needed care, she forbade her adult children from getting medical help for her. She died at home with serious pressure sores but otherwise well cared for. Law enforcement pressured the prosecutor to file charges.

Those kinds of cases kept Page awake at night. So did cases involving real crimes where she didn't think all the work of prosecuting did much good. In one such case she charged a drug-addicted grandson for financially exploiting his grandmother and got a no-contact order. But they kept seeing each other, violating the order. And he kept squeezing his grandmother for money. Page prosecuted the grandson a second time, but, she said, "prosecution just wasn't the right answer in that case. We needed something else." January 2023 marked the first criminal elder abuse prosecution to use "something else"—RISE. The case involves another grandson and grandmother, caught up in the common cycle, and wreaking discord throughout the family. If the grandson completes the inpatient drug treatment and the drug court and RISE requirements, including the restorative components, charges against him will be dropped. When Page called the grandmother to tell her that her grandson had been accepted into the program, and begun inpatient treatment, the grandmother, herself a former addiction counselor, was so relieved she wept.

Erosion of social services in the last half century—not just for the old, but for everyone—means that issues left untreated earlier in life often just get worse. They gain velocity until they collide with a cop, a prosecutor, or, sometimes, a medical examiner like Richard Harruff. Richard had told me that prosecutors and courts might not be the right venue for these cases, but until systems further upstream address them, they'll keep on coming. Better social services and more cohesive communities could buffer American families from the criminal legal system. Not dealing with social issues sooner, and better, ties us to a carceral system that has little capacity to mitigate harm, or prevent it.

Prosecution isn't built to fix social ills. Relying on it to do so hasn't worked. I'd started out as a prosecutor, but the more I saw, the more I became a preventionist. We were not going to prosecute our way out of these problems. Laws that criminalize more and more conduct may give lawmakers a platform, but they won't prevent abuse. We need better resources upstream. And prosecutors like Page need better options in the cases that do reach them.

A RESTORATIVE APPROACH

One such option has been around for a long time. Restorative justice has roots in Indigenous communities that predate European settlement in the Americas. In the Pueblo tribe, wrongdoers are brought before an elder council. "It's not taking the person out of the community and sending them to jail," says Jacqueline Gray, director of the National Indigenous Elder Justice Initiative. She explained that many tribal elders don't want the person harming them punished. "It hurts the family," she said, "and they may not have another caregiver." Instead, "people of wisdom" decide how to remedy the wrong, with a focus on what the elder wants and what resources exist to meet needs, like safe housing or respite care for the caregiver. "Wrongdoers know the community will be watching."

Restorative justice focuses on wrongdoers taking accountability for their actions and on identifying the harm they caused the victim and their community. The heart of the process is in taking steps to repair that harm and transform those involved. People define and practice restorative justice in many different ways, but in the United States, it's primarily been used in cases involving juveniles, to give them second chances and to avoid consigning them to the criminal system so young.

Use of restorative justice in elder cases has been rare, in part given the frailty of many victims and the complexity of the crimes. But given how often relationships are at the heart of both the problem and the solution in such cases, it can be a good fit when the parties are receptive and the process is rigorous and thoughtful.

At this writing, Patty and her staff have handled more than 500 RISE cases, about a quarter of them using restorative approaches, always along with RISE's other methods. They have significantly adapted the process to the exigencies of elder cases, which is why we refer to it as a restorative *approach*. Only a small number of cases have gone all the way to the culminating "conference" or "circle," a hallmark of most restorative justice practices where the harmed and harming parties meet, together with family members, supporters, and a facilitator.

In RISE, restorative approaches take many forms. In one case, a widower's granddaughter moved in with him, he thought temporarily. But she had depression, anxiety, and a serious hoarding disorder, took over his apartment, locked herself in his bedroom, and didn't leave. He was miserable and began drinking a lot. He wanted her out, but APS could only help him evict her or press trespassing charges. He wanted his home back, but he also wanted her to be okay. As the situation got more volatile, they only communicated through the RISE advocate, despite living under the same roof.

Guided by the man's goals, the advocate helped the granddaughter get treatment, find a new place, and move. The grandfather contributed funds to help her get set up in the new place. In this case, the victory was in what did *not* happen: no eviction, no criminal charges, no physical conflict, no cops, no prosecutors, no courts, no one homeless, no one guilt-ridden. RISE's restorative approach helped them resolve their conflict without resorting to legal intervention, hurting each other, or wasting resources.

Then there's the case of the retired nurse in rural Maine who declined what APS had to offer and only wanted help for her autistic son. On the evening he lost control, she called the advocate who called 911. He was arrested, charged with assault, and briefly jailed. In the usual case, he'd have ended up on the streets, eventually moved back in with his mother, and the cycle would have started anew. This time, according to the mother's wishes, the advocate helped her son get a therapist and sign up for benefits. She also helped him get a job, find an apartment, and build a network to keep on supporting him.

With her son more stable, the mom was ready to address her own needs. The RISE advocate helped her to repair perilous steps and a leaky roof, and arranged for an aide to come in to help a few times a week. She also helped the mother reconnect with people she'd lost touch with—building social support.

Finally, about a year after the original assault, the mother, son, and supporters of each one met together with a facilitator for the restorative justice conference. Because the son had honored the commitments, the charges against him were dropped. The grandmother was elated to see her granddaughter again.

Systems Neglect

Most cases APS referred to RISE involved "self-neglect," an ungenerous term for "people who couldn't manage," putting themselves or others in peril. As the advocates worked with these clients, and built trust, they often learned that there was more to the story; many also were being exploited. The RISE advocates witnessed how excruciatingly hard it could be for many older people just to navigate the details of everyday life.

We all know the stress of being on hold for forty minutes. But for most of us, that wait is an irritation. Imagine if what's at stake is getting your heat turned back on, or figuring out if your health coverage will pay for the care you need. Imagine while you're on hold that you forget your password, listen to a dozen robotic options, and then have the call drop. Now imagine doing that while cognitively impaired, half blind, and hard of hearing. For millions of older people, that's a reality of moving through the world. Those disembodied, user-unfriendly systems riddled with "administrative burdens" do real harm. One advocate said, "It's called 'self-neglect,' but it's often really 'systems neglect.'" She's right.

Conversely, when programs meet people's needs, it's not just better for the recipients but also for the providers. People doing this work want better options to meet the vast human need they see. That too is a form of "justice."

Systems Change

We intentionally built RISE to work alongside formal systems, like APS and criminal justice, so that if it worked, it might change how those systems operate. The parable of DARE, the Drug Abuse Resistance Education program, a minor celebrity in policy circles, illustrates the process. Data showed that DARE didn't reduce drug use, yet the program remained in 75 percent of schools. Why? It served other purposes: Teachers got free periods. Schools got free security.

Cops met kids on neutral turf. Those "constituents" wanted to keep the program. They also were happy to improve the services it offered. The track had been laid. They just needed to build better trains.

The DARE example helped me see a potential path in the elder justice field, too. We have infrastructure for programs like APS and victim services. We have a lot of track. But like DARE, the programs running on those tracks are rarely supported by evidence of effectiveness. Over the decades, they've ossified into the status quo. But having the track already laid is huge. Now we need better trains—that is, to conceptualize, test, and implement better models than the ones we rely on now.

Everyone was nervous as we embarked on RISE. But what's been most striking is not only how much the clients like it but also how enthusiastically advocates, APS, and criminal justice people as well as policy-makers have embraced it, not just in Maine but beyond. Everyone wants better tools to help the people involved in these hard cases. RISE is just one small step, but a hopeful one. Rigorous design, data collection, and dedication of many people can change systems. And systems change, done well, can help countless people live with less anguish and more pleasure through the entire life cycle.

Chapter 13

LAW

The law is the publique Conscience.

—THOMAS HOBBES, *Leviathan*

There was a time when I thought that our lagging norms about aging were due to an empathy deficit. I thought that telling sad stories that tugged at heartstrings would lead to compassion and improvements. But a closer look changed my mind. Empathy helps but it can't be relied on. It's too idiosyncratic and subjective. In *The Better Angels of Our Nature*, Steven Pinker argues that empathy might spark concern about overlooked groups, but "for empathy to matter, it must goad changes in policies and norms that determine how the people in those groups are treated."[1]

Goading changes in policies and norms was just what I was aspiring to do as I contemplated how to turn an idea for an elder justice law into a reality. A law, I hoped, would give people better tools to address and prevent the problem I was seeing, eventually changing behavior. The seatbelt parable again helps to illustrate the point. Laws that required car manufacturers to install seatbelts, and drivers and passengers to wear them, first changed behavior and eventually changed norms. Through the rearview mirror, such efforts look much more streamlined than they are in real life. This chapter chronicles the origins of one attempt at change-making—the Elder Justice Act—as both story and case study. Chapter 14 looks at some levers of change, especially those we were lacking, to reveal which ones we might cultivate in the future.

As fourth graders in the Washington, DC, public schools, my kids learned the song "I'm Just a Bill," about how a "sad little scrap of paper"—the anthropomorphized "Bill"—moves through Congress to become a law. Despite living in a town where that very process is the main industry, I knew little about how laws came into being. Working on the DOJ initiative had left me feeling like the sorcerer's apprentice in a deluge. Every time I got a handle on one part of the issue—like nursing homes, scams, or APS—two new ones appeared. I'd hoped to use DOJ's formidable resources to take on the problems I was seeing. When that plan fell through, I thought that getting Congress to pass a new law was our best shot at lasting structural change. But what could I do to make that happen?

The Elder Justice Act was first introduced in 2002, signed into law in 2010, not funded until 2015, and then only with a pittance. Two COVID-19 relief bills in late 2020 and early 2021 provided the EJA's first real funds. But they didn't last. As of 2023, they'd sunk back to a trifle. In that version of the story, the effort felt like a failure given the magnitude of the problems and the law's modest contributions to address them. But there's also another way to tell the story: That the Elder Justice Act's very existence illuminated the problem and how little was being done about it. That the law became a seed from which a constituency and maybe a movement began to grow.

My version of the story began at DOJ. There, for about a year, the agency's bully pulpit was trained on nursing home and elder justice issues that had lacked political constituencies or high-profile champions. It was a big deal when Attorney General Janet Reno and Deputy Attorney General Eric Holder gave speeches about the issues. Their attention validated the invisible work of people who'd spent decades in the trenches, not to mention the plight of those who'd suffered.

Having Reno and Holder engaged was progress of one kind. But then I learned about the federal resources taking on child abuse and domestic violence. There were offices at DOJ and HHS and dozens of federal experts working on the issues no matter who inhabited the White House. Federal laws appropriated hundreds of millions of dollars a year for infrastructure. By contrast, ad hoc initiatives are easy to launch and easy to kill. Suddenly, the speeches and meetings that were so exciting seemed fragile and transitory. Our house was built of straw in a brick-and-mortar neighborhood.

As the Clinton administration wound down, I searched for ways to sink roots into the federal firmament so elder justice work wouldn't disappear again. During a meeting with Attorney General Reno in 2000, I suggested that we create an Office on Elder Justice. There were models. DOJ had had an Office on Juvenile Justice and Delinquency Prevention since 1974 and an Office on Violence Against Women since 1995.

That evening, as I walked along Pennsylvania Avenue toward the Metro, a black Suburban slowed down and pulled over. Janet Reno got out and walked with me, the Suburban crawling along beside us. She instructed me to put my ideas into a memo and to send it directly to her instead of going through the customary layers of vetting. Reno was initially enthusiastic about the idea of an office, but DOJ's budget division nixed it. The very thing that appealed to me—that an office would be harder to dismantle than an initiative—was the ground for nixing it. New infrastructure would create an ongoing fiscal obligation without congressional funds to back it up.

Next, I turned to DOJ's Health Care Fraud counsel John Bentivoglio, in Eric Holder's office, who'd helped to create my position. John handled budget negotiations to divvy up health care fraud dollars. I asked him to allocate funds to the Nursing Home Initiative so I could fund experts to help with our nursing home cases and research, like the Arkansas coroner study and Laura's bruising research. Money, I argued, also would give me a toehold in the federal bureaucracy after he left. "How much do you need?" he asked. "A million bucks a year," I told him, an amount that seemed simultaneously audacious, paltry, and a great deal more than nothing. Just before leaving DOJ, he slipped a new line item—$1 million a year for the Initiative—into the budget.

During the interregnum—as the Clinton crowd departed and the Bush crowd settled in—I changed the initiative's name from Nursing Home Initiative to Elder Justice Initiative to reflect my expanding goals, and with career colleagues from several offices at DOJ and HHS, formed the federal Elder Justice Interagency Workgroup.

To my shock, the Elder Justice Initiative's budget materialized, and with it a new challenge: Money doesn't give itself away. Someone has to review the grant applications, send out the funds, and monitor the process to make sure the cash goes where it's intended to. As a litigator, I'd demanded money. Now I gave it away.

Mike Hertz, head of the Frauds section, had called the Elder Justice Initiative my "rogue operation," not entirely in jest. Being a career attorney in a litigating division with a budget and a grant portfolio was highly unusual. My work became more rogue still when in 2002 I went to Congress on loan from DOJ, my feet planted in two branches of government. Hertz and Stuart Schiffer, both by-the-books government guys, could have shut me down with little trace. But they did not.

At the time, Chuck Grassley, the Senate Aging Committee chairman, sought regular briefings from DOJ on a trio of issues: nursing homes, fraud, and bankruptcy. That meant I frequently met with Lauren Fuller, Grassley's chief investigative counsel. As our conversations became less guarded, I told her about my failed bid to create an office and my belief that lasting structural change would require a new federal law. I asked whether she might be interested in working together to draft an elder justice bill modeled on the Child Abuse Prevention and Treatment Act and the Violence Against Women Act, my models at the time.

In the spring of 2001, as Lauren and I plotted the possible contours of the law, she suddenly went silent for several months. I feared she'd changed her mind, but in fact, like millions of other Americans, she was rearranging her work life so she could care for her mother. Grassley, who by then was the highest-ranking Republican on the Senate's hard-driving Finance Committee, expected Iowa farmer hours from his staff, incompatible with the intensity of caregiving Lauren was veering toward, as we saw in Chapter 1. John Breaux, a Democratic centrist from Louisiana with a more relaxed, *laissez les bon temps rouler* office ethos, had asked Lauren to return to the Aging Committee when he took over as chair. Hill staffers rarely cross aisles or leave powerful committees for less powerful ones. But Breaux offered Lauren something she needed more, the flexibility to care for her mom. Given the rigors of readying her house—installing chair lifts and grab bars and then the caregiving itself—Lauren needed all the flexibility she could get.

Once ensconced with Breaux in July 2001, Lauren called to ask if I wanted to come work with her on elder abuse hearings. I was tempted, but there'd been little to show for two decades of hearings. I worried that my DOJ budget would disappear if I left. Though small, at that time it was the largest federal pot of money dedicated to addressing elder justice. But if Breaux was willing to introduce comprehensive legislation with real money attached, that, I told Lauren, would be worth the risk. In early 2002, Lauren called to say that Breaux wanted to introduce landmark legislation, and over lunch on Capitol Hill, she asked, "What should this law look like?" I pulled a scrap of paper from my bag and jotted down an outline of the ideas simmering in my head, under the heading: "ELDER JUSTICE ACT OF 2002."

DOJ agreed to loan me to the Senate as a "resource person" in early April as long as I kept up with my DOJ work. Lauren knew infinitely more than I did about Congress, but she was an investigator experienced in exposing problems, not in drafting bills intended to fix them. Some days, the immensity of the undertaking seemed a presumptuous folly. What did I know about writing a federal law, about Congress, about aging policy, or about fixing labyrinthine social problems? How could we absorb enough information to do it right? But there was no turning back. We'd set things in motion. Lauren was in charge of process. I was in charge of substance. We had seven weeks.

Of the more than 10,000 bills introduced in each two-year Congress, fewer than 4 percent become law.[2] "Take away bills that do things like naming post offices and designating commemorative holidays," wrote the Sunlight Foundation, "and it's probably more like one percent."[3] When Lauren told me that substantive bills took an average of seven years from introduction to enactment, we'd guffawed. Unencumbered by prior experience, we thought *our* law would be different. It had no apparent antagonists and was driven by a compelling purpose. What could go wrong?

Breaux was committed to the idea and eager to move fast. He wanted to announce the bill's contours on May 20, 2002, piggybacking on a hearing already scheduled for that day. First, we needed a name. I liked "Elder Justice Act." It was short and named what we were *for* rather than *against*. Breaux's staff and Breaux himself liked it, too. He also wanted us to describe and justify each section of the law in a "proposal" he could distribute publicly on May 20. It was a massive undertaking. We held meetings and forums to seek public input. And we researched and wrote as fast as we could, more or less around the clock. By day we foraged for food and caffeine in the Dirksen building cafeterias, and by night we scoured the fine dining options in the Senate's vending machines.

Gradually, the bill took shape with a long list of priorities. We included provisions intended to strengthen APS, expand geriatrics, form forensic centers, improve nursing homes, establish centers of excellence, reduce financial exploitation, create a federal office to coordinate and lead efforts, support law enforcement and prosecutors, collect data, and fund research, including about prevention measures. Our breakneck pace worried me.

I called a woman who'd been a lead drafter of VAWA for advice. She told me: Don't be paralyzed by doubt. Take the moment you've opened up. Do your best. Revise later.

For all my criticism of laws, and their unintended consequences, I feel keen sympathy for the people who draft them. Aspirations are easy. But translating ideas into words designed to have the force of law is a fearsome responsibility. Many times the weight of it threatened to immobilize me. But at some point, every well-intentioned drafter must quell her doubts about imperfect knowledge, imperfect compromises, imperfect predictions, and imperfect words, and just write.

I was also in the grip of culture shock. The DOJ I knew was an apolitical, rule-bound place where bland, caveat-and-footnote-riddled documents muted the drama of the cases. By contrast, Congress seemed like the Wild West. At first it seemed there were no rules, but I soon learned the rules were equally intricate, just different. I cottoned to the new freedom with one-pagers that were bold and caveat-and-footnote-free.

No part of the draft proposal could leave the office, so those who wanted to comment came in. Ken Connor, an Arkansas lawyer who'd sued nursing homes for neglect, believed vulnerable elders were treated like a "throwaway" population. Connor was then head of the conservative Family Research Council. "Those who claim to be 'pro-life' and 'pro-family,'" he said, "have a moral and social obligation to protect our elderly."[4] Lauren and I wanted the bill to have bipartisan support. Connor was an ambassador in helping to recruit Republican cosponsors, like Pennsylvania's Rick Santorum. Utah's Orrin Hatch, who'd cosponsored VAWA with then-senator Joe Biden, signed on as the lead Republican.

Several organizations that we'd hoped would be strong supporters offered tepid responses, including AARP, with its 38 million members. We feared the law would flounder without visible support from the aging field's major players, so we resorted to a bit of political theater: the press conference, a Washington set piece. We told groups that Breaux would unveil the new law at a press conference flanked by victims. The names of groups that publicly supported just the idea of the law would be distributed to the press, and a representative of the group could stand up with the victims and Breaux at the press conference. Lauren had scheduled a lineup of dramatic witnesses for the financial exploitation hearing that followed, assuring press coverage. The prospect of being MIA at the event propelled even the reluctant players to show up.

On May 20, 2002, the television crews set up their cameras early. The print media straggled in. We briefed Breaux as we walked briskly to the hearing room. Then he stood at the podium flanked by two older women victims and a phalanx of supporters behind them. Beside them stood a ten-foot timeline marking the dates of more than twenty hearings that had *not* yielded legislation.

"We hope to do more than just have another hearing," said Breaux. When he finished his remarks, he invited one of the victims to answer a reporter's question. We'd been assured she had the capacity to field questions if necessary, but at the microphone, her impassioned words veered toward incoherence. Breaux, the consummate politician, looked on with empathy and interest, no hint of impatience. Lauren and I gawked at each other. Every one of the six minutes the woman spoke felt like an hour.

For the financial exploitation hearing after the press conference, Lauren had choreographed a show. There were no people with star power who'd thrown their weight behind elder justice to have testify, but there was no shortage of people whose lives had been touched. One witness, escorted in by federal marshals, was serving a ten-year sentence for scamming old people in Idaho. His favorite trick: putting bugs on a piece of wood and telling the homeowner it "came from their attic and that I could fix the problem by spraying."[5] There was a World War II veteran targeted in a bank parking lot by a woman who soon claimed she'd fallen in love with him. She tricked him into giving her everything—all his savings and the deed to his house—and she racked up so much debt in his name he had to file for bankruptcy. APS helped him and reported the case, but law enforcement didn't investigate, and prosecutors didn't prosecute.

That day our thirty-two-page Elder Justice Act (EJA) proposal became public and went to Congress's Office of Legislative Counsel, where experts translate lofty ideas into the esoteric language of federal law. After months of wordsmithing, Breaux introduced the Elder Justice Act in September 2002 with ten Democratic and seven Republican cosponsors. Passage seemed imminent.

Lauren and I were so optimistic, we practically picked outfits for the signing ceremony. But the Democrats lost the Senate majority and Breaux his chairmanship. Still, we had high hopes for 2003. Orrin Hatch, EJA's lead Republican, became more involved, and Bob Blancato, executive director of the 1995 White House Conference on Aging, who runs an aging consulting firm, launched the Elder Justice Coalition along with allies to advocate for the law. Then Breaux announced that he planned to retire at the end of 2004.

Lauren redoubled her efforts, drawing on techniques she'd learned one summer while selling Bible reference books door to door in West Virginia. During training, an instructor had taken her face between his hands nodding her head, chin bobbing up and down, while she extolled the books' virtues. "The key was to stay positive," she learned. Never give the customer a reason to say no. "If they had concerns, you said, 'Okie dokie, I know just what you mean. But let me ask you this. . . .' And then ask a series of 'yes questions' before moving in to close the sale."

By then, I was mostly re-ensconced at DOJ and my EJA congressional work was behind the scenes. Lauren was out front, ever positive. Breaux hoped for a vote on the Senate floor but no vote came. Then he tried a last gambit, putting the EJA "on the hotline." If no senator opposed it (and none had publicly), it would pass by "unanimous consent." But someone opposed it anonymously and ran down the clock on the 104th Congress.

With Breaux gone, Lauren went to work for Wyoming Republican Mike Enzi, still pushing for the law along with supporters inside and outside Congress. But the next two Congresses that ended in 2006 and 2008 brought dispiriting déjà vu scenarios: reintroduction, mark-ups, secret holds, delays, and clocks running out. Each new session we thought, "*This* time Congress will make honest advocates of us," but were left pining.

Then things changed. The seven-year gestation for laws Lauren mentioned at the start turned out to be prescient. When Orrin Hatch reintroduced the EJA in 2009, the Obama administration supported it and Finance Committee chairman Max Baucus tucked its twenty-two page text, whittled down from the original 220, into the 2,000-page Affordable Care Act (ACA). When the ACA passed in 2010, the EJA did, too, a barnacle on a whale buffeted by the same angry storms. It got no mention at the signing ceremony nor was there any plan to implement it.

Elation about its passage was fleeting. Congress *authorized* $757 million for the EJA over four years. But authorization just puts a law's programs on layaway. Congress hadn't *appropriated* any funds for the EJA. The hundreds of billions it appropriated to implement other parts of ACA included not a dime for the EJA, and then only dribbling, rounding-error amounts from 2015 to 2020.

It was a dispiriting civics lesson. I thought that a federal law was, well, The Law. "What matters a good deal more than a statute's birth is its life," wrote the legal journalist Linda Greenhouse. "The bare statutory language that emerges from Congress is only the beginning. Stingy interpretation and enforcement can strangle a new law in its cradle, while political winds blowing in a new direction can raise it to unanticipated heights."[6]

Chastened by my miscalculation in pushing a bill into existence before we had networks and constituencies with enough power to get it enacted *with funds*, I wondered what it would take to shift the political winds. For one thing, with a huge, many-faceted social problem, people needed a common language to name it, to understand it, to know what to ask for, to coalesce around a plan, and ultimately to *do* something about it. But we had no real common language. Not yet.

Chapter 14

MOVEMENT

Change does not roll in on the wheels of
inevitability, but comes through continuous
struggle.

—MARTIN LUTHER KING

When I complained about the Elder Justice Act's foun-
dering to a political strategist friend, she said: "Your
ideas are good. You just have no political constituency."
Progress requires both substance *and* influence. We especially lacked
the latter. And it wasn't just for the EJA. That was also true for change
on many issues related to improving how we age.

The first acts of change—recognizing that something's an issue,
bringing attention to it, and getting others to care—are just the
beginnings. Real change requires sustained strategy and sweat. We
needed *voices* to bring attention to elder justice. We needed strong
organizations to turn that attention into political pressure. We
needed *tools* to turn elder justice into an issue all Americans recognized as important to them. And we needed the *electoral clout* to
make lawmakers take meaningful action. Elder justice had deficits
across the board.

Laws are usually the fruit of years of painstaking organizing and
movement building. We reversed that order with the Elder Justice
Act. The law preceded any real organizing or movement. The more I
learned about how lasting change happens, the more the gaps took
clearer shape, like, well, leafy sea dragons.

Today there are networks of people all across the country dedicated to advancing some aspect of elder justice. Despite the challenges, they keep heart and keep pushing to make things better. But they need resources and ways to leverage what they have for maximum impact. For me, seeing the gaps and challenges was hopeful. Now I had light by which to chart a course that had finally come into clearer focus.

Voices

The people most affected should be the central voices. "Nothing about us without us," exhort disability rights activists. People themselves see things differently than the professionals and family members who purport to speak for them. In particular, survivors of abuse are the most gripping and persuasive voices for change on those abuse issues. This is a challenge for the elder justice field. Few older victims can or will come forward. They are scared, ashamed, loyal, incapacitated, or dead. They inspire less empathy or hope than younger victims. And as time passes, they, in contrast to their younger counterparts, become less likely to speak out.

This makes it all the more important to engage the views and efforts of the tens of millions of family, friends, neighbors, and caregivers who witness the suffering of older people and often suffer themselves as they try to help. They have a lot to say but are rarely heard. Harnessing their stories takes vetting to make sure the details are right, distilling them into clear, compelling messages and assuring that they'll do no harm. Like the best choirs, good advocacy synthesizes many voices, both those singing the solos and those with the background harmony.

The medium and messenger can be as important as the message itself. Videos, photographs, and stories make a problem immediate and visceral in a way no report or statistics can. Images stay in our minds. Fame can serve a similar function, acting as a bullhorn that amplifies some voices and issues. Occasionally a sensational case generates public attention to an issue, but the question is what you do with that attention. The O. J. Simpson case, for example, helped set in motion events that pushed the Violence Against Women Act into law, but only because the women's movement had spent years building networks and distilling priorities. When the publicity hit, advocates were poised to use it to push lawmakers to act. Fame and attention don't magically usher in lasting change without preexisting advocacy networks, strategy, and a lot of hard work. To date, elder justice has no such networks, nor has there been a comparably notorious case.

Once they're well organized and powerful enough, advocacy groups can gain a champion to help them navigate the halls of power. Again, VAWA is instructive. Pushed by women's rights activists, then-senator Joe Biden spoke out about domestic violence and steered the Violence Against Women Act through Congress, along with hundreds of millions of dollars in appropriations to implement it. As vice president, Biden appointed a White House advisor, Lynn Rosenthal, to keep the issue in the spotlight. Rosenthal wasn't a household name, but she had Biden's ear, a White House title, and a platform. She organized events for the president and vice president to use their bully pulpits to address the problem. That validation kindled public and professional awareness and gave advocates new energy. One of Rosenthal's most lasting legacies was to weave anti-domestic violence and sexual assault measures into federal regulations and programs—steady, incremental, unglamorous change.

A lot of change happens behind the scenes. Andy Mao, who has coordinated DOJ's Elder Justice Initiative since I left the department in 2007, also operates in those federal interstices. As a career official, not a political appointee, his quiet tenure has persisted regardless of what party is in power. Andy has expanded the budget and staff for the initiative a lot, funding research, a strategic roadmap for the field, and an extensive website that makes information more broadly accessible. This type of consistent, low-profile, incremental change is important, but it's not enough to meet the stakes of the problem.

Kathy Greenlee was the country's highest-ranking elder justice champion from 2009 to 2016, as head of HHS's Administration for Community Living. Kathy rarely gave a speech without mentioning the subject. She used her bully pulpit to introduce broader audiences to elder justice and urged them to take it seriously. Still, her ability to change systems or generate new resources was limited, in part because of the lack of a powerful movement like the one that pushed and supported Biden when it came to VAWA and violence against women.

ORGANIZATIONS

Overall, organizations for which elder justice is a top priority lack the infrastructure or resources to wield significant clout. And organizations with big clout haven't made elder justice a top priority. AARP, with its thirty-eight million members, is the most influential and feared aging group in history and one of the country's most powerful advocacy organizations. Many assume it's also the leading advocate on elder abuse issues. In fact, historically, AARP has expended its political capital on issues like defending social security, Medicare, and retirement funds. In the wake of the pandemic's calamity in long-term care, AARP also brought its weight to bear on nursing home reform and staffing issues, much to the relief of other advocates. "They've really stepped up recently," one advocate told me. It also has helpful initiatives and has taken a stand on financial exploitation issues. And the foundation litigation group has been unwavering in pushing impact litigation to help older people. Still, given the vast need, a greater AARP contribution could be game-changing, and likely would have altered the fate of the Elder Justice Act.

Contrast AARP with the Elder Justice Coalition formed in 2003 to advocate for the Elder Justice Act and related laws, with some 3,000 individual and organizational members who've signed on. Whereas AARP's annual budget is $1.7 billion, the coalition's is less than $100,000, small even compared to other coalitions. Bob Blancato, its national coordinator, gives speeches, testimony, and updates about the law, and has done much to keep elder justice in the congressional eye, including working with others to urge Congress to fund the EJA with pandemic relief monies. Yet, Bob does this on top of his day job as a private consultant for a range of aging groups. Comparing the coalition's budget, staffing, website, and tools with any component of AARP or organizations like the Children's Defense Fund makes the point. Bob himself has said, "We as advocates must have a sharper edge that allows us to either be respected or feared." Right now, we're neither.

In the early days of working on the EJA, Lauren and I had hoped that powerful groups that advocate on related issues—like aging and caregiving, dementia and disability, and consumer protection and domestic violence—would become strong allies for the law. But time and time again, we were disappointed. Part of the reason for this was our own inexperience. We hadn't lined up support in advance. And the timeline was short. Still, the bill was hardly controversial and had broad bipartisan support. It felt like something bigger was going on.

I asked Henry Claypool why the most powerful groups seemed reluctant to advocate for such powerless victims. Claypool, a disability rights advocate, explained that groups often choose uncontroversial or "cute" public faces for their issues, exemplified by the Jimmy Fund for cancer and the Ryan White Act for AIDS. They open hearts and wallets, defuse aversion, and summon hope more readily than a destitute grandmother with dementia and overlong nails. It's tactical, not personal.

When considering whether to take on an issue like elder abuse, aging groups have a hard enough time gaining traction without adding the specter of abuse. Abuse groups have a hard enough time gaining traction without adding the specter of aging. Other groups don't want to take on the specter of either one, even though, or maybe because, the number of people touched by the problem—some 6 million victims a year and 30 million concerned others stressed as they try to get help—is overwhelming.

I get it. The advocacy industrial complex accrues and wields influence most effectively with tightly focused priorities and jealously guarded brands. But I was still crushed that our strongest potential allies proffered only tepid support for the law. Where they lead, others go. When they demur, others demur.

TOOLS

The elder justice movement could magnify its impact by building and harnessing tools that give other groups leverage. Part of what makes AARP and other large organizations so powerful is the tools they have and know how to wield. They have large teams of legal,

policy, and advocacy staff, government affairs experts, and lobbyists
who know the issues and the ropes and who have relationships with
the people who write laws and run agencies. They apply pressure on
every branch of government and at every level. They testify at state
and congressional hearings, and write reports that politicians actually
read. Their legal departments file impact litigation that winds its way
up through the courts. The contacts they have at state and federal
agencies give them an entrée into executive branch decision-making,
to advocate for grant programs and fund their favored bills. The elder
justice field has no advocacy entity with such tools.

Persuasive advocates can push for specific reforms because they've
researched what works. Data provides evidence for change. Without
proof that smoking causes cancer and that seatbelts save lives, there
would never have been such sweeping change in policies, and ultimately in social norms. With big cultural problems like elder abuse,
as we've seen, law enforcement and prosecution won't stop it. APS
won't stop it. The greatest reduction in cases will come from policies
we don't yet know about because we haven't yet researched them. We
do know some things. We know that more staffing prevents neglect
in nursing homes. That putting holds on accounts when there are
suspicious transactions can prevent losses. And that being socially
connected as we age protects us from mistreatment. But there will
be no large-scale prevention campaigns without credible prevention
science, which, for now, we lack. Data about the cost of the problem and of proposed solutions are also critical to the deliberations of
law- and policy-makers.

For decades we've poured billions of dollars into a hodgepodge
of unproven interventions, without collecting meaningful data about
their efficacy. We've rarely even defined *success*, much less measured
it. That's why we have so little evidence to offer anyone trying to
make responsible decisions. Every new program should be rigorously
assessed before it's replicated. Existing programs—like APS, guardianship, long-term care, and teams, as well as legal responses, from
POAs to prosecution—shouldn't be above empirical scrutiny either.

This change will take money. Money for elder justice work has
been erratic and scant, whether from government, foundation,
corporate, or individual funders. It's been an impressive feat of an

innovative elder justice field to turn modest investments into programs that have influenced practice nationwide. But overall, elder justice funding has been trifling compared to that for other issues of comparable size, harm, and cost.

Communication is also a powerful tool of change and change-makers. The designated driver campaign provides an intriguing model. It began in 1988, modeled on a Nordic social norm that the driver doesn't drink. "The communication strategy at the national level had three components," said Jay Winsten, a professor at the Center for Health Communication at Harvard's School of Public Health. "The first was news, the second was advertising. The third, which was a departure from traditional public service campaigns, was to mobilize the Hollywood creative community."[1] Winsten, who came up with the idea and led its execution, spent twenty-five weeks meeting with hundreds of Hollywood writers and producers. In the end, 160 primetime shows addressed drinking and driving. Many used the term *designated driver*. The show *Cheers* used it nine times, and put the campaign's poster—"The designated driver is the life of the party"—up on its set.

By 1992, four years into the campaign, most Americans said they'd either been a designated driver or been driven home by one. Polling suggested that the campaign was a factor in alcohol-related traffic fatalities falling from 25,000 in 1988 to 13,000 in 2009, and to 11,000 in 2020.[2] (The number has risen slightly since.) The campaign moved with remarkable speed, bypassing the usual laborious movement-building machinery, going straight into popular culture.

More conventional strategic communications can clarify and frame ideas so they resonate and encourage action. My elder justice colleagues and I have done little to promote our goals by writing op-eds, soliciting strategic coverage about our issues, or even implementing awareness-raising efforts. We've been especially slow to deploy social media, a dominant force in any communications campaign.

One trait of successful advocates, organizations, and campaigns is having the discipline to answer four questions in advance: What's the goal of the communication? Who's the intended audience? What do you want them to do? What message will get them to do what you want them to do? Once they clarify goals and draft messages, they also test them to make sure they do what they're intended to. This has scarcely happened in the elder justice field.

Articles and books can also drive change. For example, *Silent Spring* by Rachel Carson transformed how we contemplate the earth and our place on it. And investigative journalism exposing sexual abuse of children by priests, and the church's complicity in it, raised awareness and galvanized action. These were topics many believed too boring or upsetting to discuss, but their importance overcame that reluctance. So far, communicating the massive impact of elder justice and of aging itself remains challenging, despite their centrality to our lives.

Then there's the phrase *elder justice*. We did no focus groups before calling the law the Elder Justice Act. The name was borne less of tactics than of sensibility. *Justice* is a big word, encompassing ideas from punishment to mercy. The way I've defined and worked for it has evolved. For me today, it evokes fairness, dignity, and hope—a way for society to set and steer itself by values, to define rights, and to provide ways for those who are wronged to be recognized and extract meaning from society's response. The law named not only what we opposed, but what we aspired to. That aspiration is broadly shared. Since we first named the law in 2002, the phrase *elder justice* has been used by dozens of public and private entities to name initiatives, roadmaps, programs, and organizations. Yet, the daunting systemic challenges described in this book persist. The hard work of realizing the aspirations embodied by the words *elder justice* has just begun.

ELECTIONS

A final and integral tool of change that bears mention is voting in elections. Asking political candidates—local, state, and federal—to take positions while they're campaigning, and then holding them to their promises, is one way for elder justice advocates to exert more political influence. To advocate clearly and vote accordingly.

We hear that people sixty-five and older are a powerful voting bloc. And we know that people eighty-five and older are the fastest growing age group. And yet, much of the political discourse about, and advocacy on behalf of, older people focuses on three issues: social security, Medicare, and retirement funds. While those are important, a much broader array of issues determines the well-being of older people, and of those who care about and for them—like caregiving, long-term care, financial security, and isolation, just for starters. Those issues already have a massive impact on the lives of most American families. And their impact will only grow in the decades to come. We must be fiercer advocates on them, too. Older people deserve a larger, more nuanced portfolio of issues for which politicians are held accountable.

This is where the voices, organizations, and tools all come together, in service of generating powerful advocacy that turns ideas and promises into action and better lives. Elder justice should be an issue for which politicians are expected to have a platform. About which they'll get questions. And for which advocates demand concrete answers and solutions.

SEEDING CHANGE

I have my regrets about the Elder Justice Act. Among them, I wish its text had better addressed the deepest needs and complexities of the field and those it serves. I wish we'd made prevention the top priority. And made figuring out the effectiveness of the interventions we already use the runner up. Words were cut, debated, and rearranged over the years, but what became law emerged from the kernel of what we wrote in those seven weeks in 2002.

Even though the Elder Justice Act fell short of our grand early hopes, its very existence came to serve as a maypole for the field to rally around, signaling that change was possible and underway. Even before enactment, it validated the work it envisioned. *See, it's in a law. . . .* It codified the idea that wrongs against older people weren't invisible. That justice matters. It lacked appropriations, but it offered a new framework to categorize the issues, expanding the way we conceive of both the problem and its solutions. Elder justice was no longer just a matter of social services for older people or nursing home neglect but also of financial security, knowledge, health, and, well, justice. Defining the problem more broadly also offered a more expansive idea of what progress could look like.

But this is hindsight. For years, the EJA's long languishing led me to despair. I thought it would never be meaningfully funded or implemented. I changed my focus to research and writing. I wanted to gain a deeper understanding of the issues and of the obstacles that blocked the way of the law and so much more. At the outset, those obstacles felt huge, amorphous, and unyielding. But as I learned more, a broader, more hopeful spectrum of options opened up before me. Seeing the gaps more clearly was useful as I tried to translate what I learned into designing new approaches—like RISE. This book is my attempt to document what I've seen and learned.

Fortunately, others kept advocating for the EJA. New allies emerged inside and outside Congress. And then—after five years of no funds and five more years of piddling sums to implement the law—in late 2020, Congress appropriated $100 million, and in early 2021 $276 million, using COVID-19 funds. The EJA briefly became both a symbolic maypole and a real vehicle that allowed Congress to send real money to the field. But by 2023, that funding stream was dammed back to a dribble. The struggle continues.

Despite that disappointment, I also felt hope. Without the Elder Justice Act, our RISE project would not have existed. EJA money helped fund the original two-county pilot in 2018, expansion to the whole state in 2021, and expansion beyond Maine and to substance use issues in 2022. It was hardly the victory we'd dreamed of in those heady days in 2002. Still, twenty years later, there'd been some progress, nonetheless. For me personally, the feeling was surreal—a two-decades-old endeavor was funding a current one.

Over time I learned that laws, like movements, have long arcs and twisting trajectories. Typically, activists coalesce into a movement and then push through a law. But occasionally the process works in reverse. Every now and then, a law seeds ideas and hopes that help a movement crystallize and grow.

Chapter 15

MYSTERY
AND MEANING

The least of things with a meaning is worth more
in life than the greatest of things without it.

—CARL GUSTAV JUNG, *Modern Man in Search of a Soul*

I tell you it has taken me all my life
to arrive at the vision of gas lamps as angels,
to soften and blur and finally banish
the edges you regret I don't see

  —LISEL MUELLER, "Monet Refuses the Operation"

For years after the day on the river when she feared we'd abandon her on that muddy little island, my mother-in-law, Janet, lived alone. Even as she slowed down, she kept seeing new movies and reading her daily newspapers. The latest books still spilled from her shelves. She was still the cool aunt people huddled up with at family gatherings, the one who, in a few spare questions, had you spilling things you'd never told anyone, realizing things you hadn't known you felt.

When she visited us, I always went to say good night, perching beside her on the bed—it was our time to talk. One evening, as she approached ninety-five, she said, "I can't believe I've lived this long. Sometimes I wonder if someone forgot I was here." At the time I chalked it up to her surprise at still being alive. Now I think she meant something broader, what Thomas Cole, a cultural historian of aging, describes as the "cultural disenfranchisement" of later life.[1] That disenfranchisement suffuses our norms and how we perceive our own aging.

PUZZLE AND MYSTERY

When I embarked on my research for this book, I tried to read Cole's *The Journey of Life: A Cultural History of Aging*, but I put it aside. I didn't think I was writing about meaning. Yet, as I made my way from subject to subject, I had a nagging feeling that some core dimension was eluding me. Like a hiker crossing a creek, I studied the stones—was that mossy one too slippery? Would the next one wobble? I was so focused on the stones I forgot to pay attention to the water.

When I finally returned to Cole, I found him revelatory. "Aging," he wrote, "like illness and death, reveals the most fundamental conflict of the human condition: the tension between infinite ambitions, dreams, and desires on the one hand, and vulnerable, limited, decaying physical existence on the other." That conflict between our bodies and our spirits can't be "eradicated by the wonders of modern medicine or by positive attitudes toward growing old."[2]

Cole, drawing on the revelations of T. S. Eliot, explored two types of problems in life. "One kind requires the question, What are we going to do about it? And the other calls for different questions: What does it mean? How does one relate to it? The first kind of problem is like a puzzle that can be solved with appropriate technical resources and pragmatic responses."[3] These days, we primarily occupy ourselves with *aging-as-puzzle*.

The other type of problem poses deeper challenges—less puzzle than mystery. "Mysteries require meaning," Cole went on. "Born of moral commitment and spiritual reflection, the experience of meaning helps individuals to understand, accept, and imaginatively transform the unmanageable, ambiguous aspects of existence."[4]

We treat old age like a medical condition and are consumed by the multiplying puzzles of treatment, logistics, and the price of care. Our successful puzzle-solving has led to longer lives. But too often, we gain time but lose track of meaning. My primary focus in this book has also been on the puzzles. But it's in the mysteries of aging where transformation can happen for us, and where positive cultural shifts must draw their strength. Drained of meaning, late life becomes largely a series of losses. If we can re-imbue aging with meaning, there'd be a lot less suffering.

In recent decades, we've seen shifts in entrenched attitudes about race, ethnicity, gender, disability, and sexual orientation. More people have come to accept themselves, celebrate their difference, and draw strength from others who share their attributes. The processes of internal and external acceptance feed each other. As people change how they feel about themselves, they also change culture. And the changing culture in turn helps other people accept and find meaning in who they are. That's one reason movements lead with *pride*.

If being different is key to the process, maybe aging isn't different enough. It's universal. We feel little compunction about vicious slurs or jokes about old age because we're just maligning our future selves. When we ourselves are the "other," bias is permissible.

There's a paradox here. Usually, groups subjected to prejudice also have less wealth and political power. But older people, on average, have more economic and political clout than younger people. They disproportionately hold positions of power in all three branches of federal government, a complex issue beyond the scope of this book except to say that even many of those older politicians steer clear of aging issues—their constituents' and their own. *Old and proud* has no resonance in the cultural lexicon. There's no movement to liberate us from archaic ideas about old age. Our culture does little to help us construct meaning or a shared identity in aging.

Denial

A few months after we celebrated Janet's ninety-fifth birthday, her memory started faltering. It seemed sudden, but her prodigious capacities had masked the early signs. Now she needed around-the-clock care. The family vaulted into action. They visited often and everyone pitched in to hire two caregivers who alternated shifts. It was fortunate this was possible, and they were caring women, but they didn't nourish Janet's enduring curiosity about the world. She watched a lot of *Dancing with the Stars* and ate a lot of cabbage. Neither one had interested her before. Now she claimed to like both.

Although Janet had the benefit of having had choices, she'd been unable to actually choose what kind of help she'd want, from whom, or where. Now her family struggled to discern the best path for her. Not deciding is deciding, too. In our house, the kids heard many discussions about "What would Janet want?" During one, our daughter, Fiona, blurted out: "We need to talk about what *you* want. It doesn't have to be now, but soon."

I was taken aback, laughed it off, and asked for an extension. *Old is that age we are not yet.*

Denial is powerful. Some denial is okay, necessary even. We need to live at more than one speed. But too much of it can impede our consideration of big things we might be able to influence more than we know. What's lurking under the rock of denial is often fear. What we fear most about aging differs. Some of us fear losing people we love. Others of us fear disability or losing our independence. Many fear a long-term illness, especially dementia, that would make us a burden on our families. (More people fear this than dying.)

But fear can weigh us down. For a better old age, it's not aging we should fight but fear. A Harvard study of adult development found that "the old-old who love life are not exceptions—they are just healthy. As they surmount the inevitable crises of aging, [they] seem constantly to be reinventing their lives. They surprise us even as they surprise themselves. In moments of sorrow, loss, and defeat many still convince us that they find their lives eminently worthwhile. They do not flinch from acknowledging how hard life is. But they also never lose sight of why one might want to keep on living it."[5]

DEATH

Making meaning of death poses a different sort of challenge. William Breitbart, chair of psychiatry at Memorial Sloan Kettering, saw thousands of patients with cancer and AIDS. "The need to create meaning, the ability to experience meaning," Breitbart said, "was a basic motivating force of human behavior."[6] Realizing this, Breitbart designed a new kind of therapy for small groups of his patients facing end-stage cancer. In eight sessions, they were asked to reflect on questions relating to what parts of their lives they felt were most meaningful, their hopes for the future, and what parts of them they hoped would go on living after they died. They also created a "legacy project."

At the end, Breitbart gave each participant Viktor Frankl's book *Man's Search for Meaning*, in which Frankl describes how he found purpose even while imprisoned in Nazi concentration camps. Frankl, also a psychiatrist, noticed that those who believed that "life was still expecting something from them; something in the future was expected of them" were more resilient in the face of relentless terror and imminent death. "Everything can be taken from a man but one thing," Frankl wrote, "to choose one's attitude in any given set of circumstances, to choose one's own way."[7] After the meaning-focused sessions, Breitbart's patients were "less hopeless and anxious. Their spiritual well-being and quality of life improved." And those benefits got stronger with time. The period between diagnosis and death was one of "extraordinary growth."[8]

My first reaction was relief that there were proven methods of meaning-making near the end of life. My second reaction was: *Why wait?* Death doesn't have to be imminent for us to focus on meaning-making. Midcourse corrections could help us reap its benefits sooner, and for longer. In one sense, we all have a terminal illness. My father liked to say, "Life is a sexually transmitted, one-hundred-percent-fatal disease."

Stanford psychologist Laura Carstensen's research has for decades shown that we grow more content with age. Even in the pandemic, she wrote, "We observed better emotional well-being in older adults compared with their younger counterparts." This "suggests that the gains stem not from avoidance of high-stress situations—which is not possible in the time of COVID-19—but instead from prioritizing goals about meaningful aspects of life." The reason for this has to do with how we perceive time. In youth, we often feel like time lies expansive before us. But later in life, time feels more constrained. Being reminded of "the fragility of life" changes how we set priorities in favor of "emotional meaning and positive experience."[9]

In retrospect, Carstensen's work helps me to understand my mother's wishes as she felt her time waning. Gravely ill, nearing the end, and in the hospital, she yearned to see the bluebells in bloom once more. So my siblings staged a "jail break," lifting her from bed to wheelchair to van to wheelchair, wrapping her in blankets, and rolling her down the trail in search of the ephemeral blue carpets, their blossoms reaching for the sun while it lasted.

Shortly after my mother got her lymphoma diagnosis, and with accelerating insistence over her last three years, she talked about her death. She was intent on preparing us for the pragmatic and the psychic realities of losing her. When she learned that Fiona would attend college in Minnesota, she gushed, "A joyful new young life coming here just as I go," as though she was leaving on an extended trip. She wasn't without fear or grief, but she found ways to manage them because other things mattered more to her as ebbing time sharpened her goals. Those conversations she instigated felt awkward at first. With the impudence of one who thinks she still has time on her side, I rolled my eyes. But later I was grateful.

We tend to focus on the bookends of life—on birth and death. Both are shrouded in cultural and religious ritual from baby showers and baptisms to last rites and funerals. Birth and death are moments of transition when we slip into life and back out again, from the unknown back into the unknowable. They are sacred moments deserving of our attention. But what we can influence infinitely more is what happens between the bookends, not how we're born or how we die, but how we live. The power of Breitbart's sessions, and those conversations with my mother, was less about finitude and more about the prismatic impact of paying attention to how we spend the time we have.

MEANING-MAKING

As I grappled with meaning-making and the spiritual dimensions of aging, I worried I was being too Pollyannaish given the hard cases that were my starting point. But the more I learned, the more I became convinced that I'd erred in the opposite direction. I'd underestimated the importance of the ineffable. Its benefits extend well beyond the spiritual, looping back into the body and the body politics. By forging meaning in aging ourselves, we nudge the culture to do the same, one psyche at a time. Such meaning-making also increases "pro-social" behavior and even, scientists are learning, has an impact at the cellular level.

Steve Cole is a University of California, Los Angeles, professor who studies how social environments influence gene expression and our bodies' inflammatory responses. Cole started out researching loneliness and learned it put bodies into "fight or flight mode and all our stress circuits flip on" in ways harmful to our health.

Then Cole switched his focus to study the impact of happiness using definitions created by the ancient Greeks: *eudaemonia*, Aristotle's concept of living with purpose, seeking moral and intellectual fulfillment, versus *hedonia*, the pursuit of pleasure and the absence of pain. Roughly, it's the difference between meaning and pleasure, between friendship and flattery, between love and sex. Cole found that hedonic and eudaemonic activity both produced positive feelings and genomic activity in immune cells. But people who pursued meaning felt connected to something bigger than themselves. They had much lower levels of inflammation and better antiviral activity. The impact of eudaemonia was roughly the equivalent of getting enough sleep, eating a good diet, exercising, or quitting smoking. DNA is not destiny. It creates a menu of possibilities. "We have a surprising degree of unrealized control," said Cole. "One of the big opportunities is to help people remember that when they're deciding what to do with their lives or day to day."[10]

Learning about that "unrealized control" evoked in me a feeling similar to the one I get from a recurring dream I've had since childhood, a common one it turns out. In it, I discover new hidden rooms, a separate wing, or a whole new floor of my house that I hadn't known existed. Occasionally there's a lush garden, too. The rooms are spacious and lovely. One leads to another; sometimes they're dusty, or the furniture's covered, as though they've been waiting. Finding them fills me with a thrill of possibility and with bewilderment that I'd overlooked them for so long. That's much what I felt in learning about modes of meaning-making that are available to us in any season of life.

Love and Connection

"The truth," wrote Viktor Frankl about his realization in the concentration camp, is "that love is the ultimate and the highest goal
to which man can aspire. . . . *The salvation of man is through love
and in love.*"[11] Decades of studies have looked at love from countless perspectives. The unambiguously clear conclusion is that human
connection and love lengthen lives and improve both physical and
mental health. If meaning is the question, love is the answer.

In the longest-running study of human development ever done,
in a place utterly unlike a concentration camp, the answer was
much the same: 268 men who graduated from Harvard University,
between 1939 and 1944—including President John F. Kennedy and
Washington Post editor Ben Bradlee—had their health and well-
being followed lifelong, many into their nineties.[12] The findings were
summed up this way: "Happiness is love. Full stop."[13] Over time, the
study cohort was expanded to include "boys from disadvantaged and
troubled" families in Boston and 1,300 descendants of the original
group. In the 2023 update, researchers wrote that "good relationships lead to health and happiness." But, they cautioned, "those relationships must be nurtured"; like physical fitness, social fitness takes
work. They encourage taking stock of one's relationships annually.
Assess honestly "what you're receiving, what you're giving and where
you would like to be in another year," they say. "Doing this can yield
enormous benefits."[14]

But as aging narrows many people's worlds, it's not just love
we need. We also need connection, like volunteering, book clubs,
and senior centers. Researchers have found bountiful evidence for
decades about all the ways social connection improves well-being in
aging and forms a protective shield against the bad things.

How we connect was in flux even before the pandemic. Then
imperatives to socially distance changed everything, especially for
older people suddenly sequestered in their homes and rooms. Phone
calls allowed some to stay connected. And video chats let loved ones
see them and a slice of where they lived. But many older people lack
access to technology or don't know how to use it. For all its connec-
tive powers, the Internet is no substitute for real human contact and

leaves many people feeling more alone. There is much that only human beings can do for one another, that machines can't replace. The poet Walt Whitman wrote: "We convince by our presence."[15]

Purpose

Even during the most desperate of human circumstances, perhaps especially then, having purpose is central. "Being human," wrote Viktor Frankl, "always points, and is directed, to something, or someone, other than oneself—be it a meaning to fulfill or another human being to encounter. The more one forgets himself—by giving himself to a cause to serve or another person to love—the more human he is."[16]

How we find purpose may evolve as we age, but it's no less important. The way to avoid an old age that is "a derisory parody of our former existence," wrote Simone de Beauvoir, in her doleful book, *The Coming of Age*, "is to go on pursuing ends that give our life a meaning—devotion to individuals, to collectives, to causes, social, political, intellectual or creative work."[17] Like others, de Beauvoir notes that valuing the lives of others, whether by love, friendship, indignation, or compassion, also gives meaning to our own lives.

But the way we've cordoned off older people can make this harder than it should be, squandering our collective humanity. Old and young have much to give one another that is available nowhere else. When we weave back together generations that have been torn apart, the benefits flow both ways. And those benefits aren't just measured in better reading skills and happy hugs. Steve Cole's research suggests that older people who volunteered with at-risk kids also had lower levels of inflammation and better health long term.

What we know about the measurable benefits of purpose keep expanding. It lowers risks of stroke, heart disease, and dementia; it improves quality of life, sleep, heart health, walking speed, and grip strength; and it lengthens both life span and health span.

Purpose remains no less crucial as our world contracts. In a 1970s study, researchers gave a group of nursing home residents each a plant. Half of them were told a nurse would care for their plant. The other half were given responsibility for their plant—selecting it, deciding where to put it, how much to water it, and hearing a lecture on caring for it. Eighteen months later, the residents who cared for their own plants were happier and healthier. They lived longer.

Anne Basting, founder of the nonprofit TimeSlips, expands on and enriches the plant study's lessons. Anne produces plays in nursing homes, and not the fancy ones. With her mantra, "Forget memory. Try imagination," she works to bring joy and meaning to people in places from which they're often drained. In 2019, Laura Mosqueda and I took a road trip to see one of Anne's plays in Morgantown, Kentucky, a town of 2,400. The nursing home looked nondescript except for the two-foot-high, multicolored letters over the front door, reading WENDY'S NEVERLAND. The show was the culmination of a two-year project that included workshops where elders, facility staff, and local volunteers discussed *Peter Pan*'s themes. Anne then wove those themes into an original play that was staged at twelve rural Medicaid nursing homes around Kentucky. In *Wendy's Neverland*, an adaptation of the *Peter Pan* story, Wendy has indeed grown up, grown old, and now lives in a nursing home.

The pre-performance flurry could have been that of any school or community theater group. Crew distributed props and adjusted actors' fairy wings. The crocodile fastened his teeth. And the queen of the fairies had her crown placed on her head. She had been the facility's director of activities for forty years. Then a stroke turned her into a resident. She disappeared into her room. Her speech was halting, her ability to move limited, even in her wheelchair. At first, she wanted no part of *Wendy's Neverland*, but the artists coaxed her and other residents out of their rooms. The invitation to create something new together—just to create—sparked their curiosity. The nursing home filled with local musicians and theater kids from nearby high schools. Artists in residence came in from around the country.

In *Wendy's Neverland*, residents in wheelchairs weren't just parked around the periphery passively watching. They were the actors, dancers, and crew. In the grand finale, people danced in twos. The leading Lost Boy, a local high school student wearing fruit on his hat and mismatched socks, gave instructions: "Twirl to the left. Now twirl to the right. Come in. Okay, back out." For her dance partner, the queen of the fairies chose the Director of Quality of Life for the entire nursing home chain, now decked out in a tutu, a silver sparkly top, and glitter makeup. Some dancers in wheelchairs moved themselves to the music. Others paired up with someone else to help them do so.

There was silliness and profundity. There were handwritten and audio letters to Peter Pan from any resident who wanted to offer one—extolling what they missed about their youth and what they would have missed out on had they not grown up and grown old. Audience members (including Laura and me) wrote positive thoughts on decorated clouds, which hung in the lobby, and fears on metal discs, which were "eaten" by Tick Tock, the crocodile. Gifted musicians, some older themselves, played keyboard, guitar, and ukulele. Everyone sang "I'll Fly Away."

After the show, there was cake and punch for all. The lead Lost Boy told me his high school choir had performed at the facility. But those concerts were a one-way street, whereas the play was a collective project—he didn't just perform *for* the residents but *with* them. Most nursing homes are islands, or in Anne's words, places of "group solitary confinement." *Wendy's Neverland* was a bridge that brought people and life into the place and helped shift the focus from all the deficits to what people *could* still do.

Before leaving, Laura and I thanked the fairy queen and several members of the cast and crew for inviting us to their home for the show. "I doubt they get thanked often," Laura said as we drove off. That's among the starkest deprivations of long-term care: losing the chance to do things with and for others.

Curiosity and Play

We keep learning more about the expansive power of theater, its invitation to try on new ways of being—a dancer, a crocodile, a pirate, a queen. Spending time with children can also rekindle our capacity for play, one too often left behind. When our children were young, I watched in wonder when Janet played with the kids, separate and together, utterly absorbed in what they were doing. To witness them was to see play as a sacred state. Old age is a great time to relearn how to play and the relaxed, unpressured curiosity that drives and accompanies it.

Curiosity, the impulse to notice and desire to know, is the mind's motor. It's primal. In life's first moments we track objects with our eyes. And in the grip of advanced dementia, we still can take pleasure in music and stories. Anne Basting's Beautiful Questions, like those my niece Charlotte pondered together with the nursing home residents, are designed to spark curiosity. Anne's TimeSlips staff have trained hundreds of Meals on Wheels volunteers to use the questions, too. Those volunteers may be the only person the meal recipients see that day, so Anne's hope is to enrich their brief encounters with questions like: "What time of year makes you feel happy?" "Where do you connect with nature?" "What advice do you wish someone had given you?"

One piece of advice I wish I'd been given sooner is philosopher Martha Nussbaum's. She urges us not to "shrink from the needy and incomplete parts" of ourselves but instead to accept them with "interest and curiosity."[18] Our culture teaches us to rage, rage against illness, loss, and aging, while offering little support for our inevitable encounters with them. "Aging is the most interesting thing that's happened to me in the last decade," one older friend, a curious, creative person, told me. What's interesting isn't just that we age, but also how we respond to it. "As we grow older, we encounter more and more complex stories—in literature, film, visual art, music," wrote Nussbaum, "that give us a richer and more subtle grasp of human emotions and of our own inner world . . . and enhanced possibilities of real communication with others."[19] I've discovered something similar when I reread books I haven't read for decades and they seem very different than how I remember them. The books haven't changed, but I have.

It's not just with books. When I notice the first leaves falling each year, and sense summer ending, the looming cold and darkness feel like an affront. But in the woods, autumn's abundance—the colors in a minor key, the shush-shush-shush of walking through leaves— win me over. I get a supple rangy sense of time—that I'm moving through it and it's moving through me. And I wonder if I'll be able to pinpoint a moment when autumn gives way to winter.

Curiosity is optimistic. It can deepen with age, bringing with it new room to notice and new ways of noticing. Our minds still reach outward and inward and want to know and feel and learn.

Awe

When I was a little girl, I would lie awake at night, terrified by the notion that time and space went on forever. Infinity was my bogey-man. I'd try to avert my mind, but I couldn't stop thinking about the great, unending darkness. Then somewhere along the way, fear became awe. In the middle of clear, dark nights in northern Wisconsin, my siblings and I would paddle boats out into the lake and drift under the falling stars, the Pleiades, and the Milky Way. On rare occasions, we could even see the cosmic green curtains of the northern lights.

Realizing that we are tiny, transient flecks in the vast universe leaves us feeling more connected, researchers have found. My siblings and I felt it seeing the sky from the earth. Astronauts feel it seeing the earth from the sky. It's called the *overview effect*. "To see the earth as it truly is, small and blue and beautiful in that eternal silence where it floats," wrote the poet Archibald MacLeish in 1968 on seeing *Earthrise*, the first human photo taken of our planet from space, "is to see ourselves as riders on the earth together."[20]

Awe has been defined by scholar Dacher Keltner as "the emotion we experience when we encounter vast mysteries that we don't understand."[21] It's a close relative of transcendence. Studies show that awe improves our critical thinking, creativity, and health. It makes us more inclined to pro-social behavior like kindness and caring. And its impact isn't just momentary. It's better than joy or contentment in producing positive emotions that improve health and well-being over time.

What we find awe-inducing is deeply personal. For older people, faith is a common source of transcendence, one that overlaps with purpose and connection. Religion allows engagement with the divine in a way that's both individual and collective, guided by ancient rules reinterpreted through the generations and by each individual.

There are countless ways to summon awe, simple and grand, from yoga to the Rockies, from music to watching the waves roll in. What's important is "the feeling of being in the presence of something vast or beyond human scale, that transcends our current understanding of things, straddling the boundary of pleasure and fear."[22] Experiences that stretch our consciousness change us.

Neurologists have found that transcendent experiences reduce activity in the part of the brain that orients us in time and space, that differentiates between the self and the non-self. Blurring those boundaries allows us to step outside our egos and change how we perceive ourselves. It's like taking a vacation from the self. We feel both less significant and more connected. By helping us reset our sense of time and place, awe immerses us in the present. It allows us to view ourselves, and the world, with more curiosity and generosity. Feeling that we are finite animate beings in the great infinite inorganic cosmos can also reduce our fear of decline and death, and maybe aging.

Ironically, drugs, something we associate with hedonic pleasure, also can cultivate awe, producing transcendent states that transform us long after the drugs wear off. Hallucinogens—once the domain of sacred Native American rituals and counterculture youth—are now also the subjects of carefully controlled scientific research. Those studies have found that psilocybin mushrooms can reduce fear and anxiety in people who are facing imminent death, by literally altering their minds. "If you hold the strong, materialistic worldview that everything ends with the body's death . . . , then death seems like a pretty dismal prospect," said principal investigator Roland Griffiths, a professor in the departments of psychiatry and neurosciences at Johns Hopkins University and founding director of its Center on Psychedelic and Consciousness Research. But "when one has a sense of the interconnectedness of all things and a stunning appreciation of life and consciousness, whether or not you come out believing in heaven or karma or an afterlife, you can recognize the depth of our ignorance in the astounding mystery of what it is to be alive and aware."[23]

Griffiths's center also is studying the power of transcendent experiences in another context: the impact of hallucinogens on depression in people with mild cognitive impairment and early Alzheimer's disease. There's poetic convergence in the search for ways that mind-altering substances might alter the course of mind-altering diseases. Fighting fire with fire.

Storytelling

For my father, storytelling was bred in the bone. He knew how to tell them, and he loved hearing good ones. For him, there was no finer way to spend an evening than exchanging stories, told or sung, with other storytellers, especially his Irish friends and family. As he got old, at some point it dawned on me that there were lots of his stories I didn't know, that the time to hear them was running out.

Old age is a rich time for storytelling, but one that's often lost because we closet away older people, or we can't deal with the painful, unfixable parts of what they have to say, or it doesn't occur to us to ask, figuring there will be more time. So, we miss out on lots of great history, often our own. Dave Isay, founder of StoryCorps, encourages young people to carve out quiet time with older relatives to summon those stories into existence. The "simple act of listening to another person," Isay said, "could make that person feel valued, respected, and dignified."[24] The telling too can be transformative.

"Storytelling is fundamental to the human search for meaning," wrote the anthropologist Mary Catherine Bateson, "whether we tell tales of the creation of the earth or of our own early choices." The process is improvisational. We discover "the shape of our creation along the way." We are *homo narrans*—narrating humans. Our "narrative identity" grows from the stories we compose about our lives: where we come from, how we got here, where we're going.[25]

Stories have the power to reveal and heal harm, change what we deem acceptable, and give us language to understand problems. They help us imagine what resources we want and need for ourselves and others. "Literature," Susan Sontag wrote, "can train, and exercise, our ability to weep for those who are not us or ours."[26] They can help us grapple with and move beyond the painful parts. Cumulatively, experience from the many, woven into stories, can change culture and consciousness, which in turn can change politics, law, and policy. Stories are upstream from all of it. The paucity of stories about aging is a big reason why its challenges stay unacknowledged, why norms lag, why elixir remains in bottles. This is not for a lack of stories. It's because not enough of them are being told. What we pay attention to shapes our existence.

Telling those stories—arranging the good and the hard bits of our lives into sequences, braiding them into something that feels coherent—is central to how we construct meaning. Stories can bring light to people's darkness. They have the power to change those who tell and hear them. Telling stories can loosen up and animate the bits floating around inside the teller and the listener to create a new, shared story.

When I was paddling down the Brule River that day in our family flotilla, I thought I was just writing the story of a problem and its people, an accumulation of stories to tell a bigger one: how things go terribly wrong for tens of millions of people, but that there are ways to steer away from trouble—in our own lives, in our families, and in society. I wanted to show that things could be different. How things are beginning to change. How inviting and telling stories that arc over the whole of life can help us reshape the world.

What caught me off guard was how telling those stories, plumbing their lessons, would change me, too. Peering into the darkness really did reveal new patterns of light. It helped me see and then write my way into a new kind of hope both for my work and for myself. What I learned pushed me to ask harder questions about what deserves our precious attention, about what matters most, about how I spend my fleeting time.

The process is less one of grand gestures than of incremental steps. We don't just contain multitudes. We also contain continental divides. Small moves can send us in whole new directions and make a big difference in where we end up.

EPILOGUE

Consolations

I t worried him, but once my father became resigned to the fact that I'd left the security of my real job at DOJ, he became my number one supporter, if an impatient one. "I'd love to see you finish that book," he said every time I saw him, often several times a visit. Sometimes he'd add with a grin, "before I shuffle off the mortal coil." It was his favorite line from Hamlet's "To be or not to be" soliloquy. We were in a race to the death, my father and I.

I sent him draft chapters—in large font—a big lump of prose, half a ream of paper held together by a binder clip. But that wasn't what he wanted. He wanted to hold the bound thing itself in his hands. Words of his flesh. The lump wasn't a book anyway. I hadn't yet figured out how to write one. Possessed by magical notions of time, I acted like I had lots of it and stuffed it full. My days overflowed with meetings and conference calls, articles and applications, nonprofits and reports, testimony, travel, and talks. Every time some shiny new thing shimmered along I said *yes*. My mind flitted from one to the next, rarely still. "That's just my work," I thought.

My father's work life had been different. He was a one-place man, caution born of immigration, poverty, war, and an austere youth. When he was six years old, his mother was taken to the hospital. He never again saw her alive. He, who remembered almost everything, remembered almost nothing about his mother. Probably, he said later, because he felt that she had abandoned him, so he banished her from his memory, except for two details: She was jaundiced when they carried her out of the house that night. And when her body was returned, to lie in their parlor for two days, her forehead was cold when he kissed it.

His father owned a pub by John Brown's shipyard on the docks of the River Clyde in Clydebank, just outside Glasgow. As a boy, he was alone a lot—three older sisters were at boarding school, two older brothers were priests. He took refuge in Dickens's adventures and Shakespeare's verses. My grandfather, having consigned two sons to the church, nudged his bookish youngest child toward medicine.

Daddy finished first in his class at University College Dublin medical school, but in seeking an academic position there, he was rebuffed. The son of a barkeep lacked the right sort of connections. He sent off inquiries to three medical centers in the United States whose names he knew: Johns Hopkins and Bellevue weren't hiring. Mayo Clinic sent a telegram: "Start 1 April 1951." He'd found his place.

He crossed the Atlantic on the *Ile de France*, in steerage, prying open the first-class doors with a pen knife to watch movies. From New York City, he traveled on to Rochester by train, arriving with $26 in his pocket, and took a room in Nellie Baldwin's boarding house at 801 West Center Street.

A lucky tip landed him a spot in a lab with a posse of young doctors on a quest to uncover the mysteries of the heart. Those were heady days in cardiology—transplants, pig valves, mapping the heart's circuitry and flow. Before human subject protection rules forbade such things, he and his colleagues threaded catheters into their own and one another's hearts. But not without risk. He once landed in the hospital with an embolism in his big toe.

Scientific striving goes in streaks like that, interest begetting interest. Aging research, long a backwater of science, is suddenly surging these days, fueled by venture capitalists and "longevity scientists" bent on cracking the codes to long life and even vanquishing death. They fall roughly into two camps: *Healthspanners* seek "a healthier life followed by 'compressed morbidity'—a quick and painless death." They want to lengthen not just life spans but "health spans." The *immortalists* are more ambitious still. They plan to make death "optional." One project strives for eternal life where our consciousness lives on in the cloud.[1] ("Ha!" a friend told me, "life is catching up with sci-fi.") With strict rules about human testing, some longevity scientists resort to using their own bodies for experiments.

To read about their plans is exhilarating, fantastical—like plans for a Mars shot, only personal. It's the same ambition and curiosity that led my father to push catheters into his own heart—the corporeal laboratory. One kind of progress.

But most people don't need Mars. They need something more prosaic. My father, the specialist, who had always been treated by specialists, Mayo's stock-in-trade, was no different. As his medical needs multiplied and became more complex, he needed what all older adults could benefit from: good primary care. It arrived with my sister Heidi's colleague, Juan Bowen, the first doctor to breach our father's private fortress.

Daddy was a shy recluse—a motherless boy with lots of practice being alone. It was his default state. His charisma fooled people. The public man was confident, unpretentious, and blunt. He wielded humor with precision, a gift like perfect pitch. His baritone raised parties. He commanded tables and rooms. People wanted his approval. He doled it out sparingly and could be harsh, tyrannical even. He suffered neither fools nor hypocrites, and sometimes not his children either. When I "dropped out" of college or my grades weren't straight As, he barked his disapproval, telling me: "I decided to be first in my class, and I was." I wrote long letters, thinking, "If only I explain myself better . . ." But he didn't soften. He had opinions on many things, including what *we* should do with our lives, what *we* should believe. When I moved in with the man I would later marry, my father didn't speak with me for almost two years because of my open and notorious violation of the church. And him.

My siblings and I had our views, too, and when they collided with his, no one shrank from battle. Some donnybrooks lasted years. "You know what they say about Irish Alzheimer's?" he'd ask. "You forget everything except the grudge."

My mother called him her "Rock of Gibraltar," to which my brother Tim once said, "you mean he's a real hard-ass?" And he was—both rock and hard-ass. My mother was his gatekeeper. She abided not only the wit and music but also the moods, solitudes, and silences. She buffered him from the world.

Her death in 2008 left him exposed. Illness and frailty opened breaches in his perimeter through which nurses, aides, and Juan entered. In my father's late season, quality, not quantity, of life became the North Star for navigating his treatment decisions: Replace the knee to walk. Remove the cancerous bowel for continence. Fix the eyes to see. But don't mess with the large aneurysm in his belly.

During an especially rough patch after his bowel was removed, Daddy had a hard time getting to the clinic, so Juan began to see him at home. He got house calls of another sort, too. Dean Marek, a Catholic priest and Mayo chaplain, had become my mother's close friend when they worked together at the prison. Dean's house calls—saying mass and offering communion to Daddy three times a week—were a gift of faith that grew into friendship. "Your mom willed your dad to me" was how Dean put it. Both Juan's and Dean's house calls improved Daddy's quality of life immeasurably, and thereby ours, too.

Daddy had long been intimating his mortality. He was fifty-four when my sister Dena was born. In toasting her baptism, he said he hoped she could soon push two wheelchairs simultaneously, and that he wouldn't live long enough to see her get her driver's license. (On the cusp of eighteen and college, I'd crashed his car the night before.)

But he kept on living. And with the grace of time, longevity bore its gifts. We changed. He changed. Old battlefields grew over with the adult lives we hadn't ruined after all. *Peace came dropping slow.* I once asked if he remembered rebuking me: "I decided to be first in my class and I was." He shook his head and said, "Did I really say something so arrogant?"

In his last chapter of life, of frailty, of need, of forgiveness, of reconciliation, of peace, he became a kind of sweet and open we'd never seen in him before, which opened up new sweetness in us, too.

Still, longevity is unpredictable. It requires constant improvisation. On Super Bowl Sunday in 2015, Daddy got short of breath. My brother Brendan, who was visiting while Heidi was traveling, rolled him—still in his desk chair—from desk, to elevator, down to the garage, and to the car. Once at the hospital, his heart was catheterized and he landed in the cardiac care unit.

Three days later, he'd had enough and told Heidi he was going home. Brendan had left by then, so Heidi, who was on call for work, dispatched an SOS to the siblings. Daddy needed someone with him 24/7. I had the most flexible schedule, so I jumped on a plane and met them at the hospital. "You should be finishing your book," he said. "But I'm grateful you came."

As we packed up his hospital room, he told me: "I didn't have a nightcap on the first, second, third, or fourth of February. But I assure you I will on the fifth." We laughed. Back at home, he relished being back in his slippers and pants worn threadbare soft. He could watch *Jeopardy* in his favorite chair and drink a diet Sprite on ice. He used the same glass over and over, keeping it in the freezer, the bottom third a hockey puck of frozen Sprite. After dinner, he swirled his nightcap, grinning, and toasted being home: *Sláinte agus Saol agat*, Gaelic he said for "health and long life for you." But when the brandy hit the fentanyl, still sloshing in his system from the catheterization, he got delirious. I somehow got him from the dinner table to the wheelchair, to the bathroom, and to the bed. From then on, much to his chagrin and mine, I became the evening nightcap monitor. So much for autonomy.

The relief of home was fleeting. He coughed nonstop. He could barely breathe, especially when horizontal. He was exhausted and weakening but couldn't sleep. I overheard him whisper to himself, "This isn't easy." He asked me, "Is there anything else to do?" Strong words for him.

I slept, or mostly didn't sleep, on the old couch in the living room, so sun-bleached it burst its seams. That way I could hear him if he needed help, though there was little I could do. The sound of his old aluminum walker's rattle-squeak-thump punctuated the night. Once he got dressed at 2:00 a.m., went to his office, and sat at his desk. Another night he dozed in the recliner. "Oh dear God."

I was in way over my head. As I lay there, it occurred to me that I didn't know what to do if he stopped breathing. Despite everything—Daddy of sound mind, my work, eight siblings tag-teaming, house calls, a doctor-sister, and world class medicine—we hadn't made a plan.

He was still a "full code," a decision he'd made some years earlier in different health. "Full code" meant 911, resuscitation, and invasive measures. It might lock him, and us, into intubation or other procedures that could cause him a lot of suffering and likely be futile. He had wanted to get out of the hospital at any cost. A "full code" was inconsistent with that wish. If crisis struck, I didn't want to violate his instructions or cause him more unnecessary pain. I texted Heidi at 4:00 a.m. She was awake, too. We talked and texted on and off until dawn.

At noon, Juan called to see if he could stop by, but Daddy didn't want him to come. "Why not?" I asked. He loved Juan's visits. "I think my symptoms are cardiac and he'll want to hospitalize me. I don't want to go back to the hospital." I called Juan from the next room to explain his concerns, whispering, traitorous.

It was time for "the conversation." Actually, it was long overdue, but finding the right moment for it was proving hard. Finally, Daddy, Heidi, and I talked briefly, one morning, when she stopped by on her way to work. He was clear. "I don't want to go back to the hospital," he said, "but I don't want to be unfair to you all."

"This isn't about us, Daddy," Heidi said. "It's about what *you* want. No one will make you go to the hospital if you don't want to go." We agreed to discuss it further with Juan at an appointment the next day.

Daddy told Juan that he preferred not to be resuscitated or intubated if it came to that. They filled out what's called a Physician Orders for Life-Sustaining Treatment, or POLST form, a traveling medical order for seriously ill people documenting their wishes to guide anyone providing care. They discussed palliative or hospice care but ended up deciding to wait and see on that.

On our drive home from the appointment, Daddy asked me to loop past 801 West Center Street. The place where Nellie Baldwin's boarding house had once welcomed him was now a hole in the ground. I drove as close as possible. He craned his neck, peering through the chain-link fence. "I wonder what they'll put up there?" he asked. After a minute or so he said, "I've had enough. Let's go. I need a nap. And you need to get back to your book."

While he lay down, a restless, coughing affair, I sat at my mother's desk facing the stone windowsill and the brown carcass of his

desiccated cactus. Sitting there, I joined the vast chorus of caregivers—
in cars and hallways, bathrooms and offices—composing themselves,
brushing away tears for the next movement of the present illness:
meds, nurses, aides, physical therapy, meals, protein, appointments,
supplies, and wrangling with insurance. There was no chance of
writing.

By chance, there was a family gathering that weekend. My seven
siblings, and a few partners and kids, were coming to Rochester to celebrate my brother John's fiftieth birthday. The roller coaster lead-up to
the weekend had left everyone feeling like we were on borrowed time,
glad to be together. We also put together a schedule for the next few
weeks of out-of-town siblings to stay with him. He was still too frail
to be alone. Brendan and his daughter were first up. Then Patrick, the
family naturalist. On Monday, it was time for me to go. Leaving was
always hard, but that cleaving was more wrenching than usual.

Then, improbably, he got stronger. He sent us all away, declined Heidi's offer to cook or spend the night, and fired the physical therapist.
He also upped the hours of his beloved aide, mostly to get rid of us.
During commercial breaks in *Jeopardy*, he walked a "half hall," or up
and down ten stairs. And he began reciting poetry again. "One equal
temper of heroic hearts, / Made weak by time and fate, but strong in
will / To strive, to seek, to find, and not to yield."[2] He was elated to
have his privacy back.

A week later, my brother Danny visited from Minneapolis, their
Sunday routine. And, as was also their routine, Daddy chided him
for being late. Danny fried eggs and Irish bacon and helped him
video chat with family in Ireland and the United States, including
me. Saying "I love you" had been unthinkable in the austere years,
but in that last chapter of sweetness, those words were both said and
improbably uttered in return. Had I known those few minutes would
be the last time I'd speak with him, would I have said anything different? Would he have?

On Monday night his back hurt. "It might be the aneurysm,"
Heidi said. "Do you want to go to the hospital?" Daddy said a definitive no. On Tuesday morning he called her at 6:00 a.m. sharp. He'd
been up most of the night in pain, waiting for the first civil moment

to call. She went right over and tried to help him get comfortable. She again suggested the hospital. He again declined.

He lay down. He sat at his desk. He sat in the recliner, which had helped before. When that didn't work, she gave him a hand to help him get up. He seized and fell back into the chair. Heidi called Juan, Dean, and Danny. Then she texted me:

"Do you know where the POLST form is?"

"Nurse's folder or with Juan? Is there time for me to get there?"

"I don't think so."

For a minute she thought he was dead, his breathing and pulse were so faint. Then his hand brushed his lips. Dean and Juan arrived in minutes.

So it was that on that Tuesday morning, when the end came—sudden yet not sudden—Daddy was surrounded by his daughter, his doctor, and his priest. Juan stepped away. Heidi and Dean knelt beside him. Dean administered extreme unction—the blessing for the dying. Daddy whispered "amen," and died.

"He waited for Juan and Dean," Danny said later, "because he knew they'd be on time. But he knew I'd be late so he didn't wait for me."

At the funeral, my brother John sang "The Bard of Armagh." It had been my father's party piece at Irish sing-alongs in his later years. He often sang it toward the end of an evening:

> *O list to the lay of a poor Irish harper*
> *And scorn not the strings in his old withered hands,*
> *But remember those fingers, they once moved more sharper,*
> *To raise up the strains of his poor native land.*

In the last verse, he always sang my mother's name, stretching "Ruth" to the cadence of "Kathleen":

> *And when Sergeant Death in his cold arms embrace me*
> *And lulls me to sleep with sweet Erin go Bragh*
> *By the side of my dear wife, my Ruu-uth then place me*
> *Then forget Phelim Brady, the Bard of Armagh.*

Dean and my cousin Donal, a priest from Limerick, said the funeral mass. "I met Dan Connolly in the last quarter of his life," Dean said, beginning his eulogy, "in his Winter Life: that last season of a long life; a season of love more profound, no wasted energy in withholding forgiveness, a mystery for those in their prime; grace not disgrace, blessing not curse."

We processed from the church to Calvary Cemetery, alight with sun and snow. Dean and Donal said blessings as they lowered my father down next to my mother. We threw handfuls of dirt on the casket, a plain pine box made by Trappist monks. Then my brother Brendan sang out, "I'm gonna lay down my burden . . ." And the rest of us answered, the Silver Creek burbling behind us, "Down by the riverside, down by the riverside, down by the riverside. . . ." Then, "Mine eyes have seen the glory of the coming of the Lord . . ." and "Oh, I wanna go to heaven . . ." On we sang, song after song, an elevating thing no words could have achieved. Even after singing ourselves out, we stayed.

The patient gravediggers hovered close by, murmuring, smoking. This was taking longer than usual. They had a job to finish, more graves to dig. We told them to go ahead. There was no need for decorum. We knew what happened next. They lifted the Astroturf off the heap of earth, and shovel by shovel covered him over. First hollow thunks, then softer swishes of dirt on dirt, mingled with his retold jokes, our stories, and the grandkids' happy shouts. They'd found the perfect place for a snowball fight and were racing among the plots, ducking for cover behind the gravestones.

In the last decade and a half, both of my parents and my mother-in-law have died. My three children left home, completed college, and embarked on their own adult lives. For more than a quarter century, my consciousness and much of my time were dominated by the roles of being a mother, daughter, and partner and by the shifting nature of my work. Now, I faced myself anew.

I wallowed one day to my son Nathan, "I've grown old writing this book." To which he answered brightly: "You're aging while writing about aging. That's so fucking meta, Mom."

Again and again, I encountered the paradox of vulnerability as strength. I missed the dead with deep pangs, the grief a physical thing. Not long after my mother died, I went down to the river at dawn and found some solace walking along the old towpath beside it. As the most gutting grief softened, the dead became present for me again in gentler ways. My son Gabriel, who was twelve when my mother died, had predicted it then, saying, "Everyone Oma affected has some of her in them now."

I thought about my father, who kept changing to the end. "At one time I wouldn't even let my wife see me naked in the light," he'd say. "Now I take off my clothes for any woman who asks." In his last chapter, he transcended shame, gave over the scruples of the body. He accepted that frailty and need were the bargain he struck for life. He found meaning in that time and was at peace with his impending finitude. Those were gifts he gave us, too.

Why do we make our poor bodies objects of so much shameful, painful freight? We come into the world helpless, and we often leave that way, too. The rest of our lives, loss and gain, vulnerability and strength, are nestled in there together, with us constantly relearning how to make them coexist as peacefully as possible. That which we are, we are.

After our mother died, we'd asked Daddy what he wanted engraved on his side of the stone they would share—a simple granite slab lying in the grass. He suggested the stone carvers might write: "Daniel C. Connolly, 1921 to 'watch this space.'"

The time to fill in that space had come before I finished my book. In our race to the death, death won.

When my siblings and I gathered to clean out his apartment, we discovered that he had left a box for each of us, personal archeology sites. Mine contained the announcement of my birth, faded recital programs, and grade school report cards on the bottom strata. Layered on top of them, as the years accumulated, were diplomas, letters, news clippings, and that lump of early chapters I'd sent him with no evidence of having been read.

Stashed in his drawers we found cheap pens, key chains, and stacks of notepads those "charities" had sent him. My brother Danny took the dead cactus from the windowsill, which vindicated his optimism and Daddy's by turning green again.

We also found a letter in Daddy's desk, still in draft. It was addressed to "MDC," letters we decided stood for "my dear children."

"This is a letter of thanks," it began, "for your loving care, especially Heidi." He and my mother, he wrote, were grateful that we'd never been poor or hungry and relieved that my brothers hadn't been involved in any war. He was disappointed that we weren't more observant Catholics, but happy that we got along so well, and pleased that we were all "reasonably good looking, healthy in mind and body, and of above average intelligence."

He'd started off in black ink, then switched to blue, writing on both sides of the thin paper, ever frugal. Farther back in the drawer, on a page ripped in half, we found more. Along the torn top edge hung a few decapitated lower loops of letters. Below them, in black pen and pencil, were a few more sentences, then another attempt at an ending. "Love + thanks to you all."

But there was no signature, no "D." He was pondering another idea. It said, "Consolation for me in recent years," and along the bottom edge, in teal marker, larger than the rest, he'd written in all caps: "2 CONSOLATIONS." That was it. Words left mid-thought.

I carried the word and the feeling of the word around with me, part haunting, part memento. I walked with it for miles along the river, hoping that motion, water, and sky might shake loose its mysteries. What were those consolations? It's a big generous word, capable of holding dark and light, binding together suffering and comfort—a little like aging. Loss encroaches, but we're alive.

My father, his body declining and death drawing near, found consolation in the "loving care" he received and in the meaning he drew from life. Those consolations then rippled on through time from him to us, taking on new life, becoming new consolations. A legacy of peace, not regret. A type of grace.

Everywhere, everyone is aging. Everywhere, someone loves someone who is growing old. Everywhere, decent people do their best, or want to do their best, with too little help, wonder how to do right, wonder if someone will do right by them, wonder how not to be broken by it all, wonder if they will find the consolations of loving care and meaning.

That alone would be hard enough. But within many more, there lurks a darker specter—of dread and degradation, of isolation and ice floes. For some the specter is vague, for others ruinous, for all a terrible waste of precious time and life. There are so many ways it can go wrong, but also so many ways it can go right.

We can't stop aging, but we could do so much more to stop the needless suffering that attends it. Some things are simple. Others are hard. But if we bring the same ingenuity, will, and hope we've invested in lengthening life to improving it, much is possible: common consolations; a deeper, more lasting justice.

The river, too, holds its consolations, bringing me new ones each season. Its beauty keeps changing form. The trees, naked now, leave everything in sight. The water's rushing sends up a faint fresh spray that feels almost alive. Those molecules aren't alive, but mine still are, and moving toward winter. Tree and human shadows stretch along the path and entwine in the slant light.

The river flows just one way until the brackish borderland where, driven by the tides, salt water curls into fresh, atoms rearrange themselves and flow on, mingling with the infinite sea. Now fog. Now ice. Now rain. Now wave.

Another consolation.

RESOURCES

The following list of general resources includes primarily national public and nonprofit entities with information and resources that may be useful to those navigating aging. These are just a starting point. Many other resources also exist.

AARP. www.aarp.org. 1-888-687-2277.
ABA Commission on Law and Aging. www.americanbar.org/groups
/law_aging. 202-662-8690.
Administration on Community Living. https://acl.gov/programs.
202-401-4634.
Advancing States. www.advancingstates.org. 202-898-2578.
Alzheimer's Association. www.alz.org. 1-800-272-3900 (24/7 helpline).
AmeriCorps Seniors RSVP. AmeriCorps.gov.
Area Agencies on Aging (USAging). www.usaging.org. 202-872-0888.
Atlas of Care, "CareMapping." https://atlasofcaregiving.com/caremap/.
California Caregiver Resource Centers. www.caregivercalifornia.org.
Care Transitions Intervention. https://caretransitions.health/about.
Centers for Medicare and Medicaid Services. www.medicare.gov
/care-compare. 1-800-633-4227 (1-800-MEDICARE).
CoGenerate (formerly Encore.org). CoGenerate.org.
Consumer Financial Protection Bureau, Office of Older Americans.
www.consumerfinance.gov/consumer-tools/educator-tools
/resources-for-older-adults. 855-411-2372.

Consumer Voice for Quality Long-Term Care. https://theconsumer voice.org. 202-332-2275.
Diverse Elders Coalition, https://diverseelders.org, 646-653-5015.
Eldercare Locator. https://eldercare.acl.gov. 1-800-677-1116.
Family Caregiver Alliance. www.caregiver.org. 1-800-445-8106.
Federal Bureau of Investigation. www.fbi.gov/scams-and-safety /common-scams-and-crimes.
Federal Trade Commission. www.ftc.gov. 1-877-382-4357.
The John A. Hartford Foundation. www.johnahartford.org. 212-832-7788.
Justice in Aging. www.justiceinaging.org. 202-289-6976.
Kaiser Family Foundation. www.kff.org. 202-347-5270.
Meals on Wheels. www.mealsonwheelsamerica.org. 1-888-998-6325.
National Adult Protective Services Association. www.napsa-now .org. 202-541-3950 (24/7 hotline).
National Alliance for Caregiving. www.caregiving.org. 202-918-1013.
National Asian Pacific Center on Aging (NAPCA), https://www .napca.org. Helplines offered in eight languages, each with a phone number listed at https://napca.org/helpline/.
National Association of States United for Aging and Disabilities. https://thearc.org. 1-800-433-5255.
National Association of State Units on Aging. https://nasua.org. 202-898-2578.
National Caucus and Center on Black Aging (NCBA), https://ncba -aging.org, 202-637-8400.
National Center on Elder Abuse. https://ncea.acl.gov. 1-855-500-3537 (1-855-500-ELDR).
National Center on Law and Elder Rights, "About Elder Justice Toolkit." https://ncler.acl.gov/ElderJustice-Toolkit/About-Elder -Justice-Toolkit.aspx.
National Clearinghouse on Abuse in Later Life. www.ncall.us. 608-255-0539.
National Council on Aging. www.ncoa.org.
National Domestic Violence Hotline. www.thehotline.org. 1-800-799-7233 (1-800-799-SAFE).
National Elder Fraud Hotline, 877-382-4357 (HELP) and 833-372-8311.

National Hispanic Council on Aging (NHCOA), https://nhcoa.org, 202-347-9733.

National Indian Council on Aging (NICOA), https://www.nicoa .org, 505-292-2001.

National Indigenous Elder Justice Initiative, https://www.nieji.org, 701-777-6084.

National Institute on Aging. www.nia.nih.gov. 1-800-222-2225.

National Institute on Mental Health. www.nimh.nih.gov. 1-866-615-6464.

National Long-Term Care Ombudsman Resource Center. https:// ltcombudsman.org. 202-332-2275.

National Network to End Domestic Violence. https://nnedv.org. 202-543-5566.

National POLST, "POLST and Advance Directive." https://polst .org/polst-and-advance-directives/.

New York City Elder Abuse Center. www.nyceac.org. 844-746-6905 (Elder Abuse Helpline for Concerned Persons).

Office of Victims of Crime, National Elder Fraud Hotline. http://ovc.ojp.gov/program/stop-elder-fraud/. 1-833-372-8311 (1-833-FRAUD-11).

Safe Havens Interfaith Partnership Against Domestic Violence and Elder Abuse. www.interfaithpartners.org. 617-951-3980.

SAGE (Advocacy and Services for LGBTQ+ Elders). www.sageusa .org. 877-360-5428 (877-360-LGBT).

Southeast Asia Resource Action Center (SEARAC), https://www .searac.org, 202-601-2960.

Substance Abuse and Mental Health Services Administration. www.samhsa.gov. 1-877-726-4727 (1-877-SAMHSA-7) and SAMHSA helpline, 1-800-662-4357 (1-800-662-HELP).

Suicide and Crisis Lifeline. https://988lifeline.org/. 988.

US Department of Justice, Elder Justice Initiative. www.justice.gov /elderjustice. Elder Abuse Resource Roadmap: Financial. www .justice.gov/elderjustice/file/900221/download, 1-866-366-2382.

US Senate Special Committee on Aging. www.aging.senate.gov. 202-224-5364.

Women's Institute for a Secure Retirement (WISER) https://wiser women.org, 202-393-5452.

AUTHOR'S NOTE
ON NAMES, TERMS,
AND SOURCES

This is a book of nonfiction. The text is drawn from conversations with hundreds of people, the research and writing of hundreds more, as well as my own observations, work, and life. There are no conflated events or composite characters. Many bodies of knowledge contribute to the foundation on which this book builds, but ultimately, it is my attempt to make sense of what I've seen and learned.

The people whose work I've described rarely worked alone, including me. But naming everyone, and everything everyone did, would have submerged the text. I apologize to those who didn't get the credit they deserved in these pages. And I regret letting some who deserved more blame off the hook.

I generally used first names for my family and colleagues and last names for those whose published work I quoted, and followed the naming conventions used by the people I interviewed. I also edited some interview quotes for length and clarity. Some names and identifying characteristics have been changed to conceal identity and protect privacy. The first time a pseudonym is used, it appears in quotation marks.

The words we use to describe many subjects in this book—including *care*, *fraud*, and *aging* itself—keep on changing, influenced by culture, sensibility, history, politics, academia, corporate interests, and advocacy strategy. Words matter a lot. I often wished for ones that better captured the nuances, and I tried to stay away from diminishing ones. But resolving the dilemmas and debates of a language-in-flux is beyond the scope of this book and my expertise.

A list of websites and organizations that might be useful to readers is included in the Resources section, although those too are in flux and should be treated as just starting points. The programs, research, entities, and players I've described are intended to be illustrative, not exhaustive. There's much fine work deserving of attention that didn't get in these pages.

Sources for quotations and a few of the facts in the book can be found in the endnotes. Those and extensive additional sources and information can be accessed at www.TheMeasureofOurAge.com /additional-sources.

ACKNOWLEDGMENTS

In the acknowledgments to his book, *The Thing Itself: On the Search for Authenticity*, Richard Todd wrote: "Faced with the impossibility of inclusiveness, I have become no doubt wildly idiosyncratic." After lo these many years of working on this book, I feel the same way, but here goes. First thanks go to the hundreds of people, named and unnamed, who took the time to talk with me. Thank you for entrusting me with your knowledge and your stories—the happy and the hard ones. They stretched and deepened what I thought I knew. I've tried to do them justice. There would be no book without you.

Thank you to my wonderful editor, Colleen Lawrie, for believing in this book, for pushing me to reshape and improve it, and for being there every step of the way. Huge thanks also to the many others at PublicAffairs and the Hachette Book Group whose skill and contributions were essential to turning a bunch of words into a book and putting it out into the world, including Charlotte Byrne, Miguel Cervantes, Pete Garceau, Carolyn Levin, Kimberly Meilun, Joselynn Pedro, Clive Priddle, Melissa Raymond, Shena Redmond, and Jeff Williams.

Thank you to my great agent, Gail Ross, who saw the kernel of a book from the start, encouraged me to write it, stuck with me, and, together with the talented Howard Yoon, offered vital guidance along the way.

I am grateful for the institutions that have played outsized roles in my life and in this book. At the Department of Justice, where I learned to be a lawyer in the Civil Frauds Section, the Elder Justice Initiative continues to build on the Department's original mission to defend the rights of vulnerable people.

In Congress, I'm grateful to the members, staff, investigators, and research-ers dedicated to improving how we age.

At the Woodrow Wilson International Center for Scholars, I'm grateful to the stellar staff and to Linda Lannam, who provided invaluable research assis-tance and much more. As our fellowships wound down, Mary Ellen Curtain, Matthew Dallek, Robyn Muncy, Wendy Williams, and I, under the leadership of the indominable Philippa Strum, decided to keep meeting as the Red Line Group. They read the earliest, messiest snippets of this book, offered indispens-able feedback and friendship, and kept doing so until it was done.

There aren't words to properly thank the MacArthur Foundation for the life-changing fellowship that not only enabled me to write this book but also recognized that the issues in it matter. Special thanks to Marlies Carruth, Cecilia Conrad, and Christina Lovely.

It took me a while to figure out that I needed solitude to write. I'd read about the legendary artist retreats—Yaddo and MacDowell—extraordinary places that have long been wellsprings for transformative work. I am beyond grateful they took me in and transformed me too.

I am also grateful for my time in the natural beauty of the Carey Institute for Global Good, the Virginia Center for the Creative Arts, and the Heinrich Böll Cottage (in Achill Island, Ireland, where the proximity to my awesome MacNamara and Ruane cousins multiplied my good fortune).

Another gift of those residencies was the insight and inspiration offered by Rania Abouzeid, Emma Beals, David Baum, Liza Birkenmeier, Joanne Drayton, Alex Halberstadt, Trish Haretiaux, Ella Hickson, Tom Jennings, Azmat Khan, Taran Khan, Adrian Leblanc, Richard McCann, Andrew Ondrejcak, Alim Remtulla, Anastasia Taylor-Lind, Elliot Williams, and many others.

Abiding thanks to the Elder Justice Foundation's David Zimmerman and Kate Hester for supporting my work and that of others, and for investing in new ideas that really were seeds of change.

Thank you to Bonnie Brandl and Mary Twomey for never doubting that a small group of thoughtful, committed people could change the world, and for gathering a group of women to do just that. Thanks to them along with Risa Breckman, Catherine Hawes, and Alison Hirschel, with periodic consultations from Laura Tamblyn Watts, for years of Friday and January meetings, combin-ing many views to see a fuller picture. And to Bonnie, Risa, Andy Mao, and everyone else who contributed to the Elder Justice Roadmap.

I'm more grateful by the year for the neighborhood village where we raised our families, and one another, in multigenerational webs that happily persist even as they keep changing. I'm infinitely grateful too for my friends. I can't begin to name all those whose generosity pulled me through, but among them—for offering lovely places to work, healing waters, and sustenance year after year—I'm grateful to Joyce Branda, Beth Donovan, Luke Albee, Jim Grady, Bonnie Goldstein, Rachel Jacobson, Kerry and Jim Joseph, Ruth Mandel, Michael Borowitz, Maz Rauber, Charley Keyes, Ricki Seidman, Chris and Mike Taylor, Trudy Vincent, and everyone at TSD Communications.

As this book evolved, I was fortunate that early rough bits were read by sage, benevolent readers who imparted history lessons, pointed out quicksand, sharpened arguments, and said, "Keep going," including Georgia Anetzberger, Risa Breckman, Emily Goldfarb, Becky Kurtz, Nick Maduros, Steve Rickard, Laura Tamblyn Watts, and Zipporah Wiseman. (Z, I'm so sorry I didn't finish in time.)

For smart, resourceful research assistance, huge thanks to Leah Flamm, Ariel Trilling, Kylie Meier, and the incomparable Sarah Dion most of all, for, well, everything.

For house calls and phone consultations that kept finicky computers and printers running despite operator ignorance, I'm grateful to the ever patient and inventive Douglas Kebengwa.

I'm grateful to Louise Aronson, Sara Bershtel, Marc Freedman, Suzannah Lessard, Sarah MacLachlan, Tal McThenia, and Samantha Peale for kind and wise counsel when I needed it.

This book and my understanding of its subjects benefited immeasurably from the research and writing of phenomenal journalists and scholars. The issues may not generate swarms of clicks or cash, but they have everything to do with how we live. Thank you. Please keep writing.

I owe an incalculable debt of gratitude to the people whose work makes up the spine of this book, Laura Mosqueda, Ricker Hamilton, Page Ulrey, and Alison Hirschel in particular. They opened up their lives, spent hundreds of hours talking with me over a decade and a half, dug through their files, let me follow them around, and helped me to understand. Special thanks to Laura for the bottomless office hours and for helping so many people navigate not just their own aging but also that of others.

I am also grateful to the many people who did the work described in the book but were not named, as well as unnamed others who provided support or influenced my writing (whether you like it or not). This list in reality is much longer still, but for starters, I owe big thanks to: Bob Abrams, Lisa Allen, Eileen Alexander, Steve Altman, Dan Anderson, Kelly Bagby, Kevin Barr, Paula Barton, Elise Bean, Scott Beech, Bill Benson, Sue Bessette, Matthew Boller, Marie Boltz, David Boul, Tameshia Bridges Mansfield, Sarah Burger, Jason Burnett, Alex Busansky, Liz Buser, Paul Caccamise, Naomi Cahn, Jean Callahan, Jill Callahan, Jaqueline Campbell, Andy Capehart, Elizabeth Capezuti, Eric Carlson, Betsy Cavendish, Remy Cawley, Mark Childress, Jennie Chin Hansen, Kathi Church, David Corn, Lorraine Cortés-Vázquez, Ashley Cottingham-Carter, Genna Crawley, Chic Dabby, Hilary Dalin, Carol Dayton, Patty DeLoatche, K. Eric DeJong, Marti DeLeima, Donna Dougherty, Ellen Durkee, Toby Edelman, Stephanie Whittier Eliason, Alexis Espinola James, Judy Feder, Francesca Freccerro, Iris Freeman, Robert Frye, Lisa Furr, Elizabeth Gattine, Lisa Gibbs, Sue Goldberg, Amy Golen, Tracy Gray, Jeff Hall, Charles Halpern, Debora Cackler Harding, Thomas Harding, Charlene Harrington, Chris Harvie, Claudia Harvie, Alice Hedt, Candace Heisler, Melba Hernandez-Tejada, Sherri Hill, Beth Horowitz, Mary Houghton, Anne Marie Hunter, Sally Hurme, Chris Jennings, Carole Johnson, Jason Karlawish, Naomi Karp, Gavin Kennedy, Arthur Kohrman, Claire Kohrman, Lee Kohrman, Diane Krieger, Mary-Ellen Kullman, Ann Laatsch, Mark Larson, Helen Lamont, Carolyn Lerner, Peter Lichtenberg, Brian Lindberg, Ronnie LoFasso, Meg London, Susan Lynch, Maya MacGuineas, Jay Madorsky, Susan Madorsky, Leesa Manion, Ruth Marcus, Arlene Markarian, Lori Mars, Philip Marshall, Dan Marson, Jaye Martin, Julia Martinez, Alane Salierno Mason, Jennifer Mathis, Patty McFeeley (a femme fatale), Joan Meier, Emily Miller, E. Ethelbert Miller, Linda Miller, Gov. Janet Mills, Bettye Mitchell, Anne Montgomery, Meg Morrow, Sarah Morton, Carrie Mulford, Cecilia Muñez, Lisa Nerenberg, Victoria Nourse, Tom O'Briant, Bonnie Olsen, Andy Penn, Ron Petersen, Kevin Prindiville, Kathleen Quinn, Harriet Rabb, Laura Rath, Molly Reilly, Sue Renz, Leonard Roberge, Nan Robertson, Abie Rohrig, Ari Roth, Dermot Ruane, Charlie Sabatino, Kate Schechter, Andrew Schneider, David Schwartz, Cheryl Scott, Ann Shalleck, Nicole Shannon, Jeff Shreve, Eugenia Siegler, Abbe Smith, Erica Smith, Joy Solomon, William Souder, Mike Splaine, Sid Stahl, Rebecca Stoeckle, Chris Stone, Margie Sullivan, Cecil Swamidass, George Taler, Pam Teaster, Julio Urbina, Jim Vanden Bosch, Angela VonDerLippa, Edwin Walker, Deb Whitman, Mark Wiggs, Erica Wood, Wendy Wright, Mindy Young, and Ying-Ying Yuan.

Thank you to Lauren Fuller for sharing her experience of caring for her mother while also being the Elder Justice Act's tireless champion, and for *living the dream*, with so much grace.

Thank you to Ron Long from whom I learned much about banking, and whose generosity I repaid by extracting those lessons and putting them in this book.

Thank you to Stuart Schiffer and Mike Hertz for hiring me to join DOJ's honors program and who, along with Polly Dammann and George Vitelli, who spearheaded nursing home prosecutions described in this book, died far too young. Thanks also to Stuart and Mike for letting me "go rogue" with the Elder Justice Initiative, to Janet Reno, Eric Holder, and John Bentivoglio, for their integral roles in launching it, and to Andy Mao for leading and exponentially expanding it over the many years.

Thank you to Robert Butler and Rosalie Wolf for their pioneering work. I'm grateful my path crossed theirs, if too briefly. Thanks also to Linda Dawson, Jessica Lanphere-Charronsmith, Joanne Otto, and Lori Stiegel, who also died too soon, as did Carmel Dyer, who always led with love.

Working with the RISE team of creative, dedicated, fabulous people—to build and test something new and hopeful—is an ongoing privilege for which I'm grateful to David Burnes, Stuart Lewis, Geoff Rogers, and especially Patty Kimball and her team.

Thank you to Ricker Hamilton for letting us try, to Erin Salvo for being the guiding voice of APS, to Jeanne Lambrew for rigorous standards and support, and to the people of Maine's APS program for taking a chance.

Thanks also to the great RISE Alternative crew for their resolve and dedication in expanding RISE to the criminal justice system, including David Burnes, Zach Gassoumis, Tracy Gorham, Karen Heeney, Patty Kimball, Stuart Lewis, Kelsey Park, Leanne Robbin, Geoff Rogers, Tony Rosen, Suzanne Russell, Page Ulrey, and Kathy Van Olst.

One of the great gifts of this book was that it led me into the orbit of Richard Todd's wry brilliance as both an editor and a human being. Visiting him and Susan at their farmhouse was for me like walking through the wardrobe. Dick's death left a hole in the world, but among his lasting gifts was introducing me to Adrian Leblanc who has taught me more than I can thank her for.

I'm grateful also to the fantastic Julie Tate, a researcher and fact checker so good her former boss Don Graham said, "In a more just world, Julie would have several Pulitzers."

Along the way, this book benefited from superb and learned readers who brought sharp eyes and varying troves of knowledge including Anne Basting, Joyce Branda, David Burnes, Kate Kinast, Nina Kohn, Ruth Mandel, Andy Mao, Tricia Neuman, Zach Gassoumis, Sophie Kasimow, Patty Kimball, Stuart Lewis, Tony Rosen, Karl Pillemer, Geoff Rogers, Geoff Shandler, Trudy Vincent, and Kate Wilber.

At age sixteen, my amazing nieces, Charlotte and Isabelle, asked to read my manuscript, and kept asking until I relented. Then they read the whole damn thing and enlightened me with the wisdom of another age. Houston White expanded how I think about barbershops, design, community, and family. Lauren Randel aided me in poring through fragments until they cohered into more hopeful ways of understanding. Mark Steitz imparted acute guidance of many types, saving me from myself in ways large and small (or at least he tried). And Ingrid Creppell helped me sort and clarify ideas and life as, for more than a decade, we walked the trails of Rock Creek Park, mile by mile, chapter by chapter, and season by season.

I'm profoundly grateful to Amanda Bennett, David Finkel, Taran Khan, Adrian Nicole LeBlanc, John Pomfret, and Karl Vick for their deep vision, transformative counsel, and for giving me faith that there was a book in there somewhere.

My research keeps teaching me about the centrality of family and my great good fortune to have one as large, loving, unwieldy, and interesting as mine. Thank you to Danny Kohrman for the great adventure of creating our own family, raising three incredible human beings, reconfiguring the operation into friendship, and bringing Janet Kohrman into my life, the best mother-in-law any girl could have had.

Thank you to Cathryn Collins and the extended Kohrman, Madorsky, and related clans for taking me in from the get-go and for all the years since.

Thank you to Ricki Seidman for teaching me the meaning of chosen family, for being part of ours, for enduring generosities, and for being a reader, advisor, friend, and godmother extraordinaire.

Thank you to Ruth Elisabeth Westrick Connolly and Daniel Charles Connolly, who brought the fortitude, hope, and striving of immigrants to parenting, infused it with love, and who, by buying the cabin in 1969, tethered us to one another with a deep love for the natural world.

Thank you to my parents' sprawling families in more than a dozen countries on several continents and your steadfast welcoming back of the Americans.

Thank you to my siblings, Heidi, Danny, Patrick, John, Brendan, Tim, and Dena, individually spectacular humans and collectively a formidable force, and to your wonderful partners and children. Being one of you moors me in the world. Special thanks to Heidi for always being on call, for all the loving care.

Thank you most of all to Fiona, Nathan, and Gabriel. I am blown away by what incredible readers, listeners, line editors, strategists, photographers, faux pas preventers, and people you are. The book is far better for your contributions to it. As is every hour of every day. Thank you for the boundless support and love. There is nothing in my life I'm more grateful for than having you in it.

NOTES

Only direct quotes and a few additional facts are cited in these endnotes. Extensive additional sources and notes can be accessed at www.TheMeasureofOurAge.com.

PROLOGUE

1. "Ulysses," Alfred Lord Tennyson, cited in Del Plane, *College Reading in Poetry*, 305–306.
2. Butler, *Why Survive?*, 12, 3.
3. Wilkerson, *Caste*, 385.

CHAPTER 1: CARE

1. "65 and Older Population Grows Rapidly as Baby Boomers Age," *United States Census Bureau*, June 25, 2020, https://www.census.gov/newsroom/press-releases /2020/65-older-population-grows.html.
2. Steven Johnson, "How Humanity Gave Itself an Extra Life," *New York Times*, April 27, 2021, https://www.nytimes.com/2021/04/27/magazine/global-life-span.html.
3. "2020 Profile of Older Americans," *Administration for Community Living*, May 2021, https://acl.gov/sites/default/files/Aging%20and%20Disability%20in%20America /2020ProfileOlderAmericans.Final_.pdf, 5.
4. Global Health Observatory, "Life Expectancy at Birth (Years)," *World Health Organization*, accessed October 15, 2022, https://www.who.int/data/gho/data/indica tors/indicator-details/GHO/life-expectancy-at-birth-(years); "Healthy Life Expectancy (HALE) at Birth (Years)," https://www.who.int/data/gho/data/indicators/indicator -details/GHO/gho-ghe-hale-healthy-life-expectancy-at-birth.
5. "Personal Care Needs," in Tainya C. Clarke, Jeannine S. Schiller, and Tina Norris, *Early Release of Selected Estimates Based on Data From the January–June 2017 National Health Interview Survey*, National Center for Health Statistics, December 2017, https://www.cdc.gov/nchs/data/nhis/earlyrelease/earlyrelease201712_12.pdf;

Richard Johnson, "What Is the Lifetime Risk of Needing and Receiving Long-Term Services and Supports?" *Office of the Assistant Secretary of Planning and Evaluation*, April 3, 2019, https://aspe.hhs.gov/reports/what-lifetime-risk-needing-receiving-long-term-services-supports-0.

6. Richard W. Johnson, "What Is the Lifetime Risk of Needing and Receiving Long-Term Services and Supports?," *Office of the Assistant Secretary for Planning and Evaluation*, April 3, 2019, https://aspe.hhs.gov/reports/what-lifetime-risk-needing-receiving-long-term-services-supports-0.

7. Michelle R. Davis, "Despite Pandemic, Percentage of Older Adults Who Want to Age in Place Stays Steady," *AARP*, November 18, 2021, https://www.aarp.org/home-family/your-home/info-2021/home-and-community-preferences-survey.html.

8. Associated Press and NORC, "Long-Term Care in America: Americans Want to Age at Home," Associated Press-NORC Center for Public Affairs Research Issue Brief, May 2021, https://apnorc.org/wp-content/uploads/2021/04/LTC_Report_AgingatHome_final.pdf, 3.

9. AARP and National Alliance for Caregiving, "Caregiving in the U.S.," Research Report, May 2020, https://www.aarp.org/content/dam/aarp/ppi/2020/05/full-report-caregiving-in-the-united-states.doi.10.26419-2Fppi.00103.001.pdf, 4.

10. "Caregiver Statistics: Demographics," *Family Caregiver Alliance*, accessed November 11, 2022, https://www.caregiver.org/resource/caregiver-statistics-demographics/.

11. Amalavoyal V. Chari, John Engberg, Kristin Ray, and Ateev Mehrotra, "The Opportunity Costs of Informal Elder-Care in the United States: New Estimates from the American Time Use Survey," *Health Services Research* 50, no. 3 (June 2015): 871–882, https://www.rand.org/pubs/external_publications/EP66196.html.

12. Heather M. Young, Janice Bell, and Jennifer Mongoven, "Picking up the Pace of Change: Scaling Services for a Changing Caregiver Profile," *Family Caregiving Institute*, December 14, 2021, https://health.ucdavis.edu/media-resources/family-caregiving/documents/pdfs/CCRC%20Evaluation-2021-Report-Exec-Summary.pdf.

13. Aisha Adkins, "The Cycle of Care: How Generational Caregiving Disproportionately Impacts Black Women," *Generations*, August 30, 2022, https://generations.asaging.org/how-generational-caregiving-impacts-black-women.

14. Richard Schulz and Jill Eden, eds., *Families Caring for an Aging America*, National Academies of Sciences, Engineering, and Medicine Report (Washington, DC: The National Academies Press, 2016), https://nap.nationalacademies.org/catalog/23606/families-caring-for-an-aging-america.

15. AARP and National Alliance for Caregiving, "Caregiving in the U.S."

16. Family Caregiving Institute, "Picking up the Pace of Change: Scaling Services for a Changing Caregiver Profile—Evaluation of the California Caregiver Resource Centers Service Delivery and System Change," December 14, 2021, https://health.ucdavis.edu/media-resources/family-caregiving/documents/pdfs/CCRC%20Evaluation-2021-Report-Exec-Summary.pdf.

17. "Atlas CareMap," *Atlas of Care*, accessed October 15, 2022, https://atlasofcaregiving.com/caremap/.

18. "Caregivers," *Anxiety and Depression Association of America*, accessed October 15, 2022, https://adaa.org/find-help/by-demographics/caregivers.

19. Hartog, *Someday All This Will Be Yours*.

20. "Infographic About Preventing Child Abuse and Neglect," *Centers for Disease Control and Prevention*, updated March 15, 2021, https://www.cdc.gov/violence prevention/communicationresources/infographics/CAN.html; Children's Advocacy Centers of Tennessee homepage, accessed October 15, 2022, https://cactn.org.

21. "Violence Prevention," *Centers for Disease Control and Prevention*, updated June 22, 2022, https://www.cdc.gov/violenceprevention/sexualviolence/fastfact.html.

22. Martin R. Huecker, Kevin C. King, Gary A. Jordan, and William Smock, "Domestic Violence," *StatPearls*, updated July 1, 2022, https://www.statpearls.com /ArticleLibrary/viewarticle/40654.

23. Statement made to the author in 2016 by Kathleen Kelly, head of the Family Caregiving Alliance.

24. Pillemer, *Fault Lines*, 45.

25. "Home Health and Personal Care Aides," *U.S. Bureau of Labor Statistics*, accessed October 15, 2022, https://www.bls.gov/ooh/healthcare/home-health-aides -and-personal-care-aides.htm.

26. Priya Chidambaram and Alice Burnes, "10 Things About Long-Term Services and Supports (LTSS)," *Kaiser Family Foundation*, September 15, 2022, https://www .kff.org/medicaid/issue-brief/10-things-about-long-term-services-and-supports-ltss/.

27. "U.S. Home Care Workers: Key Facts," *Paraprofessional Healthcare Institute*, accessed October 15, 2022, https://phinational.org/wp-content/uploads/legacy /phi-home-care-workers-key-facts.pdf, 4.

28. "Nearly a Third of Americans Use Gray Market When Hiring Caregivers for the Elderly and Those with Dementia," *RAND Corporation*, June 21, 2021, https://www .rand.org/news/press/2021/06/21.html.

29. "Home Health and Personal Care Aides," *U.S. Bureau of Labor Statistics*, accessed November 11, 2022, https://www.bls.gov/ooh/healthcare/home-health -aides-and-personal-care-aides.htm; "Direct Care Workers in the United States: Key Facts," *PHI*, September 6, 2022, 1; https://www.phinational.org/resource/direct -care-workers-in-the-united-states-key-facts-3/; annual earnings numbers come from PHI's analysis of the American Community Survey data (2020), PHI Workforce Data Center, https://www.phinational.org/policy-research/workforce-data-center/#tab =National+Data.

30. Buch, *Inequalities of Aging*, 7.

Chapter 2: Health

1. D. D. Craves, J. D. Campbell, and D. R. Mehr, "Why Geriatrics? Academic Geriatrician's Perceptions of the Positive, Attractive Aspects of Geriatrics," *Family Medicine* 32, no. 1 (2000): 34–41, https://pubmed.ncbi.nlm.nih.gov/10645512/.

2. Gawande, *Being Mortal*, 44–45, citing Chad Boult, Lisa B. Boult, Lynne Morishita, Bryan Dowd, Robert L. Kane, and Cristina F. Urdangarin, "A Randomized Clinical Trial of Outpatient Geriatric Evaluation and Management," *Journal of the American Geriatrics Society* 49, no. 4 (2001): 351–359.

3. "Geriatrics Workforce by the Numbers," *American Geriatrics Society*, accessed October 15, 2022, https://www.americangeriatrics.org/geriatrics-profession/about -geriatrics/geriatrics-workforce-numbers.

4. "2020 Census Will Help Policymakers Prepare for the Incoming Wave of Aging Boomers," *US Census Bureau*, December 10, 2019, https://www.census.gov/library/stories/2019/12/by-2030-all-baby-boomers-will-be-age-65-or-older.html.

5. "Why Geriatrics," *American Geriatrics Society*, accessed October 15, 2022, https://www.americangeriatrics.org/geriatrics-profession/why-geriatrics.

6. Aronson, *Elderhood*, 183.

7. Aronson, *Elderhood*, 183.

8. Herman Melville, "The Encantadas," in *The Piazza Tales* (New York: Dix & Edwards, 1856).

9. "Older Adult Falls Reported by State," *Centers for Disease Control and Prevention*, updated July 9, 2020, https://www.cdc.gov/falls/data/falls-by-state.html.

10. R. S. Wilson, L. E. Hebert, P. A. Scherr, X. Dong, S. E. Leurgens, and D. A. Evans, "Cognitive Decline After Hospitalization in a Community Population of Older Persons," *Neurology* 78, no. 13 (March 27, 2012): 950–956, https://doi.org/10.1212/wnl.0b013e31824d5894.

11. Aronson, *Elderhood*, 181.

12. Aronson, *Elderhood*, 181.

13. Aronson, *Elderhood*, 182.

14. Eric A. Coleman, "The Family Caregiver Activation in Transitions (FCAT) Tool," accessed October 15, 2022, https://secureservercdn.net/72.167.242.33/253.582.my ftpupload.com/wp-content/uploads/2019/09/Family-Caregiver-Activation-in-Transitions -FCAT-tool.pdf.

15. National Academy of Social Insurance, "Designing Universal Family Care: State-Based Social Insurance Programs for Early Child Care and Education, Paid Family and Medical Leave, and Long-Term Services and Supports," 2019, https://universal familycare.org/wp-content/uploads/2019/06/Designing-Universal-Family-Care _Digital-Version_FINAL.pdf, 2.

Chapter 3: Facilities

1. "Find and Compare Nursing Homes, Hospitals and Other Providers near You," *Medicare*, https://www.medicare.gov/care-compare/.

2. Elizabeth Capezuti and Eugenia L. Siegler, "The Role of the Academic Nurse and Physician in the Criminal Prosecution of Nursing Home Mistreatment," *Journal of Elder Abuse and Neglect* 8, no. 3 (1996): 47–58, https://www.tandfonline.com/doi/abs/10.1300/J084v08n03_05.

3. Garrett E. Speaks, "Documenting Inadequate Care in the Nursing Home: The Story of an Undercover Agent," *Journal of Elder Abuse and Neglect* 8, no. 3 (1996): 37–45, https://www.tandfonline.com/doi/abs/10.1300/J084v08n03_04.

4. Ronald Whitley Costen, "Introduction," *Journal of Elder Abuse and Neglect* 8, no. 3 (1996): 1–3, https://doi.org/10.1300/j084v08n03_01.

5. David Hoffman, "Ensuring Quality of Care Through the Use of the Federal False Claims Act," *Bifocal, ABA Commission on Law and Aging* 17, no. 1 (1996).

6. Toni Heinzl, "Ex-vice President of Defunct Nursing Home Chain Cited," *Fort Worth Star-Telegram*, May 10, 2002.

7. Vladeck, *Unloving Care*.

8. "Nursing Home Care," *Centers for Disease Control and Prevention*, updated September 6, 2022, https://www.cdc.gov/nchs/fastats/nursing-home-care.htm.

9. Charlene Harrington, Anne Montgomery, Terris King, David C. Grabowski, and Michael Wasserman, "These Administrative Actions Would Improve Nursing Home Ownership and Financial Transparency in the Post COVID-19 Period," *Health Affairs*, February 11, 2021, https://www.healthaffairs.org/do/10.1377/forefront .20210208.597573/.

10. Achenbaum, *Robert N. Butler, MD*, 74–75.

11. Vladeck, *Unloving Care*, 5.

12. Amitai Etzioni, "Medicaid Woes: Exposé Is Not Reform," *New York Magazine* (January 10, 1977): 6–7.

13. Joshua M. Wiener, Marc P. Freiman, and David Brown, "Nursing Home Care Quality: Twenty Years After the Omnibus Budget Reconciliation Act of 1987," *Henry J. Kaiser Family Foundation*, December 2007, https://www.kff.org/wp-content /uploads/2013/01/7717.pdf, 13.

14. Robert Pear, "9 of 10 Nursing Homes in U.S. Lack Adequate Staff, a Government Study Finds," *New York Times*, February 18, 2002, https://www.nytimes .com/2002/02/18/us/9-of-10-nursing-homes-in-us-lack-adequate-staff-a -government-study-finds.html.

15. Special Committee on Aging, "Betrayal: The Quality of Care in California Nursing Homes," Hearings Before the Senate Special Committee on Aging, July 27 and 28, 1998, https://www.aging.senate.gov/imo/media/doc/publications/7271998.pdf.

16. "President Clinton: Improving the Quality of Nursing Home Care," *The White House*, July 21, 1998, https://clintonwhitehouse4.archives.gov/WH/Work/072198 .html.

17. Medicare Payment Advisory Commission, *Report to the Congress: Medicare and the Health Care Delivery System* (Washington, DC: MedPac, June 2021), https:// www.medpac.gov/wp-content/uploads/import_data/scrape_files/docs/default-source /default-document-library/jun21_ch3_medpac_report_to_congress_sec.pdf, 72. The MedPAC report suggests that 11 percent of nursing homes are owned by private equity, whereas another study cites 5 percent private equity ownership. Robert Tyler Braun, Hye-Young Jung, Lawrence P. Casalino, Zachary Myslinski, and Mark Aaron Unruh, "Association of Private Equity Investment in US Nursing Homes with the Quality and Cost of Care for Long-State Residents," *JAMA Health Forum* 2, no. 11 (2021): e213817, https://jamanetwork.com/journals/jama-health-forum/fullarticle /2786442.

18. Atul Gupta, Sabrina T. Howell, Constantine Yannelis, and Abhinav Gupta, "Does Private Equity Investment in Healthcare Benefit Patients?: Evidence from Nursing Homes," *National Bureau of Economic Research Working Paper* 28474, https://www .nber.org/system/files/working_papers/w28474/w28474.pdf; Robert Tyler Braun, et al., "Association of Private Equity Investment in US Nursing Homes with the Quality and Cost of Care for Long-Stay Residents," *JAMA Health Forum* (2021), https://jamanet work.com/journals/jama-health-forum/fullarticle/2786442.

19. Yasmin Rafiei, "When Private Equity Takes Over a Nursing Home," *New Yorker*, August 25, 2022, https://www.newyorker.com/news/dispatch/when-private-equity -takes-over-a-nursing-home.

20. Ava Kofman, "How Hospice Became a For-Profit Hustle," *New Yorker,* November 28, 2022, https://www.newyorker.com/magazine/2022/12/05/how-hospice-became-a-for-profit-hustle; Melissa Adridge, "Hospice Tax Status and Ownership Matters for Patients and Families," *JAMA,* May 3, 2021, https://jamanetwork.com/journals/jamainternalmedicine/article-abstract/2779070.Ò1.

21. Nicole Rupersburg, "How to Make 42% Profit Margin in Senior Housing: Eldermark CEO Craig Patnode Speaks at SLIF," *Senior Living Innovation Forum,* September 9, 2019, https://info.seniorlivinginnovationforum.com/blog/how-to-make-42-profit-margin-in-senior-housing.

22. Department of Justice, "Johnson & Johnson to Pay More Than $2.2 Billion to Resolve Criminal and Civil Investigations," Press Release 13-1170, November 4, 2013, https://www.justice.gov/opa/pr/johnson-johnson-pay-more-22-billion-resolve-criminal-and-civil-investigations.

23. Department of Justice, "Johnson & Johnson to Pay More Than $2.2 Billion."

24. Katie Thomas, Robert Gebeloff, and Jessica Silver-Greenberg, "Phony Diagnoses Hide High Rates of Drugging at Nursing Homes," *New York Times,* September 11, 2021, https://www.nytimes.com/2021/09/11/health/nursing-homes-schizophrenia-antipsychotics.html.

25. Charlene Harrington, Mary Ellen Dellefield, Elizabeth Halifax, Mary Louise Fleming, and Debra Bakerjian, "Appropriate Nurse Staffing Levels for U.S. Nursing Homes," *Health Services Insights* 13 (2020), https://journals.sagepub.com/doi/full/10.1177/1178632920934785.

26. "U.S. Nursing Assistants Employed in Nursing Homes: Key Facts," *PHI,* accessed November 4, 2022, https://www.phinational.org/wp-content/uploads/legacy/phi-nursing-assistants-key-facts.pdf.

27. "High Staff Turnover: A Job Quality Crisis in Nursing Homes," *National Consumer Voice for Quality Long-Term Care,* September 8, 2022, https://theconsumervoice.org/uploads/files/issues/High_Staff_Turnover-A_Job_Quality_Crisis_in_Nursing_Homes.pdf; Ashvin Gandhi, Huizi Yu, and David C. Grabowski, "High Nursing Staff Turnover in Nursing Homes Offers Important Quality Information," *Health Affairs* 40, no. 3 (March 2021), https://www.healthaffairs.org/doi/10.1377/hlthaff.2020.00957.

28. "U.S. Nursing Assistants Employed in Nursing Homes," *PHI;* "Direct Care Workers in the United States: Key Facts," *PHI,* September 6, 2022, 1, https://www.phinational.org/resource/direct-care-workers-in-the-united-states-key-facts-3/; annual earnings numbers come from PHI's analysis of the American Community Survey data (2020), PHI Workforce Data Center, https://www.phinational.org/policy-research/workforce-data-center/#tab=National+Data.

29. Priya Chidambaram, "Over 200,000 Residents and Staff in Long-Term Care Facilities Have Died from COVID-19," *Kaiser Family Foundation,* February 3, 2022, https://www.kff.org/policy-watch/over-200000-residents-and-staff-in-long-term-care-facilities-have-died-from-covid-19/.

30. Statement by Alison Hirschel, based on statements to her by several Michigan ombudsmen.

31. Rebecca J. Gorges and R. Tamara Konetzka, "Factors Associated with Racial Differences in Deaths Among Nursing Home Residents with COVID-19 Infection

in the US," *JAMA Network*, February 10, 2021, https://jamanetwork.com/journals/jamanetworkopen/fullarticle/2776102.

32. Committee on the Quality of Care in Nursing Homes, Board on Health Care Services, and Health and Medicine Division, *The National Imperative to Improve Nursing Home Quality: Honoring Our Commitment to Residents, Families, and Staff* (Washington, DC: The National Academies Press, 2022), https://nap.nationalacademies.org/read/26526/chapter/1. See also the Moving Forward Nursing Home Quality Coalition, https://movingforwardcoalition.org.

33. "Fact Sheet: Protecting Seniors by Improving Safety and Quality of Care in the Nation's Nursing Homes," *The White House*, February 28, 2022, https://www.whitehouse.gov/briefing-room/statements-releases/2022/02/28/fact-sheet-protecting-seniors-and-people-with-disabilities-by-improving-safety-and-quality-of-care-in-the-nations-nursing-homes/.

Chapter 4: Home

1. Cisneros at el., *Independent for Life*, xiii, 1.

2. Cisneros et al., *Independent for Life*, 3–4.

3. Wendall Potter, "To Save Billions, the Government Should Pay Doctors to Make House Calls," *PR Watch*, August 8, 2011, https://www.prwatch.org/news/2011/08/10949/save-billions-government-should-pay-doctors-make-house-calls.

4. Vladeck, *Unloving Care*, 57.

5. K. B. Wilson, R. C. Ladd, and M. Saslow, "Community Based Care in an Institution: New Approaches and Definitions of Long-Term Care," paper presented at the 41st Annual Scientific Meeting of the Gerontological Society of America, San Francisco, CA, November 1988.

6. The Green House Project homepage, accessed October 15, 2022, https://thegreenhouseproject.org.

7. Rob Waters, "The Big Idea Behind a New Model of Small Nursing Homes," *Health Affairs* 40, no. 3 (March 2021): 378–383, https://www.healthaffairs.org/doi/10.1377/hlthaff.2021.00081; Susan C. Reinhard and Edem Hado, "Small-House Nursing Homes," *AARP Public Policy Institute*, January 6, 2021, https://www.aarp.org/content/dam/aarp/ppi/2021/small-house-nursing-homes.pdf.

8. "Innovative Public-Private Partnership Bolsters Healthcare Workforce," https://www.johnmuirhealth.com/content/jmh/en/home/about-john-muir-health/press-room/community-news/2019-11-innovative-public-private-partnership-bolsters-healthcare-workforce.html, accessed November 15, 2022. John Muir Health currently pays the HCP students' tuitions. See also Health Career Pathways program, https://empoweredaging.org/healthcare-career-pathway/; https://cchealth.org/hcp/; https://opportunityjunction.org/careers/cna-training.

9. Frontline PBS, "Life and Death in Assisted Living."

10. "U.S. Assisted Living Facility Market Size, Share & Trends Analysis Report by Age (More Than 85, 75–84, 65–74, Less Than 65), Region (West, South, Midwest), and Segment Forecasts, 2022–2030," Research and Markets, April 2020, https://www.researchandmarkets.com/reports/5415610/u-s-assisted-living-facility-market-size-share#product—toc.

CHAPTER 5: MONEY

1. Federal Trade Commission, "Protecting Older Consumers 2020–2021," 32–33.

2. Federal Trade Commission, "Protecting Older Consumers 2020–2021," 32, footnote 103.

3. "Tax Scams/Consumer Alerts," *IRS*, updated September 21, 2022, https://www.irs.gov/newsroom/tax-scams-consumer-alerts; "IRS Warning: Scammers Work Year-Round; Stay Vigilant," *IRS*, February 3, 2022, https://www.irs.gov/newsroom/irs-warning-scammers-work-year-round-stay-vigilant.

4. Federal Trade Commission, "Protecting Older Consumers 2020–2021," 32.

5. Jia Tolentino, *Trick Mirror: Reflections on Self-Delusion* (New York: Random House, 2020), x, 194.

6. Gawande, *Being Mortal*, 42.

7. Gawande, *Being Mortal*, 43.

8. Mark S. Lachs, Christianna S. Williams, Shelley O'Brien, Karl A. Pillemer, and Mary E. Charlson, "The Mortality of Elder Mistreatment," *Journal of the American Medical Association* 280, no. 5 (1998): 428–432, https://jamanetwork.com/journals/jama/fullarticle/187817.

9. John Firman, Cynthia Alexis, Jacqueline Case, Marta Sotomayor, and Jim Wright, "Financial Exploitation and Consumer Fraud Workshop 2: Effective Interventions to Address Consure Fraud," in *Our Aging Population: Promoting Empowerment, Preventing Victimization, and Implementing Coordinated Interventions—a Report of Proceedings* (Washington, DC: Office of Justice Programs, December 2000), 17–18, https://www.ojp.gov/sites/g/files/xyckuh241/files/media/document/ncj_186256.pdf.

10. Inner City Press (@innercitypress), Twitter thread, July 11, 2022, https://twitter.com/innercitypress/status/1546512545585954816?s=20&t=zn35xDqtM6UMnxmlsV0cKQ.

11. *State of Washington v. Jasmine Jamrus-Kassim*, 11-1-01915-9 SEA (Superior Court of Washington for King County, 2011).

12. National Center on Elder Abuse; "Get the Facts on Elder Abuse," *National Council on Aging*, February 23, 2021, https://www.ncoa.org/article/get-the-facts-on-elder-abuse.

13. James Barron and Anemona Hartocollis, "As Mrs. Astor Slips, the Grandson Blames the Son," *New York Times*, July 27, 2006, https://www.nytimes.com/2006/07/27/us/27cnd-astor.html.

14. Colin Moynihan and Serge F. Kovaleski, "Astor's Son Surrenders on Charges," *New York Times*, November 27, 2007, https://www.nytimes.com/2007/11/27/nyregion/27cnd-astor.html.

15. S. R. Beach, R. Schulz, N. G. Castle, and J. Rosen, "Financial Exploitation and Psychological Mistreatment Among Older Adults: Differences Between African Americans and Non-African Americans in a Population-Based Survey," *Gerontologist* 50, no. 6 (2010): 744–757, https://doi.org/10.1093/geront/gnq053.

16. XinQi Dong, Ruijia Chen, Terry Fulmer, and Melissa A. Simon, "Prevalence and Correlates of Elder Mistreatment in a Community-Dwelling Population of U.S. Chinese Older Adults," *Journal of Aging and Health* 26, no. 7 (2014), https://journals.sagepub.com/doi/10.1177/0898264314531617.

17. Marguerite DeLiema, Zachary D. Gassoumis, Diana C. Homeier, and Kathleen H. Wilber, "Determining Prevalence and Correlates of Elder Abuse Using Promotores: Low-Income Immigrant Latinos Report High Rates of Abuse and Neglect," *Journal of the American Geriatrics Society* 60, no. 7 (2012): 1333–1339, https://doi .org/10.1111/j.1532-5415.2012.04025.x.

18. "Saving Our Seniors," US Senate hearing 107–105, https://www.govinfo.gov /content/pkg/CHRG-107shrg74685/html/CHRG-107shrg74685.htm.

19. Federal Trade Commission, "Protecting Older Consumers 2020–2021," 36–37, figure 8.

20. Lachs, *What Your Doctor Won't Tell You About Getting Older,* 258. (See Chapter 17, "Money and Aging," and Chapter 18, "Financial Gerontology, the Good, the Bad and the Phony.")

21. "Bill Authored by Sens. Collins, McCaskill to Protect Seniors from Scams Heads to President's Desk to Be Signed into Law," *Susan Collins,* May 22, 2018, https://www .collins.senate.gov/newsroom/bill-authored-sens-collins-mccaskill-protect-seniors -scams-heads-president's-desk-be-signed.

22. Bruce I. Carlin, Tarik Umar, and Hanyi Yi, "Deputization," National Bureau of Economic Research Working Paper 27225, May 2020, https://www.nber.org/papers/w27225.

Chapter 6: The Autonomy-Safety Conundrum

1. Richard C. Ladd, a pioneer in aging and long-term care, was the original author of this line, according to Kate Wilber, at the USC Davis School of Gerontology.

2. Cicero, *On Life and Death* (Oxford: Oxford University Press, 2017), 120.

3. Bryan Gruley, "Can a Wife with Dementia Say Yes to Sex?," *Des Moines Register,* December 13, 2014, https://www.desmoinesregister.com/story/news/crime-and-courts /2014/12/1/former-legislator-charged-raping-wife-dementia/20305991/.

4. Jane Gardam, *Old Filth* (New York: Europa Editions, 2004).

5. Maggie Jones, "The Joys (and Challenges) of Sex After 70," *New York Times Magazine,* January 12, 2022, https://www.nytimes.com/2022/01/12/magazine/sex-old-age.html.

6. "Hebrew Home at Riverdale Administration Policy and Procedure Manual: Resident Sexual Expression," *RiverSpring Health,* October 25, 2000, https://www .riverspringliving.org/wp-content/uploads/2021/10/Resident-Sexual-Expression -Policy-revised-4.2017.pdf.

7. Karl Pillemer, Emily K. Chen, Kimberly S. Van Haitsma, Jeanne Teresi, Mildred Ramirez, Stephanie Silver, Gail Sukha, and Mark S. Lachs, "Resident-to -Resident Aggression in Nursing Homes: Results from a Qualitative Event Reconstruction Study," *Gerontologist* 52, no. 1 (February 2012): 24–33, https://academic.oup.com /gerontologist/article/52/1/24/692593.

8. Jones, "The Joys (and Challenges) of Sex After 70."

9. Statement by Gretchen Sommer to reporter Heather Catallo, WXYZ, May 30, 2019, "'I just want my parents back.' Woman says company imprisoned her parents in their own home," https://www.wxyz.com/news/local-news/investigations/i-just-want -my-parents-back-woman-says-company-imprisoned-her-parents-in-their-own-home (accessed November 11, 2022). Self-dealing by guardians with respect to wards is prohibited by Michigan law. See Guardian; qualifications, MCL section 700.5313, http:// legislature.mi.gov/doc.aspx?mcl-700-5313.

10. Heather Catallo, "Court Appointed Guardianship Could Cost Macomb County Family $376,000," *WXYZ Detroit*, November 25, 2019, https://www.wxyz.com/news/local-news/investigations/court-appointed-guardianship-could-cost-macomb-county-family-376-000.

11. Kelly Rossman-McKinney, "AG Nessel Takes Unprecedented Step to Intervene in Macomb County Guardianship Case," *Michigan.gov*, September 9, 2019, https://www.michigan.gov/ag/news/press-releases/2019/09/09/ag-nessel-takes-unprecedented-step-to-intervene-in-macomb-county-guardianship-case.

CHAPTER 7: LAGGING NORMS

1. Committee on the Health and Medical Dimensions of Social Isolation and Loneliness in Older Adults, Board on Health Sciences Policy, Health and Medicine Division, Board on Behavioral, Cognitive, and Sensory Sciences, and Division of Behavioral and Social Sciences and Education, *Social Isolation and Loneliness in Older Adults: Opportunities for the Health Care System* (Washington, DC: National Academies Press, 2020), 1. Compare findings from AARP Foundation and United Health Foundation, "The Pandemic Effect: A Social Isolation Report," October 6, 2020, https://connect2affect.org/wp-content/uploads/2020/10/The-Pandemic-Effect-A-Social-Isolation-Report-AARP-Foundation.pdf.

2. Empowerline homepage, accessed November 6, 2022, https://www.empowerline.org/.

3. Laura Carstensen, Marc Freedman, and Carol Larson, "Hidden in Plain Sight: How Intergenerational Relationships Can Transform Our Future," *Stanford Center on Longevity*, June 2016, https://longevity.stanford.edu/wp-content/uploads/sites/24/2018/09/Intergenerational-relationships-SCL.pdf.

4. Alexander et al., *A Pattern Language*, 216.

5. Marc Freedman, *How to Live Forever: The Enduring Power of Connecting the Generations* (New York: PublicAffairs, 2018), 8.

6. Experience Corps homepage, accessed October 15, 2022, https://www.aarp.org/experience-corps/.

7. Soli Salgado, "Nuns and Nones Project Teaches Sisters How to Create Land Legacies for Justice," *Global Sisters Report*, April 21, 2022, https://www.globalsistersreport.org/news/environment/news/nuns-and-nones-project-teaches-sisters-how-create-land-legacies-justice.

8. Shannon E. Jarrott and Kathy Lee, "Shared Site Intergenerational Programs: A National Profile," *Journal of Aging & Social Policy*, January 31, 2022, https://www.tandfonline.com/doi/full/10.1080/08959420.2021.2024410.

9. Alexander et al., *A Pattern Language*, 216–217.

10. "The Movement to Create Great Places to Grow Up and Grow Old in America," *Grantmakers in Aging*, April 2013, http://dev.giaging.org/documents/130402_GIA_AFC_Primer.pdf.

11. TimeSlips homepage, accessed November 8, 2022, https://www.timeslips.org/. I joined the TimeSlips board of directors in 2021.

12. Becca R. Levy, Martin D. Slade, E-Shien Chang, Sneha Kannoth, and Shi-Yi Wang, "Ageism Amplifies Cost and Prevalence of Health Conditions," *Gerontologist* 60, no. 1 (2020): 174–181, https://academic.oup.com/gerontologist/article/60/1/174/5166947.

13. Scientists, poets, and philosophers from Charles Darwin to Walt Whitman to Martha Nussbaum have written about the power and universality of disgust, but there's little actual data about it, much less about its impact on aging. See, e.g., Nussbaum and Levmore, *Aging Thoughtfully*, 113–115; Nussbaum, *Hiding from Humanity: Disgust, Shame, and the Law*; Nussbaum, *From Disgust to Humanity*; and Nussbaum, "Against Disgust: Sex, Law, and the Politics of Disgust," *Boston University Law Review*, 2004. See also Molly Young, "How Disgust Explains Everything: For Psychologists Who Study It, Disgust Is One of the Primal Emotions That Define—and Explain—Humanity," *New York Times*, December 27, 2021.

14. Joint Center for Housing Studies of Harvard University, "Disabilities Among Older Adults," Chapter 3 of *Projections and Implications for Housing a Growing Population: Older Households 2015–2035*, December 13, 2016, https://www.jchs.harvard.edu/sites/default/files/harvard_jchs_housing_growing_population_2016_chapter_3.pdf, 38.

15. Aronson, *Elderhood*, 288.

16. Aronson, *Elderhood*, 288.

17. Kahneman, *Thinking, Fast and Slow*, 66, 67.

18. Richard Weissbourd, Milena Batanova, Virginia Lovison, and Eric Torres, "Loneliness in America: How the Pandemic Has Deepened an Epidemic of Loneliness and What We Can Do About It," *Harvard Graduate School of Education*, February 2021, https://mcc.gse.harvard.edu/reports/loneliness-in-america.

19. Murthy, *Together*, xix, xx, xxiii.

20. Richard Schulz and Jill Eden, eds., *Families Caring for an Aging America*, National Academies of Science, Engineering, and Medicine Report (Washington, DC: The National Academies Press, 2016), https://nap.nationalacademies.org/catalog/23606/families-caring-for-an-aging-america.

21. Murthy, *Together*, 16–19.

22. Murthy, *Together*, 17–19.

23. The Silver Line homepage, accessed October 15, 2022, https://www.thesilverline.org.uk; Murthy, *Together*, 131–132.

Chapter 8: Who to Call?

1. Suzanne K. Steinmetz, "Overlooked Aspects of Family Violence: Battered Husbands, Battered Siblings, and Battered Elderly," testimony presented to the US House Committee on Science and Technology, February 15, 1978, https://www.ojp.gov/pdffiles1/Digitization/56303NCJRS.pdf, 9.

2. Willard D. Callender and Freda Bernotavicz, *Improving Protective Services for Older Americans: National Law and Social Work Seminar Proceedings and Prospects* (Portland, ME: Center for Research and Advanced Study, University of Southern Maine, 1982), 12, 14, 100, 101.

Chapter 9: Forensics

1. Laura Mosqueda, Kerry Burnight, and Solomon Liao, "The Lifecycle of Bruises in Older Adults," *Journal of the American Geriatric Society* 53, no. 8 (2005): 1339–1343.

2. Mark S. Lachs, Christianna S. Williams, Shelley O'Brien, Karl A. Pillemer, and Mary E. Charlson, "The Mortality of Elder Mistreatment," *Journal of the American*

Medical Association 280, no. 5 (1998): 428–432, https://jamanetwork.com/journals/jama /fullarticle/187817.

3. Naomi F. Sugar, James A. Taylor, Kenneth W. Feldman, and the Puget Sound Pediatric Research Network, "Bruises in Infants and Toddlers: Those Who Don't Cruise Rarely Bruise," *Archives of Pediatrics and Adolescent Medicine* 153, no. 4 (1999): 399–403, https://jamanetwork.com/journals/jamapediatrics/fullarticle/346535.

4. US Preventive Services Task Force, "Screening for Intimate Partner Violence, Elder Abuse, and Abuse of Vulnerable Adults: US Preventive Services Task Force Final Recommendation Statement," *Journal of the American Medical Association* 320, no. 16 (2018): 1678–1687, https://doi.org/10.1001/jama.2018.14741.

5. Erik Lindbloom, Julie Brandt, Catherine Hawes, Charles Phillips, David Zimmerman, Janes Robinson, Barbara Bowers, and Patricia McFeeley, "The Role of Forensic Science in Identification of Mistreatment Deaths in Long-Term Care Facilities: Final Report," *Office of Justice Programs*, April 2005, https://www.ojp.gov/pdffiles1/nij /grants/209334.pdf, 32, 22.

6. Lindbloom et al., "The Role of Forensic Science," 20–21.

Chapter 10: Parents' Keepers?

1. *State of Washington v. Elle Barksdale Loe*, 20-1-00006-6 SEA (Washington State King County Superior Court, 2020).

2. Brian Joseph, "Bellevue Neighbors Say They Often Heard Cries from Elderly Neighbor," *Seattle Times*, August 2, 2002.

3. Michael Ko, "2-Year Term for Abuse of Elderly Dad," *Seattle Times*, November 9, 2002, https://archive.seattletimes.com/archive/?date=20021109&slug=mckinney09e0.

4. Ko, "2-Year Term for Abuse of Elderly Dad."

5. Ashley Bach, "Fatal Neglect Brings 2-Month Jail Term," *Seattle Times*, May 7, 2005, https://www.seattletimes.com/seattle-news/fatal-neglect-brings-2-month-jail-term/.

6. Press release of Bill Rehm, the son's attorney, July 7, 2003.

7. Excerpts of Ruby Wise's journals were admitted as evidence in *State of Washington vs. Christopher Wise*, No. 09-1-04552-2 SEA. Copies of the journal excerpts quoted were examined by the author. See also https://www.justice.gov/sites/default/files/elder justice/legacy/2015/07/12/Washington_State%27s_Trial_Memorandum_30pgs.pdf (prosecution brief relating to admissibility of Ruby Wise's journals). Wise's appeal denied; see https://casetext.com/case/state-v-wise-129.

8. Jennifer Sullivan, "Defendant Testifies to His Love for Mother Who Died Covered in Bedsores," *Seattle Times*, May 6, 2010, https://www.seattletimes.com/seattle -news/defendant-testifies-to-his-love-for-mother-who-died-covered-in-bedsores/; Lauren C. Williams, "Black Diamond Man Sentenced to Prison in Mother's Death from Bedsores," *Seattle Times*, July 16, 2010, https://www.seattletimes.com/seattle-news /black-diamond-man-sentenced-to-prison-in-mothers-death-from-bedsores/.

9. Williams, "Black Diamond Man Sentenced to Prison in Mother's Death from Bedsores."

10. "Elder Abuse Helpline for Concerned Persons," *NYC Elder Abuse Center*, accessed October 15, 2022, https://nyceac.org/helpline-for-concerned-persons/.

11. KOMO News Staff, "Authorities Find Woman Dead Inside Federal Way Home," *KOMO News*, January 4, 2022, https://komonews.com/news/local/authorities -find-woman-dead-inside-federal-way-home.

CHAPTER 11: HARM AND HEALING

1. Jill Lepore, "The Rise of the Victims'-Rights Movement," *New Yorker*, May 14, 2018, https://www.newyorker.com/magazine/2018/05/21/the-rise-of-the-victims-rights -movement.

2. Van der Kolk, *The Body Keeps the Score*, 53.

3. *A Mother Never Gives Up Hope: Older Mothers and Abusive Adult Sons* (Chicago: National Clearinghouse on Abuse in Later Life and Terra Nova Films, 2009), https:// terranova.org/film-catalog/a-mother-never-gives-up-hope-older-mothers-and-abusive -adult-sons/.

4. Åsa Gransjön Craftman, Anna Swall, Kajsa Båkman, Åke Grundberg, and Carina Lundh Hagelin, "Caring for Older People with Dementia Reliving Past Trauma," *Nursing Ethics* 27, no. 2 (2020): 621–633, https://doi.org/10.1177/0969733019864152.

5. Frankl, *Man's Search for Meaning*.

6. Van der Kolk, *The Body Keeps the Score*, 87–88, 352.

7. Charles P. Mouton, Rebecca J. Rodabough, Susan L. D. Rovi, Robert G. Brzyski, and David A. Katerndahl, "Psychosocial Effects of Physical and Verbal Abuse in Postmenopausal Women," *Annals of Family Medicine* 8, no. 3 (May 2010): 206–213, https:// doi.org/10.1370/afm.1095.

8. Juanita Davis and Katie Block, *Increasing Access to Healing Services and Just Outcomes for Older African American Crime Survivors: A Toolkit for Enhancing Critical Knowledge and Informing Action Within the Crime Victim Assistance Field* (New York: The National Resource Center for Reaching Victims, 2020), https://reachingvictims.org /wp-content/uploads/2020/07/Increasing-Access-Guide-1.pdf, 48.

9. Davis and Block, *Increasing Access to Healing Services*.

10. Mengting Li, Man Guo, Meredith Stensland, Merril Silverstein, and XinQi Dong, "Typology of Family Relationship and Elder Mistreatment in a US Chinese Population," *Journal of the American Geriatric Society* 67, no. S3 (2019): S493–S498, https://doi.org/10.1111/jgs.15892.

11. "Mistreatment of Lesbian, Gay, Bisexual, and Transgender (LGBT) Elders," *National Center on Elder Abuse*, 2013, https://ncea.acl.gov/NCEA/media/Publication /NCEA_RB_LGBT2020.pdf.

12. Stuart Jeffries, "Jacqueline Rose: A Life in Writing," *Saturday Guardian*, February 3, 2012, https://www.theguardian.com/culture/2012/feb/03/jacqueline-rose-life -writing.

CHAPTER 12: NEW MODELS

1. Laura Mosqueda et al., "The Abuse Intervention Model: A Pragmatic Approach to Intervention for Elder Mistreatment," *Journal of the American Geriatric Society* (2016), https://www.ncbi.nlm.nih.gov/pmc/articles/PMC5026887.

2. David Burnes, Marie-Therese Connolly, Erin Salvo, Patricia F. Kimball, Geoff Rogers, and Stuart Lewis, "RISE: A Conceptual Model of Integrated and Restorative Elder Abuse Intervention," *Gerontologist*, June 15, 2022, https://doi.org/10.1093 /geront/gnac083.

3. "Moment of Truth," *Violence Free Colorado*, June 2020, https://www.violencefree colorado.org/wp-content/uploads/2020/07/Moment-of-Truth.pdf; Elise Buchbinder,

"Moment of Truth," *End Domestic Abuse Wisconsin*, July 14, 2020, https://www.end abusewi.org/moment-of-truth/.

4. "Mental Health Treatment While Incarcerated," *National Alliance on Mental Illness*, accessed October 15, 2022, https://www.nami.org/Advocacy/Policy-Priorities /Improving-Health/Mental-Health-Treatment-While-Incarcerated.

5. "Criminal Justice Fact Sheet," *NAACP*, accessed October 15, 2022, https://naacp.org /resources/criminal-justice-fact-sheet; Ashley Nellis, "The Color of Justice: Racial and Ethnic Disparity in State Prisons," *Sentencing Project*, October 13, 2021, https://www.sentencing project.org/publications/color-of-justice-racial-and-ethnic-disparity-in-state-prisons/.

6. Leovy, *Ghettoside*, 48.

Chapter 13: Law

1. Pinker, *The Better Angels of Our Nature*, 521.

2. "Statistics and Historical Comparison," *GovTrack*, accessed October 15, 2022, https://www.govtrack.us/congress/bills/statistics.

3. Sunlight Foundation, "Only Four Percent of Bills Become Law: The Vast Majority of Bills Go Nowhere," *HuffPost*, updated December 6, 2017, https://www.huffpost.com /entry/the-vast-majority-of-bill_n_268630.

4. Testimony of Kenneth L. Connor, Senate Special Committee on Aging, October 20, 2003, https://www.aging.senate.gov/imo/media/doc/10202003.pdf, p. 31.

5. Testimony of Justin Ray White, May 20, 2002, Senate Special Committee on Aging.

6. Linda Greenhouse, "The Bittersweet Victories of Women," *New York Review*, May 26, 2016, https://www.nybooks.com/articles/2016/05/26/bittersweet-victories-of-women/.

Chapter 14: Movement

1. Jay Winsten, "Designated Driver Turns 21," *Boston Globe*, December 14, 2009, http://archive.boston.com/news/health/articles/2009/12/14/designated_driver _campaign_turns_21/.

2. "Drunk Driving," *National Highway Traffic Safety Administration*, accessed October 15, 2022, https://www.nhtsa.gov/risky-driving/drunk-driving.

Chapter 15: Mystery and Meaning

1. Cole, *The Journey of Life*, xix.

2. Thomas R. Cole and Sally Gadow, eds., *What Does It Mean to Grow Old: Reflections from the Humanities* (Durham: Duke University Press, 1986), 5.

3. Cole, *The Journey of Life*, xxiii.

4. Cole, *The Journey of Life*, xxiii.

5. Vaillant, *Aging Well*, 5; Robert Waldinger and Marc Schultz, "What the Longest Study on Human Happiness Found Is the Key to a Good Life," *The Atlantic*, January 19, 2023, https://www.theatlantic.com/ideas/archive/2023/01/harvard-happiness -study-relationships/672753/.

6. Emily Esfahani Smith, *The Power of Meaning: Finding Fulfillment in a World Obsessed with Happiness* (New York: Broadway Books, 2017), 217.

7. Frankl, *Man's Search for Meaning*, 66, 79.

8. Smith, *The Power of Meaning*, 223.

9. Laura L. Carstensen, Yochai Z. Shavit, and Jessica T. Barnes, "Age Advantages in Emotional Experience Persist Even Under Threat from the COVID-19 Pandemic," *Psychological Science* 31, no. 11 (2020): 1374–1385, https://journals.sagepub.com/doi/epub/10.1177/0956797620967261.

10. Steven Cole interview, "Purpose and Gene Expression," October 2016, https://www.youtube.com/watch?v=AvLiQ-F0gbo.

11. Frankl, *Man's Search for Meaning*, 37.

12. Liz Mineo, "Good Genes Are Nice, but Joy Is Better," *Harvard Gazette*, April 11, 2017, https://news.harvard.edu/gazette/story/2017/04/over-nearly-80-years-harvard-study-has-been-showing-how-to-live-a-healthy-and-happy-life/.

13. George E. Vaillant, *Triumphs of Experience: The Men of the Harvard Grant Study* (Cambridge, MA: The Belknap Press, 2012), 52.

14. Robert Waldinger and Marc Schultz, "What the Longest Study on Human Happiness Found Is the Key to a Good Life," *The Atlantic*, January 19, 2023; https://www.theatlantic.com/ideas/archive/2023/01/harvard-happiness-study-relationships/672753/; see also Robert Waldinger and Marc Schultz, *The Good Life: Lessons from the Longest Scientific Study of Happiness* (New York: Simon and Schuster, 2023).

15. Walt Whitman, "Song of the Open Road," in *Leaves of Grass* (Brooklyn, NY: self-published, 1855).

16. Frankl, *Man's Search for Meaning*, 100–111.

17. De Beauvoir, *The Coming of Age*, 540–541.

18. Martha Nussbaum, "Martha Nussbaum: Philosopher," in James L. Harmon, ed., *Take My Advice: Letters to the Next Generation from People Who Know a Thing or Two* (New York: Simon and Schuster, 2002), 176–177.

19. Nussbaum, "Martha Nussbaum: Philosopher."

20. Archibald MacLeish, "Riders on Earth Together, Brothers in Eternal Cold," *New York Times*, December 25, 1968, https://archive.nytimes.com/www.nytimes.com/library/national/science/nasa/122568sci-nasa-macleish.html.

21. Dacher Keltner, *Awe: The New Science of Everyday Wonder and How It Can Transform Your Life* (New York: Penguin Press, 2023), xvi.

22. Dacher Keltner, quoted in Paula Spencer Scott, "Feeling Awe May Be the Secret to Health and Happiness," *Parade*, October 7, 2016, https://parade.com/513786/paulaspencer/feeling-awe-may-be-the-secret-to-health-and-happiness/.

23. Roland Griffiths, quoted in Smith, *The Power of Meaning*, 152–153.

24. "The Act of Listening," *TED Radio Hour*, NPR, June 5, 2015, https://www.npr.org/programs/ted-radio-hour/411697251/the-act-of-listening.

25. Bateson, *Composing a Life*, 34.

26. Susan Sontag, "Literature Is Freedom," in *At the Same Time: Essays and Speeches* (New York: Farrar, Straus and Giroux, 2007), 192–209.

Epilogue

1. Tad Friend, "Silicon Valley's Quest to Live Forever," *New Yorker*, March 27, 2017, https://www.newyorker.com/magazine/2017/04/03/silicon-valleys-quest-to-live-forever.

2. "Ulysses," by Alfred Lord Tennyson.

BIBLIOGRAPHY

This book and my thinking about the subjects in it have been informed and enriched by ideas, arguments, and data in sources too numerous to fully identify here. They include the books listed below as well as articles, reports, testimony, films, and other sources, some of which appear in the text or endnotes and others in the website notes at www.TheMeasureofOurAge.com.

BOOKS

Achenbaum, W. Andrew. *Robert N. Butler, MD: Visionary of Healthy Aging*. New York: Columbia University Press, 2013.

Addams, Jane. *Twenty Years at Hull House*. New York: The MacMillan Company, 2010.

Alexander, Christopher, Sara Ishikawa, and Murray Silverstein. *A Pattern Language: Towns Buildings Construction*. New York: Oxford University Press, 1977.

Applewhite, Ashton. *This Chair Rocks: A Manifesto Against Ageism*. New York: Celadon Books, 2019. (Originally published by Networked Books in 2016.)

Aronson, Louise. *Elderhood: Redefining Aging, Transforming Medicine, Reimagining Life*. New York: Bloomsbury Publishing, 2019.

———. *A History of the Present Illness: Stories*. New York: Bloomsbury, 2013.

Athill, Diana. *Somewhere Towards the End*. New York: W. W. Norton, 2009.

Baars, Jan, and Henk Visser, eds. *Aging and Time: Multidisciplinary Perspectives*. Amityville, NY: Baywood Publishing Company, Inc., 2007.

Bancroft, Lundy. *Why Does He Do That?: Inside the Minds of Angry and Controlling Men*. New York: Berkley Books, 2002.

Basting, Anne. *Creative Care: A Revolutionary Approach to Dementia and Elder Care*. New York: HarperOne, 2020.

Bateson, Mary Catherine. *Composing a Life*. New York: Grove Press, 1989.

Becker, Howard S. *Tricks of the Trade: How to Think About Your Research While You're Doing It*. Chicago: University of Chicago Press, 1998.

Bernotavicz, Freda. *Community Role: Improving Protective Services for Older Americans*. A National Guide Series. Portland, ME: Center for Research and Advanced Study, University of Southern Maine, 1982.

Binstock, Robert H., Leighton E. Cluff, and Otto von Mering, eds. *The Future of Long-Term Care: Social and Policy Issues*. Baltimore: Johns Hopkins University Press, 1996.

Blenkner, Margaret. *Final Report: Protective Services for Older People: Findings from the Benjamin Rose Institute Study*. Cleveland: Benjamin Rose Institute, 1974.

Bonnie, Richard J., and Robert B. Wallace. *Elder Mistreatment: Abuse, Neglect, and Exploitation in an Aging America*. National Research Council Panel to Review Risk and Prevalence of Elder Abuse and Neglect. Washington, DC: National Academies Press, 2003.

Booth, Wayne, ed. *The Art of Growing Older: Writers on Living and Aging*. New York: Poseidon Press, 1992.

Boyer, Anne. *The Undying: Pain, Vulnerability, Mortality, Medicine, Art, Time, Dreams, Data, Exhaustion, Cancer, and Care*. New York: Farrar, Straus and Giroux, 2019.

Bradley, Elizabeth H., and Lauren A. Taylor. *The American Health Care Paradox: Why Spending More Is Getting Us Less*. New York: PublicAffairs, 2013.

Brandl, Bonnie, Carmel Bitondo Dyer, Candace J. Heisler, Joanne Marlatt Otto, Lori A. Stiegel, and Randolph W. Thomas, eds. *Elder Abuse Detection and Intervention: A Collaborative Approach*. New York: Springer Publishing Company, 2007.

Brawley, Otis Webb (with Paul Goldberg). *How We Do Harm: A Doctor Breaks Ranks About Being Sick in America*. New York: St. Martin's Press, 2011.

Breckman, Risa S., and Ronald D. Adelman. *Strategies for Helping Victims of Elder Mistreatment*. Sage Human Services Guides 53. Newbury Park: Sage Publications, 1988.

Bridges, Khiara M. *Reproducing Race: An Ethnography of Pregnancy as a Site of Radicalization*. Berkeley: University of California Press, 2011.

Brueggemann, Walter, and William H. Bellinger, Jr. *Psalms*. New York: Cambridge University Press, 2014.

Buch, Elana D. *Inequalities of Aging: Paradoxes of Independence in American Home Care*. New York: New York University Press, 2018.

Burdick, Alan. *Why Time Flies: A Mostly Scientific Investigation*. New York: Simon and Schuster, 2017.

Butler, Katy. *Knocking on Heaven's Door: The Path to a Better Way of Death*. New York: Scribner, 2013.

Butler, Robert N. *The Longevity Revolution: The Benefits and Challenges of Living a Long Life*. New York: PublicAffairs, 2008.

———. *Why Survive? Being Old in America*. Baltimore: Johns Hopkins University Press, 1975.

Cahn, Naomi, and June Carbone. *Red Families v. Blue Families: Legal Polarization and the Creation of Culture*. Oxford: Oxford University Press, 2010.

Callender, Willard D., and Freda Bernotavicz. *Improving Protective Services for Older Americans: National Law and Social Work Seminar Proceedings and Prospects*. A National Guide Series. Portland, ME: Center for Research and Advanced Study, University of Southern Maine, 1982.

Casey, Nell, ed. *An Uncertain Inheritance: Writers on Caring for Family*. New York: William Morrow, 2007.

Cather, Willa. *Death Comes for the Archbishop*. New York: Vintage Books, 1971. (Originally published by Alfred A. Knopf in 1927.)

Chast, Roz. *Can't We Talk About Something More Pleasant.* New York: Bloomsbury, 2014.

Cicero, Marcus Tullius. *How to Grow Old: Ancient Wisdom for the Second Half of Life.* Translated by Philip Freeman. Princeton: Princeton University Press, 2016. (Originally written in Latin in 44 BC as *Cato Maior de Senectute.*)

Cisneros, Henry, Margaret Dyer-Chamberlain, and Jane Hickie, eds. *Independent for Life: Homes and Neighborhoods for an Aging America.* Austin: University of Texas Press, 2012.

Coates, Laura. *Just Pursuit: A Black Prosecutor's Fight for Fairness.* New York: Simon and Schuster, 2022.

Cohen, Lawrence. *No Aging in India: Alzheimer's, the Bad Family, and Other Modern Things.* Berkeley: University of California Press, 1998.

Cole, Thomas R. *The Journey of Life: A Cultural History of Aging in America.* Cambridge, UK: Cambridge University Press, 1992.

Cole, Thomas, and Mary Winkler, eds. *The Oxford Book of Aging: Reflections on the Journey of Life.* New York: Oxford University Press, 1994.

de Beauvoir, Simone. *The Coming of Age.* Translated by Patrick O'Brian. New York: W. W. Norton, 1972. (Originally published in French in 1970.)

———. *A Very Easy Death.* Translated by Patrick O'Brian. New York: Pantheon Books, 1964.

Del Plane, Frances, and Adah Grandy. *College Readings in Poetry: English and American.* New York: The MacMillan Company, 1933.

Delbanco, Nicholas. *Lastingness: The Art of Old Age.* New York: Grand Central Publishing, 2011.

Desmond, Matthew. *Evicted: Poverty and Profit in the American City.* New York: Crown Publishers, 2016.

Dong, XinQi, ed. *Elder Abuse: Research, Practice and Policy.* Cham: Springer, 2017.

Douglas, Mary. *Purity and Danger: An Analysis of the Concepts of Pollution and Taboo.* London: Ark Paperbacks, 1966.

Esfahani Smith, Emily. *The Power of Meaning: Crafting a Life That Matters.* New York: Crown Publishers, 2017.

Factora, Ronan. *Aging and Money: Reducing Risk of Financial Exploitation and Protecting Financial Resources.* 2nd ed. Cham: Springer, 2021.

Fassin, Didier, and Richard Rechtman. *The Empire of Trauma: An Inquiry into the Condition of Victimhood.* Translated by Rachel Gomme. Princeton: Princeton University Press, 2009. (Originally published in French in 2007.)

Fink, Sheri. *Five Days at Memorial: Life and Death in a Storm-Ravaged Hospital.* New York: Crown Publishers, 2013.

Finkel, David. *Thank You for Your Service.* New York: Picador, 2013.

Fishman, Ted. *Shock of Gray: The Aging of the World's Population and How It Pits Young Against Old, Child Against Parent, Worker Against Boss, Company Against Rival, and Nation Against Nation.* New York: Scribner, 2010.

Foucault, Michel. *The Archaeology of Knowledge: And the Discourse on Language.* New York: Vintage Books, 1972. (Originally published in French in 1969.)

———. *Madness and Civilization: A History of Insanity in an Age of Reason.* New York: Vintage Books, 1973. (Originally published in French in 1961; originally translated into English in 1964.)

Frankl, Viktor E. *Man's Search for Meaning.* Translated by Ilse Lasch. Boston: Beacon Press, 1959. (Originally published in German in 1946.)

Freedman, Marc. *How to Live Forever: The Enduring Power of Connecting the Generations.* New York: PublicAffairs, 2018.

Friedman, Edwin. *Generation to Generation: Family Process in Church and Synagogue.* New York: Guilford Press, 1985.

Frye, W. Bruce. *Caring for the Heart: Mayo Clinic and the Rise of Specialization.* Oxford: Oxford University Press, 2015.

Fulmer, Terry, Leslie Pelton, Jinghan Zhang, and Wendy Huang, eds. *Age-Friendly Health Systems: A Guide to Using the 4Ms While Caring for Older Adults.* Boston: Institute for Healthcare Improvement, 2022.

Gardam, Jane. *Old Filth.* New York: Europa Editions, 2004.

Gawande, Atul. *Being Mortal: Medicine and What Matters in the End.* New York: Metropolitan Books, 2014.

———. *Better: A Surgeon's Notes on Performance.* New York: Picador, 2007.

———. *Complications: A Surgeon's Notes on an Imperfect Science.* New York: Picador, 2002.

Gill, Brendan, ed. *Late Bloomers.* New York: Artisan, 1996.

Gillick, Muriel R. *Old and Sick in America: The Journey Through the Health Care System.* Chapel Hill: University of North Carolina Press, 2017.

Goffman, Erving. *Asylums: Essays on the Social Situation of Mental Patients and Other Inmates.* Garden City, NY: Anchor Books, 1961.

Goodman, Ellen. "The Mary Northern Story," Parts I, II, and III. In *Close to Home,* 230–235. New York: Simon and Schuster, 1979.

Gordon, Meryl. *Mrs. Astor Regrets: The Hidden Betrayals of a Family Beyond Reproach.* Boston: Mariner Books, 2008.

Groopman, Jerome. *The Measure of Our Days: A Spiritual Exploration of Illness.* New York: Penguin Books, 1997.

Gross, Jane. *A Bittersweet Season: Caring for Our Parents and Ourselves.* New York: Vintage Books, 2011.

Gunther, Jilenne. *Navigating Your Rights: The Utah Legal Guide for Those 55 and Over.* Salt Lake City: State of Utah, 2011.

Haber, Carole, and Brian Gratton. *Old Age and the Search for Security: An American Social History.* Bloomington: Indiana University Press, 1994.

Hartog, Hendrik. *Someday All This Will Be Yours: A History of Inheritance and Old Age.* Cambridge, MA: Harvard University Press, 2012.

Hollwich, Matthias. *New Aging: Live Smarter Now to Live Better Forever.* New York: Penguin Books, 2016.

Imber, Gerald. *Genius on the Edge: The Bizarre Double Life of Dr. William Stewart Halsted.* London: Kaplan Publishing, 2010.

Insel, Thomas. *Healing: Our Path from Mental Illness to Mental Health.* New York: Penguin Press, 2022.

Johnson, Steven. *Extra Life: A Short History of Living Longer.* New York: Riverhead Books, 2021.

———. *Where Good Ideas Come From: The Natural History of Innovation.* New York: Riverhead Books, 2011.

Kahneman, Daniel. *Thinking, Fast and Slow.* New York: Farrar, Straus and Giroux, 2011.

Karlawish, Jason. *The Problem of Alzheimer's: How Science, Culture, and Politics Turned a Rare Disease into a Crisis and What We Can Do About It.* New York: St. Martin's Press, 2021.

Karlgaard, Rich. *Late Bloomers: The Power of Patience in a World Obsessed with Early Achievement.* New York: Currency, 2019.

Kass, Leon R. *Leading a Worthy Life: Finding Meaning in Modern Times.* New York: Encounter Books, 2017.

Katz, Stephen. *Disciplining Old Age: The Formation of Gerontological Knowledge.* Charlottesville: University of Virginia Press, 1996.

Keefe, Patrick Radden. *Empire of Pain: The Secret History of the Sackler Dynasty.* New York: Doubleday, 2021.

Kelly, Jean F., D. Sandoval, T. Zuckerman, and K. Buehlman. *Promoting First Relationships: A Program for Service Providers to Help Parents and Other Caregivers Nurture Young Children's Social and Emotional Development.* 2nd ed. Seattle: University of Washington, NCAST-AVENUW Publications, 2008.

Keltner, Dacher. *Awe: The New Science of Everyday Wonder and How It Can Transform Your Life.* New York: Penguin Press, 2023.

Kempe, Annie. *A Good Knight for Children: C. Henry Kempe's Quest to Protect the Abused Child.* BookLocker, 2007.

Kempe, C. Henry, and Ray E. Helfer. *Helping the Battered Child and His Family.* Philadelphia: J. B. Lippencott Company, 1972.

Kessler, David. *A Question of Intent: A Great American Battle with a Deadly Industry.* New York: PublicAffairs, 2001.

Kohn, Nina. *Elder Law: Practice, Policy, and Problems.* New York: Wolters Kluwer Law & Business, 2014.

Kosberg, Jordan, ed. *Abuse and Maltreatment of the Elderly, Causes and Interventions.* Boston: John Wright, PSG Inc., 1983.

Lachs, Mark. *What Your Doctor Won't Tell You About Getting Older: A Doctor's Guide to Getting the Best Care as You or a Loved One Gets Older.* New York: Thorndike, 2011. (Originally released as *Treat Me, Not My Age* by Viking in 2010.)

Lane, Marion S., and Stephen L. Zawistowski. *Heritage of Care: The American Society for the Prevention of Cruelty to Animals.* Westport, CT: Praeger, 2008.

Langer, Ellen J. *Counterclockwise: Mindful Health and the Power of Possibility.* New York: Ballantine Books, 2009.

Leaf, Alexander (photographs by John Launois). *Youth in Old Age.* New York: McGraw-Hill Book Company, 1975.

LeBlanc, Adrian Nicole. *Random Family: Love, Drugs, Trouble, and Coming of Age in the Bronx.* New York: Scribner, 2003.

Lehmann, Virginia (director), and Geneva Mathiasen (editor). *Guardianship and Protective Services for Older People.* New York: NCOA Press, 1963.

Leland, John. *Happiness Is a Choice You Make: Lessons from a Year Among the Oldest Old.* New York: Sarah Crichton Books, Farrar, Straus and Giroux, 2018.

Leovy, Jill. *Ghettoside: A True Story of Murder in America.* New York: Spiegel & Grau, 2015.

Levine, Carol, ed. *Living in the Land of Limbo: Fiction and Poetry About Family Caregiving.* Nashville: Vanderbilt University Press, 2014.

Levitin, Daniel J. *Successful Aging: A Neuroscientist Explores the Power and Potential of Our Lives*. New York: Dutton, 2020.

Levy, Becca. *Breaking the Age Code: How Your Beliefs About Aging Determine How Long and Well You Live*. New York: William Morrow, 2022.

Lynn, Joanne, Joan Harrold, and Janice Lynch Schuster. *Handbook for Mortals: Guidance for People Facing Serious Illness*. Oxford: Oxford University Press, 2011.

Mace, Nancy L., and Peter V. Rabins. *The 36-Hour Day: A Family Guide to Caring for People Who Have Alzheimer Disease and Other Dementias*. 7th ed. Baltimore: Johns Hopkins University Press, 2021.

MacFarquhar, Larissa. *Strangers Drowning: Grappling with Impossible Idealism, Drastic Choices, and the Overpowering Urge to Help*. New York: Penguin Press, 2015.

Martin, Del. *Battered Wives*. Volcano, CA: Volcano Press, 1976.

Mayeroff, Milton. *On Caring*. New York: Harper Perennial, 1971.

Mendelson, Mary Adelaide. *Tender Loving Greed: How the Incredibly Lucrative Nursing Home "Industry" Is Exploiting America's Old People and Defrauding Us All*. New York: Vintage Books, 1974.

Miller, Carol A. *Elder Abuse and Nursing: What Nurses Need to Know and Can Do About It*. New York: Springer Publishing Company, 2017.

Miller, G. Wayne. *King of Hearts: The True Story of the Maverick Who Pioneered Open Heart Surgery*. New York: Crown Publishers, 2000.

Montaigne, Michel de. *The Essays of Montaigne*. Translated by E. J. Trenchmann. London: Oxford University Press, 1935. (Originally written between 1570 and 1592.)

Mosqueda, Laura. *Geriatric Pocket Doc: A Resource for Non-physicians*. 2nd ed. Irvine, CA: University of California, Irvine, 2013.

Mueller, Lisel. *Alive Together: New and Selected Poems*. Baton Rouge: Louisiana State University Press, 1996.

Mukherjee, Siddhartha. *The Emperor of All Maladies: A Biography of Cancer*. New York: Scribner, 2010.

Murthy, Vivek H. *Together: Loneliness, Health and What Happens When We Find Connection*. London: Wellcome Collection, 2020.

Musemeche, Catherine. *Hurt: The Inspiring, Untold Story of Trauma Care*. Lebanon, NH: ForeEdge, 2016.

Nelson, Barbara J. *Making an Issue of Child Abuse: Political Agenda Setting for Social Problems*. Chicago: University of Chicago Press, 1984.

Nerenberg, Lisa. *Elder Abuse Prevention: Emerging Trends and Promising Strategies*. New York: Springer Publishing Company, 2008.

———. *Elder Justice, Ageism, and Elder Abuse*. New York: Springer Publishing Company, 2019.

Niebuhr, Reinhold. *Moral Man and Immoral Society: A Study in Ethics and Politics*. New York: Scribner 1932.

Nuland, Sherwin B. *How We Die: Reflections on Life's Final Chapter*. New York: Alfred A. Knopf, 1994.

———. *The Wisdom of the Body*. New York: Alfred A. Knopf, 1997.

Nussbaum, Martha C. *From Disgust to Humanity: Sexual Orientation and Constitutional Law*. Oxford: Oxford University Press, 2010.

————. *Hiding from Humanity: Disgust, Shame, and the Law*, Princeton University Press, 2006.

Nussbaum, Martha C., and Saul Levmore. *Aging Thoughtfully: Conversations About Retirement, Romance, Wrinkles, and Regret*. New York: Oxford University Press, 2017.

Olsen, Tillie. *Tell Me a Riddle*. Philadelphia: J. B. Lippincott & Co., 1961.

O'Rourke, Meghan. *The Invisible Kingdom: Reimagining Chronic Illness*. New York. Riverhead Books, 2022.

Page, Scott E. *The Diversity Bonus: How Great Teams Pay Off in the Knowledge Economy*. Princeton: Princeton University Press, 2017.

Payne, Brian K. *Crime and Elder Abuse: An Integrated Perspective*. 2nd ed. Springfield, IL: Charles C. Thomas Publisher, 2005.

Pfaff, John F. *Locked In: The True Causes of Mass Incarceration and How to Achieve Real Reform*. New York: Basic Books, 2017.

Phelan, Amanda, ed. *International Perspectives on Elder Abuse*. Routledge Advances in Health and Social Policy. London: Rutledge, 2013.

Pillemer, Karl. *Fault Lines: Fractured Families and How to Mend Them*. New York: Avery, 2020.

————. *30 Lessons for Living: Tried and True Advice from the Wisest Americans*. New York: Hudson Street Press, 2011.

Pillemer, Karl A., and Rosalie S. Wolf. *Elder Abuse: Conflict in the Family*. Dover, MA: Auburn House Publishing, 1986.

Pinker, Steven. *The Better Angels of Our Nature: Why Violence Has Declined*. New York: Penguin Books, 2011.

Pipher, Mary. *Another Country: Navigating the Emotional Terrain of Our Elders*. New York: Riverhead Books, 1999.

Pollan, Michael. *How to Change Your Mind: What the New Science of Psychedelics Teaches Us About Consciousness, Dying, Addiction, Depression, and Transcendence*. New York: Penguin Books, 2018.

Poo, Ai-jen. *The Age of Dignity: Preparing for the Elder Boom in a Changing America*. New York: The New Press, 2015.

Power, Samantha. *"A Problem from Hell": America and the Age of Genocide*. New York: Basic Books, 2002.

Puri, Sunita. *That Good Night: Life and Medicine in the Eleventh Hour*. New York: Penguin Books, 2019.

Radtke, Kristen. *Seek You: A Journey Through American Loneliness*. New York: Pantheon Books, 2021.

Rawls, John. *Justice as Fairness: A Restatement*. Cambridge, MA: The Belknap Press, 2001.

Reilly, Tim, Karin A. Mack, and Madeleine Kahn. *Age and Structural Lag: Society's Failure to Provide Meaningful Opportunities in Work, Family, and Leisure*. Hoboken, NJ: Wiley-Interscience, 1994.

Roberts, Dorothy. *Shattered Bonds: The Color of Child Welfare*. New York: Basic Civitas Books, 2002.

Robinson, Marilynne. *What Are We Doing Here? Essays*. New York: Farrar, Straus and Giroux, 2018.

Rose, Jacqueline. *On Violence and On Violence Against Women*. New York: Farrar, Straus and Giroux, 2021.

Roszak, Theodore. *The Making of an Elder Culture: Reflections on the Future of America's Most Audacious Generation*. Gabriola Island, BC: New Society Publishers, 2009.

Rothman, David J., and Sheila M. Rothman. *The Willowbrook Wars: Bringing the Mentally Disabled into the Community*. New York: Harper & Row, 1984. (Republished by Transaction Publishers in 2005.)

Rovelli, Carlo. *The Order of Time*. Translated by Erica Segre and Simon Carnell. New York: Riverhead Books, 2018. (Originally published in Italian in 2017.)

Sachs, Oliver. *Gratitude*. New York: Alfred A. Knopf, 2015.

Sandel, Michael J. *Justice: What's the Right Thing to Do?* New York: Farrar, Straus and Giroux, 2009.

Sealander, Judith. *The Failed Century of the Child: Governing America's Young in the Twentieth Century*. Cambridge, UK: Cambridge University Press, 2003.

Segal, Lynne. *Out of Time: The Pleasures and Perils of Aging*. New York: Verso, 2013.

Shakespeare, William. *The Tragedy of King Lear*. Edited by Jay L. Halio. Cambridge, UK: Cambridge University Press, 1992.

Shapiro, Joseph P. *No Pity: People with Disabilities Forging a New Civil Rights Movement*. New York: Crown Publishers, 1994.

Shay, Jonathan. *Achilles in Vietnam: Combat Trauma and the Undoing of Character*. New York: Scribner, 1994.

Sidanius, Jim, and Felicia Pratto. *Social Dominance: An Intergroup Theory of Social Hierarchy and Oppression*. Cambridge, UK: Cambridge University Press, 1999.

Skloot, Rebecca. *The Immortal Life of Henrietta Lacks*. New York: Crown Publishers, 2010.

Snyder, Rachel Louise. *No Visible Bruises: What We Don't Know About Domestic Violence Can Kill Us*. New York: Bloomsbury, 2019.

Solnit, Rebecca. *Hope in the Dark: Untold Histories, Wild Possibilities*. New York: Nation Books, 2004.

Solomon, Andrew. *Far from the Tree: Parents, Children, and the Search for Identity*. New York: Scribner, 2012.

Sontag, Susan. *AIDS and Its Metaphors*. New York: Farrar, Straus and Giroux, 1989.
———. *Illness as Metaphor*. New York: Farrar, Straus and Giroux, 1978.

Sophocles. *Oedipus at Colonus*. Translated by Robert Fitzgerald. Orlando: Harcourt, Brace & Company, 1941.

Stevenson, Bryan. *Just Mercy, A Story of Justice and Redemption*. New York: Spiegel & Grau, 2014.

Stone, Douglas, Bruce Patton, and Sheila Heen. *Difficult Conversations: How to Discuss What Matters Most*. New York: Penguin Books, 1999.

Summers, Randal W., and Allan M. Hoffman, eds. *Elder Abuse: A Public Health Perspective*. Washington, DC: American Public Health Association, 2006.

Sweet, Victoria. *God's Hotel: A Doctor, a Hospital, and a Pilgrimage to the Heart of Medicine*. New York: Riverhead Books, 2012.

Tatara, Toshio, ed. *Understanding Elder Abuse in Minority Populations*. New York: Routledge, 1998.

Taylor, R. M., ed. Elder *Abuse and Its Prevention: Forum on Global Violence Prevention: Workshop Summary*. Washington, DC: National Academies Press, 2014.

Teaster, Pamela B., and Jeffrey E. Hall, eds. *Elder Abuse and the Public's Health*. New York: Springer Publishing Company, 2018.

Teel, Allan S. *Alone and Invisible No More: How Grassroots Community Action and 21st Century Technologies Can Empower Elders to Stay in Their Homes and Lead Healthier, Happier Lives*. White River Junction, VT: Chelsea Green Publishing, 2011.

Thaler, Richard H., and Cass R. Sunstein. *Nudge: Improving Decisions About Health, Wealth, and Happiness*. Revised and expanded edition. New York: Penguin Books, 2009.

Todd, Richard. *The Thing Itself: On the Search for Authenticity*. New York: Riverhead Books, 2008.

Vaillant, George. *Aging Well: Surprising Guideposts to a Happier Life from the Landmark Study of Adult Development*. New York: Little, Brown Spark, 2002.

van der Kolk, Bessel. *The Body Keeps the Score: Brain, Mind, and Body in the Healing of Trauma*. New York: Viking, 2014.

Vladeck, Bruce. *Unloving Care: The Nursing Home Tragedy*. New York: Basic Books, 1980.

Vollmann, William, T. *Rising Up and Rising Down: Some Thoughts on Violence, Freedom and Urgent Means*. New York: Harper Perennial, 2003.

Waldinger, Robert, and Marc Schultz. *The Good Life: Lessons from the World's Longest Scientific Study of Happiness*. New York: Simon and Schuster, 2023.

Wallis, Velma. *Two Old Women: An Alaska Legend of Betrayal, Courage and Survival*. New York: Harper Perennial, 1993.

Walrath, Dana. *Aliceheimer's: Alzheimer's Through the Looking Glass*. University Park: Penn State University Press, 2013.

Weiner, Jonathan. *The Beak of the Finch: A Story of Evolution in Our Time*. New York: Vintage Books, 1995.

Welsh, Moira. *Happily Ever Older: Revolutionary Approaches to Long-Term Care*. Ontario: ECW Press, 2021.

Wilder, Thornton. *The Bridge of San Luis Rey*. New York: Perennial Classics, 1998. (Originally published in 1927.)

Wilkerson, Isabel. *Caste: The Origins of Our Discontents*. New York: Random House, 2020.

Wright, Thomas Lee. *The Family Guide to Preventing Elder Abuse: How to Protect Your Parents—and Yourself*. New York: Skyhorse Publishing, 2017.

Zehr, Howard. *The Little Book of Restorative Justice*. Intercourse, PA: Good Books, 2015.

Ziettlow, Amy, and Naomi Cahn. *Homeward Bound: Modern Families, Elder Care, and Loss*. New York: Oxford University Press, 2017.

INDEX

FIONA KOHRMAN

M. T. Connolly is widely recognized as a leading national expert on elder justice, for which she was honored with a MacArthur "Genius" Award. As head of the Department of Justice's Elder Justice Initiative, she shaped new strategies to prosecute nursing home abuses and launched a research grant program to expand evidence about what works. She conceived and was an architect of the Elder Justice Act, the first federal law to specifically address the issue, and was the lead author of the Elder Justice Roadmap that guides federal, state, and local priorities. She lives in Washington, DC.

PublicAffairs is a publishing house founded in 1997. It is a tribute to the standards, values, and flair of three persons who have served as mentors to countless reporters, writers, editors, and book people of all kinds, including me.

I. F. STONE, proprietor of *I. F. Stone's Weekly*, combined a commitment to the First Amendment with entrepreneurial zeal and reporting skill and became one of the great independent journalists in American history. At the age of eighty, Izzy published *The Trial of Socrates*, which was a national bestseller. He wrote the book after he taught himself ancient Greek.

BENJAMIN C. BRADLEE was for nearly thirty years the charismatic editorial leader of *The Washington Post*. It was Ben who gave the *Post* the range and courage to pursue such historic issues as Watergate. He supported his reporters with a tenacity that made them fearless and it is no accident that so many became authors of influential, best-selling books.

ROBERT L. BERNSTEIN, the chief executive of Random House for more than a quarter century, guided one of the nation's premier publishing houses. Bob was personally responsible for many books of political dissent and argument that challenged tyranny around the globe. He is also the founder and longtime chair of Human Rights Watch, one of the most respected human rights organizations in the world.

•　　•　　•

For fifty years, the banner of Public Affairs Press was carried by its owner Morris B. Schnapper, who published Gandhi, Nasser, Toynbee, Truman, and about 1,500 other authors. In 1983, Schnapper was described by *The Washington Post* as "a redoubtable gadfly." His legacy will endure in the books to come.

Peter Osnos, *Founder*